Sabah from the Ground

The **ISEAS – Yusof Ishak Institute** (formerly Institute of Southeast Asian Studies) is an autonomous organization established in 1968. It is a regional centre dedicated to the study of socio-political, security, and economic trends and developments in Southeast Asia and its wider geostrategic and economic environment. The Institute's research programmes are grouped under Regional Economic Studies (RES), Regional Strategic and Political Studies (RSPS), and Regional Social and Cultural Studies (RSCS). The Institute is also home to the ASEAN Studies Centre (ASC), the Singapore APEC Study Centre and the Temasek History Research Centre (THRC).

ISEAS Publishing, an established academic press, has issued more than 2,000 books and journals. It is the largest scholarly publisher of research about Southeast Asia from within the region. ISEAS Publishing works with many other academic and trade publishers and distributors to disseminate important research and analyses from and about Southeast Asia to the rest of the world.

◆ ◆ ◆

The **Strategic Information and Research Development Centre (SIRD)** is an independent publishing house founded in January 2000 in Petaling Jaya, Malaysia. The SIRD list focuses on Malaysian and Southeast Asian studies, economics, gender studies, social sciences, politics and international relations. Our books address the scholarly communities, students, the NGO and development communities, policymakers, activists and the wider public. SIRD also distributes titles (via its sister organisation, **GB Gerakbudaya Enterprise Sdn Bhd**) published by scholarly and institutional presses, NGOs and other independent publishers. We also organise seminars, forums and group discussions. All these, we believe, are conducive to the development and consolidation of the notions of civil liberty and democracy.

Sabah from the Ground

The 2020 Elections and the Politics of Survival

Bridget Welsh, Vilashini Somiah and Benjamin YH Loh
(editors)

SIRD
Strategic Information and Research Development Centre

This edition is published in 2021 by
Strategic Information and Research Development Centre
No. 2 Jalan Bukit 11/2, 46200 Petaling Jaya, Selangor, Malaysia
Email: gerak@gerakbudaya.com
Website: www.gerakbudaya.com

and

Co-published in Singapore in 2021 by ISEAS Publishing
ISEAS – Yusof Ishak Institute, 30 Heng Mui Keng Terrace, Singapore 119614
Email: publish@iseas.edu.sg
Website: bookshop.iseas.edu.sg

Perpustakaan Negara Malaysia / Cataloguing-in-Publication Data

Sabah from the Ground : The 2020 Elections and the Politics of Survival /
Bridget Welsh, Vilashini Somiah and Benjamin YH Loh. (editors).
ISBN 978-967-2464-24-2
1. Elections–Malaysia–Sabah.
2. COVID-19 Pandemic, 2020-.
3. Sabah (Malaysia)–Politics and government.
I. Welsh, Bridget.
II. Vilashini Somiah.
III. Loh, Benjamin Y.H.
324.60959521

ISEAS Library Cataloguing-in-Publication Data
A catalogue record for this book is available from the ISEAS Library

Cover design by Janice Cheong
Layout by Janice Cheong

Printed by Vinlin Press Sdn Bhd
2 Jalan Meranti Permai 1
Meranti Permai Industrial Park
Batu 15, Jalan Puchong
47100 Puchong, Selangor, Malaysia

Contents

PART 3: CAMPAIGNING

PART 4: RESULTS

This book is dedicated to the memory of

Datuk Thasius Sipanggol Joeman, 1940-2021

Terrance Maximus Tangit, 1967-2021

and to all those who lost their lives during the Covid-19 pandemic in Sabah and Malaysia.

Foreword

A Defining Role for a New Malaysia Forgone?

There has never been so much written on and researched about an election in Sabah. The chapters of this book deal with the many issues that have bedeviled Sabah politics from the time of its entry into Malaysia. The former Warisan Plus government infused the campaign with a style reminiscent of the freshness that the late Adenan Satem brought into Sarawak's politics. It also rekindled hopes of a 'second coming' for the New Malaysia touted by Pakatan Harapan during the 2018 General Election, and its short time in government. The chapters are a good read on the dynamics of Sabah politics and provide pointers, perhaps, on why the new dawn of Sabah politics may not yet see the light of day any time soon!

Illegal immigration, which has been billed as the mother of all problems in Sabah during previous elections, reared its ugly head in Sabah politics soon after the declaration of independence and the formation of Malaysia. Robust politicking especially involving the Muslim and non-Muslim Bumiputeras generated policies which changed the demography of the state. Clandestinely implemented by officials either at the behest of the government, or at least its acquiescence, these moves have been, uncharacteristically for a government policy initiative, a roaring success.

The numerous elections held for both Parliament and the state assembly have failed to produce any fixed solution to the immigration issue. A Royal Commission of Inquiry was set up to look into this but until today nothing of significance has been undertaken to address the issue. It calls for sincerity and seriousness on the part of the governments and pragmatism from amongst Sabahans adversely affected by the influx of illegal immigrants, many of whom have now secured citizenship through dubious means.

Perhaps a Truth and Reconciliation Commission can be considered to facilitate a national healing and a lasting solution. The government and perpetrators of a redefined Sabah demography can own up to their actions. Sabah can accept its fair share of the immigrants with the rest distributed between the other states. As an assurance of its commitment to racial and religious harmony, the state government can take steps to return to the constitutional provisions as of Malaysia Day 1963. Sabah then did not have an official religion. With the immigration issue out of the way, the state can then focus on strengthening its economy and the eradication of poverty.

The strong presence of Kuala Lumpur has continued to exert its influence on the outcome of elections in Sabah, as well as on the composition of the ensuing government. The fight for power at the centre has spilled over to the states and it does appear that this will be a feature of Malaysian politics for some time to come. Sadly, this will divert the attention of winning parties away from the business of providing good governance – as the eyes of the victorious will be trained towards another victory in the next battle. For Sabah, the overdependence of state leaders on political support from Kuala Lumpur will compromise the pursuit of states' rights, which were a very significant part of the election campaign.

The perennial issues of Sabah politics are thriving. The same issues will flow seamlessly into the elections ahead. What is interesting to note is that the natives of Malaysia from the third largest island in the world are articulating issues openly. In the past, the loud voices in the debate were from the non-Muslim communities but today the Muslim Bumiputera are also at the forefront demanding state rights and articulating the need to steer the country towards building a nation for all Malaysians. Perhaps herein lie the pointers for the search of the lost soul of the nation. Can Malaysian Borneo rise to the occasion? Doesn't the Sun rise from the East!

Bernard Giluk Dompok
Chief Minister of Sabah 1998-1999

Foreword

Learning from Sabah

It is my pleasure to accept this invitation to write a foreword for *Sabah from the Ground*. My identity and roots will always be tied to my place of birth, my beloved land of great beauty and individuality. This book offers a variety of perspectives focused on contemporary Sabah politics from academicians, journalists and activists. It is good to see more scholarly attention on Sabah, especially from young Sabahan scholars in the collection.

From my perspective, Sabah politics offers important lessons for the rest of Malaysia.

Generally, political development in Sabah is more mature than that in the Semenanjung (Peninsula). In the 14th General Election in 2018 and the 16th Sabah state election in 2020, we saw peaceful transitions from one administration to another despite fiery campaign periods, and without recourse to protracted post-election crises. Politicians have put aside their differences to come together and work for the people of the state. Sabah has had five peaceful transitions of power, and while some of these have faced challenges, there has been a willingness to accept the role of the opposition and new governments throughout. Sabahans have embraced political change, long before the Semanunjung. When Sabahans have been unsatisfied, they have voted out governments. We are more evolved as voters because of our willingness to accept different political leadership.

And although Sabahans tend to be passionate about the parties they support (or don't), we have developed a reputation for being a very united people. This is because Sabah practices a politics of accommodation; racial and religious identities are celebrated differently in Sabah from the Semenanjung. Sabahans recognise that their differences are to be embraced not effaced. We appreciate our diversity and know that our diversity is a strength. We listen to each other – a theme in Dr Benjamin YH Loh and Yi Jian Ho's chapter on Sabah's digital space. The Semanunjung has a lot to learn from Sabah's greater ethnic tolerance and inclusion.

This is not to say that we do not have problems associated with race and religion, which will happen given the prominence of racial politics in Malaysia and the migrant problem in the state. I believe the broader appeals to Sabahans for Sabah strengthens unity in the state and we share a common desire for the uplifting of development and wellbeing for all Sabahans across different races and religions.

When we go out to vote, we consider a range of issues. Sabahans consider personality, leadership and the response to their social conditions such as the challenges of rural livelihoods. The book's attention to different factors influencing voting corresponds to the different realities on the ground. Ethnic preferences are less important, as Dr Bridget Welsh's chapter in this book explains well. Dr Arnold Puyok's attention to the role of personality in rural areas is also accurate.

And so, I believe there must be a continuous call for Sabahan rights that transcends party lines. The *rakyat* do not need more leaders who are only interested in playing politics all the time, but instead need more serious, dependable statesmen, working to keep the administration in good form. We must collectively work towards more state autonomy and resources from the federal government in an effort to focus on better development projects and outcomes.

Sabahans are united in wanting more commitment from the federal government to address the imbalance in economic development. These needs are not unfounded, and if addressed, the effects of change impact not just socio-economic conditions of Sabahans but also all Malaysians. For example, with the Covid-19 pandemic impacting our economy and society, there should be more focus in ensuring that Sabahans are given the tools to combat digital poverty, where communities are not afforded ICT infrastructure or skills. Many young people in Sabah can benefit from gaining more digital literacy through access to smart devices and high-speed Internet access. Empower your weakest and you will empower all.

My professional ethos has always been to fight for what I believe is right and good for Sabah. I have met and worked with many from different sides of the political divide, and while we may have had our differences, we believe that there is always more that can be done for Sabah. I found the discussion on civil society in the book especially valuable and know that we need to collectively work with civil society to address the challenges Sabah faces.

The collection edited by Drs Bridget Welsh, Vilashini Somiah and Benjamin YH Loh sees Sabah in her uniqueness and diversity. This book helps mark a time in our history and a new political era of change and transformation. Capturing the ongoing political transformations in a period of change offers insights on how to move Sabah and Malaysia forward. The book will be an essential reference for Sabahans and those interested in Sabah politics for years to come.

Salleh Said Keruak Ph.D JP
Chief Minister of Sabah from 1994 to 1996

Acknowledgments

In the wake of the Sabah 2020 state elections, we, the editors, found ourselves discussing in great detail the drivers and outcomes of the campaign. Sabah, unlike other parts of Malaysia, has always been a political puzzle, difficult for many on the outside to decipher. As the three of us continued unpacking and piecing together what we knew of local leadership and governance, we were also confronted by the need to acknowledge the shifts and changes occurring in Sabah's politics from the ground. Sabahans and friends of Sabah, all of whom experienced the 2020 state elections first-hand, could offer great insights into how that influenced local politics thereafter.

This book was then formulated as a way to bring together scholars, experts, and intellectuals working on Sabah to provide current and contemporary views of the state. While there have been seminal and important works about Sabah in the last half century, these are few and far between, especially in recent years. And so, we began this project keeping in mind the importance of filling in what we can of the obvious gap in the literature on Sabah.

We would first like to thank two important Sabah leaders that have contributed forewords to the book. Both former chief ministers of Sabah from different parties, Salleh bin Md Said Keruak and Bernard Dompok, were kind enough to take time out of their busy schedules to offer short commentaries for this book and contemporary Sabah politics. These leaders join others among the Sabah political elite who were generous with their time and feedback. While the list is long and many prefer to remain anonymous, we would like to especially acknowledge those assisted with the book through offering insights in interviews or assistance: Abdul Rahman Dahlan, Bung Moktar Radin, Chan Foong Hin, Nixon Habi, Adrian Lasimbang, Wilfred Madius Tangau, Martin Tommy and Yong Teck Lee.

We believe that a book on Sabah politics requires plural voices. We have gathered a large and eclectic group of extraordinary writers from various walks of life, all with rich experiences with Sabah's economy, society, and politics; we are very grateful for their important contributions. We have writers representing various civil society organisations (CSO) in Sabah. In the chapters written by Beverly, Nelson, Asraf, Mahirah, Fiqah, and Auzellea, they cast a spotlight on the important and necessary work that often goes unnoticed in protecting and improving the lives of both average and marginalised Sabahans. The efforts of CSOs are often taken for granted and we are pleased to give these selfless organisations the due recognition they deserve and we could not have done so without the help of these authors.

We are also truly fortunate to include political analysts and commentators who were willing to share their invaluable insights in this book. We are thankful to Joe, Tsu Chong and Philip for providing insightful and comprehensive summaries of the contextual issues that set the stage in Sabah. The chapters from Ei Sun, Amanda, and Rahimin provide novel and revelatory looks into narratives of the Chinese and Muslim communities of Sabah. These contributions all add texture and depth to our understanding of this highly plural state. Public commentators are not properly recognised for their on the ground knowledge and accessible contributions to knowledge. We hope that by including them here their role in adding to knowledge will be more appreciated.

Their analyses join a wonderful group of academic colleagues. The chapters by James, Marcilla, Tony, Arnold and Trixie represent some of the best works by Sabah academics. As editors, we would also like to thank our co-writers in our respective chapters, Yi Jian, and Aslam, both of whom are young talented academics and names to look out for in the future. We look forward to further collaborations with all of our contributors in the future. We thank them for their patience in the editing process, the unbelievable timeliness in responding to queries and their support in making this collection come together as it has.

This book would not have been realised were it not for the support and confidence given by our publishers, the Strategic Information and Research Development Centre (SIRD)/Gerakbudaya and the ISEAS–Yusof Ishak Institute (ISEAS). Given the challenges of operating under the Covid-19 restrictions, Gerakbudaya continues to play an important role in the dissemination of knowledge in Malaysia; accepting this book project for publication reflects their commitment to pursuing understanding even when they are being financially challenged. ISEAS's agreement to co-publish reflects their prominent role in enriching understanding of Southeast Asia as a whole.

At ISEAS, its head of publishing Ng Kok Kiong has been gracious and supportive. Gerakbudaya's editorial team under the tenacious Pak Chong gave us the much-needed refinement and encouragement to get this book in shape and to assist us with a timely publication. We are very thankful to the dedicated work of Janice Cheong and William Tham for assisting with the book cover/typesetting and in the minutiae of publishing, respectively. Special thanks are extended to Charles Brophy, a scholar in his own right and the captain of this book's publishing process. He was the lynchpin that pulled the different individuals together in the publishing process and helped tremendously to improve the quality of the book. We certainly could not have completed it without him – and in the publication process he is our hero.

There has also been help behind the scenes. The collection benefitted from the assistance of Jillian Simon who helped prepare the bibliography and Guo who assisted with the data analysis. Special thanks are also extended to all those who shared electoral data (you know who you are and will get a complimentary book), allowing for a comprehensive analysis of the results. We recognise the hard work of all involved and apologise if we have invertedly left anyone out.

Last, but definitely not least, we must thank the people of Sabah. *Sabah from the Ground* would not have been possible without the kind support of the people of Sabah whose stories and history inspired each article in the book. We would like to dedicate the book to those who have lost loved ones during this difficult time. Two of our authors lost family members while this book was being written – Beverly Joeman lost her beloved father Thasius Sipanggol Joeman, and Trixie Tangit lost her beloved brother Terrance Maximus Tangit. Both men were keen to read the book and their loss is felt deeply as part of our collective family in this collection. At the time of publication, Sabah and Malaysia as a whole continues to face challenges from the COVID-19 pandemic. Sabah has been the hardest hit. This is why we also dedicate this collection to those who have lost their loved ones to Covid-19 in Sabah and Malaysia as a whole. Our hearts go out to all of you and your families.

We thank the readers of this book in advance. We hope that this book will stimulate debate and discussion. We apologise for any errors in the collection and welcome feedback. We hope that our efforts encourage more scholarship on Sabah and Sabahans. The editors' focus on the agency of ordinary Sabahans – in the politics of survival – reflects our confidence and appreciation of how Sabahans are rising above, with dignity and decency, and continuing to dream for a better future that they deserve.

Benjamin YH Loh Vilashini Somiah Bridget Welsh
8 April 2021

Introduction

Sabah Goes to the Polls

Bridget Welsh, Benjamin YH Loh and Vilashini Somiah

On 29 July 2020, Chief Minister Shafie Apdal dissolved the state assembly to pave the way for Sabah's 16th state elections. These 'snap' polls, after only 26 months in government, were called to prevent the takeover of the government by Shafie's long-time rival Musa Aman, who had served as chief minister of the state for 15 years and whom Shafie had ousted from power after the 2018 General Election (GE14). The night before, Musa had gathered 33 state assemblypersons ('*Kumpulan 33*') in his house as a show of support, and was pressuring Sabah Governor Juhar Mahiruddin to swear his government in as he allegedly had the numbers for a majority. The federally aligned Musa, whose roots in the United Malays National Organisation (UMNO), long tenure in office and connection with Prime Minister Muhyiddin Yassin of Perikatan Nasional (PN) had the advantage in his efforts to woo defections to his side. All of the 46 criminal charges for corruption and money laundering filed against him had been put aside a month earlier in June, giving him the opportunity to galvanise his allies and attempt a takeover of the state government.[1] Rather than have a second 'Sheraton Move', reminiscent of Pakatan Harapan's loss of government in February, Shafie turned the decision over to the electorate. When the election results came in on the night of 26 September, Shafie and his Warisan Plus coalition, comprising his party Warisan, the Democratic Action Party (DAP), Parti Keadilan Rakyat (PKR) and the United Progressive Kinabalu

---

1 Nurbiati Hamdan, 'Former Sabah CM Musa Aman acquitted of 46 charges of corruption, money laundering', *The Star*, 9 June 2020, https://www.thestar.com.my/news/nation/2020/06/09/former-sabah-cm-musa-aman-acquitted-of-46-charges-of-corruption-money-laundering

Organization (UPKO), had lost power to the newly formed Gabungan Rakyat Sabah (GRS), a nine-party alliance helmed by new Chief Minister Hajiji Noor from Bersatu, the prime minister's party.[2]

The 2020 Sabah state election (also referred to as PRN2020 below) was a hard-fought campaign, and national attention, resources and party supporters concentrated on Sabah. For many in Peninsular Malaysia, the focus on this Borneo state was a necessary learning experience – the recognition of Sabah's diversity and the state's important differences from other parts of Malaysia. For others, this was more of the same – politicians fighting for power and the spoils of power – often at the expense of everyday citizens. The tragic reality of the spread of Covid-19 around Sabah's polls, leading to 'super-spreaders' of the virus and a deadly third wave – which many blamed on the politicians themselves[3] – has reinforced cynicism and, in many ways, overshadowed the important dynamics of the election. Yet for the 1.2 million Sabahans who were engaged in the election through campaign appeals and mobilisation, the election provided an opportunity to participate in a political process that has long been driven by elite interests and rivalries so aptly on display in the 'Sheraton Move'. Despite the political fatigue and Covid-19 risks, two-thirds of registered voters (66.6 per cent) came out to vote, shaping a decisive result that led to Sabah's fifth change in government and the return of Barisan Nasional (BN)/UMNO into power in a new alliance and in a secondary role.

How did this happen? Was this the product of the decisions of leaders and campaign outcomes, or was this driven by structural conditions tied to federal-state relations, political legacies and underlying socio-economic factors? Explaining the events of the Sabah 2020 state elections – campaign, results and implications – is at the core of this book. In order to do so, we take a broader lens than the usual post-election analyses. Given the relative dearth of analysis and understanding of Sabah politics, we – scholars, analysts, journalists and social activists – discuss the wider context and

---

2 GRS was formed on 13 September with the PN parties of Bersatu, STAR, SAPP and PAS, and BN, which comprised of UMNO, PBRS and MCA. PBS also joined, making nine parties in total.

3 'Suhakam: Politicians, Campaigners least compliant with Covid-19 SOPs during Sabah polls,' *Malay Mail*, 21 January 2021, https://www.malaymail.com/news/malaysia/2021/01/21/suhakam-politicians-campaigners-least-compliant-with-covid-19-sops-during-s/1942682.

different currents of Sabah's politics. Our aim is to place PRN2020 within a broader context of changing political dynamics in the state, and in Malaysia more generally. Importantly, all of the book's contributors were on the ground during the Sabah campaign, with the majority of them originating from Sabah itself. The chapters individually, and the book collectively, aim to offer a more 'on the ground' perspective, to reinterpret and reflect on Sabah's contemporary politics.

Reviewing Results

The heart of the discussion centres on the election: a political contest on many levels. For Sabahans, this election was about who would lead their state as rivalries and personalities faced off. When Musa Aman was not slated as a candidate, the contest became one of Shafie against a long list of GRS alternatives, from UMNO's Bung Moktar and Bersatu's Hajiji Noor to Parti Solidariti Tanah Airku Rakyat Sabah (STAR)'s Jeffrey Kitingan and dark horses such as Bersatu's Masidi Manjun. The personalities were tied to different parties, with long political histories, different agendas and similar ambitions. This was the second time a non-BN allied government was aiming to hold onto power. In 1994, while winning the election, Joseph Pairin Kitingan's Parti Bersatu Sabah (PBS) lost out to defections which allowed the BN (dominated by UMNO) to come back into government.[4] In 2018, when no one party won a majority, defections – in this case from UPKO, which was the same party that had formed after splitting off from PBS twenty-four years earlier – played a role in shoring up a new Shafie-led government. It would be defections from all of the parties in his alliance that would threaten Shafie's downfall in July 2020 and serve as a catalyst for the polls.

The GE14 vote had been one largely against UMNO and its leadership nationally.[5] Concerns about corruption, ethnic exclusion, religious freedom[6]

---

4 James Chin, 'The Sabah State election of 1994: end of Kadazan unity', *Asian Survey* 34, no. 10 (1994): 904-915.

5 See James Chin, 'Sabah and Sarawak in the 14th General Election 2018 (GE14): local factors and state nationalism', *Journal of Current Southeast Asian Affairs* 37, no. 3 (2018): 173-192 and Arnold Puyok, 'The Appeal and Future of the 'Borneo Agenda' in Sabah,' in Johan Savaranamuttu, Hock Guan Lee, and Mohamed Nawab Mohamed Osman (eds), *Coalitions in Collision: Malaysia's 13th General Elections*, (KL & Singapore: ISEAS & SIRD, 2016), 199-220.

6 Arnold Puyok, 'Rise of Christian political consciousness and mobilisation,' in

and inadequate sharing of resources fueled frustrations and anger after a long tenure in office for the party and fifteen years of Musa Aman as chief minister. The state-based party Warisan capitalised on the national call for 'change' and state nationalism to win seats, allying itself with Pakatan Harapan locally and nationally to take office. Warisan/PH came into power with a litany of promises for reform and deliverables, many of which they failed to realise or deliver, and spent only 26 months in office. In fact, many of these promises were impossible to deliver, while others illustrated the serious governance challenges Sabah faced as a state on Malaysia's periphery, long neglected in terms of development, with inadequate control over its resources and facing persistent inequalities.

For those in Peninsular Malaysia the contest was about national leadership. The Sabah contest was one in which the February-ousted Pakatan Harapan opposition was pitted against Muhyiddin's PN. Shafie was seen to be holding the mantle for reform, and his decision to dissolve the assembly was lauded as a step for democracy as opposed to PN's 'backdoor' takeover. From across the South China Sea, the contest was portrayed as 'good versus evil' with Shafie's 'unity' call and prioritisation of everyone over one community or religion as part of a righteous narrative. Even after the September loss, he is still a contender to lead Malaysia, and PRN2020 increased his national profile. Many Warisan and PH supporters believed that not only would Muhyiddin be tested, but he would also be rejected by voters.

This discourse stood in stark contrast to the perception of the election as an opportunity for the prime minister and his party to show their popularity, strengthen their party's fortunes and consolidate their leadership nationally. While Muhyiddin aimed to show he was in charge and claim a mandate for this from Sabah, his (then) main ally UMNO saw Sabah as an arena to strengthen their comeback which had been boosted in their victory in the Kimanis January 2020 by-election. For PN party supporters, who came in droves from Kuala Lumpur to support the various PRN2020 campaigns, Sabah's polls were an affirmation of their control and an endorsement of their leadership. National ambitions were close at hand throughout the contest.

For many ordinary Sabahans, especially those living on the ground, the

---

Meredith Weiss (ed), *Routledge handbook of contemporary Malaysia* (Routledge, 2015), 60-72.

election was about themselves – their hopes and dreams intertwined with grievances and concerns about displacement. As with Malaysia on a whole, there were different perspectives about the election, often tied to partisan loyalties and views of the federal-state relationship. For many Sabahans, there was little regard for who ruled in Putrajaya, or even Kota Kinabalu for that matter, as they looked to their own local representatives as their conduit to government and services. Many felt that it did not matter who was in office at all, as they struggled with managing everyday life during a pandemic and an economic downturn. While leaders from the peninsula saw an opportunity for themselves, some Sabahans saw the election as an opportunity for change, continuity or new forms of patronage. Concerns about unity touted in Bangsar were less salient than maintaining dignity in the face of economic hardship in Telupid or Lamag. As the election approached, there was excitement as Sabahans understood that PRN2020 would be a competitive contest, with no clear winner from the outset.

When the ballots were counted the results showed three important trends. Foremost, that Warisan Plus had lost. It had only secured 32 seats, compared with GRS which had won 38. With the three additional pro-GRS independents winning,[7] GRS had secured a stable majority, even without the additional six nominated seats it could add constitutionally to the state assembly. Second, GRS's victory was a collective one, where all of the major parties contributed, as shown in Table 1. UMNO won the most seats, followed by Bersatu, PBS and STAR. One of these parties leaving GRS could affect the coalition's stability and this forced difficult rambunctious negotiations on positions on election night. Of the GRS parties, Bersatu gained the most, securing a political base in another state outside of Johor and consolidating a foothold in Borneo. Ironically, the party Mahathir Mohamad created and insisted should be allowed into Sabah helped to bring down his political ally, Shafie. While UMNO might have won the most seats, it lost three seats compared with 2018 (largely due to the defections it experienced to Bersatu).

[7] The pro-GRS candidates that won were Rubin Balang of Kemabong, Ruddy Awah of Pitas and Masiung Banah of Kuamut.

Table 1: Sabah 2020 Election Results by Party

	Votes	% Votes	Seats	% Seats	Changes in Seats
Gabungan Rakyat Sabah (GRS)	**316,049**	**43.2**	**38**	**52.1**	7
United Malays National Organisation (UMNO)	122,358	16.7	14	19.2	-3
Malaysian United Indigenous Party (Bersatu)	86,383	11.8	11	15.1	11
United Sabah Party (PBS)	49,941	6.8	7	9.6	1
Homeland Solidarity Party (STAR)	35,586	4.9	6	8.2	4
United Sabah People's Party (PBRS)	9,687	1.3	0	0.0	-1
Warisan Plus	**317,541**	**43.4**	**32**	**43.8**	**3**
Sabah Heritage Party (Warisan)	186,749	25.5	23	31.5	2
Democratic Action Party (DAP)	69,477	9.5	6	8.2	0
People's Justice Party (PKR)	28,372	3.9	2	2.7	0
United Progressive Kinabalu Organization (UPKO)	29,473	4.0	1	1.4	-5

Finally, Warisan Plus's defeat was not a devastating one, at least not in terms of the numbers. Warisan held its political ground, winning 22 seats, with its coalition partners DAP and PKR maintaining their seats. UPKO, which was not originally allied with Warisan/PH in GE14, lost the most seats (5), and 11 of the 12 it contested. These seats were never in Warisan Plus's hands in the first place, as they were originally won by UPKO while it was in BN in 2018. This said, the loss speaks to the challenge Warisan Plus had in reaching out across communities, notably to the Kadazan, Dusun and Murut (KDM) communities, and the lack of appreciation of the need to do so before the campaign began. The last-minute distribution of land titles, for example, was not able to sway many with longer-standing grievances.[8] The results suggest that Warisan Plus was not ready for the 'snap' polls in

[8] Tarrence Tan, 'Native land rights a hot topic as Sabah polls approach,' *The Star*, 28 August 2020, https://www.thestar.com.my/news/nation/2020/08/28/native-land-rights-a-hot-topic-as-sabah-polls-approach. For a broader understanding of these issues see: Amity A. Doolittle, *Property and politics in Sabah, Malaysia: Native struggles over land rights*, (University of Washington Press, 2011).

that there were clear areas of governance which had not been addressed. The incumbent's campaign promises of the past would come under scrutiny.

Recognising Resentments

The authors in this collection offer a range of explanations for the outcomes – the turnover, the losses and victories and the meaning of the results for Sabah politics, Sabahans and Malaysians. We do not agree on many points, nor should we. The aim is to provide insights that go beyond narrow explanations such as those outlined above – that the outcome was the product of the shortcomings of one political party or even a particular community. PRN2020 should be understood to be the outcome of a multitude of factors, reflecting the realities of Sabah politics before the election, dynamics in the campaign itself and ongoing changes taking place within the society and polity at large – including those occurring in Malaysia as a whole. What our collection urges the reader to do is to adopt different lenses to understand and see Sabah – its complexity and contrasts.

Despite Sabah's central role in forming Malaysia and the dynamism of the state's politics, comparatively little has been written about its elections and politics, more generally, especially when compared to its southern neighbor Sarawak or Peninsular Malaysia. It is almost as if the 'Land Below the Wind' has been passed by, echoing the neglect many Sabahans feel in the inadequate attention the state has received in terms of resources and services. Some of the important books on the state's politics, such as the account of former Sabah Attorney General Herman Luping, are banned,[9] and many others are just not available at a cost that most Sabahans can afford. Malaysia's national history books leave out meaningful discussion of Sabah leaders and peoples – indeed, treating Sabah as the periphery. Nevertheless, as government archival material about the 1960s has become available and social media has expanded, there is now more discussion about the state's history and politics. This book's discussion aims to be a part of these ongoing discussions and hopefully enriches and provokes debate.

A place to start is to recognise that many of the narratives of Sabah politics are largely those of its elite and may themselves be limited. This can

9 Herman Luping, *Sabah's Dilemma: The Political History of Sabah, 1960-1994* (Magnus Books, 1994).

be said, for example, about the '*Ketuanan Melayu*' discourse in Peninsular Malaysia,[10] as historical interpretations about social-political contracts, rights and realities are often told by those in power. As many Malays and non-Malays can attest to, the story of power in Malaysia is more than a racialist frame of superiority. Lived experiences are often disconnected from politicised narratives, while the narratives themselves remain politically salient.

This said, the main political narrative in Sabah is one of resentment. Discussion centres around the Malaysia Agreement of 1963 (MA63).[11] This document, written nearly sixty years ago, is portrayed as embedding the rights of Sabahans and it is argued that if the different provisions within this agreement are restored, Sabahans will get access to the resources and rights they deserve. The anguish of years of injustice has concentrated on an agreement of the past – leading to an outpouring of activism and mobilisation around state nationalism to 'correct' the federal-state relationship. There are indeed many who believe in 'time travel', hoping that a return to the past can set Sabah on a different path.

This idealism in no way takes away from the reality of legitimate grievances. Sabahans have, for years, openly vented their unhappiness that there was no fulfillment of MA63, except partially in relation to immigration, and have not had their status restored as an equal partner that formed the Federation. The agreement was written with specific memorandums for each Bornean territory to ensure a safe and successful decolonising process as well as to clearly articulate equal terms for the formation of the Federation between the territories. Over time, the value of the MA63 has eroded, with a rewording of the agreement reducing both Sabah and Sarawak to mere states in 1976.

The issues have long been about more than those in the document. History has brought witness to underlying distrust and indignities. Sabah

---

10 James Chin, 'From Ketuanan Melayu to Ketuanan Islam: UMNO and the Malaysian Chinese', in Bridget Welsh (ed.) *The End of UMNO* (Petaling Jaya: SIRD, 2016), 226-273.

11 Vilashini Somiah, 'What Is the MA63? And Why It Is Important to Sabah and Sarawak', *New Naratif*, 8 October 2020, https://newnaratif.com/comic/what-is-ma63/ and James Chin, 'The 1963 Malaysia Agreement (MA63): Sabah and Sarawak and the Politics of Historical Grievances', in Sophie Lemiere (ed.) *Minorities Matter: Malaysian Politics and People*, (Singapore: ISEAS-Yusof Ishak Institute, 2019), 75-91.

has been perceived by BN as a 'fixed deposit' state for many years, in which political support from the state was crucial for the coalition's continuous survival at the federal level – and at times for the survival of UMNO leaders.[12] And Sabah's history bore witness to federal intervention in state politics[13] on multiple occasions, often without history being properly told. From mysteries in helicopter crashes to the Project IC of the 1980s involving social engineering through immigration,[14] the federal-state relationship has been a troubled one intertwined with inequality and a perceived lack of respect.[15]

After over 58 years, the resource-rich state of Sabah remains one of the most underdeveloped states in Malaysia. It has the highest poverty rate based on the 2019 Poverty Line Income (PGK) calculation.[16] Sabah is lagging behind the Klang Valley by 40 years in terms of infrastructure and development.[17] Allocations for development under BN have increased throughout the years but socio-economic growth is low, with high unemployment and low wages.[18] Sabah's economy relies on the extraction of

---

12 Arnold Puyok and Piya Raj Sukhani. 'Sabah: breakthrough in the fixed deposit state', *The Round Table* 109, no. 2 (2020): 209-224 and James Chin and Arnold Puyok, 'Going against the tide: Sabah and the 2008 Malaysian general election', *Asian Politics & Policy* 2, no. 2 (2010): 219-235.

13 James Chin, 'GE14 In East Malaysia: MA63 and Marching to a Different Drum,' in Daljit Singh and Malcolm Cook (ed.) *Southeast Asian Affairs 2019* (Singapore: ISEAS-Yusof Ishak Institute, 2020), 211-222.

14 RCI Commissioners, *Report of the Commission of Enquiry on Immigrants in Sabah*, Kota Kinabalu, Malaysia (2014), http://legacy.sapp.org.my/rci/RCI-Eng.pdf.

15 James Chin, 'Politics of federal intervention in Malaysia, with reference to Sarawak, Sabah and Kelantan', *Journal of Commonwealth & Comparative Politics* 35, no. 2 (1997): 96-120.

16 Avila Geraldine, 'Sabah Ranks as Malaysia's Poorest State, Again,' *New Straits Times*, 20 September 2020, https://www.nst.com.my/news/nation/2020/09/625711/sabah-ranks-malaysias-poorest-state-again.

17 M. Niaz Asadullah and Jeron Joseph, 'Concern over Rising Inequality in Sabah,' *The Edge Markets*, 6 September 2018, https://www.theedgemarkets.com/article/concern-over-rising-inequality-sabah.

18 'Seeking Economic Transformation in Sabah,' *The Malaysian Insight*, 4 July 2018, https://www.themalaysianinsight.com/s/70347 and 'Greater trouble ahead if Sabah economy not managed well warns think tank,' *Free Malaysia Today*, 19 September 2020, https://www.freemalaysiatoday.com/category/nation/2020/09/19/greater-trouble-ahead-if-sabah-economy-not-managed-well-warns-think-tank/.

raw materials, as the stunting of children's growth and malnutrition from the inadequate access to affordable nutritious food for the population festers.[19] There is also a large gap between the rich and poor in Sabah.[20] Income and wealth are concentrated around Kota Kinabalu, Sandakan and Tawau, largely through investment and tourism. Rural areas remain largely poor, with no access to clean water, electricity, and roads. Many – too many – live in conditions of squalor that are not acceptable.

From Kuala Lumpur, Sabah is seen through quite different lenses. The hardships and inequalities are construed in a framework by those in power that see Sabah's struggles as their own with their federally oriented solutions. When it does not conform, efforts are invested to make it do so. Since Sabah's entrance into the Malaysian Federation in 1963, UMNO has been seen as wanting Sabah to replicate the BN model of Peninsular Malaysia, in seeing the two principles of Malay supremacy (*Ketuanan Melayu*) and, from the 1970s, Islamic supremacy (*Ketuanan Islam*) adopted.[21] This was especially so since the largest native Sabahan communities, the KDM and Chinese, were non-Muslims. Immigration, seat allocations, leadership and wealth, it was understood, should be controlled and distributed to assure that Sabah conformed to federally construed ideals. Over time, policies and practices become less responsive to Sabah's diversity and local conditions. For example, even though Malaysia employs an affirmative action policy to uplift the economically disadvantaged, 90 per cent of these privileges are given to Peninsular Malays, some to Sabah Muslims, and rarely to non-Muslims.[22] This is in spite of the fact that poverty in Sabah crosses ethnic lines. Those that challenge this framing and these practices with calls for

---

19 Wan Manan Wan Muda, Jomo Kwame Sundaram and Tan Zhai Gen, *Addressing Malnutrition in Malaysia*, Khazanah Research Institute, September 2019, http://www.krinstitute.org/assets/contentMS/img/template/editor/Discussion%20Paper_Addressing%20Malnutrition%20in%20Malaysia.pdf.

20 Martin Ravallion, *Ethnic Inequality and Poverty in Malaysia Since 1969*. No. w25640, National Bureau of Economic Research, 2019.

21 James Chin, 'Exporting the BN/UMNO model,' in *Routledge Handbook of Contemporary Malaysia*, 83-92.

22 Azlan, Romzi Ationg, Jualang Gansau, and Andreas Totu, 'Ethnohistorical Analysis on the Resurgence of Multiracial Political Ideology through "Sabah for Sabahan" Slogan in Sabah, Malaysia,' ASEAN/Asian Academic Society International Conference (2018), 186–94.

autonomy or even a substantive review of MA63 are seen to be challenging federal power.

Therein lies the tug of war between the federal government and Sabah. The federal government sees Sabah as an important supply state which it must control tightly to mould in its own image. In contrast many, although not all, Sabahans want more autonomy and envision a different future for the state. The elite conversations on MA63 reflect this contestation. For those on the ground, a history of marginalisation and neglect brings home the imbalanced federal-state relationship.

Revealing Reasons

It is thus not surprising that explanations of Sabah politics often begin with a focus on ethnic and state nationalism. In the 1980s and 1990s scholars pointed to the rise of KDM empowerment through the rise of PBS led by Joseph Pairin.[23] The empowerment of this KDM/state-based party led to its cooptation by BN and later the entrance of UMNO into Sabah. Ironically, the resentment over representation, displacement and autonomy grew stronger, not just among the KDM community.[24] The anger was increasingly directed at UMNO. From 2008 onwards a state nationalism movement gained momentum, driven by state-based parties such as STAR and Warisan, with the aim of ending UMNO's control of Sabah in its sights. This happened in GE14.[25] At the same time, UMNO developed its own political base in Sabah, tied to party machinery, patronage and the changing demography of the state. A political polarisation of Sabah politics also took root, with many UMNO supporters viewing Kuala Lumpur as a means for advancement – and, for others, survival. When one looks at the popular vote over the last few elections in Sabah (43.2 per cent GRS versus 43.4 per cent

---

[23] James Chin, 'Going east: UMNO's entry into Sabah politics', *Asian Journal of Political Science* 7, no. 1 (1999): 20-40.

[24] James Chin and Arnold Puyok, 'Going against the tide: Sabah and the 2008 Malaysian general election', *Asian Politics & Policy* 2, no. 2 (2010): 219-235.

[25] Arnold Puyok, 'Ethnic Factor In The 2008 Malaysian General Election: The Case of The Kadazan Dusun (KD) In Sabah', *Jebat: Malaysian Journal of History, Politics & Strategic Studies* 35 (2020): 1-16 and Arnold Puyok and Tony Paridi Bagang, 'Ethnicity, Culture and Indigenous Leadership in Modern Politics: The Case of the KadazanDusun in Sabah, East Malaysia', *Kajian Malaysia: Journal of Malaysian Studies* 29 (2011): 177-97.

Warisan Plus in 2020) it is clear that there is a divided electorate, and that there are differences within Sabah itself over the federal-state relationship.

These differences highlight the need to adopt multiple explanations to understand Sabah politics. Six heuristic lenses have been primarily applied by different scholars. The first and more prominent contemporary interpretation emphasises state nationalism – the growing division between the federal and state governments.[26] This underscores the adoption of state-based parties and political rhetoric around MA63. Second, and arguably even more salient over multiple elections, are appeals to ethnic nationalism, from KDM rights to loyalties around religion.[27] Early scholarship on Sabah politics emphasised the differences of local communities and how these identities shaped political mobilisation and engagement.[28] Sabah – like most of Malaysia – has political parties that rely on particular ethnic appeals, and repeatedly voting has been understood along ethnic lines. Studies regularly focus on the political behavior of a particular community – a lens three of our contributors adopt in the chapters of our book.

---

[26] See the following for good discussions of the federal-state relations broadly: Regina Lim, *Federal-state Relations in Sabah, Malaysia: The Berjaya Administration, 1976-85* (Singapore: Institute of Southeast Asian Studies, 2008); Francis Loh Kok Wah, 'Restructuring federal–state relations in Malaysia: from centralised to co-operative federalism?' *The Round Table* 99, no. 407 (2010): 131-140; Mohammad Agus Yusoff, 'The politics of centre-state conflict: The Sabah experience under the ruling Sabah Alliance (1963-1976)', *Jebat: Malaysian Journal of History, Politics & Strategic Studies* 26 (2020); James Chin, 'Politics of federal intervention in Malaysia, with reference to Sarawak, Sabah and Kelantan', *Journal of Commonwealth & Comparative Politics* 35, no. 2 (1997): 96-120; Tricia Yeoh, *Federal-State Relations under the Pakatan Harapan Government* (Singapore: ISEAS-Yusof Ishak Institute, 2020). See the following for discussion of the relationship in campaigns: Bruce Gale, 'Politics at the Periphery: A Study of the 1981 and 1982 Election Campaigns in Sabah', *Contemporary Southeast Asia* 6, no. 1 (1984): 26-49; Sabihah Osman, 'Sabah state elections: implications for Malaysian unity', *Asian Survey* 32, no. 4 (1992): 380-391; Mohamad Nawab Mohamad Osman, 'A Transitioning Sabah In A Changing Malaysia', *Kajian Malaysia* 35, no. 1 (2017): 23-40.

[27] See, for example, Farish A. Noor, 'The 13th Malaysian general elections from a Sabah perspective', *The Round Table* 102, no. 6 (2013): 541-548 and Arnold Puyok and Tony Paridi Bagang, 'Ethnicity, Culture and Indigenous Leadership in Modern Politics: The Case of the KadazanDusun in Sabah, East Malaysia', *Kajian Malaysia: Journal of Malaysian Studies* 29 (2011): 177-97.

[28] Robert Milne, 'Patrons, clients and ethnicity: The case of Sarawak and Sabah in Malaysia', *Asian Survey* 13, no. 10 (1973): 891-907.

Research on Sabah has also led the way in a focus on personality and patronage.[29] Personal ties and the performance and accessibility of local leaders has consistently been emphasised. Sabah's low population, its geography with a large share of Sabahans living in rural and remote areas, and the state's challenging social conditions which reinforce reciprocal ties have underscored a focus on hierarchical relationships. These explanations are often intertwined with ethnicity, with the central role of the *Huguan Siou*, the paramount leader of the KDM, highlighted. The entry of UMNO into Sabah has extended the discussion about patronage further, drawing attention to party machinery and the expansion of vote buying and money politics.[30] Corruption has been seen to become an integral part of Sabah politics. Other scholars have highlighted the role of developmentalism – development promises – as a means to woo support.[31]

These varied explanations broadly fall into two paradigms – those that highlight political narratives for mobilisation and those that centre on vertical political engagement. Research that draws attention to the federal-state relationship prioritises more systemic inequalities. What is striking about our understanding of Sabah politics is how much is left out. Sabahans are given little agency – instead they are acted upon or mobilised by elite political narratives or politicians. The role of elites is prioritised. There is little attention paid to differences among Sabahans beyond ethnicity, and to a lesser extent the urban-rural divide. Sabah is acknowledged to be unique, but Sabah politics has been seen narrowly.

Rethinking Analysis

This book aims to move beyond these approaches. While acknowledging these established scholarly frameworks is useful and relevant for understanding Sabah politics – as many of the chapters in the book show – they are inadequate.

---

29 See Faisal S. Hazis, 'Patronage, Power and Prowess: Barisan Nasional's Equilibrium Dominance in East Malaysia', *Kajian Malaysia: Journal of Malaysian Studies* 33, no. 2 (2015): 1-24.

30 James Chin, 'Going east: UMNO's entry into Sabah politics', *Asian Journal of Political Science* 7, no. 1 (1999): 20-40.

31 Francis Loh Kok Wah, 'Developmentalism and the limits of democratic discourse' in Francis Loh Kok Wah and Khoo Boo Teik (eds), *Democracy in Malaysia: Discourses and Practices* (London: Curzon, 2002), 19-50

The shortcomings fall into three categories. Generally, these approaches often underestimate the pluralism within Sabah – the differences of views within ethnic communities, and the importance of other social cleavages. Intentionally, the essays in this collection engage with different forms of identity and different perspectives. Special attention is placed on the role of generational, gender and class differences. An integral part of this is the inclusion of scholars from different academic disciplines outside of political science, notably anthropology, communication and economics, and the inclusion of journalists and activists. The contributors use different methods of analysis. While some base their arguments on data from ethnography or quantitative data from election results, others rely on building their arguments from interviews, historical interpretations as well as from personal experience. The only common thread is the shared experience of being on the ground during PRN2020.

Second, we aim to contextualise the discussion within a wider context of changing politics in Sabah. Elections decide who governs (when there is not an Emergency declaration) but they are often aberrations. This collection addresses a wide range of issues and themes that have been and continue to be relevant in the Sabah space; topics of ethnicity, belonging, economy, governance, indigeneity, activism and leadership, with many of the issues overlapping. We bring in discussions, for example, of policies and civil society activism to enrich the context of Sabah politics. Not only do these areas influence the election through who runs, the agendas and grievances, but they persist long after the election is over, shaping the lived experiences of politics.

By going wide, the additional aim is to bring the voices of more Sabahans into the discussion. We recognise that many of our contributors are members of the elite themselves, but their attention to youths, the less disadvantaged and more marginalised groups aims for greater inclusivity. By starting from an appreciation of difference, we work to unpack the systemic processes and conditions found in Sabah that may have limited previous attempts to discuss Sabah's politics at large. Multidisciplinary work allows us to understand quandaries both from the top-down and the bottom-up, helping us to build knowledge and challenge current thinking. Ultimately, whether complementing or contrasting, the chapters in the collection offer an opportunity to rethink Sabah's past, present and future. By no means is our collection fully representative of the issues involved, but it aims to move the analysis forward.

Reading Ahead

We have divided the chapters into four interconnected sections: context, narratives, campaigning and results. The breakdown of the sixteen chapters into these sections provides an easy way to understand the Sabah election for both those unfamiliar and familiar with Sabah. Many of the chapters recontextualise or take alternative views of longstanding issues and concerns.

We start the discussion with attention to context by looking at Shafie's Warisan/PH government in office. The first chapter by Chan Tsu Chong offers insights into the successes and failures of the former government. It was clear that the Warisan/PH administration had high hopes for success. And, as Chan notes, there were many successes. However, poor economic performance and a failure to follow up on campaign promises, especially greater state autonomy, left the government vulnerable going into the elections, ultimately contributing to its defeat.

The second chapter by Johan Arriffin Samad tackles the difficult issue of MA63 and state autonomy more broadly. He highlights the many attempts to restore the original agreement by numerous parties and shows that progress was made in the past few years, especially under Warisan/PH, but serious gaps and obstacles remain. Johan's chapter outlines the contentious issues facing the current PN Muhyiddin/Hajiji governments and in the process illustrates that the state's national narrative remains strong.

Economic conditions were also impactful in the 2020 election. James Alin and Marcilla Malasius look at the problem of high unemployment in the state. Even factoring for the Covid-19 economic downturn, they found that unemployment rates were rising due to unrealistic expectations, mismanagement and latent issues under Warisan/PH's governance. While the Warisan/PH government recognised the issue and implemented a heartfelt campaign to promote jobs, their performance in power fell short, and arguably was destined to fall short given structural problems facing Sabah's economy.

Representing civil society organisations (CSOs), Beverly Joeman, Nelson Dino and Asraf Sharafi Mohammad Azhar write about the roles these organisations play in representing Sabahan interests against corrupt and inefficient governance. Their chapter highlights the role of civil society as a political 'third force' to provide a check-and-balance against governmental and political powers, and to serve regular Sabahans who are left behind at the grassroots level. In particular, they draw attention to mobilisation around the environment, electoral reform and social inequality, especially the treatment of undocumented persons.

Two chapters specifically address the thorny issue of immigration and undocumented persons in Sabah – arguably the most prominent issue shaping the narrative of Sabah politics.[32] Tied to perceptions of displacement and belonging, this issue provokes strong emotions and remains at the core of the state's politics. While labeling includes 'illegal', 'irregular' and 'PTI/PATI' (abbreviations for *pendatang asing tanpa izin* or foreign migrants without permission) we use 'irregular migrants' in this book insofar as possible. Vilashini Somiah and Aslam Abd Jalil offer an insightful chapter on how regional differences in Sabah, between the west and the 'treacherous' east, influence narratives and shape politics. Using interviews with youths, Trixie Tangit finds that young voters are not as driven by ethnocentric politics. They prefer candidates who embrace pluralism and are focused on representing the communities rather than themselves.

Looking at the PRN2020 campaign, journalist Philip Golingai presents first-hand accounts from Sabah politicians over their strategies and rhetoric to engage with the electorate. With interviews conducted after the election, both government and opposition representatives reflected on their successes and failures during the campaign and what the future holds for Sabah. Benjamin YH Loh and Yi Jian Ho take a closer look at how social media campaigning took place in these elections and analyse the impact of 'cybertroopers' on online discussions. While cybertroopers were out in force, their impact was not as devastating as in Peninsular Malaysia. They show that social media both reflected and expanded political space in Sabah. In her first individual chapter, Bridget Welsh provides an analysis of campaigning on the ground during the elections. Based on ethnographic observations and interviews, she lays out the highly contrasting approaches employed by both Warisan Plus and GRS and shows that a 'Sabah style' of campaigning emerged, tied to masculinity and the exploitation of local conditions on the ground. Undi Sabah leaders Mahirah Marzuki, Fiqah Roslan, and Auzellea Kristin Mozihimin write about their experiences with Undi Sabah and their efforts to engage with the youths during the

---

32 Catherine Allerton, 'Contested statelessness in Sabah, Malaysia: Irregularity and the politics of recognition', *Journal of Immigrant & Refugee Studies* 15, no. 3 (2017): 250-268.

campaign. They show that youths played a major role in the elections, and that despite growing engagement, more is needed to strengthen engagement with younger voters.

The final section of the book turns to the results. Bridget Welsh begins the discussion with a detailed study of the electorate and voting behavior along different social cleavages. She finds that the impact of gender and class differences have been inadequately appreciated and argues that a more holistic approach is needed for a better understanding of voting. She turns to the results, suggesting that changes from the addition of 13 new seats, postal voting and turnout did influence outcomes in the competitive contest, but notes that persistent patterns in voting along polarised lines are becoming more entrenched.

Three chapters adopt the traditional ethnic lens to understand the electoral outcome. Oh Ei Sun and Amanda Yin Yeo take a historical look, exploring why Chinese Sabahans stood so firmly behind Warisan Plus despite the fact that Peninsular Chinese were growing disheartened with PH. They discuss how Chinese Sabahans contrast to their counterparts in Sarawak and Peninsular Malaysia. They argue that Chinese Sabahans are more self-reliant and less dependent on government support, which affords them greater agency to vote based on larger ideals rather than simple self-preservation. Arnold Puyok and Tony Paridi focus on the 'KDM factor' in the campaign. They describe how the homogenisation of the KDM community dilutes and diminishes their nuanced political participation. At the same time, they argue that the communities focus on personalities rather than political dogma, and as a voting bloc they adopted more conservative voting patterns. Mohd Rahimin Mustafa examines how Islam is shaping Sabah politics and how Muslim politics has evolved, with cooperation and divisions both evident in PRN2020. He argues that the dynamics among Muslim Bumiputera are being shaped by Peninsular Malaysia, but simultaneously, conditions within Sabah itself and competition among elites are transforming the state's politics.

Finally, to conclude the book, Bridget Welsh, Benjamin YH Loh and Vilashini Somiah reflect on the fallout from the election. The end of the elections did not signal a return to normalcy in Sabah as Covid-19 cases rose precipitously, leading to a third wave of infections throughout Malaysia. The new GRS government, which faced bitter infighting immediately after winning, left Sabah without a strong leadership to see it through the coronavirus crisis. Our conclusion discusses what this new government spells for Sabah and Malaysia's future. In the process we bring together the various findings of the contributors, and flesh out a different, more ordinary, people-centred approach for understanding Sabah politics moving forward – the politics of survival.

Part 1

Context

Chapter 1

Warisan Plus in Government: A Retrospective from the Campaign and Beyond[1]

Chan Tsu Chong

Politics in Sabah has always been feisty. The 14th General Election (GE14) in 2018 saw a change of government at the federal level for the first time, but Sabah has experienced changes of government before. Nevertheless, the 2020 Sabah state election (PRN2020) was an unpleasant surprise, not least because it was caused by an attempted takeover in the midst of the Covid-19 pandemic. This eventually led to a third wave of infections in Malaysia.

At the centre of PRN2020 was Parti Warisan Sabah (Warisan), a relatively new party, only officially established in October 2016.[2] It was formed by Shafie Apdal after he was sacked from the cabinet for questioning the 1MDB Scandal. Warisan and its allies from Pakatan Harapan (PH) were able to organise themselves and capitalise on the political opportunity afforded by GE14. They formed the government after GE14 and were in power for 26 months, until the sudden dissolution of the state assembly in July 2020. In PRN2020, Warisan and Shafie Apdal were still popular in Sabah, but they failed to defend their position and were ousted by the hastily established Gabungan Rakyat Sabah (GRS) coalition.[3]

---

1 The author would like to thank the editors for their suggestions and comments on the chapter, and Bridget Welsh for always being a supportive mentor.

2 To be exact, Warisan was formed via a takeover and relaunch of Parti Pembangunan Warisan Sabah, a dormant political party.

3 The GRS consists of parties from the Barisan Nasional (BN) coalition, Perikatan Nasional (PN) coalition, and Parti Bersatu Sabah (PBS).

This chapter seeks to provide readers with an overview of PRN2020 in the context of Warisan and the key political issues in Sabah. Here, I focus on how Warisan was affected by, and dealt with, five key issues: (1) party hopping and patronage; (2) economic development; (3) state nationalism and federal-state relations; (4) statelessness and undocumented immigration; and (5) ethnic politics. These issues are of course not exhaustive, but they were, based on my field observations, pertinent during PRN2020.[4] These issues have shaped Sabah politics in many ways before PRN2020. It is necessary, therefore, to analyse the issues in a wider timeframe. Throughout this chapter, I focus on three time points for analysis: (1) GE14 in 2018; (2) Warisan's 26 months in power as the state government; and (3) PRN2020.

I argue that Warisan capitalised on key political issues during GE14, but was never in a dominant position during or after GE14. Indeed I argue that Sabahans were mainly voting *against* BN, UMNO in particular, as opposed to voting *for* Warisan. While the Warisan government had some key successes in addressing these issues, they were set back by poor coordination, implementation and communication. Voters in PRN2020, therefore, were unable to relate to Warisan's successes and were drawn by other considerations.

Party Hopping and Patronage

PRN2020 was set in motion when several assemblypersons from the Warisan-PH-UPKO coalition crossed over to support UMNO's former chief minister, Musa Aman. But party hopping is not new in Sabah. In 1985, Parti Bersatu Sabah (PBS) won the state elections and formed the government, but an election was forced less than a year later in 1986 after several of its assemblypersons defected to the United Sabah National Organisation (USNO). History repeated itself in the 1994 state elections. PBS won the elections with a two-seat majority, but several of its assemblypersons crossed

[4] The field observations were based on my visit to Sabah from 11-23 September 2020. I was based in Tawau and made trips to the neighbouring constituencies. The observations include: monitoring the campaign activities and materials of candidates, unstructured interviews with candidates, party workers and voters, as well as media monitoring, especially local dailies. After PRN2020, I followed up with some of the party workers to seek their views on the outcome of the elections.

over again, resulting in UMNO forming the government.[5]

Likewise, in GE14, Warisan did not win the state elections per se. The result was essentially a tie with BN winning 29 seats and Warisan, together with its PH partners, also winning 29 seats. The other two seats were won by Parti Solidariti Tanah Airku Rakyat Sabah (STAR). In terms of the popular vote, Warisan and PH collectively obtained 45.93 per cent of the vote share compared with BN's 40.97 per cent. On the night of the elections, the incumbent Chief Minister Musa Aman, announced that BN had obtained a simple majority, with the support of Jeffrey Kitingan's STAR party. Warisan announced not long after that it has obtained the support of six assemblypersons from BN – four from UMNO and two from United Pasokmomogun Kadazandusun Murut Organisation (UPKO). With the crossovers, Shafie Apdal was sworn in as the chief minister on 12 May 2018.

How did voters react to the party hopping incident that triggered PRN2020? A large section of voters were naturally angry about the crossovers and attempted political takeover. In one instance, the Democratic Action Party (DAP) organised a frog-themed dinner in Kota Kinabalu, where candidates symbolically roasted frogs in protest against party hopping. Such sentiment, however, was mostly contained in urban areas. In an interview after the elections, a local DAP leader from a rural constituency reflected that voters in semi-rural and rural areas do not perceive party hopping as a problem.[6] He opined that some voters there even felt that party hopping was beneficial because it allowed their representative to access funds for development. At the same time, some local Sabahan parties argued that Warisan had a taste of their own medicine.[7] They referred to the fact that Warisan did not win GE14 and instead enticed crossovers from BN. Warisan candidates rebutted this by arguing that the scenario was different because it was before a government was formed. Likewise, Jeffrey Kitingan, nicknamed 'King Katak' (King Frog) for his regular party hopping throughout his career, lamented in an interview that he had been wrongly

---

[5] For more details see: Mohamed Nawab Mohamed Osman, 'A Transitioning Sabah in a Changing Malaysia,' *Kajian Malaysia* 35, no. 1 (2017): 24–28.

[6] Anonymous DAP leader from Sabah, personal communication, 9 October, 2020.

[7] 'Hypocrisy of Warisan Is Now Clear, Says Gagasan', *Daily Express*, 23 June 2020, https://www.dailyexpress.com.my/news/154695/hypocrisy-of-warisan-is-now-clear-says-gagasan/.

labelled as a *katak* because he had never crossed over to make a government collapse.[8]

Voters in general were apathetic and sceptical towards the debate over party hopping during PRN2020. There was a sense that party hopping was an established norm and part of the political culture: those who were exasperated about party hopping felt powerless to do anything about it, and on the other hand, there were voters who did not perceive it as a problem. Out of the 19 assemblypersons who defected since being elected in 2018 (some of whom double-defected i.e. in 2018 and again in 2020), only seven of them did not get re-elected in PRN2020, of which five stood as independent candidates.[9]

The context of party hopping is important for several reasons. It goes beyond moralistic corruption and reflects the deep-rooted nature of patronage in Sabah's politics. Ruling parties in Sabah, especially BN in the past decade, have relied on public institutions, resources, and favours in order to maintain support among the people and the government.[10] The timber industry, for example, was utilised to establish clientelist networks among politicians, business elites and the electorate.[11] Assemblypersons cross over to other parties to maintain power, support and patronage networks. As I shall further explain in the proceeding sections, political patronage is also interlinked with state-federal relations.

Dismantling patronage culture requires fundamental changes in the way politics and the economy is organised. Warisan's 26 months in government were perhaps too short to drive such changes. Nevertheless, Shafie Apdal took several steps to address patronage politics and corruption during Warisan's tenure. Among the key reforms were related to the timber

8 Philip Golingai, 'When Is Party-Hopping Okay? Jeffrey Kitingan Speaks', *The Star*, 13 August 2020, https://www.thestar.com.my/opinion/columnists/one-mans-meat/2020/08/13/when-is-party-hopping-okay-jeffrey-kitingan-speaks.

9 Andrew Ong, 'Sabah Voters Are Kind to Defectors', *Malaysiakini*, 27 September 2020, https://www.malaysiakini.com/news/544239.

10 For further details see: Faisal S. Hazis, 'Patronage, Power, and Prowess: Barisan Nasional's Equilibrium Dominance in East Malaysia', *Kajian Malaysia* 33, no. 2 (2015): 1–24.

11 Teresa Maria Chala, 'The "Green Gold" of Sabah: Timber Politics and Resource Sustainability' (PhD thesis, The University of Melbourne, 2000), http://hdl.handle.net/11343/35977.

industry. He banned the export of logs in an attempt to curtail the timber cartels that have long monopolised the industry. The government reactivated the Illegal Logging Crackdown Committee to act against corruption among bureaucrats and logging companies, leading to several raids by the MACC.[12] The state government sought to catalyse downstream industries, such as furniture factories, to create jobs for locals. During PRN2020, these reforms were often highlighted during rallies, especially by Shafie Apdal. Voters, especially those in the vicinity of logging areas such as Tawau and Sandakan, understood the issue well and responded positively when reforms were explained.

On the other hand, old habits die hard – patronage politics was still practiced under Warisan's rule. The state government made political appointments to state entities and companies. Allocations to state assemblypersons were still limited to government representatives only, and this created pressure for those in the opposition to access those resources. Eventually, more assemblypersons crossed over and joined Warisan, followed by a wave of defections at the grassroots level, and Warisan welcomed the party hoppers.[13]

Economic Development

During PRN2020, economic development, or rather the lack of it, was still a major concern among voters. In Tawau, youths I spoke to lamented the lack of opportunities and 'buzz' in the town centre. This has caused most youths to head towards Peninsular Malaysia or Singapore to develop their careers. The Warisan-DAP candidate there, Justin Wong, pledged to empower entrepreneurship and rejuvenate the city, and this was well-received among the locals.

Sabah, on the whole, suffers from underdevelopment. The state has the highest absolute poverty rate in Malaysia – at 19.5 per cent compared

---

12 Tracy Patrick, 'MACC Raids Sabah Forestry Department, Timber Firms', *Free Malaysia Today*, 2 August 2018, https://www.freemalaysiatoday.com/category/nation/2018/08/02/macc-raids-sabah-forestry-department-timber-firms/.

13 See, for example: '7,206 Ahli UMNO Keluar Parti, Sertai Warisan', *Astro Awani*, 9 December 2018, https://www.astroawani.com/berita-malaysia/7206-ahli-umno-keluar-parti-sertai-warisan-193120.

with the nation's average of 5.6 per cent.[14] It suffers from a lack of basic infrastructure, such as roads, water and electricity, owing to years of mismanagement and neglect. When I was in Sabah during the elections, I witnessed two separate water supply disruptions. The locals were frustrated, but they appeared fatalistic and brushed it off as a normal occurrence, signifying their deep cynicism of the government's ability to resolve basic infrastructure issues.

During Warisan's tenure in government, one of its foci was to develop the production sector to drive economic growth. This was important because economic development models have emphasised the importance of industrialisation as an engine of growth.[15] In other words, industrialisation is essential for generating greater economic productivity and growth in the long run. To put this into context, Sabah's economic structure is highly dependent on mining and quarrying activities (petroleum) and has a very low industrial capacity. The contribution of the manufacturing sector in 2019 stood at 7.6 per cent of the GDP, as compared with the national average of 22.3 per cent.[16]

One of the initiatives by the Warisan government was the ban on the export of logs in order to promote growth in downstream activities, such as furniture manufacturing. This has led to increased private investment for the sector and created more job opportunities.[17] Another example is the launch of Sabah's first home-grown cooking oil brand, leveraging on the state's existing palm oil sector. Instead of merely producing and selling raw palm oil, Sabah now has the capability to process, bottle and market palm-based cooking oil which has a higher value. The Warisan government also allocated funds from their annual budget to encourage entrepreneurship among youths.[18]

---

14 Department of Statistics, Malaysia, 'Household Income and Basic Amenities Survey Report 2019', July 2020.

15 See, for example, Nicholas Kaldor's three growth laws: Servaas Storm, 'Structural Change', *Development and Change* 46, no. 4 (1 July 2015): 670–74.

16 Department of Statistics, Malaysia, 'Laporan Sosioekonomi Negeri Sabah 2019', 2020.

17 See, for example, Cynthia Baga, 'Log ban bearing fruit', *Daily Express*, 22 September 2019, https://www.dailyexpress.com.my/news/140884/log-ban-bearing-fruit/

18 Ilona Andrew, 'Sabah grants RM2 million for youth entrepreneurship', *Borneo Today*, 19 November 2019, https://www.borneotoday.net/sabah-grants-rm-2-million-for-youth-entrepreneurship/.

The Warisan government was also successful in negotiating for more funds from the federal government. Sabah is entitled, under the Federal Constitution, to a special grant from the federal government. The grant was supposed to be 40 per cent of net revenue derived by the federal government from the state, but the amount of grant money had remained unchanged and unreviewed since 1974. In the PH's budget for 2020, the special grant was doubled from RM26.7 million to RM53.4 million,[19] although it was still below what was anticipated by the state government. Under the PH government, the development allocation for Sabah also increased from RM4.1 billion in 2018 to RM5.1 billion in 2020. These development expenditures, when translated into projects, are also a major part of the patron-client relationship at the state and grassroots levels. A key contributing factor to Warisan getting into power in GE14 was via defections, tied to the presumption that it would be able to maintain and create new patronage networks, given that Warisan was allied with PH who were then the federal government. This condition was, of course, no longer present following the 'Sheraton Move' in 2020, leading to the fall of the Warisan government not long after.

Warisan's efforts and policies to strengthen the economy did not feature prominently during PRN2020. Candidates focused more on generalised sentiments such as state nationalism. The underlying issue is that most voters did not feel that life was better, economically, under the Warisan government. Bread-and-butter issues, such as poverty and unemployment, showed little improvement during Warisan's tenure. Of course, Warisan was not all to blame. The Covid-19 pandemic aside, two years was hardly sufficient for socio-economic transformation. Sabah's economic problems are also linked to other socio-political dimensions, as I shall further explain below.

State Nationalism and Federal-state Relations

The Malaysian Agreement 1963 (MA63) provides several safeguards to Sabah's (and Sarawak's) sovereignty and autonomy. This covers matters such as state immigration, language, finance and education. However,

---

19 This amount has reverted back to RM26.7 million under the PN government's budget for 2021.

over the years, the position and autonomy of Sabah has eroded and the federal government often intervened in Sabah's internal politics.[20] This has intensified state nationalism in the form of 'anti-federal' sentiments, and federal-state relations continue to affect Sabah's politics in many ways.

In GE14, national politics mattered and had an impact on local sentiments. The elephant in the room was of course the 1MDB Scandal.[21] The scandal, coupled with bread-and-butter issues such as the Goods and Service Tax (GST) and a high cost of living, created a strong resentment towards BN among voters nationally. The opposition in Sabah was able to capture the opportunity by contextualising these issues with reference to local concerns. Shafie's arrest by the Malaysian Anti-Corruption Commission (MACC) in 2017, after he openly challenged the then Prime Minister Najib Razak and formed Warisan, was seen by many Sabahans as a form of political persecution and oppression by Peninsular Malaysia against Sabahans.[22] The anti-BN sentiment was also affected by BN and Sabah UMNO's increasing unpopularity. Many, including his supporters, felt that Chief Minister Musa Aman had been in power for too long.[23] He was seen as being subservient to UMNO to maintain his position and therefore not willing to demand greater state autonomy and seek recognition on issues such as oil royalties or citizenship.

On the other hand, local opposition parties continued championing 'Sabah for Sabahans,' contending that the people of Sabah should be represented by local Sabahan parties. One of the key local parties during

---

[20] James Chin, 'Federal-East Malaysia Relations: Primus-Inter-Pares?', in Andrew J. Harding and James Chin (eds.) *50 Years of Malaysia: Federalism Revisited* (Singapore: Marshall Cavendish Editions, 2014), 152–85.

[21] The 1MDB Scandal is a corruption scandal involving the former Prime Minister Najib Razak. Allegedly, USD4.5 billion had been laundered through a series of complex transactions and companies around the world. For further details, see: Randeep Ramesh, '1MDB: The Inside Story of the World's Biggest Financial Scandal,' *The Guardian*, 28 July 2016, http://www.theguardian.com/world/2016/jul/28/1mdb-inside-story-worlds-biggest-financial-scandal-malaysia.

[22] Tracy Patrick, 'Shafie's Arrest Could Be a Blessing to Warisan', *Free Malaysia Today*, 21 October 2017, https://www.freemalaysiatoday.com/category/nation/2017/10/21/shafies-arrest-could-be-a-blessing-to-warisan/.

[23] James Chin, 'Sabah and Sarawak in the 14th General Election 2018 (GE14): Local Factors and State Nationalism', *Journal of Current Southeast Asian Affairs* 37, no. 3 (2018): 173–92.

GE14 was STAR. This party was led by Jeffrey Kitingan, who had been building his political movement around state nationalism and Kadazan, Dusun and Murut (KDM) support since the 12th General Election in 2008.[24] Warisan also capitalised on state nationalist sentiments by promising to restore Sabah's rights and the MA63, and this was echoed by Pakatan Harapan at the federal level. As such, Warisan successfully established themselves as a strong and credible party to win the state and federal elections (together with PH), as opposed to the smaller local parties who failed to form credible alliances.[25]

During PRN2020, Warisan and GRS took opposing positions in terms of state nationalism. On one hand, Warisan decried that the PN-led federal government had again interfered in Sabahan politics and attempted to bring down a government elected by the people. Shafie Apdal, in his campaign speeches, rallied voters to protect Sabah's rights and autonomy against Peninsular Malaysia's interference. This caused complications with his allies in PH who are seen as Peninsular Malaysian parties. The PH component parties mobilised many of their national leaders to campaign as they were popular among voters, especially in urban areas. One national leader from PH was left angered when his Sabahan colleague commented that the campaign was too Peninsular-centric because of the presence of national leaders.[26] Likewise, Warisan leveraged such state nationalist sentiments in negotiating seats and the use of a common logo with the PH parties.

On the other side, GRS did not appeal much to state nationalism. It was clear from the outset that their biggest selling point was federal-state alignment. Prime Minister Muhyiddin Yassin called upon voters to choose parties that held federal power so that the new state government could have a close relationship with, and continued support from, the federal government for development.[27] Warisan reacted by accusing the prime minister of making a threat: that the federal government would not support Sabah if its people did not vote for his coalition. Yet, voters, especially in

---

24 James Chin and Arnold Puyok, 'Going Against the Tide: Sabah and the 2008 Malaysian General Election', *Asian Politics & Policy* 2, no. 2 (2 April 2010): 224.

25 Arnold Puyok and Piya Raj Sukhani, 'Sabah: Breakthrough in the Fixed Deposit State', *The Round Table* 109, no. 2 (2020): 213.

26 Anonymous Member of Parliament, personal communication, September 2020.

27 Hariz Mohd, 'Vote for Those Who Hold Federal Power - Muhyiddin Tells Sabahans', *Malaysiakini*, 16 September 2020, https://www.malaysiakini.com/news/542851.

semi- and rural areas, resonated with GRS's appeal. GRS went into the elections without having a clear chief ministerial candidate, but this was evidently of secondary importance to voters when compared to the appeal of federal-state alignment. On the ground, many campaign materials featured Muhyiddin Yassin's portrait more prominently than the candidates or Sabahan leaders. In Kalabakan, I spoke to a voter who did not know who this 'Datuk' (Muhyiddin Yassin) on the election banner was, but despite that he claimed that he would vote for the 'federal government' to ensure development. This shows that patronage and federal-state relations are instinctive to voters at the grassroots level.

While in power, the Warisan state government and PH federal government took steps to restore MA63 and gain greater autonomy for Sabah and Sarawak. The Special Cabinet Committee on MA63 was set up in September 2018. The government announced that 17 out of 21 issues brought forth by the Sabah and Sarawak state governments in relation to MA63 have been agreed upon. These issues include, among others, export duties on timber, regulation of electricity and gas, human resources, land matters and judiciary powers.[28] These reforms are tangible steps that would strengthen the administration and autonomy of the state governments in the long run. However, the Warisan and PH government had major weaknesses in communicating their successes to the public and, instead, were often drawn into adverse narratives by the opposition.[29] The MA63 reforms were no exception. Success stories, especially those that were technical in nature, were not communicated through meaningful ways that were relatable to the people. During PRN2020, voters did not relate to the MA63 reforms undertaken by Warisan and PH, neither did the candidates speak much about them.

However, this is not to say that Warisan had a smooth and strong working relationship with the PH-led federal government. Politically, Warisan has never been an official member of the PH coalition. Warisan protested against the entry of Mahathir Mohamad's party, Parti Pribumi

---

28 Parlimen Malaysia, 'Parliament Hansard, Dewan Negara for 10 December 2019', 2019: 6-17.

29 Nathaniel Tan, 'Is Pakatan Failing Due to Bad Communications Strategy?', *The Star*, 18 February 2020, https://www.thestar.com.my/opinion/columnists/all-the-pieces-matter/2020/02/18/is-pakatan-failing-due-to-bad-communications-strategy.

Bersatu Malaysia (Bersatu), into Sabah as the move risked displacing Warisan's political position in the state. Nevertheless, Bersatu made its way into Sabah despite the unhappiness among Warisan leaders and supporters.[30] Five Members of Parliament and eight assemblypersons from UMNO Sabah, including the present Chief Minister Hajiji Noor, eventually joined Bersatu.

Another central issue which remained unresolved was the petroleum royalty. For Sabah, the royalty is the biggest contributor to the state's revenue (projected at 40.6 per cent of revenue or RM1.7 billion in 2020). The state has been receiving only 5 per cent in petroleum royalties, and politicians have criticised this as an example of the unequal partnership between the Borneo states and Peninsular Malaysia. PH promised in their GE14 manifesto to increase the petroleum royalty to 20 per cent, only to backtrack and say it was 'really not workable'.[31] GRS echoed the same sentiment during PRN2020, arguing that Sabah may never get the 20 per cent petroleum royalty but there are other ways around it.[32] The difference, however, was that GRS did not want to over-promise and face the same challenge as PH did with its GE14 manifesto.

GRS was correct in that there may be other ways to increase Sabah's revenue from petroleum. For example, the Warisan government followed Sarawak's move to introduce a 5 per cent sales tax on petroleum products. This was an effective alternative to increase the state's income from petroleum. To put this into perspective, the sales tax was expected to increase the state's revenue by 14 per cent in 2020.[33] Out of the nine oil and gas companies in Sabah, only Petronas, the national oil and gas company,

---

30 Julia Chan, 'Bersatu Enters Sabah, Mixed Feelings All Round', *Malay Mail Online*, 6 April 2019, https://www.malaymail.com/news/malaysia/2019/04/06/bersatu-enters-sabah-mixed-feelings-all-round/1740348.

31 'Dr M: 20pct Oil Royalty for Sarawak, Sabah 'Really Not Workable', *Borneo Post Online*, 27 September 2019, https://www.theborneopost.com/2019/09/27/dr-m-20pct-oil-royalty-for-sarawak-sabah-really-not-workable/.

32 Stephanie Lee, 'Sabah May Never Get 20% Oil Royalty, but There Are Other Ways to Get What Is Owed to the State, says Bung Moktar', *The Star*, 17 September 2020, https://www.thestar.com.my/news/nation/2020/09/17/sabah-may-never-get-20-oil-royalty-but-there-are-other-ways-to-get-what-is-owed-to-the-state-says-bung-moktar.

33 Olivia Miwil, 'Sabah Expects Monthly RM50 Million Revenue from Tax Collection of Oil and Gas Products', *New Straits Times Online*, 21 April 2020, https://www.nst.com.my/news/nation/2020/04/586234/sabah-expects-monthly-rm50-million-revenue-tax-collection-oil-and-gas.

resisted and did not pay the sales tax. Petronas is a state-owned company, which meant that the PH government would have been involved, in one way or another, in not recognising and withholding the petroleum sales tax. It was only after PRN2020 that the new government announced that Petronas would pay RM1.3 billion in sales tax to Sabah in 2020.[34] The new government has claimed credit over the issue, arguing that Warisan was not serious in pursuing the petroleum tax as they did not want to offend former Prime Minister Mahathir Mohamad and their federal partners.[35]

Statelessness and Irregular Migration

Statelessness and illegal immigrants (commonly referred as *pendatang asing tanpa izin*, PATI) have been a key point of political contention in Sabah. The crux of differences relate to the large number of non-citizens in Sabah, estimated at one million (25.6 per cent) in comparison to the state's total population of 3.9 million in 2020.[36] Many of them can be traced to refugees from the Sulu Archipelago who were permitted to stay and work in Sabah in the early 1970s.[37] Previous state governments, especially the USNO and BERJAYA governments, were alleged to have encouraged further immigration and resettlement by Filipino Muslims to strengthen their political positions.[38] This was further exacerbated by the Project IC syndicate, which systematically gave citizenship and identity cards to immigrants.[39]

---

[34] Petronas had initiated a judicial review to challenge the legality of the petroleum sales tax by the Sarawak state government. The Kuching High Court decided, on 13 March 2020, that the sales tax was valid. Petronas further appealed the case, but the appeal was subsequently withdrawn on the instructions of the PN government. See: Sulok Tawie, 'Sarawak CM Claims Petronas Told to Withdraw Court Appeal against Paying Sales Tax', *Malay Mail Online*, 12 June 2020, https://www.malaymail.com/news/malaysia/2020/06/12/sarawak-cm-claims-petronas-told-to-withdraw-court-appeal-against-paying-sal/1874927.

[35] 'Shafie Didn't Pursue Petroleum Sales Tax for Fear of Offending Dr M, Says Former Asst Minister', *Free Malaysia Today*, 11 November 2020, https://www.freemalaysiatoday.com/category/nation/2020/11/11/shafie-didnt-pursue-petroleum-sales-tax-for-fear-of-offending-dr-m-says-former-asst-minister/.

[36] Department of Statistics, Malaysia, 'Current Population Estimates, Malaysia 2020,' July 2020.

[37] Puyok and Sukhani, 'Sabah: Breakthrough.'

[38] Mohamad Osman, 'A Transitioning Sabah,' 30.

[39] Catherine Allerton, 'Contested Statelessness in Sabah, Malaysia: Irregularity and the

After GE14, the PH and Warisan governments attempted to address statelessness and immigration issues. They sought to introduce the Pas Sabah Sementara (Sabah Temporary Pass, PSS) to streamline the documents being used by immigrants in Sabah.[40] The PSS was met with intense backlash, not least because the opposition was successful in using the issue to their advantage. The PATI issue is highly emotive amongst Sabahans. Many see the migrants as a major threat to their rights, identity, and economic opportunities. Many felt that the previous governments have exploited the issue for their political purposes at the expense of the people.

The height of these attacks was during the Kimanis by-election in January 2020. Warisan and PH were heavily accused by their opponents of trying to use the PSS to legitimise the migrants as citizens and to alter the state's ethnic balance. This further fuelled the rhetoric that Warisan is a 'PATI party'. Three days before polling day, several NGOs organised an anti-PSS rally to oppose the policy, and the rally attracted the attendance of over 500 people. The PSS became, arguably, the biggest issue during the by-election and contributed towards Warisan's loss.[41] Several days after losing the by-election, the Warisan government announced that the PSS would be scrapped.

For those who are stateless in Sabah, it is a lived reality of despair, destitution and insecurity.[42] The fact is that this perennial issue is tied to complex socio-historical legacies. One of the main problems was the overlapping legal documentation system, which the PSS sought to resolve. The problem, with regards to the backlash against Warisan, was not with the design of the PSS per se. Rather, Warisan lost control of the narrative from the get-go. In this respect, Warisan shared many problems faced by the PH federal government, especially in terms of communication and

---

Politics of Recognition', *Journal of Immigrant & Refugee Studies* 15, no. 3 (2017): 261-262.

40 Under the present system, there are three different legal documents for an immigrant: the IMM13, *Kad Burung-Burung and Sijil Banci*. For further details on this, see: Chong Eng Leong, 'The Facts on Sabah IMM13, Burung Burung and Sijil Banci', *Borneo Today*, 27 June 2020, https://www.borneotoday.net/the-facts-on-sabah-imm13-burung-burung-and-sijil-banci/.

41 Martin Vengadesan, 'BN's PSS Tactics Played a Part in Kimanis Win', *Malaysiakini,* 19 January 2020, https://www.malaysiakini.com/news/507618.

42 Allerton, 'Contested Statelessness', 250–68.

coordination. The government announced the PSS programme without enough consideration of the technicalities and long-term plans to address the issue, thus creating more fear than reassurance.

Warisan ought to have known that the PATI issue was a highly political and emotive one. Politically, statelessness is intertwined with public resentment towards the PATIs. During GE14, BN was seen as part of the problem for their failure and reluctance to resolve the issue and association with Project IC and electoral fraud.[43] This was among the main local factors which led to voters punishing BN during GE14, and likewise Warisan during the Kimanis by-election. Yet, not much consultation was conducted to generate valuable buy-in and feedback from the public before the PSS programme was announced. During the Kimanis by-election, one Warisan vice-president was even in denial, arguing that the PSS was a non-factor and voters had no problems accepting it.[44] The use of anti-immigrant rhetoric against Warisan continued in PRN2020 (as described in Chapter 5 by Vilashini Somiah and Aslam Abd Jalil) although to a lesser extent compared with the Kimanis by-election. However, perceptions, once formed, are hard to shrug off. The 'Warisan equals PATI party' stigma was strong among voters, and Warisan had to repeatedly defend themselves on the issue.

Ethnic Politics

Sabah politics are complex not least because of the state's intricate multi-ethnic and multi-religious make-up. In general, there are three main communities:[45] (1) the indigenous KDM communities, who are mostly

---

43 The Royal Commission of Inquiry on Illegal Immigrants in Sabah has confirmed the existence of Project IC, where citizenship and identity cards were granted to immigrants to bolster electoral support for UMNO. Over 60,000 of those highlighted in the Royal Commission of Inquiry as having problematic identity cards were found to be registered as voters. For further details, see: Jimmy Wong et al., 'Over 60,000 Potentially Dubious Voters in the Electoral Roll Based on Dubious Old IC Numbers Highlighted in the Sabah RCI', *DAP Malaysia*, 2013, https://dapmalaysia.org/statements/2013/03/19/17106/.

44 Olivia Miwil, 'Warisan Says PSS Non-Issue in Kimanis by-Election', *New Straits Times Online*, 4 January 2020, https://www.nst.com.my/news/nation/2020/01/553472/warisan-says-pss-non-issue-kimanis-election.

45 These three groupings are indeed an over-simplified way to analyse the ethnic breakdown and relations in Sabah. As the other chapters in this book will highlight, the ethnic breakdown in Sabah is far more complex, with numerous ethnic and sub-

Christians; (2) the indigenous Bajau, Suluk, and Malay communities, who are mostly Muslim; and (3) the Chinese community. Sabahans of different faiths, particularly Buddhists and Christians, often take pride for having less ethnic tension compared to Peninsular Malaysia, and ethnic polarisation is often seen as part of Peninsular culture. This is true in that no single community is the majority or dominant over any other in Sabah, and day-to-day ethnic relations are less contentious in nature. Yet, identity politics has been a key factor in Sabah's elections and politics.

In GE14, support for BN in Sabah had been on the decline, especially towards Musa Aman and UMNO, who were perceived as corrupt and weak in defending Sabahans' interests across all communities.[46] Warisan, having just established itself as a party, realised the strategic importance of ethnic-based support. Shafie Apdal had strong support from the Muslim Bajau-Suluk community, owing to his established political base on the east coast. But he wanted Warisan to also have the support of other communities in Sabah. This led to the recruitment of Darrel Leiking from PKR, who was seen as someone who could draw support from younger KDM voters, and Junz Wong from DAP, to draw support from the Chinese community.[47] Warisan attempted to bring different groups together, especially the various KDM and Muslim communities, but enduring distrust was a major obstacle as many held long-standing feelings of displacement and neglect.[48] The voting pattern in GE14 showed that there was a swing of support towards Warisan from the Bajau-Suluk, Malay-Muslim, Chinese and Murut communities, but the Kadazan-Dusun moved towards BN.[49]

Similar ethnic dynamics were at play during PRN2020. Warisan's main theme for the electoral campaign was 'In God We Trust, Unite We Must'. This theme was adapted from the one previously used in GE14 – 'In God We Trust, Change We Must' – which arguably contributed to Warisan's

---

ethnic groups. Here, I use these three groupings for a broad analysis only.

[46] Farish A. Noor, 'The 13th Malaysian General Elections from a Sabah Perspective', *The Round Table* 102, no. 6 (December 1, 2013): 541–48.

[47] Chin, 'Sabah & Sarawak in the 14th General Election 2018', 175-177.

[48] Bridget Welsh, 'Is Sabah Ready for Political Change?', *Malaysiakini*, 26 April 2018, https://www.malaysiakini.com/columns/421636.

[49] Bridget Welsh, 'Warisan Swing: How It Helped "win" Sabah in GE14', *Malaysiakini*, 23 September 2020, https://www.malaysiakini.com/columns/543711.

successful campaign during that election.[50] The shift of emphasis, from 'Change' to 'Unite' in PRN2020, served two main purposes. First, it was used during the campaign to appeal to state nationalism: that Sabahans must unite against federal intrusion. Second, it was a counter against allegations that Warisan was a Bajau-Suluk party, especially given that Shafie Apdal was often attacked for allegedly being a PATI of Bajau ancestry. These played to the underlying distrust of the Bajau-Suluk community. The Suluks and Bajaus were historically seafarers from the Philippines and Indonesia, but they have settled in Sabah for a long period of time.[51] The issue was made more complicated when intertwined with the influx of refugees from southern Philippines beginning in the 1980s and the granting of citizenship via the Project IC syndicate. Local politicians and parties from the KDM community have long felt that these were all part of a systematic ploy to reconstruct the ethnic-religious balance, and therefore political power, to be more in line with the demographics at the federal level.[52]

Most of the Warisan party activists that I spoke to on the east coast were generally confident that they could maintain the support of urban and Muslim communities, but they were worried about the KDM areas. They mentioned that ethnic politics in Sabah may not be as open and pronounced as Peninsular Malaysia, but at the local level, such sentiments do appeal to primordial instincts of insecurity and group loyalty.

Nevertheless, the unity narrative established by Warisan was successful in many ways. It was a clear and strong message that resonated with people on the ground. Even simple policy measures by the Warisan government, such as an additional public holiday on Christmas Eve, aroused great appreciation among the people during PRN2020. It lifted the standing of Shafie Apdal and Warisan not just in Sabah but nationally. The unity message remains alive beyond the state elections. Several movements, such as the youth-led Sabah Unity Movement,[53] have continued advocating the message. In the context of Malaysia, where ethnicity and religion are often

---

50 Geraldine Tong, 'From Change to Unity, Warisan's Evolving Message in Sabah Polls', *Malaysiakini*, 12 September 2020, https://www.malaysiakini.com/news/542346.

51 Farish Noor, 'The 13th Malaysian General Elections', 542-544.

52 Kamal Sadiq, 'When States Prefer Non-Citizens over Citizens: Conflict over Illegal Immigration into Malaysia', *International Studies Quarterly* 49, no. 1 (2005): 101–22.

53 For more info on the Sabah Unity Movement, see https://sabahunitymovement.com/.

used to divide, Warisan's message of unity and inclusiveness has been very much needed, showing that such narratives can indeed be a strong and viable alternative in politics.

Concluding Reflections

The five key issues discussed in this chapter sought to provide readers with an overview of PRN2020 in relation to Warisan. The issues are not new to Sabah politics, but they continued to feature prominently in recent elections. The issues worked in Warisan's favour during GE14, yet the results of GE14 were more of a vote against BN as opposed to a vote for Warisan. Despite this, voters' expectations were high after GE14 as they looked forward to the new government fulfilling the promises they made.

The Warisan government had some key successes on those issues, such as a greater allocation from the federal government. However, there were also major challenges in terms of coordination, implementation and communication. Many of the reforms, such as the restoration of the state's autonomy under MA63, were slow and had little immediate impact on the ground. On the other hand, controversial issues, such as the PSS policy, were not coordinated and communicated well, resulting in a severe backlash against the government. Warisan was also beset by political instability (and destabilisation) at the federal level within the PH coalition, which eventually led to PRN2020. Nevertheless, Warisan's tenure in government was indeed too short to be assessed fairly as many of the issues are complex and long-term in nature.

PRN2020 was a close and competitive contest between Warisan and GRS. Warisan, however, was not able to capitalise on its successes in government. There were very few tangible things that voters could relate to, and they did not feel that life was necessarily better under the Warisan government. In this respect, Warisan's tenure was, perhaps, a missed opportunity. GRS had its weaknesses too, such as infighting within the alliance, but it managed to rebrand itself and moved away from the anti-BN legacy. It leveraged issues to their advantage, such as appealing to the necessity of state-federal political alignment.

The dust has settled for now, but Malaysia is still in the midst of political uncertainty, of new trajectories and configurations. In this respect, Warisan will continue to play a critical role in Sabah and Malaysia. At the time of writing, Warisan has announced that the party plans to expand to Peninsular

Malaysia.[54] During the vote for the government budget in 2021, Warisan had boycotted the vote at the committee stage in an attempt to censure Anwar Ibrahim's last-minute decision to not call for bloc voting at the policy stage. There is also continuing momentum to position Shafie Apdal as the next prime ministerial candidate from the opposition.[55] Will we see Warisan leading the way in the next elections? Much is yet to unfold, but Sabah will certainly remain a vibrant arena in Malaysian politics.

54 'Shafie Nudges Opposition to Muster Courage for Change', *Malaysiakini*, 12 December 2020, https://www.malaysiakini.com/news/554938.

55 Ibid.

Chapter 2

The 1963 Malaysia Agreement: Pakatan's Failed Restoration and Perikatan's Fledgling Initiatives

Johan Arriffin Samad

Introduction

The Malaysia Agreement 1963 (MA63) is of important historical significance to Sabah but has unfortunately not been given the attention it rightfully deserves. This is especially so as over the past few decades, many citizens in the Borneo states (Sabah and Sarawak) have felt that their rights under MA63 have been violated. They harbour distrust towards the federal government in a Peninsular-dominated Malaysia and are troubled by the imbalance in the federal-state relationship. The call for the federal government to fulfil its MA63 obligations from many prominent Sabah politicians,[1] opposition parties,[2] and NGOs[3] tends to surface during every election, but in recent years, MA63 has increasingly reverberated around the political arena. The 14th General Election (GE14) of May 2018 saw the

[1] Nancy Lai, 'Sabah Federal Ministers Must Prioritize MA63 Implementation – Rahman', *Borneo Post Online*, 11 March 2020, https://www.theborneopost.com/2020/03/11/sabah-federal-ministers-must-prioritize-ma63-implementation-rahman/.

[2] Zam Yusa, 'MA63 Focus for Opposition's GE14 Manifesto in Sabah', *Free Malaysia Today*, 12 August 2017, https://www.freemalaysiatoday.com/category/nation/2017/08/12/ma63-focus-for-oppositions-ge14-manifesto-in-sabah/.

[3] Peter Sibon, 'Sarexit Gathering Aims to Pressure DUN to Pass Referendum Bill, Say Organisers', *Dayak Daily*, 1 November 2018, https://dayakdaily.com/sarexit-gathering-aims-to-pressure-dun-to-pass-referendum-bill-say-organisers/.

opposition parties of Sabah and Sarawak hoping to end Barisan Nasional (BN) rule and secure campaign promises from the Pakatan Harapan (PH) coalition for increased autonomy over religious matters, education and health, as well as greater control over development agendas, and this expectation of progress ran especially high after PH won that election.

Sentiments for change have strengthened. A survey by the Merdeka Centre showed an increase in dissatisfaction over Putrajaya's efforts in protecting the interests of Sarawak and Sabah despite major strides made in restoring their rights under MA63.[4] Many Borneo Malaysians who are frustrated by the non-fulfilment of MA63 and the current federal-state relationship, at the extreme end, are calling for independence.[5] Words and terms like 'colonised' or 'marginalised by Malaya' are often used to describe the betrayal by the federal government. Those feeling disenfranchised by the dominance of federal politics are using nationalistic slogans like 'Sabah for Sabahans' and 'Sarawak for Sarawakians' to distinguish themselves from 'Malaya' (the Peninsula). Activists have admitted to exploring ways of seceding from Malaysia as a last resort if Putrajaya fails to honour its legal obligations under MA63.[6] But it is dangerous to create a secessionist movement if grievances are not addressed.[7]

Prior to the formation of Malaysia, the late Tun Fuad Stephens[8] from Sabah, and other leaders from Sarawak, negotiated safeguards for the Borneo

---

4 Lim How Pim, 'Dissatisfaction over Putrajaya's Efforts in Protecting Sarawak, Sabah's Interests Increased Last Year – Survey', *Borneo Post Online*, 5 January 2020, https://www.theborneopost.com/2020/01/05/dissatisfaction-over-putrajayas-efforts-in-protecting-sarawak-sabahs-interests-increased-last-year-survey/.

5 Piya Sukhani, 'What's Behind Calls for Independence in Sabah?' *The Diplomat*, 3 April 2019, https://thediplomat.com/2019/04/whats-behind-calls-for-independence-in-sabah/.

6 James Chin, 'Is Malaysia Heading for "BorneoExit"? Why Some in East Malaysia Are Advocating for Secession,' *The Conversation*, 29 September 2020, https://theconversation.com/is-malaysia-heading-for-borneoexit-why-some-in-east-malaysia-are-advocating-for-secession-146208.

7 James Chin, 'The 1963 Malaysia Agreement (MA63): Sabah And Sarawak and the Politics of Historical Grievances,' in Sophie Lemiere (ed.) *Minorities Matter: Malaysian Politics and People*, Vol. III (Singapore: SIRD/ISEAS–Yusof Ishak Institute, 2019) 75-92.

8 P. J. Granville-Edge, *The Sabahan: the Life & Death of Tun Fuad Stephens*, Rajen Devadason ed. (Kota Kinabalu: Family of the late Tun Fuad Stephens, 2008).

states to allay fears that they might be dominated by another colonial master or become a vassal state of Malaya. The 20-point safeguards for Sabah[9] and 18 points[10] for Sarawak contained in the Inter-governmental Committee Report (IGC) were listed as preconditions for forming Malaysia. All these points were supposed to be embedded in the new Federal Constitution and become basic tenets or the building blocks of the Borneo states' rights. Many early leaders of Sabah, including Tun Fuad Stephens and Tun Mustapha, have criticised the central government for 'whittling' away the 20-points safeguard.[11] The 20 and 18 points have not been fully implemented to the satisfaction of the people of the Borneo states. It remains a contentious issue which has yet to be resolved.[12]

During GE14, Parti Warisan Sabah (Warisan), led by Shafie Apdal and its state coalition partners, Parti Keadilan Rakyat (PKR) and the Democratic Action Party (DAP), won the Sabah state elections and forged a loose alliance with the PH government at the federal level.[13] The newly established state-federal relationship was advantageous for Sabah's pursuit of the MA63 agenda. Upholding and empowering the basic rights of the people of Sabah based on the terms of MA63 topped the list as one of the 13 main points of Warisan's manifesto.[14]

---

9 Herman J. Luping, *Sabah's Dilemma: (the Political History of Sabah); (1960-1994)*, Kuala Lumpur: Magnus Books (1994). Sabah's 20 points in the IGC report were: 1. Religion; 2. Language; 3. Constitution; 4. Head of Federation; 5. Name of Federation; 6. Immigration; 7. Right of Secession; 8. Borneanisation; 9. British Officers; 10. Citizenship; 11. Tariffs and Finance; 12. Special Position of Indigenous Races; 13. State Government; 14. Transitional Period; 15. Education; 16. Constitutional Safeguards; 17. Representation in Federal Parliament; 18. Name of Head of State; 19. Name of State; 20. Land, Forests, Local Government, etc. Sarawak's 18 points were similar to Sabah's 20 points.

10 Karen Bong and Wilfred Pilo, 'An Agreement Forged and Forgotten', *Borneo Post Online*, 16 September 2011, https://www.theborneopost.com/2011/09/16/an-agreement-forged-and-forgotten/.

11 Jeffrey G. Kitingan and Maximus J. Ongkili (eds.) *Sabah, 25 Years Later, 1963-1988* (Kota Kinabalu, Sabah: Institute for Development Studies (IDS), 1989).

12 Richard A. Lind, *My Sabah: Reminiscences of a Former State Secretary* (Kota Kinabalu, Sabah: Natural History Publications, 2003).

13 Suzianah Jiffar, 'Warisan Will Work Only with Pakatan Harapan for GE14: New Straits Times', *New Straits Times*, 2 April 2018, https://www.nst.com.my/news/nation/2018/04/352101/warisan-will-work-only-pakatan-harapan-ge14.

14 'Basic, State Rights Top Warisan's 13 Concerns: Daily Express Online – Sabah's

Federal-state Revenue Sharing Issues

One of the most important areas of contention involves control over funds. Point no. 11 in the IGC report relates to tariffs and finance, whereby North Borneo (as Sabah was formerly called) should retain control of its own finances, development and tariffs, and should have the right to its own taxation and to raise loans on its own credit. Sabah and Sarawak combined cover 198,070 square kilometres or 60 per cent of Malaysia's land mass and require significant funding for development purposes. Because state governments are only able to derive the bulk of their revenues from limited sources such as land, property, agriculture and forestry, they depend heavily on federal funding for development.[15] Despite showing a slight improvement compared with four years ago, Sabah continues to record the highest poverty rate in the country. Latest government figures show that the state's poverty rate was at 19.5 per cent in 2019, down from 23.9 per cent in 2016.[16] By simple calculations, based on the percentages quoted, more than 760,000 people of its 3.9 million population are living in poverty.

Both Sabah and Sarawak are the major producers of oil and gas in Malaysia and the federal government has secured the bulk of petroleum rents extracted from these two oil-producing states. Sabah alone produces 50 per cent of the nation's oil.[17] The Petroliam Nasional Berhad (Petronas), Malaysia's leading oil and gas company, has paid out RM488 billion in dividends to the government since its establishment in 1974. In 2019, the total amount of dividends paid out by Petronas was RM54 billion, including a special dividend of RM30 billion.[18] In comparison, petroleum cash

---

Leading News Portal', *Daily Express*, 28 April 2018, https://www.dailyexpress.com.my/news/124383/basic-state-rights-top-warisan-s-13-concerns/.

15 Tricia Yeoh, *Reviving the Spirit of Federalism: Decentralisation Policy Options for a New Malaysia*, Institute For Democracy and Economic Affairs, April 2019, https://www.ideas.org.my/wp-content/uploads/2019/04/PI59-Reviving-the-Spirit-of-Federalism.pdf.

16 'Sabah, Kelantan Record Highest Poverty Rates', *Malaysiakini*, 3 December 2020, https://www.malaysiakini.com/news/553618.

17 Avila Geraldine, 'Shell Excel in Oil Extraction from Sabah Deepwaters' *New Straits Times*, 8 November 2017, https://www.nst.com.my/business/2017/11/300512/shell-excel-oil-extraction-sabah-deepwaters.

18 'Govt to Receive RM34 Billion Dividend from Petronas in 2020', *New Straits Times*, 3 November 2020, https://www.nst.com.my/news/nation/2020/11/637510/govt-receive-rm34-billion-dividend-petronas-2020.

payments to Sabah and Sarawak, for the period of 2008 to August 2020, were RM13.2 billion and RM25.3 billion respectively. The disproportionate sharing of the oil proceeds has created a development divide between the Borneo states and Peninsular Malaysia.[19]

The PH government has recognised the disparity in revenue sharing and doubled the special grant to Sabah and Sarawak as provided under Section 112D of the Federal Constitution. Tabling the Budget in October 2019, Minister of Finance Lim Guan Eng said that the government had, for the first time, proposed to increase this rate, doubling it for 2020 to RM53.4 million for Sabah and RM32 million for Sarawak. The grant had not been reviewed since 1969 even though the provision of the Federal Constitution stated that a review ought to be done every five years. He added that the government planned to double the rate again to RM106.8 million for Sabah and RM64 million for Sarawak within five years.[20]

Despite the doubling of grants, the Federal government remained silent on a revenue item unique to Sabah under a constitutional requirement. Under Part IV, Section 2 (1) of the Special Grants to the States of Sabah and Sarawak, Sabah is entitled to 40 per cent of the tax revenue derived from the state. In November 2019, a group of senior party leaders from different political parties in Sabah demanded that Putrajaya honour the Federal Constitution and pay the revenue entitlement stipulated.[21] The disproportionate distribution of wealth, rent-seeking of oil resources from oil producing states, failure to comply with constitutional requirements and Sabah continuing to be the poorest state in Malaysia, are situations which have created serious anger against the federal government.

---

[19] 'Petroleum Payments to Sabah, Sarawak, Terengganu & Kelantan Totalled RM61.32b from 2008 to 2020', *The Edge Markets*, 2 November 2020, https://www.theedgemarkets.com/article/petroleum-payments-sabah-sarawak-terengganu-kelantan-totalled-rm6132b-2008-2020.

[20] Lim How Pim, 'Budget 2020: Fed Govt Doubles down on Special Grant for Sarawak, Sabah', *Borneo Post Online*, 11 October 2019, https://www.theborneopost.com/2019/10/11/budget-2020-fed-govt-doubles-down-on-special-grant-for-sarawak-sabah/.

[21] The demand was made in a joint statement issued by Kimanis MP Anifah Aman (former Foreign Minister), Keningau MP Jeffrey Kitingan, Tamparuli Assemblyman Jahid Jahim, Kiulu Assemblyman Joniston Bangkuai, Yong Teck Lee (former Sabah Chief Minister), Wilfred Bumburing (former Tuaran MP) and Francis Goh (former Malaysian Chinese Association (MCA) chairman).

Pakatan Harapan's MA63 Promises

This angst was the driving force opposing BN's rule of the state and contributed to the election of PH. On 9 May 2018, the BN government, dominated by the United Malays National Organisation (UMNO), which has been in power since 1957, was toppled and replaced by PH. The PH government promised a better deal for Sabah and Sarawak in its election manifesto.[22] This was perhaps the best opportunity for the Borneo states to seek resolutions on MA63, especially on areas of greater autonomy and increases in revenue for development.

Under Pillar 4 of PH's manifesto, the coalition criticised the UMNO-led BN government for not fulfilling the demands of the people of Sabah and Sarawak based on MA63 during the time it was in power. In every election campaign, UMNO and BN have made many empty promises regarding changes and reforms while large shares of the Borneo states' wealth were channelled to federal coffers. In view of this, the PH government set up a Cabinet Committee to review and monitor the fair implementation of MA63 within the first 100 days of its administration. PH was committed to restoring Sabah and Sarawak to their rightful places in line with MA63 in order to protect the unity of the Federation.

A Commission with representatives from the Peninsular, Sabah and Sarawak with expertise in relevant matters was established. The Commission was directed to provide detailed reports to the government within six months from the date of establishment, and for immediate execution. The Commission's terms of reference were to review and propose measures to rectify: 1) the status of MA63 based on current legislation; 2) efforts to enhance the understanding of the people on MA63 through the national education system; 3) implementation of the concept of federalism for the three territories within Malaysia; 4) the rights of Sabah and Sarawak to revenue from their natural resources such as oil and gas; and 5) administrative rights – the share of funds that rightfully belongs to Sabah and Sarawak.[23] Out of the five items, the main thrust would still be the fair

[22] Nadzri Muhamad M. N., 'The 14th General Election, the Fall of Barisan Nasional, and Political Development in Malaysia, 1957-2018', *Journal of Current Southeast Asian Affairs* 37, no. 3 (2019): 139–71.

[23] Phyllis Wong, 'PH to Keep Its Word on MA63', *Borneo Post Online*, 24 May 2018, https://www.theborneopost.com/2018/05/23/ph-to-keep-its-word-on-ma63/.

share of revenue from its oil and gas resources, grants and taxes under the agreement, alongside autonomy or administrative rights.

The PH coalition's election manifesto was signed by Tun Mahathir, who was Prime Minister of Malaysia for 23 years (1981-2003) under UMNO/BN, and again for less than two years (2018-2020) under PH. In the foreword he wrote for the manifesto, Mahathir acknowledged for the first time that Borneo state rights have been trampled upon and that he 'attempted' to right the wrong. The irony is that Mahathir was the longest serving prime minister of Malaysia and did nothing to restore the rights of Sabah and Sarawak during his first premiership. Most Sabahans have a love-hate relationship with Mahathir and blame him for the influx of illegal immigrants into the state (the PATI issue, see also Chapters 1 and 5) which has changed the demographics of Sabah and for allegedly re-engineering the religious make-up of the state population in favour of Islam. While the past chief ministers of Sabah were equally to blame for the situation, Mahathir is seen as the main culprit. He was also disliked for implementing the Sabah chief minister's two-year rotation system between 1994-2004 to resolve unity problems in the state, which some regarded as a huge mistake.[24] Due to his lack of popularity, Mahathir was not welcomed to Sabah during GE14 (or for the recent state elections) for fear of jeopardising the opposition's chance to wrestle the state government from BN.

The PH manifesto points to a prime minister of 23 years admitting that he has not fulfilled the safeguards bargained by Bornean leaders prior to forming Malaysia. Critics may view his admittance of MA63 failures as another election ploy to win the hearts and minds of the people of Sabah and Sarawak. Despite Sabahans' weariness of Mahathir, the change of government brought new hope and optimism that this time it would be different. Mahathir admitting his failures was a step in the right direction and what remained was for PH to deliver its promises to the people.

Despite Mahathir's rocky relationship with Sabah, PH made good by delivering their MA63 manifesto promises. In December 2019, deputy minister in the Prime Minister's Department, Mohamed Hanipa Maidin, told the Dewan Negara that a total of 21 matters were tabled by the Sarawak and Sabah governments at the Cabinet special committee meeting to

---

[24] Herman J. Luping, 'Rotation of CM a Big Mistake', *Daily Express*, 19 September 2010, http://www.dailyexpress.com.my/read/418/rotation-of-cm-a-big-mistake/.

review the implementation of the MA63, and 17 of them had been jointly approved.[25] But there still remained issues up for discussion between Mahathir, Sabah Chief Minister Shafie Apdal and Sarawak Chief Minister Abang Abdul Rahman Zohari, which included the oil royalty and petroleum payments; oil minerals and oil fields; the Territorial Sea Act 2012 (Act 750); and states' rights over the continental shelf.

According to Mohamed Hanipa, the 17 matters that were agreed upon were: 1) claims to export duties for logs and forest products in Sabah; 2) the regulation of gas and electricity distribution in Sarawak and Sabah; 3) the implementation of federal works in Sarawak and Sabah; 4) the labour force in Sarawak and Sabah; 5) state authority over health issues in Sarawak and Sabah; 6) the administration of Sipadan and Ligitan Islands in Sabah; 7) agricultural and forestry issues; 8) federal financial obligations under the joint list; 9) the review of special gifts; 10) fishing, inshore and offshore fisheries; 11) ownership given to federal land in states; 12) legal authority on environment and tourism; 13) Article 112 of the Federal Constitution (Increase in Employment); 14) the delegation of power to the Sabah and Sarawak Courts; 15) the jurisdiction of the chief judge of Sabah and Sarawak, the autonomous administration of Sabah and Sarawak courts, and the experience of Borneo judges to hear appeals filed in a Borneo state; 16) the appointment of the judicial commissioner; and 17) stamp duties imposed on transfer instruments, charges, and land lease under Sarawak and Sabah land ordinances. The report of the Cabinet Special Committee was to be tabled at the Cabinet Meeting after which a special announcement would be made by Mahathir.

These 21 points should not be confused with the 20 points contained in the 1962 IGC[26] report and should be regarded as an updated list of demands under the MA63 negotiated by Sabah and Sarawak chief ministers under the PH government. PH's attempt to resolve the MA63 grievances was perhaps the only real opportunity to sort out these issues after 57 years. Before the PH government could announce the findings of the MA63 Committee,

---

[25] 'MA63: 17 Issues Resolved, 4 Still Being Discussed, Says Hanipa', *Malay Mail*, 10 December 2019, https://www.malaymail.com/news/malaysia/2019/12/10/ma63-17-issues-resolved-4-still-being-discussed-says-hanipa/1817903.

[26] *Malaysia: Report of the Inter-Governmental Committee*, (Kota Kinabalu, Sabah: Government Printing Department, 1962)

they were ousted on 29 February 2020 due to political infighting and were replaced by Perikatan Nasional (PN), led by new Prime Minister Muhyiddin Yassin, Mahathir's former deputy.

Attempts to Amend Article 1(2)

A similarly unfinished situation emerged in efforts to amend the Federal Constitution. One of the main arguments on MA63 was the claim of equal status by Sabah and Sarawak as signatories to the agreement. Without Sabah and Sarawak, there would be no Malaysia; Singapore left on 9 August 1965. The two states (North Borneo and Sarawak) claimed to be equal partners of Malaysia after signing MA63 with other sovereign nations – Great Britain and Northern Ireland, the Federation of Malaya and Singapore.[27]

In October 2016, a leading BN component party in Sarawak apologised for having supported the amendment to the Federal Constitution in 1976 that led to the downgrading of the state from its previous sovereign status. The Sarawak United People's Party (SUPP) Secretary-General, Ting Chew Yew, admitted that his party made no objections at the time and had helped to pass the amendment to Article 1 of the Federal Constitution in 1976 through Act A354, which saw Sarawak downgraded from Region 2 in the Federation of Malaysia, to being one of 13 states in Malaysia. As a result, the federal government has curtailed the disbursement of federal funds for Sarawak and Sabah to the level of a state, rather than as two of the three founding partners.[28]

The Bill to amend Article 1(2) of the Federal Constitution as equal partners was tabled in Parliament in April 2019.[29] Law Minister VK Liew pointed out that it was the constitutional amendment in 1976 that altered the status of Sabah and Sarawak, a change that has remained for 43 years. The amendments were tabled in line with PH's election manifesto of

---

[27] 'Malaysia: Agreement to Form Malaysia and Draft Constitution', *International Legal Materials* 2, no. 5 (1963): 816-70.

[28] 'Sorry, Says Sarawak Party for Downgrading Status in 1976', *Free Malaysia Today*, 20 October 2016, https://www.freemalaysiatoday.com/category/nation/2016/10/20/sorry-says-sarawak-party-for-downgrading-status-in-1976/.

[29] Muguntan Vanar, 'Liew: Bill to Amend Constitution a Major Step to Restoring Sabah and Sarawak's Equal Status', *The Star Online*, 29 July 2019, https://www.thestar.com.my/news/nation/2019/04/02/liew-bill-to-amend-constitution-a-major-step-to-restoring-sabah-and-sarawaks-equal-status.

bringing the Borneo states to their original position in 1963. Liew suggested returning to the original version of Article 1(2) of the Federal Constitution: 1) the Federation shall be known, in Malay and English, by the name Malaysia; 2) the States of the Federation shall be (a) the States of Malaya, namely Johor, Kedah, Kelantan, Malacca, Negeri Sembilan, Pahang, Penang, Perak, Perlis, Selangor, and Terengganu; and (b) the Borneo States, namely Sabah and Sarawak.

The PH government's effort to amend the Federal Constitution to restore the original status of the Borneo states failed to get two-thirds majority support in the Dewan Rakyat. Out of 197 MPs who attended the Dewan Rakyat, 138 MPs voted for the Bill, while 59 abstained. The Bill required a two-thirds majority or the agreement of 148 MPs to pass under Article 159 of the Federal Constitution.[30] Surprisingly, Sarawak, which would have benefitted from the amendment, was accused of being the spoiler, as they had wanted to include 'pursuant to the Malaysia Agreement 1963' and were adamant that the phrase be included in the main clause of Article 1(2) of the Federal Constitution and not in the explanatory notes.[31] Nancy Shukri, an MP from Sarawak, said that they did not oppose the amendment, but merely abstained from voting as it did not contain those words. Whether it was just objections over polemics or a critical legal term that necessitated its inclusion, Sarawak MPs denied the restoration of the Borneo states as equal partners and lost an opportunity to turn back the clock. The Borneo states are unlikely to get a second chance.

U-Turning on the Oil Royalty Pledge

PH was given a chance on areas of oil royalty, and these also did not materialise. The biggest revenue promise in the PH manifesto was to increase the oil royalty for all oil-producing states from an existing 5 per cent to 20 per cent. Sabah and Sarawak saw this as a low hanging fruit that

30 Adam Aziz, 'No Two-Thirds Majority for Bill to Make Sabah, Sarawak Equal Partners', *The Edge Markets*, 9 April 2019, https://www.theedgemarkets.com/article/no-twothirds-majority-bill-make-sabah-sarawak-equal-partners.

31 Sharon Ling, 'Constitutional Amendment Must Include "Pursuant to MA63" before GPS Will Vote for It, Says Nancy Shukri', *The Star Online*, 14 January 2020, https://www.thestar.com.my/news/nation/2020/01/14/constitutional-amendment-must-include-pursuant-to-ma63-before-gps-will-vote-for-it-says-nancy-shukri.

could be realised very quickly. Mahathir said that this was one of the fairer steps to distribute income from petroleum resources which would then allow both states to take on more development expenditure responsibilities at the state level.

In July 2018, Mahathir announced in Parliament that oil-producing states would receive 20 per cent of oil royalties as stated in PH's election manifesto.[32] However, Mahathir backtracked a week later and clarified that the proposed 20 per cent oil royalty would be based on Petronas's profit from oil and gas. This is different from the current practice where the 5 per cent of oil royalty paid to Sabah and Sarawak is based on gross revenue.

Former Economic Affairs Minister, Azmin Ali, warned that Petronas may cease operations if it accedes to demands for the 20 per cent oil royalty to be paid based on gross production instead of net profit.[33] In another statement, Azmin said the proposed oil royalty cannot be implemented yet as it contravenes the Petroleum Development Act 1974. It will also take time as the provisions of the Act need to be amended first.[34] As early as August 2018, as pressure built up for the PH government to deliver its promises, Mahathir admitted that the government was having a hard time fulfilling its election pledges as it made 'too many promises', believing it would not win the May 9 polls.[35] Mahathir's confession that PH 'did not expect to win' set the tone for the difficult negotiations ahead to restore Bornean rights in accordance with MA63.

Frustrations were building up in the Borneo states. In September 2018, Finance Minister Lim Guan Eng stated that legacy issues from the previous government were preventing the implementation of promises made under the PH manifesto, especially in terms of the oil royalty for Sabah and

---

32 Chester Tay and Sangeetha Amarthalingam, 'Dr M: Oil-Producing States to Get 20% Royalties', *The Edge Markets*, 19 July 2018, https://www.theedgemarkets.com/article/dr-m-oilproducing-states-get-20-royalties.

33 'Azmin: End of Petronas If Royalty Set at 20pct Gross Value', *Malaysiakini*, 25 July 2018, https://www.malaysiakini.com/news/435812.

34 '20 Pct Oil Royalty Payment Cannot Be Implemented Yet – Azmin', *Borneo Post Online*, 26 July 2018, https://www.theborneopost.com/2018/07/25/20-pct-oil-royalty-payment-cannot-be-implemented-yet-azmin/.

35 'We over-promised, Dr M Tells Ruling MPs', *Free Malaysia Today*, 17 August 2018, https://www.freemalaysiatoday.com/category/nation/2018/08/17/we-over-promised-dr-m-tells-ruling-mps/.

Sarawak.[36] He blamed the past excesses of the previous BN government in the aftermath of the 1MDB kleptocracy case, which has left the country in a bad financial situation. The statement by Lim was interpreted as an emphatic 'no' to the increase in oil royalty.

In September 2019, Mahathir (who was attending the 74th Session of the United Nations General Assembly), in a dialogue session with fund managers at the JP Morgan headquarters in New York, extinguished any hope of the Borneo states having their oil royalty raised to 20 per cent, saying that it was not workable.[37] He said giving 20 per cent would in effect kill Petronas, the goose that lays golden eggs for the federal government through taxes and dividends.

In December 2019, the flip-flop on the oil royalty continued with Mahathir stating that the government was considering selling stakes in energy giant, Petronas, to states where the company's oil and gas fields were, in a bid to raise funds for the debt-laden government.[38] Such a move, he said, would also give states such as Sarawak and Sabah a say in the running of Petronas. Mahathir confessed that the government could not meet the demands made by the states for a quadrupling of the royalty. In a December 2019 opinion article, P. Gunasegaram estimated that if the oil producing states wanted to take just a 5 per cent stake in Petronas, it would cost some RM50 billion. Thus, taking a significant stake in Petronas by states such as Sabah, Sarawak, and Terengganu would be out of the question because the federal government simply would not be able to afford it.[39] The petroleum royalty is a significant revenue for the Borneo states. For Sabah's 2020 revenue budget, the oil royalty is expected to remain the highest contributor,

---

[36] 'Sabah, Sarawak Oil Royalty Promises Hindered by Legacy Issues, Says Guan Eng,' *Malay Mail*, 13 September 2019, https://www.malaymail.com/news/malaysia/2019/09/13/sabah-sarawak-oil-royalty-promises-hindered-by-legacy-issues-says-guan-eng/1790178.

[37] 'Dr M: 20pct Oil Royalty for Sarawak, Sabah "Really Not Workable"', *Borneo Post Online*, 27 September 2019, https://www.theborneopost.com/2019/09/27/dr-m-20pct-oil-royalty-for-sarawak-sabah-really-not-workable/.

[38] Joseph Sipalan, Krishna N. Das, and Matthew Tostevin, 'Malaysia Considering Selling Stakes in Petronas to Provinces: Mahathir', *Reuters*, 10 December 2019, https://www.reuters.com/article/us-malaysia-politics-mahathir-petronas-i-idUSKBN1YE0TX.

[39] P. Gunasegaram, 'Should Petronas, Worth Almost RM1 Trillion, Be Listed?' *Malaysiakini*, 13 December 2019, https://www.malaysiakini.com/columns/503471.

with revenue estimates of RM1.7 million, accounting for 40.6 per cent of the state's revenue.

Perikatan's Fledgling Initiatives

The 'Sheraton Move' federal government took over and has shown similar reluctance in addressing the imbalances with the Borneo states. In forming his PN cabinet, Muhyiddin Yassin appointed political veteran, Maximus Ongkili, as minister in the Prime Minister's Department in charge of Sabah and Sarawak affairs. Ongkili had once been detained under the Internal Security Act in the 1990s for allegedly wanting to take Sabah out of Malaysia.[40] Ongkili announced that one of his main tasks was to solve issues regarding MA63 within six months.[41] He claimed that the previous government tried to amend Article 1(2) of the Federal Constitution for Sabah and Sarawak to restore their status as equal partners but failed because it did not include in detail the terms as per the original MA63, and thus left it open to interpretation.[42]

At the top of Ongkili's agenda were issues pertaining to petroleum payments and infrastructure development in the state and the outstanding payment of the 40 per cent net revenue to Sabah since the 1970s, which will bring billions of ringgit back to the state in total. Petroleum royalties and the 40 per cent tax were already part of PH's negotiations on Borneo rights. Ongkili's statements above confirmed that the priority and focus of MA63 was related to revenue.

Ongkili's statements have been treated with scepticism as successive governments have promised to resolve the MA63 issues with little result. They were dismissed as 'political talk.' The progress on MA63 under PN has

---

40 Ongkili was Deputy Director of the Institute for Development Studies (IDS), a government think-tank at that time, and was suspected of engaging in activities detrimental to the country's security. *Malaysia: Detainees in Sabah*. Human Rights Watch, 18 October 1991, https://www.hrw.org/reports//pdfs/m/malaysia/malaysia91o.pdf.

41 'Ongkili Hopes to See MA63 Issues Solved in 6 Months', *The Malaysian Reserve*, 13 March 2020, https://themalaysianreserve.com/2020/03/13/ongkili-hopes-to-see-ma63-issues-solved-in-6-months/.

42 Durie Rainer Fong, 'Restoring Equal Status to Sabah, Sarawak My First Priority, Says Ongkili', *Free Malaysia Today*, 12 March 2020, https://www.freemalaysiatoday.com/category/nation/2020/03/12/restoring-equal-status-to-sabah-sarawak-my-first-priority-says-ongkili/.

been slow and there is no continuity on what has been previously discussed during PH's time. The Parliamentary committee that was initiated by the PH government was dismissed as being unnecessary.[43] Ongkili's deputy, Hanifah Hajar Taib, has announced that the MA63 findings under the PH government have now been classified as official secrets under the Official Secrets Act 1972 and would not be made available to the public.[44] For the moment, the government maintains its stand that there is no need for the final report to be distributed to the public as the content is technical in nature and involves sensitive matters. As such, the status of the document will remain as an official secret and is to be treated as such as provided by the law. Opposition leaders and critics have panned this announcement as another delaying tactic. Anger and frustrations are continuously mounting. After 57 years in Malaysia, Sabah and Sarawak leaders questioned why there is a need to make the MA63 Report a secret as 17 items have already been agreed upon and are ready for implementation. The outstanding matters may take longer to resolve due to legal issues.[45]

Muhyiddin Yassin, on Malaysia Day 2020, at a celebration held in Sibu, announced the formation of a special council on MA63, to be chaired by himself, with the chief ministers of Sarawak and Sabah among its members. He said that the council would discuss issues related to the rights of Sabah and Sarawak in accordance with MA63. This, he said, included the position of Sabah and Sarawak as '*rakan sekutu*' (equal partners); states' rights under Article 112 of the Federal Constitution, MA63 and the IGC report; in addition to security and education. Opposition party leaders responded that they have heard such speeches many times before, but delivery has always fallen short.[46]

---

[43] Martin Carvalho, Hemananthani Sivanandam, Rahimy Rahim, and Tarrence Tan, 'Hanifah: No Need for Parliament Committee on MA63 Implementation', *The Star Online*, 10 August 2020, https://www.thestar.com.my/news/nation/2020/08/10/hanifah-no-need-for-parliament-committee-on-ma63-implementation.

[44] Soo Wern Jun, 'No Need to Make Cabinet's Final MA63 Report Public, Parliament Told', *Malay Mail*, 17 November 2020, https://www.malaymail.com/news/malaysia/2020/11/17/no-need-to-make-cabinets-final-ma63-report-public-parliament-told/1923357.

[45] Kelvin Yii, 'More Transparency Needed from Govt on Sabah-Sarawak Rights', *Malaysiakini*, 11 August 2020, https://www.malaysiakini.com/columns/538245.

[46] 'Muhyiddin's MA63 Announcement Disappointing - DAP', *Borneo Post Online*, 17

On 2 December 2020, the Special Council on MA63 convened its inaugural meeting and approved the formation of three committees that will be dealing with various matters important to Sabah and Sarawak. The matters that will be discussed include issues on the constitution and equal status; security and illegal immigrants; socio-economic matters; and the implementation of the 12th Malaysia Plan. The Council Members were briefed on the latest development on actions taken pertaining to MA63, as well as on the decisions made by the previous Cabinet Committee. Ongkili said that 17 out of the 21 issues identified by the council had been considered in detail, and the remaining four were still under deliberation. Out of the 17, three are considered solved, namely timber export duties and forest products for Sabah, the issue of Sipadan and Ligitan Islands in Sabah and forestry issues. The remaining 14 points, which include the gas, labour and stamp duties, need further deliberations as they involve amendments to laws and regulations.[47]

The change of government has brought in different views and dynamics on MA63 issues. It is a setback for Sabah and Sarawak that both hope to see the MA63 issues resolved as quickly as possible, especially in the areas of revenue sharing and state autonomy.

The 2020 Sabah State Election

In July 2020, several elected representatives from the Warisan-led government defected in support of former Chief Minister Musa Aman.[48] Shafie Apdal was forced to call a snap election after Musa claimed that he had a simple majority of 33 assemblymen to form a government in a 60-seat state legislature. The 2020 state election was held with 13 new seats added to the Sabah State assembly (now 73 seats in total). A record number of candidates (447, including 56 independents) and more than a dozen

---

September 2020, https://www.theborneopost.com/2020/09/18/muhyiddins-ma63-announcement-disappointing-dap/.

47 'Muhyiddin Chairs First MA63 Special Council Meeting', *Daily Express*, 3 December 2020, https://www.dailyexpress.com.my/news/162533/muhyiddin-chairs-first-ma63-special-council-meeting/.

48 Avila Geraldine, 'Shafie Dissolves State Legislative Assembly, Calls for Snap Election [NSTTV]', *New Straits Times*, 30 July 2020, https://www.nst.com.my/news/politics/2020/07/612753/shafie-dissolves-state-legislative-assembly-calls-snap-election-nsttv.

political parties fought it out in numerous multi-cornered contests. Warisan Plus comprising Parti Warisan Sabah, DAP, PKR, Amanah and the United Progressive Kinabalu Organisation (UPKO) were up against a new coalition Gabungan Rakyat Sabah (GRS) consisting of BN, PN, and the United Sabah Party.

Shafie campaigned on a platform that local parties must have control over the state to advance the MA63 agenda and to continue with his development plans for Sabah. Muhyiddin Yassin, who visited Sabah frequently during the election campaign, issued subtle threats (much like the BN government of the past), saying that Sabahans should choose a state government that is aligned with the federal government to facilitate the administration and development of the state.[49] He said that Sabah would be more successful if it was run by PN, together with the parties aligned with it.[50]

The subject of MA63 was on the agenda for many of the candidates who pledged that they would fight towards restoring the status of Sabah and Sarawak as equal partners in Malaysia, as per the original demands of the agreement.[51] To drum up support for the GRS coalition, Muhyiddin announced that the government would form a special council to resolve issues on MA63, which included increasing royalties of natural resources such as oil and gas and offering Sabah more administrative rights over areas like health and education.[52] While the issue of MA63 is important, there exists a significant divide between the urban-educated and rural residents in understanding or even caring for the history and implications of the agreement. Warisan did not capitalise on the doubling of the grant or the

---

49 'Muhyiddin's MA63 Announcement Disappointing – DAP', *Borneo Post Online*, 17 September 2020, https://www.theborneopost.com/2020/09/18/muhyiddins-ma63-announcement-disappointing-dap/.

50 'Muhyiddin: Choose Sabah Government That Is Aligned with Federal Government', *Malay Mail*, 17 September 2020, https://www.malaymail.com/news/malaysia/2020/09/17/muhyiddin-choose-sabah-government-that-is-aligned-with-federal-government/1904100.

51 'Sabah Election: Focus Will Be on Economy, MA63 and Development – Academic', *Borneo Post Online*, 18 September 2020, https://www.theborneopost.com/2020/09/19/sabah-election-focus-will-be-on-economy-ma63-and-development-academic/.

52 Amir Yusof, 'Parties Play up "Sabah Identity", Economic Development to Woo Voters in State Polls', *Channel News Asia*, 22 September 2020, https://www.channelnewsasia.com/news/asia/state-election-sabah-identity-malaysia-agreement-1963-13132640.

21 points negotiated by Shafie under the PH government, where the federal government agreed to 17 out of the 20 points negotiated. The GRS victory suggests that while the 'Sabah for Sabahans' campaign and the push for the Borneo state's autonomy under MA63 were important, bread-and-butter concerns still could not be displaced at the ballot box.[53]

As the election campaign progressed, especially in urban and semi-urban settings, Warisan's campaign took on a unity theme.[54] Shafie's campaign message was simple enough – to build an inclusive Sabah without the divisive racial or religious rhetoric within the federation.[55] 'We are here to build a nation, not a particular race or religion,' along with the hashtag '#SabahansUnite', became Warisan's mantra, posted on larger-than-life billboards featuring Shafie's profile.[56] Shafie's unity theme was well received by social media and among urban folks. But it failed to convey Shafie's development agenda for the state. Muhyiddin used a different tack with his intimate '*Abah*' (father) posters, presenting himself as a fatherly figure that would take care of his Sabah family.[57]

In its 26 months in power, Warisan failed to convince the electorate that it had the capability to turn the economy around and chart a new future for Sabah. People were concerned that Sabah, impacted by Covid-19, would be starved of development funds if Warisan stayed on the sidelines and was not aligned with the federal government. GRS's election campaign

---

53 James Chin, 'Commentary: Sabah's Surprise Results – and How Warisan Lost Big in State Elections', *Channel News Asia*, 28 September 2020, https://www.channelnewsasia.com/news/commentary/sabah-election-results-how-warisan-lost-big-grs-won-huge-13156026.

54 Joe Samad, 'Reflections on the Sabah Election Outcome', *Free Malaysia Today*, 30 September 2020, https://www.freemalaysiatoday.com/category/opinion/2020/09/30/reflections-on-the-sabah-election-outcome/.

55 Julia Chan, 'As Clock Ticks down to Sabah Election, a Laser-Focused Shafie Apdal Keeps Calm and Campaigns on for Warisan', *Malay Mail*, 25 September 2020, https://www.malaymail.com/news/malaysia/2020/09/25/as-clock-ticks-down-to-sabah-election-a-laser-focused-shafie-apdal-keeps-ca/1906409.

56 Emmanuel Santa Maria Chin and Julia Chan, 'In Billboard War, Warisan Pushes Unity While Perikatan Banks on Cult of Personality', *Malay Mail*, 17 September 2020, https://www.malaymail.com/news/malaysia/2020/09/17/in-billboard-war-warisan-pushes-unity-while-perikatan-banks-on-cult-of-pers/1903893.

57 Liew Chin Tong, 'The Cost of Muhyiddin's Overreach in Sabah', *Malaysiakini*, 24 September 2020, https://www.malaysiakini.com/columns/543886.

focused on the lack of basic infrastructure, the failure of the Warisan state government to revive the ailing Sabah economy as well as the need to have a close relationship with the central government in Putrajaya. GRS wasted no time in pointing out the poor record of economic growth under Shafie's leadership. The state's gross domestic product (GDP) was at its lowest – 1.5 per cent in 2018 and 0.5 per cent in 2019, compared with 8.3 per cent in 2017 under the previous government.[58] While some people were buoyed by Shafie's unity message, others lost confidence in his leadership and were doubtful that Warisan could turn the economy around.

Although MA63 was important for the state's future, it was not the main issue discussed in the election campaign. Other issues like nativist sentiments on undocumented foreigners in Sabah contributed to Warisan's loss.[59] Lower voter turnout of 67 per cent and pandemic campaign restrictions did not help Warisan's situation. The official election results saw GRS winning 38 seats, Warisan Plus 32 and Independents 3.[60] That Shafie's stand did not align with PN at the federal level was also said to be Warisan's downfall. His campaign speeches to vote for local parties fell flat. UMNO has been in Sabah since 1991, and Musa Aman was chief minister for fifteen years. In February 2019, Parti Pribumi Bersatu Malaysia (Bersatu) announced their entry into Sabah despite a tacit understanding between Mahathir and Shafie that Bersatu would stay out of Sabah. Mahathir, as Bersatu Chairman, explained that problems arose when UMNO leaders left the party in Sabah and chose not to join Warisan, but many applied to join Bersatu at the national level, hence the need to establish Bersatu in Sabah. There were grumblings on Warisan's side, but Shafie had to accept the reality of the situation. Sabahans were already used to Malayan parties as part and

---

58 Kenneth Tee, 'Sabah's GDP Growth to "Plummet to Zero" If Warisan Continues to Run State, Bung Moktar Claims', *Malay Mail*, 16 September 2020, https://www.malaymail.com/news/malaysia/2020/09/16/sabahs-gdp-growth-to-plummet-to-zero-if-warisan-continues-to-run-state-bung/1903765.

59 Tashny Sukumaran, 'Malaysia's Sabah State Elections: What Issues Will Decide the Polls?' *South China Morning Post*, 23 September 2020, https://www.scmp.com/week-asia/explained/article/3102576/malaysias-sabah-state-elections-what-issues-will-decide-polls.

60 '(LIVE) SABAH DECIDES 2020: Final Tally GRS 38, Warisan Plus 32, Ind 3', *Borneo Post Online*, 26 September 2020, https://www.theborneopost.com/2020/09/26/live-sabah-decides-2020-final-tally-grs-38-warisan-plus-32-ind-3/.

parcel of its political landscape; even Warisan Plus consists of non-Sabah parties, such as PKR and DAP. The irony was that by letting Bersatu into Sabah, it became the leading partner to displace him.

Conclusion

While MA63 was not the central issue during PRN2020, it continues to test the federal-state relationship in terms of deliverables and expectations. The Borneo states will continue to pressure the federal government as equal partners under MA63 on equitable sharing of revenue, oil and gas rights as well as autonomy on health and education. The previous PH government had started the process of the review and implementation of MA63 and now the responsibility has passed on to the PN government to deliver. Muhyiddin has reiterated that Sabah and Sarawak are equal partners of the Federation but has not committed to whether Article 1(2) will be re-tabled in Parliament at a future date. To-date, Sabah remains one of the 13 states of Malaysia.[61]

The PN government has started the process of forming committees to review the 21 items negotiated by the chief ministers of Sabah and Sarawak. With the Sarawak state elections due in 2021 and the strong possibility of Muhyiddin calling for a general election not too long after that to solidify his position, the non-resolution of MA63 issues will be played up even more.[62] Parti Bumi Kenyalang (PBK) of Sarawak has already declared its platform to fight for Sarawakian independence and will try to force a unilateral declaration of independence against Malaya if their demands are not met.[63]

Muhyiddin will be under a great deal of pressure to please Gabungan Parti Sarawak (GPS). The GPS coalition, although not part of PN, has supported Muhyiddin's government with 18 seats and with his razor-thin margin in Parliament, and GPS has exploited the situation to their

---

[61] 'Sabah One of 13, Not Four, States – MP,' *Borneo Post Online*, 10 July 2012, https://www.theborneopost.com/2012/07/10/sabah-one-of-13-not-four-states-mp/.

[62] Justin Ong, 'Muhyiddin Says Sabah Poll Could Set Stage for General Election,' *Malay Mail*, 18 September 2020, https://www.malaymail.com/news/malaysia/2020/09/18/muhyiddin-says-sabah-poll-could-set-stage-for-general-election/1904446.

[63] Lian Cheng, 'PBK to Contest Solo in All Urban and Semi-Urban Seats in PBN12,' *Dayak Daily*, 3 December 2020, https://dayakdaily.com/pbk-to-contest-solo-in-all-urban-and-semi-urban-seats-in-pbn12/.

advantage.[64] Five out of the 13 demands relating to Sarawak's rights under MA63 have been fulfilled, according to Sarawak Assistant Minister of Law, State-Federal Relations and Project Monitoring Sharifah Hasidah. The demands range from federal grants, the regulation of gas and the delegation of powers.[65]

Sarawak has also taken Petronas to court over the non-payment of the petroleum sales tax in November 2019. The Sarawak state won the case,[66] resulting in Petronas paying Sarawak RM2.96 billion in arrears for the 2019 assessment on the export of petroleum products in an out-of-court settlement. Sabah expects to collect RM1.25 billion in petroleum sales tax from Petronas in 2021, as announced by Deputy Chief Minister Jeffrey Kitingan with the blessing of Muhyiddin, who agreed to this after a discussion with the GRS-led state government. According to Jeffrey, the tax proceeds collected from Petronas will be spent on infrastructure, human resources and economic development.[67] The previous Warisan state government had already imposed a 5 per cent sales tax on oil and gas since April 2020, which has now become law.[68]

Objectively, despite Muhyiddin's precarious position in Parliament, the new Sabah government now aligned with Putrajaya has brought immediate dividends in oil tax revenue. Based on the Sarawak example, a combination of legal suits and political alignment with Putrajaya can be leveraged by both Sabah and Sarawak leaders to get Putrajaya to fulfil its MA63 obligations, especially in the areas of state autonomy and revenue sharing. Down the

---

64 Sharon Ling and Stephen Then, 'GPS Affirms Support for Muhyiddin', *The Star Online*, 21 June 2020, https://www.thestar.com.my/news/nation/2020/06/22/gps-affirms-support-for-muhyiddin.

65 Goh Pei Pei, '5 Of 13 Demands Related to MA63 Fulfilled, Sarawak Assembly Told', *Free Malaysia Today*, 11 November 2020, https://www.freemalaysiatoday.com/category/nation/2020/11/11/5-of-13-demands-related-to-ma63-fulfilled-sarawak-assembly-told/.

66 'Sarawak Sues Petronas over State Sales Tax', *Bernama*, 21 November 2019, https://www.bernama.com/en/news.php?id=1791986.

67 Muguntan Vanar, 'Sabah Aims to Collect RM1.25bil in Tax from Petronas', *The Star Online*, 8 November 2020, https://www.thestar.com.my/news/nation/2020/11/09/sabah-aims-to-collect-rm125bil-in-tax-from-petronas.

68 'After Petronas Settles Sarawak's SST, Shafie Says Sabah's Tax Must Be Paid Too', *Malay Mail*, 18 September 2020, https://www.malaymail.com/news/malaysia/2020/09/18/after-petronas-settles-sarawaks-sst-shafie-says-sabahs-tax-must-be-paid-too/1904516.

road, Putrajaya needs to prove its sincerity in wanting to settle the issue of MA63 and establishing a genuine partnership with Sabah and Sarawak.

Chapter 3

The Unemployment Problem during the Warisan Plus Administration

James Alin and Marcilla Malasius

Introduction

When Warisan Plus took power in May 2018, the general public felt hope for the future of Sabah. One wish was for the new government to solve the unemployment problem. On 11 July 2018, Chief Minister Shafie Apdal announced that his economic policies would improve the people's well-being and living standards by creating 600,000 new jobs by the year 2023.[1] Job creation, according to Shafie, was a means to an end, ensuring that every Sabahan would be able to enjoy the benefits of development.

'Is it possible to create 600,000 new jobs in five years?' asked his staunch critics. During the Kimanis by-election in January 2020, UMNO accused Warisan Plus of not solving the unemployment problem. A few days before polling day, Warisan held a large campaign gathering in Membakut. Outside the town hall, the Human Resources and Education Departments put on lavish career talks and a jobs carnival. Then State Minister for Human Resources Yusof Yacob, in his opening remarks, told the crowd of young people that jobs were plentiful during the Warisan Plus administration.[2]

---

1 Shafie's speech was read by his Deputy Chief Minister cum Minister of Commerce and Industry Datuk Seri Wilfred Madius Tangau, during the launching of the Sabah Small Industry Festival in Tamparuli town. Refer to 'State Government aims 600,000 new jobs', *Daily Express*, 12 July 2018, http://dailyexpress.com.my/news.cfm?NewsID=125733.

2 'Kimanis By-Election: Dr Yusof Denies Threatening Government Officials', *New Straits Times*, 11 January 2020, https://www.nst.com.my/news/politics/2020/01/555632/

The crowd was obviously more interested in the free flow of food and entertainment, all at the taxpayers' expense. Although Warisan had the government machinery (money and mass media) at their disposal, they lost Kimanis to UMNO. Warisan apparently failed to convince voters.

From that time, Warisan Plus came under constant scrutiny from the opposition. Among the most vocal critics were Haji Hajiji Mohd Noor,[3] currently the chief minister, and ex-Chief Minister Musa Aman. Voters were increasingly critical towards Warisan as well. Based on our attendance at campaign speeches, unemployment was one of the most popular themes during the state election held in September 2020 (PRN2020). Accusations were thrown at Warisan Plus; they were accused of failing to manage the economy and for causing employment to grow to new heights. As a rebuttal to this criticism, Warisan Plus included in their manifesto the assertion that they had successfully created 83,100 new jobs.[4]

The snap September election was held during a recession, after six months of Covid-19 Movement Control Orders (MCO). And so, a recession and high unemployment rate were used by the Gabungan Rakyat Sabah (GRS) in campaigning against their convenient scapegoat, Warisan Plus. Voters were bombarded with messages sent through social media, loaded with veiled political threats. The consistent theme: unless and until Sabahans vote for GRS, the economy of Sabah would worsen.[5]

---

kimanis-election-dr-yusof-denies-threatening-govt-officials

3 Anna Vivienne. 'Sabah Economy is Sluggish at 0.5 Percent Under Warisan administration – Hajiji,' *BorneoNews.Net*, 16 August 2020, https://borneonews.net/2020/08/16/sabah-economy-is-sluggish-at-0-5-percent-under-warisan-administration-hajiji/

4 Refer to pamphlet '*Pencapaian Kerajaan Warisan*' (Achievement of Warisan Government), available on FB Shafie Apdal and on FB Friends of Shafie Apdal. This author was at the venue when Datuk Seri Shafie Afdal announced that under his government, 83,100 new jobs had been created. That same day, it was repeated by his deputy, Peter Anthony at another rally for N.42 Melalap, Tenom, to support the DAP candidate. See Borneo Post Reporter, 'Melalap Incumbent Peter Faces Radin, Four Others,' *Borneo Post Online*, 13 September 2020, https://www.theborneopost.com/2020/09/13/melalap-incumbent-peter-faces-radin-four-others/

5 He, together with four other candidates, used this tactic to blame the incumbent government with a common theme: 'the Warisan government failed to solve unemployment'. See Jo Timbuong, 'Sabah Polls: Musa says Crucial for State to be Aligned with Federal Administration When Campaigning for GRS', *The Star*, 18 September 2020, https://www.thestar.com.my/news/nation/2020/09/18/sabah-polls-

Against such a background, this chapter will analyse official secondary data on unemployment and job vacancies and focus on four important issues: (1) the unemployment problem Warisan inherited; (2) the severity of unemployment during the Warisan Plus government; (3) Warisan Plus's policy strengths and weaknesses on employment and (4) the costs of unemployment. We close by discussing the implications of our findings. Unemployment was important during the election and negatively affected Warisan, but it cannot be solved easily. Unemployment is a perennial problem in Sabah and is itself a significant social cost. It needs to be better understood for Sabah to move forward.

Inheriting Unemployment: The unemployment problem in 2017

Back in 2017, during the Barisan Nasional (BN)-UMNO administration, the unemployment rate was at a record high of 5.6 per cent, equivalent to 107,500 unemployed persons in Sabah.[6] One-fifth of the unemployment in Malaysia was reported in Sabah. Warisan, then in the opposition, criticised BN-UMNO for failing to address the rising army of the unemployed. It was a very popular rhetoric during the 2018 election. Many politicians have preconceived ideas about unemployment. They believe it can be solved by simply changing the legislators and that it should be eliminated at all costs. The first step in deconstructing these assumptions is to find out who the unemployed in Sabah are.

Unemployed persons refer to the kind or type, whereas the unemployment rate measures changes in the supply of labour. This change occurs in temporal (e.g. from 2017 to 2018) and spatial dimensions (e.g. urban and rural). The Malaysian Department of Statistics classifies the unemployed into two groups: The active type (those not working but who are available for work and actively looking for work) and the inactive type (those persons who are not looking for work).

The unemployment rate is therefore a proportion of the unemployed population in a labour force.[7] Ipso facto, an unemployment rate of 5.6 per

---

bung-moktar-hopes-musa-aman-will-campaign-for-bn.

6 *Yearbook Statistics Malaysia 2016* (Kuala Lumpur: Department of Statistics Malaysia, 2017), 201.

7 Labour force refers to those during the reference week, who are between 15 to 64 years old and who are either employed or unemployed. Outside of the labour force are

cent means that only an average of 94 persons out of every 100 persons seeking employment were able to find employment in 2017. In Sabah this was equivalent to 101,050 job seekers who were not hired. The remaining six out of every 100 persons was equivalent to 6,450 unemployed persons; whatever they do and no matter how skilled or experienced they are, they were not able to secure employment in 2017.

The unemployment rate is a useful indicator for gauging changes (increases or decreases) in the supply of labour. An unemployment rate of 3 per cent or below is acceptable and is called the natural rate of unemployment (NAIRU). When the unemployment rate is within this range, an economy is said to be in full employment. An unemployment rate of zero is not possible. Until today, Sabah has never experienced an unemployment rate of 3 per cent or below. But it can be done. Malaysia as a whole has been within NAIRU or at full employment for the past 22 years (1995-2017) while Sarawak has been in full employment for the past 14 years. Unemployment in Sabah, by comparison, was the most severe.

Recall that an unemployment rate records changes in the supply of labour. A 5.6 per cent increase in unemployment suggests the same proportion of increase in the supply of labour, which means we are halfway to gauging the severity of unemployment in 2017 compared with the year before or after. To gauge the other half, we must find out what happened to the demand for labour. For this we turn our attention to job vacancies. In 2017 there were 128,100 job vacancies and 107,500 unemployed individuals in Sabah. More than enough vacancies were available. As shown in Table 1, Sabah under the BN-UMNO administration was experiencing unprecedented economic growth. The labour market during these three years was vibrant.

Unemployment during the Warisan Plus Government

BN-UMNO left office in May 2018, leaving 107,500 unemployed people behind through April 2018. A heavy responsibility was passed onto the Warisan Plus government. By the time Warisan Plus took control of the

---

those neither employed nor unemployed, particularly housewives, students, retired, disabled persons and those not interested in looking for a job.

Table 1: Growth and Unemployment Sabah, 2014-2017

	GDP growth (%)	Unemployed persons	Unemployment rate (%)	Job vacancies
2014	5	79,500	4.7	141,324
2015	6.30	92,300	5	193,408
2016	4.70	103,300	5.4	120,676
2017	8	107,500	5.6	128,100

Source: DOSM-Sabah and authors' estimates

economy it was already declining. Gross domestic product (GDP) growth was at a meagre rate of 1.5 per cent, only slightly higher than the dismal growth of 1.2 per cent in 1999 (in the aftermath of the Asian Financial Crisis). In 2018 GDP shrank 6.5 per cent in just one year, a drastic decline.[8] Most alarming was the unemployment rate of 5.8 per cent, equivalent to 112,200 unemployed individuals.[9] There were 0.2 per cent or 4,700 more unemployed people compared with 2017. Job vacancies also decreased by 35 per cent, creating a serious situation. With only 44,848 job vacancies, there were not enough employment opportunities for the 112,200 able, willing and searching for jobs.

Table 2: Growth and Unemployment Sabah, May 2018-September 2020[10]

	GDP growth (%)	Unemployed persons	Unemployment rate (%)	Actual job vacancies
2018	1.5	112,200	5.8	44,848
2019	0.5	117,100	5.9	53,262
2020	0.5	117,800	6	83,100

Source: DOSM-Sabah and authors' estimates

8 Department of Statistics Malaysia, Official Portal, https://www.dosm.gov.my/v1/index.php?r=column/cone&menu_id=dTZ0K2o4YXgrSDRtaEJyVmZ1R2h5dz09

9 Ibid.

10 Job vacancies for April and May 2019 not available, and the authors estimated it to be 4,762 job vacancies. Welsh and Cheng estimated 15,523 job vacancies (January to July 2020) or 17.2 per cent of the targeted job vacancies. Bridget Welsh and Calvin Cheng, 'Malaysian youth on the unemployed front line,' *Malaysiakini*, 18 April 2020, https://www.malaysiakini.com/columns/521283

Warisan Plus's Record on Unemployment

In July 2018, the Warisan Plus government announced that they intended to create 600,000 new jobs by 2023. Chief Minister Shafie made the announcement through a speech, three months after he took office. The speech was read by Deputy Chief Minister cum Minister for Commerce and Industry Wilfred Madius Tangau during the launching of the Sabah Small Industry Festival in Tamparuli town.[11] This event was organised to kick-start the One District One Small Industry (OD1SI) programme. According to Tangau, his ministry would formulate and implement flagship district products under the supervision of a Coordination Committee. Emphasis was given to small and medium enterprises because they contribute 36.3 per cent to GDP and provide 66 per cent of the jobs in Sabah. The OD1SI was designed to promote local products and boost local confidence in these products.

As we have suggested, the target was achievable. Distributed over five years, at least 120,000 job vacancies should have been created per annum. Because Warisan Plus governed for only six months in 2018, the target should have been 60,000 new jobs. However, until the end of December 2018, there was no follow-up on the OD1SI. By the end of 2018, based on our calculations, only 62.6 per cent of that yearly target of job creation was achieved. Vacancies were also not adequately filled. Despite efforts taken by employers to search for new recruits and to make job offers more attractive, we calculated that an average of two out of every 100 vacancies, or 2,690 vacancies, were not filled. Looking back, one could say that OD1SI was really a blunt instrument; no significant new jobs were created.

We also witnessed job losses as a result of policy changes. On 23 May 2018, the Warisan Plus government imposed an export ban on sawlogs and sawn timber.[12] According to Shafie, it was a temporary measure to ensure sufficient supply of materials for local industries and to provide jobs for unemployed youths. In the previous year, Sabah exported 529,500 cubic metres, generating a revenue of RM562.5 million for both sawlogs and sawn timber.[13] The exported volume was equivalent to 30 per cent of the total

---

[11] The author attended this event.

[12] Chief Minister Shafie's press statement reported by Julia Chan, 'Shafie Bans Exports of Sabah Logs', *Malay Mail*, 23 May 2018, https://www.malaymail.com/news/malaysia/2020/12/22/new-sabah-govt-mulls-lifting-ban-on-export-of-timber-logs/1934243.

[13] Department of Statistics Malaysia, Official Portal, 'File External Trade Sabah 2017-

volume of timber logs, the remaining 70 per cent became raw materials for downstream local industries. There are two plausible reasons why that 30 per cent was exported; firstly, downstream industries in Sabah have a smaller or more limited processing capacity compared to Peninsular Malaysia. Secondly, the exported sawlogs were made of a species of timber which was coveted in the international market.

As shown in Table 3 below, the blanket ban imposed higher costs on companies exporting sawlogs or sawn timber. In reality, the exporting of sawlogs is not their main business; the core of their operation is in downstream operations: processing sawlogs and sawn timber into immediate inputs and higher value-added products mostly for export (e.g. engineered timber products, furniture components or various panel-based products). They were only exporting unprocessed sawlogs and sawn timber when international market prices were higher. In this case, a blanket ban was simultaneously hurting and benefitting the targeted companies.

Table 3: Impact of Export Ban on Sawlogs and Sawn Timbers, 2017

	Cost*	Benefit**
Volume of exports ('000 cubic metres)	529.5	662,093
Export valued at F.O.B (MYR million)	562,509	1,149,804
Total workers	7,000	4,000
Malaysian workers	6,200	2,680
Malaysian youth workers aged 19 to 30	2,800	800
Malaysian workers aged above 30	4,200	3,200
Non-Malaysian workers	980	1,320
Job vacancies per annum	400	200

* Exporters of sawlogs and sawn timber
** Local downstream industries

Source: Authors estimates using data compiled from Internal Files of Sabah Furniture Association and their website newpages.com.my; various internal reports of Sabah Timber Industries Association; Federation of Sabah Industries (FSI) and Federation of Malaysian Manufacturers Sabah. Representative Office, Yearbook Statistics Sabah 2017; The State Budget 2019 tabled by the Warisan Plus government in November 2018

2018', https://www.dosm.gov.my/v1/index.php?r=column/cone&menu_id=dTZ0K2o4YXgrSDRtaEJyVmZ1R2h5dz09

As shown in Table 3, the blanket ban imposed a huge cost, and interrupted the business of exporting sawlogs and sawn timbers, resulting in 7,000 workers losing their jobs. Of these, 86 per cent were Malaysian and the remaining 14 per cent were foreign workers. Of the Malaysians who lost their jobs, 40 per cent were youths aged between 19 to 30 years old. This industry created on average 400 new jobs per annum. The expected beneficiaries of the ban were the downstream exporters of veneer sheets and plywood plus furniture which were producing 662,093,000 cubic metres and employing 4,000 workers of which 67 per cent were Malaysian and the remaining 33 per cent foreigners. Of this total, 20 per cent were youths. The rest were semi-skilled and managerial workers aged above 30. Although downstream businesses were larger in size, they create on average only 200 new jobs per annum because half of their operation workers have been replaced by machines and automation. Being capital-intensive, they are able to produce higher value-added products for export which bring in larger profits. They tend to hire more educated Malaysian workers. On the other hand, exporters for sawlogs and sawn timber were more labour intensive, therefore they were more likely to hire unemployed youths without regard for their education background.[14] Unemployed youths with a tertiary education have a higher probability of getting a job from exporters of sawlogs.[15]

There was a substantial loss in revenue to the Sabah state revenues as well.[16] In 2018 the royalties from sawlogs and sawn timber were RM149.5

---

[14] From *Statistics Yearbook Sabah 2017*, Kuala Lumpur: Department of Statistics Malaysia (2018), 50-51. We know that, of the total unemployed persons in Sabah, 91 per cent (97,825) were youths (aged 15 to 34). It is also known that from the total unemployed, 66 per cent (70,950) have completed primary and secondary schooling, 26 per cent (27,950) have tertiary education but 8 per cent (8,600) have no formal education. The education attainment of unemployed youth is not known. For an excellent overview on the unemployment among youths in 2020 see Bridget Welsh and Calvin Cheng, 'Malaysia's Youth on the Unemployed Frontline', *Malaysiakini*, 18 April 2020, https://www.malaysiakini.com/columns/521283.

[15] Local higher learning institutions have produced 1,200 to 1,500 graduates yearly, most specialising in forestry and wood-based technology. See Sabah Timber Industries Association, 'STIA proposes questions for State Government consideration', *Borneo Post Online*, 28 April 2020, https://www.theborneopost.com/2020/04/28/stia-proposes-questions-for-state-govt-consideration/

[16] YB Masiung Banah (ADUN for N. 39 Sugut, then from UPKO) posed questions in the State Legislative Assembly, asking why there was a decrease in revenue from royalties

million or 3.5 per cent of state revenue. This was much lower compared with RM160 million in 2017. The export ban was supposed to benefit the downstream industries to engage in structural change, but they hired fewer workers. At the same time, the ban was forcing a sector which provided many jobs and created more job vacancies to close. Many of the middle-aged employees of the affected companies either quit, were laid off through the Voluntary Separation Scheme (VSS) or had their pay cut. They had been working for a long time with companies who had signed hundred-year timber concession contracts during the previous BN-UMNO government. Warisan Plus refused to renew these contracts or issue a new Form 1 License (to take forest produce) and Form IIB License (to take forest produce from alienated land on the prepayment of royalties) for companies who had signed contracts during the previous government, including four high profile companies.

The first, Jawala Plantation Sdn Bhd, a timber plantation company employing 72 workers (more if the six directors and subcontractors are included), had signed the concession contract in 2015 (it was supposed to expire in 2115).[17] Second, Rentak Hasil Sdn Bhd, a trading company exporting crude palm oil (CPO), kernel palm oil (KPO) and wood products, signed in early 2018 (it was supposed to expire in 2118) a joint venture with Sabah Softwood Berhad which employed 4,000 estate workers. Third, Boonrich Sdn Bhd, a teak plantation business, employed 57 full-time staff (more if their contractors are included). On 1 June 2017, Boonrich received from the Sabah Department of Forestry a registration certificate to supply

of forestry-timber. He said up to June 2018, only RM80 million was collected. He requested it to be investigated but Chief Minister Shafie categorically refused. See Kristy Inus, 'Log Export Ban Poses No Serious Repercussions on State revenue: Shafie', *New Straits Times*, 3 July 2019, https://www.nst.com.my/news/nation/2018/07/386931/log-export-ban-poses-no-serious-repercussions-state-revenue-shafie.

17 Jawala Plantation signed concession contracts to log 11,000 ha of Class II Commercial Forest Reserves (FR) of Kalabakan. Concession contracts for logging larger areas of 50,000 ha inside the same FR were 50 per cent owned by Sabah Softwoods Sdn Bhd, a subsidiary of Sabah Foundation, which is under the chief minister's office and 50 per cent owned by Rentak Hasil Sdn Bhd. See Sabah Softwoods Berhad, 'SSB | Sustainability', http://www.softwoods.com.my/sustainability.html and Jawala Incorporated, *Replanting Sabah's Forest for Future Generations: Annual Report 2020*, Labuan FT: Jawala Incorporated (2020), https://links.sgx.com/FileOpen/Jawala%20Inc%202020%20Annual%20Report.ashx?App=Announcement&FileID=637997

and export timber not from natural forests but from the company's own (alienated) land.[18] They were pioneers in plantation forestry and since 1992 had commercially planted 220,000 teak trees on their own land in Sandakan. Between 6 September 2018 and 11 January 2019, Boonrich sent seven letters to the Forestry Department and Chief Minister's Office, seeking clarification and an exemption from the ban. But the requests for exemption were rejected. On 7 March 2019, Boonrich filed a summons at the High Court of Sabah and Sarawak, sued and demanded damages of RM91.6 million from the first defendant i.e. the Chief Conservator of Forests and the second defendant i.e. the Sabah state government. This case is still ongoing.

In 2016, Sabah Forest Industries Sdn Bhd in Sipitang closed down. The owner, Ballarpur Industries, lost more than RM300 million. SFI was in deep financial trouble. Its 2,000 employees suffered job insecurity and irregular or delayed wage payments, and 500 of them were temporarily laid off or resigned. Later in 2017 the BN-UMNO administration appointed Grant Thornton Consulting (GTC) as Receiver and Manager (R&M). A company named Pelangi Prestasi Sdn Bhd (PP) agreed to take over and signed a sales and purchase agreement on 9 March 2018 to acquire 98 per cent of the assets and land titles of SFI from Ballarpur Industries. One month before that, the BN-UMNO government (the state owns 2 per cent of SFI) agreed to approve new timber licenses once PP fulfilled the terms and conditions of the SPA. So, as promised, PP paid RM120 million (10 per cent of RM1.2 billion) in which RM23.1 million of the deposit was used to settle unpaid wages for January to March 2018.[19]

---

[18] Coverage for this case, 'State Government is Sued for RM91m Over the Log Export Ban', *Daily Express*, 12 March 2019, https://www.dailyexpress.com.my/news/132260/state-govt-is-sued-for-rm91m-over-the-log-export-ban/; 'Now Sabah Government Tangled in Suit Over Log Exports', *Free Malaysia Today*, 13 March 2019, https://www.freemalaysiatoday.com/category/nation/2019/03/13/now-sabah-government-tangled-in-suit-over-log-exports/. Profile of Boonrich in Rahimatsah Amat and Christian Schriver, *Legal Source Certification Assessment (Audit) Report for Global Plantations Ltd. In Sabah*, (Kota Kinabalu: NEPCon Global Region Office, 2014), https://preferredbynature.org/sites/default/files/2018-02/SFI%20LS%20Assessment%20public%20summary%2015.pdf.

[19] Payment was for arrears, overtime etc. Pelangi Prestasi agreed to pay a premium of 16 per cent (above market value) for acquisition of SFI which recorded losses of RM354.7 million in the 2017 financial year.

This reprieve[20] was short-lived. The new Warisan-led government decided to call for an open tender again and with it was a new precondition for approving the new timber licenses. Then PP filed an injunction with the High Court of Malaya requesting a status quo until the disposal of the suit. Later on, PP filed for a judicial review. Both filed a civil suit against SFI, Grant Thornton and Lee & Man Paper Manufacturing Limited (LMPM).[21] Grant Thornton and LMPM retaliated by filing for a restraining order against PP. On 6 February 2020, the said court allowed SFI to transfer the proceedings to another judge. This legal battle is far from over, the future of SFI employees was, and still is, in limbo. Having cancelled the previous contracts, the Warisan-led government, through its investment arm, Yayasan Sabah, signed two separate Memorandums of Understanding (MOUs) with the logging and timber companies of their choice. First, on 3 March 2019 between ICSB (Perhutanan) and Priceworth International Berhad (PIB is 30 per cent owned by Rakyat Berjaya Sdn Bhd, a subsidiary of Yayasan Sabah Group which manages its forest concession area) and second on 7 October 2019 between Rakyat Berjaya and Priceworth International Berhad.[22]

Warisan Plus characterised unemployment in the 2019 Budget debate of November 2018 as the product of job seekers' choosy attitudes and the mismatch between existing qualifications and available jobs. The economic situation worsened further. Growth in 2019 shrank to 0.5 per cent.[23] It

---

[20] Reprieve is a legal term referring to a postponement or cancellation of a punishment

[21] Pelangi Prestasi was not in the pulp and paper business, this is probably why the Warisan-led government favoured LMPM to partner with SFI. The CEO of Lee & Man Paper, a large paper company based in Hong Kong, Mr Edmund Lee, announced in October 2018 that HK$5.1 billion (RM2.6 billion) in factories would be opened at Sepang with a production capacity of 700,000 metric tonnes (m.t.) of paper and 550 m.t of pulp. On 7 March 2019, officials of SFI and GTC attended a visit to the SFI plant by the delegates from LMPM. See Justin Kor, 'Heading Down South: Lee and Man Paper expands into Malaysia', *South China Morning Post*, 23 October 2018, https://www.scmp.com/presented/news/asia/topics/china-conference-sea/article/2167000/heading-down-south-lee-and-man-paper.

[22] Justin Lim, 'Innoprise to own 30% of Priceworth under log supply agreement,' *The Edge Markets*, 7 October 2019, https://www.theedgemarkets.com/article/innoprise-own-30-priceworth-under-log-supply-agreement

[23] 'Laporan sosioekonomi Sabah 2019,' Department of Statistics Malaysia (2019), https://www.dosm.gov.my/v1/uploads/files/1_Articles_By_Themes/National%20Accounts/GDPbyState/2020/Laporan_Sosioekonomi_Sabah_2019.pdf.

was by far the lowest in recent history. The expansionary fiscal stimulus of only RM418.7 million did not stimulate production, so few new jobs were created. Subsequently, the unemployment rate remained at 5.8 per cent.

On December 2018, the Warisan Plus Cabinet announced their decision to terminate six contracts to manage 58 water treatment plants (WTPs) that was signed during the previous BN-UMNO government, effective from 15 January 2019. According to Deputy Chief Minister and State Minister for Infrastructure Development Peter Anthony, the contracts were terminated because the state government could not afford to pay the 'too high' charges.[24] He said that the Water Department would take control over all WTPs and absorb the 1,335 employees of the affected companies. Two days before the termination date, employees of Arawira, 94 of them stationed in Segaliud, Sandakan, and 39 in Milau, Kudat, held a picket protest. Water supply was disrupted, causing complaints from industry and consumers. In response, they were accused of sabotaging the State government. Six companies requested a meeting with the Water Department to solve the matter amicably, but they were turned down. On 12 February 2019, five firms filed separate suits against the government for wrongful termination of their contracts and demanded damages totalling RM254 million. The Water Department's Director Amarjit Singh was named as the first Defendant and the State government as the second Defendant.[25] Until now, none of the employees of the previous contractors were absorbed by the Sabah Water Department. It seems unlikely that the State Public Service Department would be able to accommodate them, given that many new posts cannot

---

[24] Larry Ralon, 'Up To Water Concessionaire Companies to Sue: Peter', *Daily Express*, 16 February 2019, https://www.dailyexpress.com.my/news/131288/up-to-water-concessionaire-companies-to-sue-peter/

[25] The contracts were valid for the next 13 years and five months but they were unduly terminated. It is allegedly a gross violation of the contracts. They demanded damages as the following (1) Arawina Sdn Bhd in its statement of claim maintained that they have fully complied with terms of the agreement since 2011 and filed two suits, RM30.9 million and RM37.9 million; (2) Sahabat Megajuta = RM60.9 million; (3) Yuda Water = MYR51.1 million; (4) BYT Vision = RM42.8 million; (5) Harmony Water = RM30.2 million; (6) Akal Kukuh Sdn Bhd mulled to file suit later. See details in Tracy Patrick, 'Five Water Firms Demand RM254 Million Compensation from Sabah Government', *Free Malaysia Today*, 12 February 2019, https://www.freemalaysiatoday.com/category/nation/2019/02/12/5-water-firms-demand-rm254-mil-compensation-from-sabah-govt/.

be easily created. Besides, the Sabah Water Department (State Water Authority) is already employing 1,191 state civil servants. Absorbing those experienced and skilled technicians would come in handy if the Department was operating all the water treatment plants by themselves.[26] In the end, the contracts were awarded to new companies such as Rintis Dinamik Sdn Bhd.[27] So the intention behind the termination was clear: not for the Department to take over but for Warisan Plus to select new contractors of their choice.

Table 4: Revenues and Costs of Water Treatment Plants, Sabah

Items	Notes	Operation/ Variable cost	State revenue received
(A) maintenance work, to fix wear and tear on equipment	amount paid by the State	200,000	330 million (7.7% of state revenue in 2018)
or purchase spare parts for damaged parts of water pumps, piping, main storage tanks			
lodging, electricity and other utilities	paid by six contractors	30,000	
(B) Contractors purchased bleaching agent chemical such as chlorine,	paid by six contractors	?	
filtering equipment etc., all for treating raw water			

[26] Many of employees of the contractors hold essential certificates to work for water treatment plants including the Drinking Water Treatment Process Competency Test, Water Sampling Protocol Competency Test, Water Laboratory Management, Water Treatment Plant Operator Competency Levels 1 and 2 etc. The majority of staff in the Sabah Water Department, 44 (management); 38 (executive); 994 (non-executive) and 115 (meter readers) do not have the technical qualifications to operate water treatment plants, including the management.

[27] Rintis Dinamik Sdn Bhd sub-contracted RM124.7 million to Salcon Engineering Sdn Bhd to expand the capacity i.e. Trunk Main Pipeline and Storage Tank to 160 million litres a day (from 80 MLD) of the Telibong II water treatment plant in Tamparuli, see Surin Murugiah, 'Salcon Jumps 9.26% on Securing Sabah Water Treatment Contract', *The Edge Markets*, 20 March 2019, https://apps.theedgemarkets.com/article/salcon-jumps-926-securing-sabah-water-treatment-contract.

Items	Notes	Operation/ Variable cost	State revenue received
labor charges for scheduled cleaning of tanks			
(C) Monthly wages for 1,335 full time employees of six contractors	paid by six contractors	4,005,000	
Insurance for employees/plants			
Cost (A) + (B) < Revenue		230,000	330 million

Source: Authors' estimates using data from Water Department of Sabah, *Sabah Statistics Yearbook 2017* and three of the six contractors.

The water treatment plants did not yield the revenue they should have. As shown in Table 4, a large proportion of the operation expenditures (Opex) incurred in 54 water treatment plants were paid by the State Water Authority with a smaller portion paid by the six contractors. The sole owner of water treatment plants is the Sabah Water Department and the six contractors' tasks as specified in the contract are to operate them, to pump raw water from sources such dams, reservoirs or rivers, treating or filtering it from pollutants or other impurities. In 2019, the State budgeted Special Expenditures of RM2.045 billion to pay for items related to infrastructure and maintenance. The state earned RM330 million, considerably larger than the RM254 million in fees to be paid to the service contractors. Water revenue should have been higher but there was the serious problem of non-revenue water. Non-revenue water in 2019 and 2020 amounted to RM300 million in losses respectively. Leakages, breakages and thefts along the distribution system are rampant.[28] The effect is that a failure to address underlying issues undercuts revenue and job growth.

In early 2019, the Warisan Plus cabinet decided to cease issuing and renewing licenses for slot machines (jackpot machines).[29] Local authorities

---

28 The Malaysian Water Association, *Water Malaysia Magazine: Clean Water for All*, no. 37, (2020).

29 Under the Public Entertainment Ordinance (Ordinance Hiburan Awam) Sabah 1958, local authorities can issue licenses for 45 kinds of public entertainment, including slot machines, as their important source of income. The fee is RM800 per machine monthly for corporate clubs (including golf and country clubs, horse race outlets) and

sent notices to 50 such outlets informing them that their licenses for slot machines (e.g. one-armed bandits, fruit or poker machines) would not be renewed from the end of 2019. Deputy Chief Minister and State Minister for Local Government and Housing Jaujan Sambakong said the decision was based on the views of the community at large and that gambling activities contributed to many social ills in the state. In October 2019, hundreds of employees held a demonstration in Kota Kinabalu. It was organised by an in-house trade union, the Welfare Association of Recreation Club Employees. Yap How Nam, the president of the union, said Chief Minister Shafie had not responded to their requests for a meeting to discuss the matter. The 3,000-strong members of the union (plus their 15,000 dependents) had been working for jackpot outlets for a long time and were now concerned about losing their livelihoods. He questioned why 4D lottery outlets were not subjected to such rules. In November 2019, many of the affected companies filed applications for a judicial review over the State government's decision. It has not been resolved at the time of writing.

The costs and benefits of the jackpot license cancellations are summarised in Table 5. We make the following observations: many jobs were lost, most of those who lost jobs had low educational backgrounds, making it harder for them to immediately shift to different occupations at a time when jobs are scarce. The jobs in slot machine outlets did not pay much in terms of wages but they did provide a great sense of security, pride and livelihood. Secondly, based on our calculations, the state government was willing to sacrifice RM3,840,000 per annum in revenue from slot machine licenses, which is not a small amount. The outlets were located in Kota Kinabalu, Sandakan, Tawau, Penampang, Putatan, Tambunan, Keningau and Lahad Datu. These local authorities were running budget deficits totalling RM5,842,000. Without the revenue from slot machine licenses, the budget deficit would increase 34 per cent and potentially impact the services provided by local governments. Thirdly, the cost of the decision was not equitably distributed. There was a private cost incurred insofar as the jobs sacrificed had a higher value to low-income people. It also affected the employees on a personal level, hence they felt victimised and betrayed.[30]

RM200 per machine monthly for association clubs (such as Sabah Polo Association, Sandakan Turf, etc.).

[30] '*Kami Undi Warisan, Kini Kena Buang Kerja*', (translated as 'We voted for Warisan,

Fourthly, while enforcement was pretty easy and low cost, there were other costs. With outlets closed and slot machines no longer available, gamblers have moved underground to illegal options. Social ills have not been solved and have arguably increased due to illegality. There are good substitutes i.e. legalised gambling such as the lottery (e.g., Lotto, Sports Toto, Sandakan Turf Club 4D, Diriwan etc.). The lottery outlets are still operating under the jurisdiction of the federal government.[31] In 2019 the State received RM60 million (the same amount in 2018) from taxes on the sale of lottery tickets, draws and prizes.[32] With the benefit of hindsight, the policy should have been adopted differently. Workers in the now-closed outlets bore the brunt of the decision.

Table 5: Cost and Benefit of Not Renewing Jackpot Licenses (2018)

Cost
Employment for 3,000 Sabahans = monthly salary RM6,000,000
Benefit / Revenue (Licenses for Corporate Clubs)
RM3,840,000 (400 slot machines x RM800 x 12 months)

Source: Authors' estimates using data from Welfare Association of Recreation Club Employees.

Now we have been fired', message written on the banners used during demonstration), 7 October 2019, Wikisabah.blogspot.com and 'Why close business operated by Chinese despite strong support for Warisan from Chinese community', Tan Sri T.C. Goh cited in 'Reduce the slot machines clubs, not close them', *Daily Express*, 17 September 2019, https://www.dailyexpress.com.my/news/140587/reduce-the-slot-machine-clubs-not-close-them/. Tan Sri Goh Tian Chuan is the vice president of the Federation of Chinese Association Sabah and the owner of Everise Venture, the company which manages Sandakan Turf Club. He is now a member of the Sabah Economic Advisory Council under the new Bersatu-led government. The Chairman for this Advisory Council is Tan Sri David Chu Sui Kiong, owner of Clubhouse Jackpot Double Up.

31 Casinos and gaming are legal businesses but are in a heavily taxed and regulated sector. The subtle differences between slot machines (known as public entertainment or recreation) and gambling in the casino are explained in *Malaysia's Gaming Tax Act 1972 and Service Tax 2018: Guide on Betting and Gaming*, Putrajaya: Royal Malaysia Customs Department (2018), https://mysst.customs.gov.my/assets/document/1.%20Guide%20on%20betting%20&%20Gaming_230818%20rev3.pdf.

32 'The 2020 Sabah Budget Speech', delivered on 15 November 2019 by Chief Minister and Finance Minister of Sabah Shafie Apdal. See Chief Minister's Office website, www.sabah.gov.my, https://sabah.gov.my/cms/sites/default/files/file-upload/STATE-BUDGET-SPEECH-2020.pdf.

So far, we have explained how Warisan's policy U-turns caused noticeable increases in the number of jobless people in a period of lower demand for labour from both the public and private sectors. The demand for labour from the public sector is derived from two sources: (1) the report that 100,000 people applied for 401 government job vacancies, advertised from January to July 2019;[33] (2) in September 2019 there were 273 new posts of various grades in the state civil service still available, and from 958 vacancies opened in 2018 only 685 were filled by September 2019.[34] These posts were created to accommodate the newly formed Ministry of Law and Native Affairs and the district office of Kalabakan. The entire exercise cost RM71.09 million (a portion of Recurring Expenditure of RM1,371.94 million):[35] creating civil service jobs is surprisingly costly to taxpayers.

The Department of Labour, Sabah, reported that between January to March 2019 there were 7,143 new vacancies advertised by the private sector.[36] According to another source, there were 46,119 job vacancies available from June to December 2019.[37] Data on job vacancies for April and May were not available, but we know that in 2019 there were at least 53,262 job vacancies. To make up for the incomplete data on the demand for labour, we must rely on assumptions extrapolated from limited information; firstly, we assume with a high probability that the number of people looking for jobs was larger than available job vacancies; secondly, unemployed people have a strong preference for government jobs and thirdly, even with low growth, the economy was able to create at least 2,381 job vacancies monthly.[38] Therefore we estimate that the total job vacancies by the end

33 '100,000 apply for just 401 Sabah Govt vacancies,' *Daily Express*, 18 July 2019, https://www.dailyexpress.com.my/news/138037/100-000-apply-for-just-401-sabah-govt-vacancies/

34 'The 2020 Sabah Budget Speech', 19.

35 'The 2019 Sabah Budget Speech', delivered on 9 November 2018 by Shafie Apdal, Chief Minister's Office website, www.sabah.gov.mywww.sabah.gov.my/cms/?q=en/content/state-budget-speech-2019.

36 *Career Roadshow March 2019 Report*, (Kota Kinabalu: Labour Force Department Sabah), 3, https://www.dailyexpress.com.my/news/139442/3-000-jobs-up-for-grabs-at-sabah-career-tour/

37 Refer to Table 4 in Bridget Welsh and Calvin Cheng, 'Emerging Humanitarian Covid-19 Crisis in Sabah,' *Malaysiakini*, 25 October 2020, https://www.malaysiakini.com/columns/548026

38 Estimated using data for Malaysia. For details see, 'Press Release: Employment

of 2019 were likely around 58,024 jobs. In short, unemployment worsened in 2019. The Warisan Plus government missed the target, once again, by a large margin.

The quarterly data that were released up until October 2020 by the Department of Statistics was the national data. Data by state was not included. Up until the third quarter, Malaysia's economic growth was negative 3.1 per cent (GDP down to RM900 billion, valued at purchasing power parity).[39] Malaysia's GDP is a sum of three parts of different sizes, the GDP of Peninsular Malaysia being the largest, that of Sarawak the second largest (10 per cent) and Sabah the smallest. Sabah contributes only 6 per cent to the national GDP.

There is a high probability that Sabah's GDP was positive in the first quarter but turned negative in the second quarter. Here is why: the labour markets went through significant changes during the first and second months of 2020. The demand for labour from tourism, hospitality and its related sub-sectors slowed down due to declining tourist arrivals. All non-essential economic activities were stopped with immediate effect after the Covid-19 MCO was enforced from 18 March until 6 June 2020. During this period, much of the economy was suspended, and real production diminished although many people worked from home. Businesses re-opened in April. By June, even when many outlets resumed normal office hours, business didn't return to the period before the MCO. As a result, many people have lost their jobs.[40] The highest reduction in employment was in the service sector, in areas such as accommodation, food and beverages, entertainment, recreation and parks (mountain guides for Kinabalu National Park). On 7 July 2020, Sabah's then Minister of Human Resources Yusof Yacob said that 4,900 people from 128 companies registered with the Ministry had lost their jobs due to the MCO.[41]

Statistics Second Quarter 2020', Department Statistics Malaysia, 13 August 2020, https://www.dosm.gov.my/v1/index.php?r=column/cthemeByCat&cat=439&bul_id=bnk1UFhEelFxd2F2dUFYK2hKTXc2UT09&menu_id=Tm8zcnRjdVRNWWlpWjRlbmtlaDk1UT09.

39 Ibid.

40 For an excellent journalistic coverage on this issue, see Amir Yusof, 'Help us Get Back Our Jobs', *Borneo Bulletin*, 22 September 2020, https://borneobulletin.com.bn/help-us-get-back-our-jobs/.

41 Jason Santos, 'Close to 4,900 in Sabah Lost Jobs Due to Lockdown, says minister',

While many old jobs were destroyed due to the closing of businesses because of the policy U-turns and the MCO, there were also new (but fewer in number) jobs created by e-commerce, e-hailing taxis, e-delivery and other IT related activities. By the time of the election in September, there were ominous signs of a jobless recovery, with a hangover from a recession; real output resumed but employment did not grow. Often growth that is caused by technological change is responsible for destroying rather creating new jobs, more so for the capital-intensive IT sectors. Consider this; while the old-style taxi drivers lost their business entirely, e-hailing and e-delivery were thriving. The majority of the old-style taxi drivers became unemployed instead of switching to driving MyCar or Grab passengers.

There are other important observations from the situation above. Apart from making a mess with their policy U-turns, Warisan Plus also wrongly predicted that Sabah's GDP would be able to grow 4 to 5.1 per cent in 2020.[42] Even accounting for the pandemic, this prediction was too optimistic. As explained above, growth was positive at 0.5 per cent in the first quarter but negative at -3.1 per cent in the second and third quarters. It is probable that the economy will modestly recover, with positive growth of 0.5 per cent by the end of 2020 – far lower than assumed. A similar mistake was made in 2019. Warisan predicted that growth would increase between 5 to 6 per cent.[43] It turned out to be only 0.5 per cent.

Economic theory argues that slowdowns in growth are associated with rising unemployment. Sabah's GDP was negative in the first and second quarters of 2020 so it could be associated with an additional 702 unemployed people (351 jobless people in each quarter). So, there should be at least 117,800 unemployed persons in 2020. During the election in September, Warisan Plus claimed to have successfully created 83,100 job vacancies, equivalent to achieving 92 per cent of the targeted job vacancies. Another study estimated that there were only 15,523 job vacancies from January to July 2020,[44] which means that Warisan achieved only 17.2 per cent of the targeted job vacancies (summarised in Table 2). Now we have

Free Malaysia Today, 7 July 2020, https://freemalaysiatoday.com/category/nation/2020/07/07/close-to-4900-in-sabah-jobless-due-to-lockdown-says-minister/.

42 'The 2020 Sabah Budget Speech', 16.

43 'The 2019 Sabah Budget Speech', 14.

44 Welsh and Cheng, 'Malaysia's Youth on the Unemployed Frontline'.

a more complete picture of the labour market supply. The implications are clear; out of desperation, most new entrants often resort to taking jobs not to their liking, skills or qualifications. Put simply, they lower their expectations (in terms of wages), as they cannot afford to be choosy. While many are not happy with their current job, they have no other choice but to put up with a pay cut just to make ends meet. They end up as cheap workers.[45] Due to slow business, employers are reducing the number of employees even though they are productive workers. And if business picks up later, employers would be very careful in recruiting staff. There is a lot of cheap labour to choose from anyway.

Costs of Unemployment

In any given year, there are always unemployed persons stuck in long periods of joblessness, while many others, given time, will eventually be employed. We first estimate the opportunity cost for this type of unemployment. Opportunity cost for the long spell of unemployment during BN-UMNO's administration in 2017 was large. As summarised in Table 6 below, opportunity costs were even larger during the Warisan Plus government. Long spells of unemployment represent a loss of output in consumer goods and services which could have been avoided. This loss is substantial when the gap between actual and potential GDP is calculated.

Next, we calculated the gap by including all unemployed persons, not just those experiencing long spells of unemployment. We found that the unemployment of 5.6 per cent had caused the real output in 2017 to shrink by as much as RM10,852.52 million. The RM10 billion is a loss due to inefficiency. Sabah's GDP in 2017 could have been higher than it was (RM77,518 million). If not because of the severe unemployment, economic growth during the Warisan Plus government could have been higher too. The loss in GDP caused by unemployment during 2018 to September 2020 is presented in Table 6 below. In short, a slight increase in unemployment could cause large inefficiencies because labour was not employed, and hence has no productivity.

45 The unemployment rate does not measure involuntary under-utilised skills or under-employment, which is an interesting topic in its own right.

Table 6: Opportunity Costs due to Unemployment, May 2018 to September 2020

	Opportunity cost for long spell of unemployment	Loss in GDP
BN-UMNO		
2017	158,902,200	10,852.52 million
Warisan Plus		
2018	174,096,252	12,142.88 million
2019	182,676,000	12,264.30 million
2020	208,217,602	12,300 million

Source: Authors' estimates: 2017 is estimated as follows: at a 6 per cent unemployment rate there were 6,450 unemployed persons multiplied by 2017's GDP per capita of RM24,636. Counting the 6 per cent who suffer from long spells of unemployment, but with the remaining 101,050 not included, they will be employed in the end. 2018 is estimated as follows: 6,732 unemployed persons multiplied by 2018's GDP per capita of RM25,861. 2019 is estimated as follows: 7,026 unemployed persons multiplied by 2019's GDP per capita of RM26,000. 2020 (up to September) is estimated as follows; 8,246 unemployed persons multiplied by 2020's (3rd Quarter) GDP per capita of RM25,250.74.

Concluding Remarks

Sabah's unemployment developed slowly from 1997 and it worsened over time. In 2017 the number of unemployed people was high compared with 2016, but much less than the job vacancies, which is why there was no shortage of jobs. This was not the first time that this happened. Actually, the supply of labour being less than the demand for labour occurred from 2014 to 2017.

In looking at the Warisan Plus government, firstly, unemployment was very severe. There was a serious shortage of jobs. During GE14, the Warisan Plus government made promises including solving the unemployment problem. Having governed Sabah for two years, their performance did not meet expectations and they failed dismally to achieve their promises. Policy U-turns incurred much higher costs than their intended benefits. In fact, they exacerbated the unemployment problem and to a certain extent further damaged the economy.

Secondly, a shortage of jobs reached acute levels during the Covid-19 lockdown and its aftermath. There was double trouble: a sudden increase in the number of unemployed people and a sudden decrease in job vacancies. During the lockdown – except for those in essential services and front-liners – no one was allowed to go out to work. Thirdly, the unemployment rate far exceeded the NAIRU level, and Sabah's economy was far from having full employment. Again, this is not the first time Sabah's labour market has been in a tight situation, where labour supply far exceeds demand. It has happened 30 times in the State's history between 1980 to 2010. Unemployment during these 30 years was of the same kind, but of a different magnitude compared with during Warisan Plus's time.

Fourth, the target set by Warisan Plus in 2018 was actually achievable. In the past, the Sabah economy was able to produce over 100,000 job vacancies per year for seven consecutive years from 2011 until 2017. The target should have been 60,000 jobs in 2018 because they had only six months that year due to the elections. They governed for one full year in 2019 so the target should have been 120,000, and they had up to September 2020, so the target should have been 90,000 jobs. During the Warisan government, which lasted only 26 months, there was a total of 154,520 job vacancies. They only achieved 57.2 per cent of their target.

The economy was adversely affected by unemployment from 2018 until 2020. However, our calculations did not include other social costs such as wasted talent and the unrealised productivity of unemployed people. So too with the costs of misery or frustration experienced by unemployed individuals, as well the burden to families and friends who had been supporting them. More could have been done to address the situation, with more realistic targets and greater appreciation of the effects of policy U-turns on the economy.

Chapter 4

Voices of Civil Society Organisations in Sabah Politics

Beverly Joeman, Nelson Dino and Asraf Sharafi

Introduction

Civil society organisations (CSOs) are synonymous with support for democracy, human rights and civil rights. This is true also in the case of Sabah-based CSOs which play a constructive role in raising awareness and empowering the people of Sabah. CSOs contribute to a system of checks-and-balances on the government, regardless of who is in power. This encompasses the protection of fundamental liberties, the protection of human rights and educational outreach. There are lots of ways in which CSOs have been pursuing their advocacy: raising awareness through voter education campaigns, workshops, training, webinars and even using the arts in making their voices heard. Others are more vocal about voicing out their concerns by organising flash mobs, peaceful protests, handing out memorandums and the like.

More importantly, CSOs provide checks-and-balances to keep the government of the day accountable and to remind them that the people are watching. They try to bring to the public issues that would otherwise be left unnoticed, and to make sure that the genuine spirit of democracy and human rights is upheld and respected. They also bring the government to the table to engage with people as part of the decision-making process.

In this chapter, we analyse how CSO advocacy in Sabah affects politics, especially in light of the 2020 Sabah state election (PRN2020) which saw the incumbent Warisan Plus coalition, including Parti Warisan Sabah (Warisan), the Democratic Action Party (DAP) and United Progressive

Kinabalu Organisation (UPKO) lose to the Perikatan Nasional (PN)-aligned Gabungan Rakyat Sabah (GRS). By land area, Sabah is the second largest state in Malaysia and is probably the state with the most fluid political situation. It has seen frequent changes of government, from the United Sabah National Organisation (USNO) to Parti Bersatu Rakyat Jelata Sabah (BERJAYA), Parti Bersatu Sabah (PBS), Barisan Nasional (BN), Warisan Plus and most recently GRS. In this piece, we show how, in the context of this volatile political scene in Sabah, some CSOs have made their voices heard. CSOs have fought hard over the years to raise issues and navigate the changes of government, sometimes to no avail. Many issues still haunt Sabah, although the politicians in charge have changed. This is the case, for example, where the state government continues to impose mega dam projects that would harm the livelihoods and traditions of local communities.

Some complex issues such as statelessness, which have existed in Sabah since the 1970s, are repeatedly used as tools for bartering as politicians project themselves as true and loyal Sabahans who will fight for Sabahans' rights against migrants. Communities that are affected by statelessness in Sabah include inland indigenous communities that lack documentation and recognition. However, it is the coastal and seafaring indigenous communities from the east coast who have become the main targets for hate speech and fear-mongering in political campaigns.

Other issues are more institutionalised, focussing on reforming the electoral process and promoting progressive democracy in Sabah. There is also mobilisation from youth-based CSOs that are playing a more prominent role. These youth groups counter the view that youths or *anak muda* do not care about politics. Although to some extent this is true (as it is of all age groups), during the election there were youth organisations that tried to influence voters and promote inclusion, especially targeted at youth voters, with their activism and advocacy. This suggests that CSO activism will have a bright future as it is flourishing among the young, and that older CSOs will have future leaders to replace them, bringing more creativity and dynamism.

To understand the future of CSOs in Sabah it is necessary to look back, to discuss the evolution of Sabahan civil society, and examine some of the most important contemporary issues shaping politics, most recently in the context of the 2020 state polls.

Voices from the Forest and the River

The CSO movement has deep roots in Sabah, but in the last decade it has started to take a more recognisable form. There are more open calls for support and a closing of ranks amongst NGOs which work together in the same network of friends and comrades. In Sabah, the NGO community is a small circle of people. Anyone who dares to speak up against the government is labelled a troublemaker, and is subject to intimidation, doxing[1] and harassment from the police and pro-government supporters. The last decade witnessed many activists being harassed, such as those from Bersih 2.0, PACOS, Pangrok Sulap, Borneo Komrad of Universiti Malaysia Sabah (UMS) and so on. These attacks have reinforced solidarity and increased outpourings of public support. People understand that CSOs prioritise grassroots and community issues. They also understand that issues must be resolved meaningfully, not just through superficial legal or institutional remedies.

For instance, consider the issues raised by the inland indigenous peoples, particularly in relation to protecting their native land rights and livelihoods against mega dams. In 2008, the BN Sabah state government granted approval for a feasibility study to be carried out for the building of a mega dam situated in Ulu Papar, Sabah: the Kaiduan Dam. In 2015, Joseph Pairin Kitingan, who was then state infrastructure development minister, suggested that by 2030 the dam would be able to supply water to millions from Kota Kinabalu to Papar, Kinarut, Tuaran and beyond, and would avert a serious water crisis.[2]

The dam was proposed to be built within the boundary of the Crocker Range Park area, affecting nine villages in total (Timpayasa, Terian, Tiku, Buayan, Pongobonon, Babagon Laut, Timpango, Kalanggaan and Long Kogungan). When the villagers, numbering some 1,500, were informed about the proposed Kaiduan Dam, they quickly formed an action committee called the Taskforce Against Kaiduan Dam (TAKAD), led by Nousi Giun, a villager from Terian, who put up fierce protests against the dam, which would take away native customary land rights, livelihoods and sustenance.

---

1 Publicising private information about individuals, usually on the Internet.

2 Jenne Lajiun, 'Urgent need for Kaiduan Dam', *Borneo Post*, 24 March 2015, https://www.theborneopost.com/2015/03/24/urgent-need-for-kaiduan-dam/.

It would also see their indigenous lands submerged and force them to be relocated.

Before Kaiduan Dam, there was the Babagon Dam, built in the Upper Moyog area in 1997, displacing indigenous communities of Kampung Kintup, Nunuk, Tiung and Mogilan. In August 2019,[3] a former Jawatankuasa Keselamatan dan Kemajuan Kampung (Village Development and Security Council) chairman, Nelson Malon, spoke about the unfulfilled promises which included a *balai raya* (community hall), cemetery and chapel. The quality of compensation can be seen in the poor road conditions and dilapidated houses at Kampung Tampasak, where the communities were relocated to in 1994, and the ancestral graves were submerged. While all titled lands and inundated areas were compensated, the areas under the water catchment, both titled and customary, have not been compensated because they were not gazetted. The irreplaceable loss faced by the communities is documented in a 2013 film *The Sunken Graves*,[4] made by Mohd Nizam Andan and Nelson Raymond.

Learning from the Babagon Dam situation, TAKAD forged on despite continuous harassment from the authorities. One of their defenders, Galus Ahtoi, was summoned by the police and was investigated regarding a Facebook post objecting the Kaiduan Dam project.[5] Lessons were also learnt from Orang Asal communities of Sungai Asap displaced by the Bakun Dam in Sarawak.[6]

Leaning on the concept of free, prior and informed consent (FPIC), the villagers said that they were not consulted about the building of Kaiduan Dam. They were given confusing and inadequate information from the government, with claims that the dam project had not been approved even though the contractor had already entered the affected villages to conduct

---

3 Oswald Supi, 'Don't move before Govt offers Papar dam compensation', *Daily Express*, 28 August 2019, http://www.dailyexpress.com.my/news/139930/ngo-don-t-move-before-govt-offers-papar-dam-compensation/.

4 Nizam Andan, *The Sunken Graves* (film), Borneo Eco Film Festival (Subtitled) (2013), https://bit.ly/TheSunkenGraves.

5 'Police probe activist over Kaiduan Dam project post on Facebook', *Borneo Post*, 16 February 2016, https://www.theborneopost.com/2016/02/16/police-probe-activist-over-kaiduan-dam-project-post-on-facebook/.

6 'Sungai Asap: BN's Final Betrayal', *Sarawak Report*, 23 April 2013, https://www.sarawakreport.org/2013/04/sungai-asap-bns-final-betrayal/?

an Environment Impact Analysis (EIA).[7] To protect their rights, TAKAD, together with PACOS Trust, held a traditional blessing ceremony, planted a *batu sumpah* (oath stone), held a Catholic mass right on the land where the Kaiduan Dam was to be built and planted a cross to mark the blessed land in 2010. For the indigenous people, although many have converted to Christianity or other religions, their traditional beliefs are deeply entrenched when it comes to seeking divine intervention and protection on matters of land and wellbeing.

Fast forward to 2016. As strong winds of change blew across the nation's political landscape, a new political party, Parti Warisan Sabah (Sabah Heritage Party), was formed. In order to win over the voters of Penampang, particularly in Moyog, the Warisan candidates for N.20 Moyog, Jenifer Lasimbang, and P.174, Darell Leiking, took to the villages promising to scrap the Kaiduan Dam if they were voted in. This promise may have contributed to Lasimbang's 4,442 and Leiking's 23,473 vote majorities in the 14th General Election (GE) on 9 May 2018. Such was the weight of the promise to protect ancestral lands to the people of Moyog. Importantly, if the construction was pushed through, it would destroy the ancestral ecosystem of the indigenous people that contains indigenous knowledge, interconnected with the people's indigenous beliefs, existence and rituals.

However, the euphoria of having a new Warisan-led state government dissipated when Peter Anthony, the State Infrastructure Development Minister, announced on 3 August 2018 that there would be no more Kaiduan Dam, but announced a RM2 billion Papar Dam instead, spanning over 522 hectares, to be built in Kampung Bisuang.[8] The location was later changed to Kampung Mondoringin, Papar. Then Chief Minister Shafie Apdal had earlier announced that the construction of the Papar Dam would not be on the same site as the Kaiduan Dam project[9] but geo-maps showed that

7 Nousi Giun, 'Letter to Friends, Campaigners', International Work Group for Indigenous Affairs (IWGIA), April 2010, https://www.iwgia.org/images/newsarchivefiles/0135_Action_Committee_Against_Kaiduan_Dam_coverletter.pdf.

8 Hayati Dzulkifli, 'RM2b Papar Dam to resolve West Coast woes', *Daily Express*, 3 August 2018, http://www.dailyexpress.com.my/news/126301/rm2b-papar-dam-to-resolve-west-coast-woes/.

9 Bernama, 'New dam must be able to tackle water supply problems — Mohd Shafie', *Borneo Post*, 7 August 2018, https://www.theborneopost.com/2018/08/07/new-dam-must-be-able-to-tackle-water-supply-problems-mohd-shafie/.

while it was not at the exact same location, it was nearby, and the same nine villages would again be adversely affected.

Figure 1: Kaiduan and Papar Dams
Source: 'Save Ulu Papar' Facebook page, 9 July 2019[10]

TAKAD once again leapt into action, led by Diana Sipail, their spokesperson, along with Save Ulu Papar, PACOS Trust, and Bersih 2.0 (Sabah). On 1 August 2019, 200 residents from 10 villages around Papar and Penampang converged to protest the Papar Dam.[11] A Catholic mass was held and a cross was erected on the exact spot of the cross planted 10 years ago to protest the Kaiduan Dam. Affected villagers again reiterated their stand against any mega dams on their ancestral lands and would not consider any form of compensation over the loss of their native customary land rights, livelihoods and sustenance, and urged the government to seriously consider the Water Catchment Plan proposed by UMS geologist

[10] 'Save Ulu Papar' Facebook, 9 July 2019, https://www.facebook.com/SaveUluPapar/photos/a.538661702913290/2301944303251679/?type=3&theater.

[11] Durie Rayner Fong, 'Protesters seek divine intervention to halt Papar dam project', *Free Malaysia Today*, 1 August 2019, https://www.freemalaysiatoday.com/category/nation/2019/08/01/protesters-seek-divine-intervention-to-halt-papar-dam-project/.

Professor Dr Felix Tongkul[12] to conserve and improve water catchments, and to arrest the state's non-revenue water (NRW) losses which were said to be at 52 per cent.[13]

In PRN2020, due to the U-turn decision by Warisan to install the Papar Dam after promising to cancel the Kaiduan Dam, voters in the affected villages spoke about their disappointment. Jackly Lasimin, who hails from Kampung Bisuang and is the spokesperson of Save Ulu Papar, said that this decision would haunt Warisan in the state elections.[14] Villagers have warned decision makers about the 'curse of the seven generations' should the controversial dam be continued.[15] On the other hand, it must also be noted that there are 'organised' dam supporters too.[16] On 11 July 2019, a group of pro-Papar Dam supporters led by Juil Nautim, the deputy president of KDM Malaysia, gathered in Papar town. When the gathering went viral on social media, Save Ulu Papar's Jackly showed that the pro-dam supporters were neither residents nor indigenous communities from the affected villages. On 3 September 2020, several individuals were quoted in *Borneo Today* saying that the people of Papar wanted the dam to be built because of the water woes that they have faced for years.[17] But ironically, none of the communities from the nine affected villages were interviewed. The president of KDM Malaysia is Warisan's Peter Anthony; Juil Nautim later became the Warisan candidate for a new seat, N.27 Limbahau, in PRN2020, and won with a 2,523 majority.

---

12 Jason Santos, 'Reservoir better than building dam, says Sabah expert', *Free Malaysia Today*, 23 October 2019, https://www.freemalaysiatoday.com/category/nation/2019/10/23/reservoir-better-than-building-dam-says-sabah-expert/.

13 NST Team, 'Sabah's non-revenue water problem is the worst because Shafie did not address it', *New Straits Times*, 22 March 2018, https://www.nst.com.my/news/nation/2018/03/348078/sabahs-non-revenue-water-problem-worst-because-shafie-did-not-address-it.

14 Stephanie Lee, 'Papar Dam decision will haunt Parti Warisan Sabah, says activists', *The Star*, 2 September 2020, https://www.thestar.com.my/news/nation/2020/09/02/papar-dam-decision-will-haunt-parti-warisan-sabah-says-activists.

15 Kow Gah Chie, 'Dusun villagers warn of "7-generation curse" if Papar Dam is built', *Malaysiakini*, 21 September 2020, https://www.malaysiakini.com/news/543432.

16 Tracy Patrick, 'Papar residents come out in support of RM2 bil dam', *Free Malaysia Today*, 11 July 2019, https://www.freemalaysiatoday.com/category/nation/2019/07/11/papar-residents-come-out-in-support-of-rm2-bil-dam/.

17 Suraidah Roslan, 'Penduduk Papar mahu empangan dibina untuk atasi masalah bekalan', *Borneo Today*, 3 September 2020, https://www.borneotoday.net/penduduk-papar-mahu-empangan-dibina-untuk-atasi-masalah-bekalan/.

In what looked like a stern warning from Peter Anthony,[18] NGOs such as PACOS were cautioned that organisations that received most of their funding from international sources should abide by the law and regulations of the state and should not be allowed to incite the people. In fact, it was advised that NGOs with international funding should seek the government's approval for all activities. Anthony proposed that the Act governing NGOs be updated. Bersih 2.0 (Sabah) issued a statement condemning the policing of civil society, citing Article 10 of the Federal Constitution to uphold freedom of speech.[19] Citizens on the lower rungs of society have only their voices as a channel to criticise and disapprove of government policies that ignore the interests of the communities, and CSOs such as PACOS, TAKAD and Save Ulu Papar will continue to represent the communities affected by mega government projects, and echo the voices of the communities to the larger public.

Jannie Lasimbang, a human rights activist and a newcomer to politics in 2018, stood on a DAP ticket for N.19 Kapayan in GE14 and garnered the highest vote per constituency of 19,558 votes (72 per cent), and the biggest majority vote of 13,163. Under immense public pressure to make a statement on the building of the Papar Dam, Jannie reiterated her stand that the government must uphold native land rights.[20] She mentioned that it was her prerogative to ensure that the communities affected by the dam were protected. The courage to maintain her stand, while being part of the Warisan-led government as the deputy minister of the Sabah Ministry of Law and Native Affairs, could have contributed to the increase in voter confidence. The voters of N.25 Kapayan voted Jannie to be their *wakil rakyat*

---

18 Jenne Lajiun, 'Not enough water supply by 2024 – minister', *Borneo Post*, 9 July 2020, https://www.theborneopost.com/2019/07/09/not-enough-water-supply-by-2024-minister/.

19 Bersih Steering Committee, 'Do not threaten to silence civil society', *Bersih 2.0*, 10 July 2019, http://www.bersih.org/press-statement-bersih-2-0-sabah-10-july-2019-do-not-threaten-to-silence-civil-society/ and Natasha Joibi, 'Sabah Bersih takes minister to task for attempting to silence civil society', *The Star*, 10 July 2019, https://www.thestar.com.my/news/nation/2019/07/10/sabah-bersih-takes-minister-to-task-for-attempting-to-silence-civil-society.

20 Julia Chan, 'Sabah assistant minister says respect native's rights in controversial Papar dam project', *Malay Mail*, 3 July 2019, https://www.malaymail.com/news/malaysia/2019/07/03/sabah-assistant-minister-says-respect-natives-right-in-controversial-papar/1767885.

(people's representative) again in PRN2020, resulting in a larger percentage of support, winning 15,052 votes (77.4 per cent) with a majority of 13,163 votes.

Jannie has always been well respected by the voters of Kapayan and Penampang by virtue of her human rights track record in being appointed as Sabah SUHAKAM commissioner, secretariat director (and later secretary general) of JOAS, vice-chair of Bersih 2.0 and an expert member of the UN-EMRIP, having worked on the United Nations Declaration on the Rights of Indigenous Peoples (UNDRIP) and the UNDRIP Outcome Document as well as being the Secretary General of Asia Indigenous Peoples' Pact prior to entering the world of politics. She is also known to have campaigned against the controversial dam alongside PACOS, JOAS and TAKAD.

The Orang Asal connection to the river is timeless, and the belief in the traditional practice of river conservation (*tagal*) is immense, even in modern times. In the case of the Babagon Dam, international instruments such as the UNDRIP (which did not exist in 1994) were not yet widely used. (UNDRIP was adopted by the United Nations on 13 September 2007.) Indigenous rights were hardly discussed; PACOS (1997) and JOAS (1996) were just finding their voices. Today, there is extensive research on the irreversible environmental impact and damage of mega dams, earthquake risks,[21] conservation and preservation of water catchments, the application of international instruments and the growing national and international support network such as through Save Rivers, Land Rights Now, ASEAN People's Forum, AICHR, the United Nations and the like. Leveraging on the lessons of the Babagon Dam has resulted in more systematic, solid and informed protests against mega dams.

The issue of Kaiduan/Papar Dam has reached an international audience, up to the level of the United Nations, as it was mentioned at the Permanent Forums in New York, the Expert Mechanisms of the Rights of Indigenous Peoples (EMRIP) Forum and the Business and Human Rights Forum in Geneva. Several open letters have been written by TAKAD, MOUs have been submitted and protests such as the 'Idle No More' walk, Bersih 4 and 5 rallies, the Women's Rights and Climate Change gatherings were held in

[21] David Thien, 'Earthquake risk from proposed Papar Dam', *Daily Express*, 12 November 2019, https://www.dailyexpress.com.my/news/143173/earthquake-risk-from-proposed-papar-dam/.

Sabah. The numerous protests held by the villagers, and documentation of the controversial dams since 2008 have proven that the voices of the people, albeit in the interior, were magnified by media, activists and researchers.

As of the end of December 2020, more than three months after PRN2020, the issue remains unresolved by the GRS government, possibly due to its concentration on Covid-19 cases, food aid and the Conditional Movement Control Order (CMCO). The new state infrastructure minister is Bung Moktar, who swapped portfolios with Masidi Manjun on 29 September 2020. Again, this situation not only puts the people in limbo but slows services to the communities. Villagers are also having trouble moving forward as the issue of environmental protection of their land remains at risk, affected by the waves of change for 'progress', like the development of the beach or coast in Tanjung Aru.

Voices from the Land for the Sea

The estimated RM7.1 billion Tanjung Aru Eco Development (TAED) was first announced in 2013 when Sabah's previous chief minister, Musa Aman (2003-2018) launched the project. He said that it was a strategic initiative with strong state and federal support to create a new gateway to unique tourist attractions in Sabah. Accordingly, the master plan also placed emphasis on community facilities, open spaces and landscaping, and is supported by many sustainable environmental features.[22] When the Terms of Reference of the Special Environment Impact Analysis (SEIA) were displayed to the public in July 2014, they were met with strong objections from half of the respondents.[23] There were concerns around public access to the beach, arguments that the project should be relocated and calls that Tanjung Aru Beach ultimately belongs to the people of Sabah. When TAED became more known to the larger public, a group of concerned

---

22 Wong King Wai, 'City & Country: Tanjung Aru Eco Development to rehabilitate public spaces and attract investment', *The Edge Malaysia Weekly*, 20 November 2014, http://www.theedgeproperty.com.my/content/city-country-tanjung-aru-eco-development-rehabilitate-public-spaces-and-attract-investment.

23 Wong Lie Lie, Tania Golingi and Claus Pedersen, 'Proposed Tg. Aru Eco Development, Kota Kinabalu, Sabah. Special Environmental Impact Assessment – Terms of Reference', DHI Water & Environment (M) Sdn Bhd, 15 October 2014, http://www.epd.sabah.gov.my/v1/images/specialeia/SEIA11/Addendum%201.pdf?type=file.

environmental organisations (WWF Malaysia, Land Empowerment Animals People [LEAP], PACOS Trust, Pusat Belia Youth-PREP Alamesra, Sabah Environmental Protection Association, Sabah Women's Action Resources Group and Save Open Spaces Kota Kinabalu) formed the Tanjung Aru Action Group 2.0 (TAG) and demanded that the beach and the Prince Philip Park remain as a public space. Harjinder Kaur Kler, who headed TAG, said that the group wanted to ensure that Tanjung Aru beach is developed according to the needs of the public, voiced scepticism at the plans and claimed that public access to the beach and park would become limited.[24]

In a move to garner the public's support and confidence for Warisan, the promise to scrap the TAED project was made by Warisan candidate for N.17 Tanjong Aru, Junz Wong. In February 2017, Wong announced that the TAED was a no-go if Warisan gets the mandate of the people to govern Sabah.[25] After releasing a press statement, Wong continued to speak up against TAED on his social media platform.

However, after winning the Tanjung Aru seat, Wong declared in June 2019 that he was never against TAED, saying that the BN government had already spent RM90 million on TAED, and that it would be a waste if the project was dropped altogether. Peter Anthony earlier disclosed that the multi-billion-ringgit project was to go ahead, even with the blessing of Shafie Apdal.[26] Jefferi Chang and SM Muthu from Save Open Space KK continued to speak up in an open letter to the CM against the project, urging the new government to conserve Tanjung Aru Beach and to turn it into a large park, saying that any developments should not degrade or devalue the beach. In July 2019, a public picnic event, Occupy Tanjung Aru Beach, was organised at the Prince Philip Park to protest Warisan's decision to continue the controversial TAED. Save Open Space KK, Bersih 2.0 (Sabah), TAKAD,

---

[24] Julia Chan, 'RM7.1b Sabah beachfront development plans draws conservationists' ire', *Malay Mail*, 3 September 2014, https://www.malaymail.com/news/malaysia/2014/09/03/rm7.1b-sabah-beachfront-development-plan-draws-conservationists-ire/739369.

[25] The BorneoToday Team, 'TAED is a "no go" under a Warisan government, reassures Junz Wong', *Borneo Today*, 17 February 2017, https://www.borneotoday.net/taed-is-a-no-go-under-a-warisan-government-reassures-junz-wong/.

[26] Durie Rainer Fong, 'Multi-billion ringgit Tanjung Aru Eco-Development project to start soon, says minister', *Free Malaysia Today*, 25 June 2019, https://www.freemalaysiatoday.com/category/nation/2019/06/25/multi-billion-ringgit-tanjung-aru-eco-development-project-to-start-soon-says-minister/.

Bentarakata and several other activists, as well as members of the public, came together for the event.

Towards the end of 2019, some residents of Kampung Tanjung Aru Lama, Sembulan, Kepayan and Putatan, led by Mansor Abdullah, decided to form a group that would defend Tanjung Aru Beach at all costs. Thus Komuniti Indah Tanjung Aru (KITA) was formed and registered. This group came about when news of an updated TAED plan arrived, and included reclaiming almost one kilometre from the sea. Augustine Wong, a landscape architect and urban designer from Penampang, released a commentary noting that the Malaysian EIA needed to address the environmental, social and cultural perspectives, not just the economic and technical factors, of the proposed project.[27] He questioned if holistic elements had been taken into consideration when the government decided to go ahead with the project. The members of KITA capitalised on Junz's failed election promises to stop TAED and campaigned for another political candidate in the snap election. While Wong retained the Tanjung Aru seat, his majority dropped from 4,610 to 3,147 votes.

The Tanjung Aru Beach has been named as one of the world's best locations to view the sunset. Thousands of photographs have been shared on social media, and Sabah Tourism Board Chairman, Joniston Bangkuai, said the board continually promoted the beach to tourists, locals and foreigners alike.[28] Before Covid-19 and the MCO crippled the tourism industry, it was easy to find hundreds of tourists and beach lovers there, and many Sabahans have a sentimental attachment to the beach. This is why the protest against TAED to protect Tanjung Aru Beach must be continued by the people, who are the true stakeholders of the beach.

Save Open Space KK's Jefferi Chang and SM Muthu as well as KITA continue to fight to defend Tanjung Aru Beach, to protest against mega development projects that will cause irreversible environmental damage, change shorelines and close the beach to the public for generations to come.

---

27 Augustine Wong Chee Ming, PLA, 'TAED masterplan must be sustainable in long term', *Daily Express*, 8 December 2019, http://www.dailyexpress.com.my/read/3356/taed-masterplan-must-be-sustainable-in-long-term/.

28 Olivia Miwil, 'Spectacular sunset in Tanjung Aru', *New Straits Times*, 17 October 2017, https://www.nst.com.my/news/nation/2017/10/291949/spectacular-sunset-tanjung-aru.

By ignoring these voices, the unheard and ignored voices of the coastal indigenous people from the sea would also be ignored, as not only would the future of their children be put at stake but the future of their environment and marine resources, as well as their economic and cultural development.

Voices from the Sea: The Coastal Indigenous People

The problems of the coastal people extend across Sabah. Statelessness is a perennial problem in the state due to poverty, ignorance and legal issues. The ethnicity or race of these 'stateless' children, most of whom live in coastal areas and are legally recognised in the Sabah State Ordinance 1952 as 'native', and are hence indigenous peoples of the coastlines or the Orang Asal Pesisir.[29] But this 1952 Native Ordinance is not seen as a legal instrument to complement the Registration of Births and Deaths Ordinance 1966, aimed at resolving documentation issues. Although statelessness has long been acknowledged as a problem by elected political leaders, they do not have specific policy positions to address them. There are bureaucratic problems which have made it harder for disadvantaged people to obtain identification cards for their children and this needs to be resolved. But due to the sensitivities involved, resolving this issue is very complex.[30]

On 3 June 2018, the Human Resources Development for Rural Areas (DHRRA) organised a workshop in Kota Kinabalu to deal with Sabah's documentation issues. It was attended by the representatives of 21 CSOs. As these CSOs are familiar with what is happening on the ground, they proposed recommendations to the state government on how to resolve these issues because there are many Sabahans who do not have documents.[31] Even SUHAKAM met with then Chief Minister Shafie Apdal in April 2018 to extend help in finding a pragmatic solution to these issues and working with federal agencies. The chief minister agreed to work with SUHAKAM

---

29 Tracy Patrick, 'Who's a native in Sabah? State Minister defers an answer', *Free Malaysia Today*, 14 June 2018, https://www.freemalaysiatoday.com/category/nation/2018/06/14/whos-a-native-in-sabah-state-ministry-defers-an-answer/.

30 M Fakhrull Halim, 'Sekolah Alternatif: A school for Semporna's invisible children', *Malaysiakini*, 26 September 2020, https://www.malaysiakini.com/news/544148.

31 Avila Geraldine, '21 NGOs to assist in resolving issue of stateless people in Sabah', *New Straits Times*, 3 June 2020, https://www.nst.com.my/news/nation/2018/06/376213/21-ngos-assist-resolving-issue-stateless-people-sabah.

as an interlocutor for the realisation of human rights.[32]

Political will amongst politicians is needed. Citizens in Sabah have long been sceptical of any government steps to provide citizenship to undocumented and stateless people. Such moves can be seen as a political strategy by the ruling party to increase their voting base. However, solving this problem needs more than just a political decision. It needs a humanitarian act to ensure no children are left behind. In 2019, the government announced the new 'Zero Reject Policy' that allows stateless children to register for public schools. However, the stateless children whose parents do not have documents are not allowed to enter public schools because at least one parent has to be a Malaysian citizen. Thus, solutions should go beyond curing symptoms. They should instead address the issues at their roots. If not, the stateless children will still be in an unfortunate situation when trying to access education, freedom of movement and employment opportunities as well as healthcare.[33]

The Advocates for Non-discrimination and Access to Knowledge (ANAK) provide paralegal advice, access to basic rights and conduct research on statelessness. It argues that there is a greater possibility that these children will grow up to be functioning, contributing members of society through education. Because they also desire to live decent and normal lives.[34] Two of the CSOs that work on the issue of stateless children among the coastal indigenous people in different districts of Sabah are Borneo Komrad and Cahaya Society. They built alternative schools in the communities of the 'invisible children' who do not have any legal documents. Aside from illiteracy, the communities also face problems accessing clean water because the main pipe is not connected to their homes. The status of their houses is unclear too, as they were often built on state land without a permit. The government's responsibility to provide facilities

---

32 Avila Geraldine, 'Suhakam to help Sabah solve stateless problem', *New Straits Times*, 15 April 2019, https://www.nst.com.my/news/nation/2019/04/479695/suhakam-help-sabah-solve-stateless-problem.

33 Crystal Teoh, 'We have a Zero Reject Policy, so what's next?', *Centre for Public Policy Studies*, 1 April 2019, https://cpps.org.my/publications/we-have-a-zero-reject-policy-so-whats-next/.

34 Robin Augustin, 'How to reduce stateless numbers in Sabah', *Free Malaysia Today*, 17 April 2018, https://www.freemalaysiatoday.com/category/nation/2018/04/17/how-to-reduce-stateless-numbers-in-sabah/.

has been largely neglected.[35] There is no help available as the areas they built their houses on are unrecognised as kampung land, or are not gazetted.

Borneo Komrad is a collective of educated and motivated youths who came together to provide free education programmes for stateless and undocumented children 'because education is power'.[36] They believe that 'education is a right for all', not only for citizens of Malaysia. Even though former Education Minister Dr Maszlee Malik used this slogan and confirmed that there are about 1,184 undocumented children in Sabah in the public school system, a citizenship identification document from one of the parents is still required for a child to be admitted to school.

Borneo Komrad is a youth collective of different ethnic backgrounds (Bugis, Suluk, Bajau, Malay, Brunei and Sungai) that provides lessons on human rights, languages, sex education and basic hygiene skills, emphasising their slogan '*Sekolah di Air, Impian di Gunung*' (Schools at Sea, Dreams in Mountains). This slogan was incorporated into a woodprint by Pangrok Sulap, a collective of Dusun and Murut artists, musicians and social activists dedicated to raising public issues through their art. This woodprint design was then printed on T-shirts and bags which were sold to the public by Borneo Komrad to raise funds for their alternative schools. The slogan is highly poetic, with the schools they built floating on the murky-looking sea, with the view of mountains silhouetted in the distance.[37] Borneo Komrad, like Iskul Sama DiLaut Omadal, provides basic literacy for stateless children as well as bringing aid during the Covid-19 outbreak.[38]

Cahaya Society, like Borneo Komrad, is a youth collective of different ethnic backgrounds. In October 2019, they urged the government to understand the issues of the people without identification documents or are stateless in Sabah by taking into account the historical, socio-cultural,

---

35 Chelsea Justalianus Lim, 'How a school for stateless children brought clean water to Sabah villages', *Malaysiakini*, 10 January 2020, https://www.malaysiakini.com/news/506642.

36 Mohd Asyraf bin Abd Hamid, 'Even with the difficult future, everyone has the right to dream a little', *C-asean*, 29 January 2020, https://www.c-asean.org/?op=post-detail&c=48.

37 Ibid.

38 Iskul Sama diLaut Omadal, 'Letter: Iskul hopes to help bring aid to stateless community in Sabah island', *Malaysiakini*, 30 March 2020, https://www.malaysiakini.com/letters/517672.

political and multi-ethnic factors to find resolutions to the problems in accordance with the law. This came in response to the aforementioned statement by Dr Maszlee Malik. At the same time, Cahaya Society also urged the media to stop promoting 'hate campaigns' which demonise these undocumented and stateless communities.[39]

The Cahaya Society runs an alternative education programme and provides stateless children with a safe space to learn, and sees an even more worrying pattern where children work in construction, factories, as bag carriers in the market, in the fishing industry and on the jetties. They are subjected to various safety, security and health risks, not only at a personal level, but also at a community level. They can easily be exploited and manipulated into becoming part of the sex trade, extremist movements and other criminal activities. Despite taking the risk to teach these children, Cahaya Society highlights discrimination against CSOs and stateless children, particularly in Sandakan. These worries were documented and submitted to Dr Fernand de Varennes, the UN special rapporteur of minority rights, in August 2019.[40]

In September 2019, the Pakatan Harapan (PH) government announced a plan to start the process of resolving the statelessness problem through the issuance of the Sabah Temporary Pass (Pas Sementara Sabah, PSS). It was a single high-security card, meant to weed out fake document holders. However, it became a hot issue in the January 2020 Kimanis by-election. The BN coalition and parties aligned with it, including PBS and Sabah STAR, called for PSS to be scrapped. They insisted that the move would dilute the demographics of the indigenous people of Sabah and held a protest in Membakut town with their election message: a vote for Warisan is a vote for PSS.[41] This message was becoming popular over social media, and Warisan

---

39 Asrin Utong, 'Respon kepada kenyataan YB Menteri Pendidikan bersangkut isu kanak-kanak tanpa dokumen di Sabah', *Borneo Komrad*, 4 October 2019, https://borneokomrad.com/kenyataan-rasmi-cahaya-society/.

40 Koordinator Cahaya Society, 'Cahaya Society menyerahkan surat kepada Special Rapporteur United Nation (UN)', *Borneo Komrad*, 3 August 2019, https://borneokomrad.com/cahaya-society-menyerahkan-surat-kepada-special-rappoerteur-united-nation-un/.

41 Muguntan Vanar, Stephanie Lee and Kristy Inus, 'PSS – Sabah's hot button issue', *The Star*, 14 January 2020, https://www.thestar.com.my/news/nation/2020/01/14/pss--sabahs-hot-button-issue.

lost the Kimanis seat. But this was not the main reason for Warisan's defeat. The people in the constituency had yet to embrace the PH administration. There were concerns about Warisan's new agriculture policy,[42] Warisan candidates had a track record of undelivered promises, PH's promise to abolish higher education loans angered young voters[43] and the campaign highlighted the leadership of the party instead of their candidate.[44] Statelessness received media coverage, but it was not the primary concern of voters.

During a working visit to the state on 15 June 2020, Minister of Home Affairs Hamzah Zainudin proposed the IMM13 (social visit pass for refugees) as a single document to resolve the statelessness issue in Sabah.[45] The Warisan-led government was against this. Shafie Apdal said that the use of such a document was not proper since stateless people hold various other documents such as the Federal Special Task Force census certificate, as well as the Kad Burung-Burung issued by the state government in the 1980s and 1990s.[46]

Hamzah Zainuddin retracted the plan on 5 August 2020 in a Parliamentary session, stating that the government did not intend to issue more IMM13 passes to undocumented people in Sabah. However, on 8 August, Hamzah announced a major crackdown to resolve the 'illegal immigrant' (as the stateless are referred to) issue. When asked if he knew

---

42 Bernama, 'Warisan lost Kimanis because voters haven't embraced PH, says Dr M', *Free Malaysia Today*, 19 January 2020, https://www.freemalaysiatoday.com/category/nation/2020/01/19/warisan-lost-kimanis-because-voters-havent-embraced-ph-says-dr-m/.

43 Durie Rayner Fong and Jason Santos, 'There were telltale signs Warisan would lose in Kimanis, say analysts', *Free Malaysia Today*, 19 January 2020, https://www.freemalaysiatoday.com/category/nation/2020/01/19/writing-is-on-the-wall-for-warisan-after-defeat-in-kimanis-say-analysts/.

44 Kenneth Tee, 'Why did Warisan lose Kimanis? Too much focus on Shafie, failed strategies, says think tank', *Malay Mail*, 19 January 2020, https://www.malaymail.com/news/malaysia/2020/01/19/why-did-warisan-lose-kimanis-too-much-focus-on-shafie-failed-strategies-say/1829547.

45 'DAP: Is Hamzah sincere about solving problem?', *Borneo Today*, 6 August 2020, https://www.borneotoday.net/dap-is-hamzah-sincere-about-solving-problem/.

46 Muguntan Vanar, 'Shafie Apdal: IMM13 is for refugees, not long-staying migrants', *The Star*, 18 June 2020, https://www.thestar.com.my/news/nation/2020/06/18/shafie-apdal-imm13-is-for-refugees-not-long-staying-migrants.

that the detention centres were full during the Covid-19 pandemic, Hamzah stated that the ministry had to start from somewhere in order to solve the issue.[47]

Before the announcement of a major crackdown, STAR's president, Jeffrey Kitingan, echoed Hamzah Zainuddin's announcement to resolve documentation issues. He saw this as a positive first step and the most appropriate single document to group the Burung-Burung and Banci Cards.[48] During these announcements, PRN2020 had been scheduled to take place on 26 September 2020.[49] After PRN2020, during a Parliamentary session on 17 November 2020, the minister for the Prime Minister's Department, Mohd Redzuan Md Yusof, answered the inquiry about the documentation issue in Sabah, stating that the government would pursue the issuance of IMM13 as a single document to replace other documents as Hamzah Zainuddin had announced on 14 June 2020.[50] But no implementation dates and guidelines were announced.

The issue of stateless and undocumented peoples has been used time and again in the interest of the politicians and political parties. The ruling government, in suggesting legalising stateless and undocumented people, has been labelled as 'pro-migrant' by their rivals. In GE14, the Kimanis by-election and PRN2020, the battle cry was often 'Sabahans for Sabah' or 'Sabah for Sabahans'. Leiking, in his campaign for the Moyog seat, said 'I believe we are all Sabahans regardless whether you are from any other ethnic group in Sabah, we all share this little island together.'[51] This gave

---

[47] Sherell Jeffrey and Stefyanie Myla Michael, 'Must start somewhere on illegals: Hamzah', *Daily Express*, 9 August 2020, http://www.dailyexpress.com.my/news/156759/must-start-somewhere-on-illegals-hamzah/.

[48] Stephanie Lee, 'IMM13 most appropriate document to solve illegal immigration woes in Sabah, says Jeffey Kitingan', *The Star*, 16 June 2020, https://www.thestar.com.my/news/nation/2020/06/16/imm13-most-appropriate-document-to-solve-illegal-immigration-woes-in-sabah-says-jeffrey-kitingan.

[49] Rafiqah Dahali, 'PRN2020 pada 26 September', *Berita Harian*, 17 August 2020, https://www.bharian.com.my/berita/nasional/2020/08/722164/prn-sabah-pada-26-september.

[50] Safrah Mat Salleh, 'IMM13 kekal dokumen tunggal ganti Sijil Banci dan Burung-Burung', *Utusan Borneo*, 19 November 2020, https://www.utusanborneo.com.my/2020/11/19/imm13-kekal-dokumen-tunggal-ganti-sijil-banci-dan-burung-burung.

[51] Durie Rayner Fong, 'I'm Kadazan but a Sabahan first, says Warisan's Leiking', *Free Malaysia Today*, 13 September 2020, https://www.freemalaysiatoday.com/category/nation/2020/09/13/im-kadazan-but-a-sabahan-first-says-warisans-leiking/.

hope to the people that inclusive politics are possible. Yet many candidates still fostered toxic fear-mongering by using 'illegals', the voiceless stateless communities, as the main ammunition for their campaign, tacitly appealing to specific ethnic groups to gain their votes.

For CSOs who champion the cause of 'education for all', which is entangled with the issue of statelessness, their voices have become louder. On 27 October 2020, Jefry Musa, a teacher at Iskul Sama DiLaut Semporna, an alternative school affiliated with Borneo Komrad, sent out a distress call to government agencies through social media.[52] Jefry and his fellow teachers were worn down. It had been nine days since the first Covid-19 positive case was announced in Pulau Omadal by the Ministry of Health, but they received no guidelines or help to manage patients on the island. Fellow activists and many CSOs networked to amplify his plea. On 28 October 2020, Jefry appeared on Astro Awani alongside the president of MERCY Malaysia, and soon after the Semporna District Health Office contacted Iskul Sama DiLaut Omadal to discuss possible ways forward to break local transmissions on the island.

The voices of these CSOs and others are crucial in raising the issues of stateless and undocumented people, and Pangrok Sulap, through their woodprint art, have brought attention to statelessness. These issues require hard work with both the federal and state governments, and additional assistance from other international agencies and civil society.

Voices from the Street: Marching Towards Free and Fair Elections

Hard work is second nature for Sabah's CSOs. Perhaps one of the most well-known is Bersih 2. This organisation is synonymous with national mass rallies and calling on the *rakyat* (people) to march on the streets. Bersih 2 succeeded in mobilising tens of thousands of people to gather and speak with one voice to demand clean and fair elections for Malaysia. Bersih 2 started their campaign with eight demands for a cleaner and fairer election: cleaning of the electoral roll, reforming postal ballots, requiring the use of indelible ink, adopting a 21-day minimum campaign period, ensuring free

[52] Jefry Musa, *Facebook*, 27 October 2020, https://www.facebook.com/100001230962325/posts/3703988742985455/?d=n and Iskul Sama DiLaut Omadal, *Facebook*, 27 October 2020, https://www.facebook.com/732606673528808/posts/3174863062636478/?d=n.

and fair access to the media, strengthening public institutions as well as stopping corruption and dirty politics.[53] The Bersih 2 and Bersih 3 rallies were held in 2008 and 2011 respectively. The impact of people marching in the streets saw the government of the day – BN – accede to their demands. The Election Commission of Malaysia agreed to implement the use of indelible ink during GE13.[54]

Although many associate Bersih 2.0 with Peninsular Malaysia, Bersih 2.0 actually spread its wings to Sabah with the Bersih 3 to Bersih 5 rallies from 2011 onwards. Sabah-based NGOs and CSOs organised Bersih 3 in Kota Kinabalu in 2012, and from there they continued to mobilise people in Bersih 4 Kota Kinabalu (B4KK-2015) and Bersih 5 (B5KK-2016). The demands of Bersih 5 differed slightly as the Sabah CSOs demanded the empowerment of Sabah and Sarawak.[55] Bersih 5 was the first Bersih rally that contained specific demands from Sabah and Sarawak for their rights as enshrined in the Malaysia Agreement 1963, as well as to uphold Sabah's and Sarawak's dignity through the realisation of a true democracy that would not be affected by vote buying, fear and abuse of state resources and government machinery.

Apart from the mass mobilisation of people on the streets, Bersih 2.0 pushed to reform the electoral system and to educate voters on democracy and elections. The electoral watchdog also mobilised *Pemantau Pilihan Raya* (Election Observers), a civil society initiative to monitor the election since the Election Commission did not recognise Bersih 2.0 as accredited observers.[56] During GE13 and GE14, the Election Observer teams were deployed to most of the states in Peninsular Malaysia, and Sabah and Sarawak, covering 70 seats in GE13 and 30 zones in GE14.

In the run up to PRN2020, to make democracy in Sabah healthier and

---

53 Bersih 2.0 Steering Committee, 'Our 8 Demands', *Bersih 2.0*, http://www.bersih.org/about/8demands/.

54 Nigel Aw, 'EC okays indelible ink and advance voting for GE13', *Malaysiakini*, 19 December 2011, https://www.malaysiakini.com/news/184484.

55 Bersih 2.0 Steering Committee, 'What is BERSIH 5: 5 demands for institutional reform', *Bersih 2.0*, 14 September 2016, http://www.bersih.org/what-is-bersih-5-5-demands-for-institutional-reform/.

56 Bernama, 'SPR Kaji Panggil Pemerhati Antarabangsa pada PRU akan datang', *The Star*, 11 July 2011, https://www.mstar.com.my/lokal/semasa/2011/07/01/spr-kaji-panggil-pemerhati-antarabangsa-pada-pru-akan-datang.

more progressive, and to improve Sabah's political culture, Bersih 2.0's Sabah chapter offered to organise a Chief Minister Candidates' Debate.[57] According to their press statements, they invited five candidates said to be eyeing the coveted position: Shafie Apdal (Warisan), Bung Moktar Radin (UMNO Sabah), Anifah Aman (Parti Cinta Sabah, PCS), Pandikar Amin Mulia (USNO Baru) and former incumbent of Sabah, Chong Kah Kiat (Liberal Democratic Party, LDP). Although the invitations were sent before the nomination day, none of the candidates accepted except for USNO Baru's Pandikar Amin Mulia.[58] This showed that either Sabah's politicians were not ready to debate their policies, or it showed how tough the battle was during PRN2020. Either way, Sabahans missed the chance to watch the candidates face off in a presidential-style debate.

As in the Sandakan 2019 and Kimanis 2020 by-elections, Bersih 2.0 (Sabah) also sent their election observer teams to monitor the state polls. This team consisted of 26 observers deployed to monitor 33 state seats, from Pulau Banggi to Semporna. Bersih 2.0 (Sabah) also had a team to monitor online campaigns by the candidates (*Laporan Pemerhati Pilihan Raya Umum Negeri Sabah Kali ke-16*, Bersih 2.0).

It did not take long for the electoral watchdog to highlight important issues during the campaign. On 12 September 2020 – nomination day – Bersih 2.0 highlighted the need for Sabahans' living and working outside of Sabah to come home and vote. There was a discussion between the National Security Council (NSC) and the Health Ministry as to whether to impose compulsory quarantine for all returnees to the peninsula from PRN2020.[59] Bersih 2.0 was of the view that this should not be done as it

---

[57] Bersih 2.0 Steering Committee, 'Bersih 2.0 ready to organise Sabah Chief Minister candidates debate', Bersih 2.0, 11 September 2020, http://www.bersih.org/press-statement-of-bersih-2-0-11-september-2020-bersih-2-0-ready-to-organise-sabah-chief-minister-candidates-debate/.

[58] Bersih 2.0 Steering Committee, 'Debate cancelled, only one panel agree to participate', *Bersih 2.0*, 17 September 2020, http://www.bersih.org/press-statement-from-bersih-2-017-september-2020debat-cancelled-only-one-panel-agree-to-participate/.

[59] Bersih 2.0 Steering Committee, 'Compulsory quarantine for Sabah returnees may further suppress Sabahans' right to vote and underscores the urgent need for postal/absentee voting', Bersih 2.0, 12 September 2020, http://www.bersih.org/bersih-2-0-12th-september-2020-compulsory-quarantine-for-sabah-returnees-may-further-suppress-sabahans-right-to-vote/.

would discourage voters, election workers, health workers and election observers from carrying out their responsibilities. This issue would also have larger implications for the functioning of electoral institutions and democracy itself. Therefore, Bersih 2.0 urged the Election Commission to open a category for postal or absentee voting to some voters, who due to work and studies were not living within or near their place of voting.

Closer to polling day, campaigning became more aggressive. Top politicians from Peninsular Malaysia flooded into Sabah, including Prime Minister Muhyiddin Yassin. In one of his field visits in Beaufort, he handed a mock cheque of RM60 million to fishermen and farmers. This is a common sight in Malaysian politics. Politicians in the government usually use government money to their advantage in elections to influence voters, but Bersih 2.0 considers this form of voter engagement an election offence.[60]

After the dissolution of the Sabah State Assembly, the caretaker Chief Minister Shafie Apdal still travelled across Sabah, from Kudat to Tawau, to hand out land titles to the people. Bersih 2.0 criticised him for the abuse of state resources in campaigning as it violated the principle of free and fair elections.[61] One of the issues in the state election was the presence of confused voters who did not know whom to vote for. This was largely true for youths and first-time voters. One cause of this confusion was the issue of party hopping that underscored why there was a snap election in Sabah. There were talks at the grassroots level as to whether the voters should vote based on political parties or candidates. Bersih 2.0 organised one forum to discuss this topic from a youth perspective.[62] Many concerns were raised by the panellists as the youths demanded that politicians or candidates be more dignified and loyal to the electorate, and to focus on the people's grievances.

One of the most important issues in PRN2020 was how the political parties conducted their campaigns. Many strategies were devised and implemented. This was the focus of Bersih 2.0's election observers. Some campaign activities undertaken by the candidates involved handing out cash

---

60 Bersih 2.0 Steering Committee, 'Is Muhyiddin bribing voters in Sabah?', *Bersih 2.0*, 18 September 2020, http://www.bersih.org/press-release-from-bersih-2-018th-september-2020-is-muhyiddin-bribing-voters-in-sabah/.

61 Annabelle Lee, 'As polls loom, Shafie crisscrosses state armed with native land titles', *Malaysiakini*, 12 August 2020, https://www.malaysiakini.com/news/538393.

62 Diskusi Borneo, 'PRN2020: Undi Calon atau Undi Parti?', *Bersih 2.0 Facebook*, 15 September 2020, https://www.facebook.com/BERSIH2.0/videos/330015541447210/.

to voters, usually carried out one or two days before polling day. Giving out cash to voters is an open secret in elections, especially in Sabah. Strategies included going from house to house with voter slips, or disbursing money at political parties' headquarters or *markas*. From Bersih 2.0's report, there were 16 observations of bribery committed by political parties and independent candidates.[63] The report of their election observation has been submitted to the Election Commission.

There remain concerns on how elections are carried out by key actors, including the Election Commission, political parties, public institutions, authorities and voters. Elections are the heart of democracy and they must be conducted in a clean, free and fair manner. The conduct of elections has been included as an indicator of good governance and democracy, such as in the World Bank Governance Indicators (WGI)[64] and the Economist Intelligence Unit (EIU) Democracy Index.[65] As there are not many CSOs focusing on the conduct of elections, Bersih 2.0 still plays a vital role as the nation's electoral watchdog to ensure that elections are clean and fair. Failures in the electoral process have dire consequences for our democracy and the legitimacy of the government, since elections are the largest medium for people to elect their government.

Voices of the Youth: New Mobility in Sabah's Political Sphere

The largest share of voters are youths. A popular view in Sabah is that youths do not care about politics and prefer to focus their energy on less serious things. Politics is seen as 'old-people's talk', more suitable for their parents' generation than theirs. There is also a high level of political cynicism, with many reflecting that although there was a change of state government, their overall quality of life did not increase significantly, and politicians are viewed

---

63 '*Laporan Pemerhatian Pilihan Raya Umum Negeri Sabah Kali ke-16*', Bersih 2.0, 14 October 2020, https://www.bersih.org/wp-content/uploads/2020/10/Laporan-Pemerhatian-Pilihan-Raya-Umum-Negeri-Sabah-Kali-Ke-16.pdf.

64 'Worldwide Governance Indicators', https://info.worldbank.org/governance/wgi/Home/Documents.

65 'Global democracy in retreat', *The Economist Intelligence Unit*, 21 January 2020, https://www.eiu.com/n/global-democracy-in-retreat. The Democracy Index is based on five categories: electoral process and pluralism; the functioning of government; political participation; political culture; and civil liberties.

as only being interested in power grabbing among themselves. These issues are seen to distance youths from politics.

However, during PRN2020, there was a rise in youth-based groups that directly and indirectly influenced youths to participate in the election, empowering them to be more critical of politicians, be they in opposition or government. They bring fresh perspectives without being accused of siding with parties on either side of the political divide. We can categorise their activism during the election from at least three angles.

The first is how youths mobilised voters to come back home from Peninsular Malaysia and Sarawak.[66] The group, known as Pulang Mengundi Sabah, is an extension of Pulang Mengundi Mahasiswa, comprising student activists and youths from Sabah and Peninsular Malaysia. They launched their campaign to help Sabahans residing in Peninsular Malaysia and Sarawak to come home and vote. Among their members are student groups such as Suara Mahasiswa, Kelab Sastera Mahasiswa UMS (KARMA) and Borneo Komrad from UMS. They launched their donation drive on 26 August 2020 with the aim of funding flight tickets for student-voters and working voters under 35 years old and earning below RM3,000 monthly.[67]

The team required some information from applicants before they were approved. Among the requirements were their identity card numbers, to check whether they were registered voters with the Election Commission. They managed to raise RM75,438 and received almost 6,000 applications, out of which 3,441 met the criteria. With the amount of funds raised, they managed to send 214 youth voters home to vote.[68] No doubt Pulang Mengundi Sabah has encouraged Sabahan youths and students to participate in the electoral process. Most of the funded voters sent photographs of their marked index fingers to show that they voted in the election.

Another angle of youth activism is political education. The most noticeable group is Undi Sabah[69] (Vote Sabah). Undi Sabah is mobilised by

---

66 '#PulangMengundiSabah: Crowdfunding to help young Sabahans travel home to vote', *Malaysiakini*, 10 September 2020, https://www.malaysiakini.com/news/541991.

67 See 'Pulang Mengundi Sabah', Facebook, https://www.facebook.com/PulangMengundiSabah/ and Ibid.

68 Interview via WhatsApp with Masdania Mokhtar, 'Pulang Mengundi Sabah' member by writer Asraf Sharafi Mohammad Azhar.

69 See 'Undi Sabah' on Facebook (powered by Undi18), https://www.facebook.com/undisabah

young activists from diverse backgrounds, who provided information and raised awareness about politics, elections and voting to Sabahans. Compared with before GE14, youths were more inclined to campaign for political parties and were less focused on political education. PRN Sabah showed how Undi Sabah had brought new ways to engage youths in political discussions, voice out their demands and consider their choices in politics. More on Undi Sabah's movement can be seen in Chapter 10.

A third angle is the youth art groups. These groups try to distance themselves from politics as much as possible. They produce art to criticise politicians and political policies if they are not pro-*rakyat*. One notable group is Pangrok Sulap, which has been consistently critical of social and environmental issues, and has also criticised the Kaiduan Dam and Papar Dam projects using their woodprint banners and posters. During this election, Pangrok Sulap raised certain issues that mirrored the youths' political cynicism. They produced sharp messages with their woodcut art and printed them on posters. Messages such as '*Pilih Wakil Rakyat Macam Pilih Durian Atau Tarap, Dua-Dua Bermusim Kadang Dua-Dua Buruk!*'[70], '*Ada Aspal Ada Undi, Yang Selalu Berjanji Siou Noh!*'[71] and '*Hanya Kerna Rebut Kerusi, Kita Semua Mati*',[72] among others. Their posters have gone viral on social media and some were printed on T-shirts by popular demand. Their messages are seen as fighting corrupt and dirty politicians who only care for their coffers rather than protecting the interests of the *rakyat*.[73] Pangrok Sulap's visual art shows that politicians are openly monitored and evaluated by youths, who continue to scrutinise them and will speak up without fear or favour.

---

[70] Translation: 'To choose a people's representative is like choosing durian or tarap, both are seasonal, and sometimes both are rotten'. Tarap (*Artocarpus odoratissimus*) is a fruit that is native to Borneo.

[71] Translation: 'Give us asphalt, we will vote for you. For those always promising, our apologies.'

[72] Translation: 'Just because you are fighting for seats, we all die.'

[73] Chan Kok Leong, 'Sabah artists use artwork to "fight" dirty politicians', *The Malaysian Insight*, 18 September 2020, https://www.themalaysianinsight.com/s/273260.

Figure 2: Pangrok Sulap's artwork, including one in support of Bersih 2.0's proposal to have a Recall Election (Pilihanraya Pecat Wakil Rakyat) to end party hopping.

Source: Pangrok Sulap's Facebook page.

Conclusion

In PRN2020, CSOs played a pivotal role in shaping the narrative and mobilising voters around key issues, from land rights and the inclusion of stateless peoples to electoral reform and youth mobilisation. In many cases, CSO mobilisation influenced the outcome. CSOs, however, engage in politics before and after any election, as their role involves bringing issues to the public and promoting a fairer and better Sabah, extending well beyond the short campaign period.

Sabah's CSOs will expand, decline and maybe rebrand themselves as time goes on. We have seen many CSOs becoming inactive after some time, or when they have resolved issues or are re-strategising, given the ever-shifting political situation in Sabah. CSOs are also not spared from acts of intimidation by uniformed authorities misusing their power. Conditions in Sabah have led some CSO members to become frustrated when their comrades join politics and become their opponents. Many stop fighting altogether but others choose other methods, such as joining the government to try and help change policies from within.

In Sabah, the CSOs need to work to bridge inland, coastal and seafaring indigenous communities, from the west and east coasts, so they can understand Sabah as a whole – not only from their own local perspectives. Moving forward, CSOs will work with local politicians to remind them that when their forefathers agreed to create Malaysia in 1963, it wasn't solely the voices of the coast but also the voices of the mountain ranges that agreed. It was a will from the east and west, from their homeland, their *Tanah Air*. And the collective consciousness of being a Sabahan is tied to two greater elements of the earth – the land and the sea.

CSOs who always fight for the cause of justice, humanity and fairness must stay vigilant in these trying times for democracy, either locally, nationally or globally. The need to ensure that human beings from all ethnic backgrounds are treated equally is real. CSOs will not stop their march to fight for all indigenous people's rights as human beings in Sabah, be they from inland, riverine, rural, mountain range, urban, sea, coastal and island communities. Their basic rights to life are equal and they should be able to participate in the society whether they are affected by political disasters or statelessness, whilst being equal in the eyes of the law of the country and the natural law of God.

No single human being must be left behind in modern day Sabah. CSOs in Sabah need to continue fighting hard to uphold democracy by making sure that institutions within a democratic framework are functional and accountable to the people. As part of the CSO community, we believe that freedom of speech, which is enshrined in Article 10 of the Federal Constitution, must be upheld, as it is, too, part of the Universal Declaration of Human Rights.

Part 2

Narratives

Chapter 5

Incessant Political Narratives: Perilous Migrants and the Treacherous East

Vilashini Somiah and Aslam Abd Jalil

Introduction

The tourist paradise of Semporna, located on the southeastern-most tip of Sabah, was heavily monitored during the election for hosting several political heavyweights, including then incumbent chief minister and Parti Warisan Sabah[1] president, Mohd Shafie Apdal. With a population of approximately 155,000,[2] Semporna was flooded with targeted political posters and flags throughout the town, a scenario similar to that found in many other districts in the state. The messages throughout the district were direct but not particularly controversial, playing on unity politics and autonomy from the federal government.

Missing from these posters were the oft-discussed migration problems that were plastered throughout the west coast of Sabah. The overall population of Sabah comprises 11.3 per cent (3.2 million) of the total Malaysian population of 28.3 million.[3] Of that, the Malaysian government has reported that Sabah is 'host to the highest proportion of non-Malaysian

1 Parti Warisan Sabah, or Sabah Heritage Party, is a local party which was founded on 17 October 2016.

2 Department of Statistics Malaysia, 2020.

3 Helen Benedict Lasimbang, Wen Ting Tong, and Wah Yun Low, 'Migrant Workers in Sabah, East Malaysia: The Importance of Legislation and Policy to Uphold Equity on Sexual and Reproductive Health and Rights', *Best Practice Research: Clinical Obstetrics & Gynaecology* 32 (2016): 113-123.

citizens at 27.7 per cent (886,400)',[4] specifically from the Philippines and Indonesia. Their presence in Sabah has resulted in their utilisation for a series of alleged offences, notably the illicit and systematic granting of citizenship, phantom voting and the swelling of the informal sector, all of which have often been described as complicated and difficult to solve due to a lack of political will.[5]

Although not physically present in these posters, there existed an anxiety not lost on the locals, and as one taxi driver explained: 'Warisan cannot be at fault for the migration issue we have in Sabah, they were only in power for two years, unlike BN[6] who were in power for so long.' He continued to lament about how the subject was cheap fodder for those who were anti-Warisan, dragging ordinary citizens like himself into the larger anti-migrant narrative. The accusation of a pro-migrant political party that had briefly run the state weighed heavily on many east coasters who saw themselves villainised in this effort.

However, on the other side of the Sabah coast, in the state capital of Kota Kinabalu, anti-migrant messages were made explicit in campaign speeches and publicity materials. One particular poster that had gone viral during the campaign was sponsored by the Liberal Democratic Party, which promised its voters in the district of Inanam 'a Sabah free of PTIs'.[7] Some of the voters who had seen the posters expressed shock and occasional disgust but agreed

---

4 Ibid.

5 Vilashini Somiah, 'Romantic Whispers: When Relationships Mobilise Political Agency in the Sabah Elections', in Sophie Lemiere (ed.) *Minorities Matter: Malaysian Politics and People Volume III* (Singapore: ISEAS–Yusof Ishak Institute, 2019), 36-51. Catherine Allerton, 'Contested Statelessness in Sabah, Malaysia: Irregularity and the Politics of Recognition,' *Journal of Immigrant & Refugee Studies* 15, no. 3 (March 2017): 250-268; Anne-Marie Hilsdon, 'Migration and Human Rights: The case of Filipino Muslim Women in Sabah, Malaysia', *Women's Studies International Forum*, 29, no. 4 (2006): 405–416; Kamal Sadiq, 'When States Prefer Non-Citizens over Citizens: Conflict over Illegal Immigration into Malaysia', *International Studies Quarterly*, 49, no. 1 (2005): 101-122.

6 Barisan Nasional or National Front was in power at Sabah state level for most of the years after Sabah joined Malaya to form Malaysia except from 1985-1994 when PBS was in power and from 2018-2020 when Warisan/PH was in government and at federal level from independence until 2018.

7 PTI and PATI are acronyms in Bahasa Malaysia for *Pendatang Tanpa Izin* or 'illegal' migrants.

that the message reflected a growing concern of stranger danger amongst residents that even they shared. As one resident put it: 'I don't like the way they said it because it is harsh, but I do want a more orderly Sabah.'

The anti-migrant narrative in Sabah has long been used by all sides of the local political arena as political ammunition. These anti-migrant messages were said to be generationally and ethnically targeted; either expressed boldly or explicitly for older Sabahans of Kadazan, Dusun and Murut background (referred to locally as KDM), or muted and disguised as unity politics for a younger, more progressive audience. Voters from both the east and west of Sabah experienced the campaign in very different ways, simply because these spaces are translated and interpreted differently by political parties. This clear difference in using and responding to the Sabah migration issue is key in understanding what it means to be associated with the 'other' and how that can continue to impact future elections to come.

This chapter will unpack why and how a xenophobic discourse continues to exist in Sabah, by taking into consideration the socio-political divisions between the east and west coast. It will also show how this was exemplified in the 2020 Sabah state election, believed by many locals to be an obvious product of corruption and desperation by both federal and local powers. Data for this article were gathered through a multi-sited ethnographic approach that ran simultaneously in the greater Kota Kinabalu and Semporna Districts. While speaking to local voters and residents, the authors also ran observational analyses in these areas during the campaign and on election and post-election day in September 2020, and had further support through the use of secondary data such as newspaper articles, policy papers and scholarly materials. Ultimately, this paper argues that Sabah politics is informed by layered, diverse and complex ethnic narratives, that have often been used for political ammo. Divisions exist between both the east and west of Sabah simply because the geopolitics has been rooted in the convenient but necessary villainising of the other.

Background

Malaysia's rapid economic growth is highly reliant on migrant labour, both documented and undocumented, especially in 3D (dirty, dangerous and difficult) sectors which are shunned by the locals.[8] In 2020, it was recorded that there were 2,960,400 documented non-citizens out of 32,657,300 of the total population of Malaysia.[9] Malaysia's porous borders make irregular movements between neighbouring countries relatively easy, facilitated by lax border controls and corrupt officials. At present, it is estimated that the numbers of undocumented migrants in the country stand at between two million[10] and six million;[11] the range in these estimates highlights a problem in transparency and sufficient public data. Sabah has the highest proportion of non-citizens as its residents, including migrants and refugees mainly from Indonesia and the Philippines who have become temporary migrants, stateless and permanent residents. Due to the different status and complex nature of this population, this chapter will refer to this group as 'irregular migrants'.

For the past few decades, Malaysia has been hosting hundreds of thousands of people who were forcibly displaced from their home countries to seek safety, starting from the Indochinese boat people in the 1970s to the recent arrival of Middle Eastern refugees. As of the end of August 2020, the United Nations High Commissioner for Refugees (UNHCR) had registered 178,140 refugees and asylum-seekers in Malaysia.[12] Although Malaysia has stressed that they are temporary, refugees have been living in this country for generations, leading to statelessness, especially in Sabah. Many

---

8 P. Iruthayaraj D. Pappusamy, 'Migrant Workers Contribution towards the Malaysian Economic Transformation', *Asian Conference on Globalization and Labor Administration: Cross-Border Labor Mobility, Social Security and Regional Integration* (2014). https://islssl.org/wp-content/uploads/2014/12/Pappusamy_2014_Asian_Conf.pdf.

9 Department of Statistics, *Current Population Estimates, Malaysia, 2020*, Department of Statistics Malaysia, 2020, https://www.dosm.gov.my/v1/index.php?r=column/cthemeByCat&cat=155&bul_id=OVByWjg5YkQ3MWFZRTN5bDJiaEVhZz09&menu_id=L0pheU43NWJwRWVSZklWdzQ4TlhUUT09.

10 International Organization for Migration (IOM), 'IOM Malaysia Info Sheet: Migration,' IOM, May 2019, https://www.iom.int/sites/default/files/country/docs/malaysia/iom_malaysia_infosheet_may2019.pdf

11 United Nations High Commissioner for Refugees, 'Statement by Philip Alston, United Nations Special Rapporteur on extreme poverty and human rights, on his visit to Malaysia, 13-23 August 2019', Ohchr.org, 23 August 2019, https://www.ohchr.org/en/NewsEvents/Pages/DisplayNews.aspx?NewsID=24912&LangID=E.

12 'Figures at a Glance in Malaysia', UNHCR, 2020, https://www.unhcr.org/en-my/figures-at-a-glance-in-malaysia.html.

migrants from neighboring countries migrate to Sabah due to geographic proximity and socio-economic stability. Specific to migrants from the Philippines, however, migration happens because they are fleeing unrest. The conflict in the southern Philippines in the 1970s had forced around 72,000 Moro Muslims from Mindanao to seek refuge in Sabah.[13] Based on humanitarian grounds and economic interests, Sabah absorbed these newly arrived migrants because they provided a ready pool of human capital that was much needed in order to spur economic growth – particularly in the logging, plantation and construction sectors.[14]

Adding to this is also a claim that Sabah had once belonged to the Philippines, becoming a 60-year-old dispute over the state's sovereignty. In 2013, an incursion by the now defunct Sulu Sultanate took place in the coastal district of Lahad Datu, demanding for Sabah to be returned to them. The incursion witnessed the death of approximately 70 militants, armed forces and civilians, and led Malaysia to increase its efforts against foreign threats on the east coast in the form of the Eastern Sabah Security Command (ESSCOM).

But as the years have gone by, the influx of these peoples has been difficult to trace and identify due to the illicit nature of their arrival,[15] leading the Malaysian government to intervene through various management programmes of non-citizens in the 1980s and 1990s.[16] Amidst continuous political and economic instability, local Sabahans have expressed grave concerns over the growing numbers of migrants and have demanded immediate action. The Malaysian government responded by enforcing repatriation, and from 1990 until 2017, over half a million irregular migrants had been deported from Sabah.[17]

---

13 Gerhard Hoffstaedter, 'Place-making: Chin refugees, citizenship and the state in Malaysia', *Citizenship Studies* 18, no. 8 (2014): 874.

14 Azizah Kassim, 'Filipino Refugees in Sabah: State Responses, Public Stereotypes and the Dilemma over Their Future', *Southeast Asian Studies* 47, no. 1. (2009): 52-88.

15 UNHCR, 'Ending statelessness in Malaysia', 2020, https://www.unhcr.org/endingstatelessness-in-malaysia.html.

16 Azizah Kassim, 'Filipino Refugees in Sabah'.

17 'Kenyataan Media Sempena Mesyuarat Jawatankuasa Induk Pengurusan Warga Asing Di Sabah (Jkpwas-Induk) Bil. 1/2017', Ministry of Home Affairs, 2017, http://www.moha.gov.my/index.php/en/maklumat-korporat22-4/kenyataan-media-kdn/3234-.

Migration Frameworks and Demographic Engineering

It is important to note that the legal frameworks on migration in Malaysia have been heavily criticised and critiqued for enabling authorities to socially engineer the demography of Sabah for years. Malaysia is not a signatory country to the refugee convention, the convention on migrant workers and convention on statelessness. Malaysian laws classify illicit migrants, the undocumented and refugees as 'illegal migrants' and this automatically strips them of their rights as 'legal' people. Rather, Malaysia's management of irregular migrants is ad hoc and occurs on a case by case basis, including in the case of Moro refugees in Sabah. Section 55 of the Immigration Act 1959/63 and Section 4 of the Passports Act 1966 give power to the minister to exempt a group of people from any provisions of these Acts. The southern Philippines refugees were legalised by the amendment of the Passports Act 1966 by the addition of Passport Order (Exemption)(No.2)(Amendment) 1972, which became effective on 12 September 1972 by the deputy prime minister, who was also home minister.[18] Initially, these refugees were issued with HIF22, with a yearly fee of RM20, before changing it to PL(S)IMM13 with a yearly fee of RM90.[19] IMM13 holders are allowed to be employed legally and stay in Sabah and Labuan temporarily.

In 1999[20] and 2007[21] respectively, the minister of Home Affairs proposed that all Filipino refugees holding IMM13 passes residing in Sabah be granted permanent residency, which caused some backlash. As of September 2018, 101,355 individuals have been issued with IMM13 cards, with 99,055 registered in Sabah and 2,300 Syrians in Peninsular Malaysia.[22] The Malaysian Federal Constitution's Second Schedule section 1(e) states that 'every person born within Malaysia who is not born a citizen of any country' is a Malaysian citizen by operation of law.[23] Unfortunately, this part of the

---

[18] Arkib Negara Malaysia, *Pengeluaran PL(S) IMM13 baru dalam tempoh 1 hari, Konvensyen Kumpulan Inovatif dan Kreatif 2012 Kementerian Dalam Negeri*, (n.d.), 15.

[19] Ibid., 34.

[20] Ibid.

[21] Dewan Rakyat, 'Penyata Rasmi Parlimen bil. 29', 20 June 2007, 87, https://www.parlimen.gov.my/files/hindex/pdf/DR-20062007%20-%20edit.pdf.

[22] Parlimen Malaysia, 'Isu bancian pemegang kad IMM13', 1 November 2018, 1, https://www.parlimen.gov.my/files/hindex/pdf/KKDR-01112018.pdf.

[23] Federal Constitution of Malaysia, 168, http://www.agc.gov.my/agcportal/uploads/files/

law has been extremely difficult to apply due to its technicalities.[24]

Azizah Kassim[25] outlined the resettlement programmes initiated by both the Federal and State Governments with the assistance of UNHCR by opening 34 villages, as the Chief Minister's Office intended to absorb these refugees permanently into Sabah. Consequently, in 1987 UNHCR ceased its ten-year operation in the state because the resettlement programmes had managed to integrate the refugees into the local population and they were granted temporary residence and a work permit.[26] This means that these Filipinos are no longer considered 'refugees', rather they are 'persons of concern' or former refugees who form the larger pool of the stateless population in the state, of which the exact number is unknown.[27]

Authorities have estimated half a million or more undocumented people in the state.[28] Without any legal status, a person is not eligible to be resettled to a third country through the UNHCR – one of the three durable solutions[29] that Malaysia always prefers for the refugee population.[30] Historically, Sabah was known to have a larger and more dominant Christian majority, mainly from its KDM and Sino population. The social and political engineering in Sabah through Project IC started by absorbing the alleged Muslim migrants by granting them citizenship in an apparent act to change the demography of Sabah to become a Muslim-majority state.[31] Additionally, conversion to Islam or the adoption of Muslim names were

---

Publications/FC/Federal%20Consti%20(BI%20text).pdf.

24 Rodziana Mohamed Razali, 'Addressing statelessness in Malaysia: New hope and remaining challenges', Statelessness Working Paper Series No. 2017/9, Institute on Statelessness and Inclusion, 2017, https://files.institutesi.org/WP2017_09.pdf.

25 Azizah Kassim, 'Filipino Refugees in Sabah'.

26 UNHCR, 'Filipino refugees in Sabah', UNHCR, 2016, https://reporting.unhcr.org/node/9993.

27 UNHCR, 'Ending statelessness in Malaysia'.

28 Muguntan Vanar, 'Sabah seeks to resolve issue of stateless people in the state', *The Star*, 16 November 2018, https://www.thestar.com.my/news/nation/2018/11/16/sabah-seeks-to-resolve-issue-of-stateless-people-in-the-state/.

29 For more information on durable solutions for refugees, see https://www.unhcr.org/en-my/durable-solutions-in-malaysia.html.

30 Bernama, 'Govt identifying countries willing to receive refugees', *The Star*, 8 September 2020, https://www.thestar.com.my/news/nation/2020/09/08/govt-identifying-countries-willing-to-receive-refugees.

31 Kamal Sadiq, 'When States Prefer Non-Citizens over Citizens', 101-122.

facilitating factors that eased this process and thus there was a resentment amongst the Christian indigenous populations over their rapidly eroding political power.

Unfortunately, the Filipino migrants in Sabah are in a state of limbo because they are neither wanted by the Philippines nor accepted by Malaysia despite being born and bred in Sabah.[32] In 2012, the Malaysian Government launched the Royal Commission of Inquiry on Immigrants in Sabah after being pressured by Sabah-based parties and the public. The inquiry gave attention to the massive increase of Sabah's population within a few decades, specifically those who obtained identity cards, migrant workers, illegal migrants and refugees. It was concluded that Project IC was 'more likely than not' to have been conducted by senior officers of the National Registration Department issuing Malaysian identification documents under the orders of their superiors, as testified by witnesses, which was of course denied by the politicians named.[33] To date, there is no clear solution that resulted from the report.

In 2019, whilst Sabah was still under Warisan/PH, the Pas Sementara Sabah (PSS) or Temporary Sabah Pass was introduced to replace the existing variety of documents held by over 136,055 recorded migrants in Sabah,[34] namely the IMM13 issued by the Immigration Department, the Burung-Burung Card (Kad Burung-Burung) issued by the Chief Minister's Department and Census Certificates issued by the Federal Special Task Force (FSTF).[35] It was estimated these pass holders, together with their dependents and children, would total around 600,000 individuals.[36] The

---

32 Azizah Kassim and Ragayah Haji Mat Zin, 'Policy on irregular migrants in Malaysia: an analysis of its implementation and effectiveness', PIDS Discussion Paper Series, No. 2011-34, Philippine Institute for Development Studies (PIDS), Makati City, 2011, https://www.econstor.eu/handle/10419/126870.

33 Government of Malaysia, *Report of the Commission of Inquiry on Immigrants in Sabah*, 2012, http://legacy.sapp.org.my/rci/RCI-Eng.pdf.

34 Hayati Dzulkifli, 'Sabah Temporary Pass: Focus is on 136,000 foreigners', *Daily Express*, 26 November 2019, http://www.dailyexpress.com.my/news/143904/focus-is-on-136-000-foreigners/.

35 Muguntan Vanar, Stephanie Lee and Kristy Inus, 'PSS - Sabah's hot button issue', *The Star*, 14 January 2020, https://www.thestar.com.my/news/nation/2020/01/14/pss--sabahs-hot-button-issue.

36 Hayati Dzulkifli, 'Sabah Temporary Pass: Focus is on 136,000 foreigners', *Daily Express*, 26 November 2019, http://www.dailyexpress.com.my/news/143904/focus-

policy recommendation was mooted by the previous Barisan Nasional (BN) government,[37] and later politicised during the Kimanis by-election when rival politicians alleged that such a policy would legalise migrants in a manner akin to Project IC of the 1980s.[38] The fear-mongering campaign garnered strong support for the BN candidate.[39] Ironically, a few months after that, the newly formed Perikatan Nasional government also announced that it would streamline all the existing documents held by foreigners[40] and those without proper documentation were to leave Sabah immediately.[41] However, the newly appointed Deputy Chief Minister of Sabah Jeffrey Kitingan was quick to dismiss the similarity between the migrant regularisation plan in the state and the PSS.[42] Instead, the government claims to be providing nothing more than a short-term solution for employers who demand more workers to fill labour shortages in sectors affected by Covid-19 pandemic.[43]

---

is-on-136-000-foreigners/.

[37] Bernama, 'Keputusan keluarkan pas di Sabah bukan dibuat mendadak', *Malaysiakini*, 17 December 2019, https://www.malaysiakini.com/news/503957.

[38] CNA, 'Illegal immigration a hot-button issue in crucial Sabah by-election', *Channel News Asia*, 17 January 2020, https://www.channelnewsasia.com/news/asia/malaysia-sabah-kimanis-by-election-pss-illegal-immigrants-pass-12274988.

[39] Anil Netto, 'What went wrong for Pakatan Harapan at Kimanis?' *Aliran*, 19 January 2020, https://aliran.com/thinking-allowed-online/a-kipahit-experience-whither-ph/. Bridget Welsh, 'Why Warisan Plus Lost – a Preliminary Analysis', *Malaysiakini*, 29 September 2020, https://www.malaysiakini.com/columns/544346.

[40] Syahidatul Akmal, Dunya, 'IMM13 jadi dokumen perjalanan tunggal warga asing di Sabah', *Sinar Harian*, 14 June 2020, https://www.sinarharian.com.my/article/87793/BERITA/Nasional/IMM13-jadi-dokumen-perjalanan-tunggal-warga-asing-di-Sabah.

[41] Luqman Arif Abdul Karim, 'Segera tinggalkan Sabah jika tiada dokumen sah', *Berita Harian Online*, 4 August 2020, https://www.bharian.com.my/berita/nasional/2020/08/717959/segera-tinggalkan-sabah-jika-tiada-dokumen-sah.

[42] Asyikin Asmin, 'Pemberian pas sementara kepada PATI diputar belit: Jeffrey', *Sinar Harian*, 21 October 2020, https://www.sinarharian.com.my/article/107773/EDISI/Sabah-Sarawak/Pemberian-pas-sementara-kepada-PATI-diputar-belit-Jeffrey.

[43] Izwan Abdullah, 'Pemutihan pendatang di Sabah jika ada permintaan dari majikan', *Berita Harian Online*, 31 October 2020, https://www.bharian.com.my/berita/wilayah/2020/10/748495/pemutihan-pendatang-di-sabah-jika-ada-permintaan-dari-majikan.

The 'Treacherous East' Political Narrative

As such, the social tensions that exist in Sabah today can be traced back to multiple overlapping problems greatly involving the migrant presence. The east coast is regarded by those living outside it as an inhospitable and volatile space, especially due to its proximity with bordering nations, such as the Philippines and Indonesia. Many respondents in the west coast of Sabah believe this to be the reason behind a slew of other security issues apart from illicit migration, such as drug trafficking and sightings of extremist groups like the Abu Sayyaf.[44] Furthermore, the rich blend of maritime cultures amongst east coast communities has resulted in many sharing similar ethnicities and heritages with irregular migrants. This phenomenon has unfairly led to many east coast residents described as a potential security threat to the state of Sabah. For example, communities of Bajau and Suluk ethnic groups in particular share similar cultural and religious roots with people in the Philippines. A common belief by Sabahans from both ends of the coast is that Project IC has resulted in the once majority Christian and 'indigenous' communities being dominated by Muslim migrants from neighbouring states.

The earlier BN-led state governments were heavily criticised by Sabahans and the opposition for having urban and middle-class centric policies and lacked any autonomy against federal powers. However, when Warisan took over in 2018, non-supporters were concerned that leadership and support, in the form of their party president, came primarily from the east coast. This new political climate brought up different anxieties amongst different communities; east coast communities defending their presence in and belonging to the state, west coast communities fearing an exacerbated loss of indigeneity and rights and migrant communities dreading further persecution in light of everything.

Thus, resentment for the 'treacherous' east became low hanging fruit for members of the BN (and Perikatan Nasional[45] coalition) in the state elections, which was ironic considering these criticisms had previously

---

44 Abu Sayyaf is a jihadist militant group based in the south-western Philippines. This group had launched attacks and kidnappings in Sabah territory and beyond.

45 Perikatan Nasional (National Coalition) was formed ad hoc in early 2020 after a power struggle that saw the fall of Pakatan Harapan (Alliance of Hope) government at the federal and state levels.

stemmed from their time in government. This became an opportunity to revive the never ending 'dinosaur issue' of 'illegal' migration.[46] Throughout the campaign period, Warisan was accused of being a party of illicit migrants[47] that aimed to direct development and other opportunities to the east coast. This accusation was countered by Warisan, reminding voters and members of the opposition that they were steadfast in creating a united Sabah, all of which was made possible by members of their permanent secretaries who were indigenous persons of Kadazan and Dusun ethnic descent.

Nevertheless, while this may seem like customary political banter in Sabah, many Sabahans from the east have expressed the negative impact such narratives had. With a stereotype of being dangerous, foreign-filled and disloyal to the state of Sabah, residents of the east have often lamented their precarious positions and often blame it on the weak will of their politicians. One Tawau resident, who worked as a restaurateur, expressed fatigue in often reading about accusations of an east coast invasion into the state administration. He explained: 'I'm fed up. Are we so unwanted by everyone on the other side that this story keeps making headlines? We are Sabahan's too, *mau jugak kami yang bagus-bagus* (we also want good things to happen).'

Anti-migrant messages in the 2020 State Election

The election campaign period had transformed into a battlefield of identity politics fueled by politicians who capitalised on the divide for their own gains. Ironically, despite the anti-migrant narrative, none of the political parties provided voters with a comprehensive solution for solving the irregular migrant issue, despite the issue being raised since the 1980s elections.[48] As expected, anti-migrant messages were circulated aggressively,

---

[46] Durie Rainer Fong, 'As Sabah election looms, a host of issues take centre stage', *Free Malaysia Today*, 6 September 2020, https://www.freemalaysiatoday.com/category/nation/2020/09/06/as-sabah-election-looms-a-host-of-issues-take-centre-stage/.

[47] Tarrence Tan, 'Sabah polls: Warisan Plus leaders warn Sabahans against illegal immigrant rhetoric in campaigns', *The Star*, 14 September 2020, https://www.thestar.com.my/news/nation/2020/09/14/sabah-polls-warisan-plus-leaders-warn-sabahans-against-illegal-immigrant-rhetoric-in-campaigns.

[48] Muguntan Vanar and Tarrence Tan, 'Need for a solution to Sabah's migrant problem', *The Star*, 6 September 2020, https://www.thestar.com.my/news/nation/2020/09/06/

Figure 1: A campaign billboard for Chong Kah Kiat from the Liberal Democratic Party (LDP), seen in the Inanam constituency. Chong was the 13th Chief Minister of Sabah and became minister of the Prime Minister's Department during Mahathir's first period of premiership.

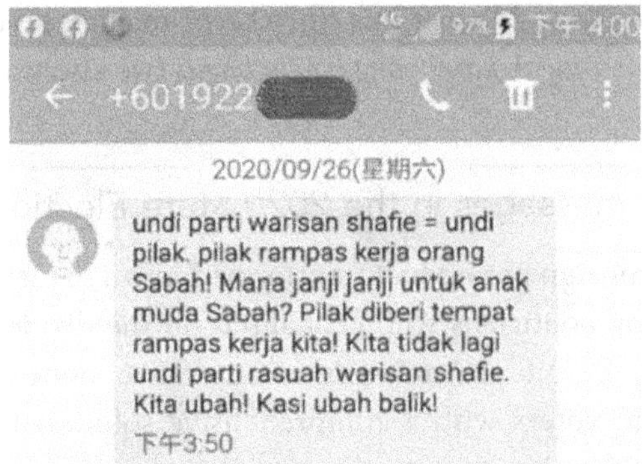

Figure 2: A screenshot of an SMS by an unknown sender uploaded on Facebook which translates to: 'A vote for Shafie's Warisan = Vote for the pilak.[49] Pilaks have taken jobs away from Sabahans! Where were the promises for Sabahan youths? 'Pilaks were given a chance to take away our jobs! We will no longer vote for a corrupted Shafie's Warisan party! We want change! We will switch back!'

---

need-for-a-solution-to-sabahs-migrant-problem.

49 'Pilak' is a derogatory term used to refer to irregular migrants in Sabah.

where some messages were more daring and blatant, playing up voter frustrations in the east coast of Sabah. This, however, was also perceived as an act of desperation by members of Warisan and their supporters.

It is not difficult to understand how xenophobic messages can trigger such a reaction. Most of Sabah suffers from a considerable lack of infrastructure and services from decades of neglect from the federal government. Bad roads and poor public transportation hamper connectivity even within the state itself. In 2019, Sabah's broadband penetration rate per 100 inhabitants stood at 83.8 per cent[50] and with an 80.7 per cent mobile-broadband penetration rate.[51] While still less than that of the peninsula, online connectivity was enough for political campaigning to be carried out through social media, which includes WhatsApp, Facebook and YouTube. Unfortunately, the anonymity of social media has made it easier for controversial content to be shared more widely.[52] With many voters claiming to receive numerous texts and messages feeding direct propaganda, most of which were untruths and venomous speculations. This is nothing new as WhatsApp has been a powerful tool to disseminate hate speech that is utilised during the elections.[53] Unfortunately, the effort to curb hate speech and 'fake news' would be extremely difficult either because it was too rampant or both parties across the political divide benefitted from such a strategy. The sentiment on the ground generally focused on the 'intrusion of PATI' and whoever won should solve the issue by hook or by crook.

---

[50] MCMC, '1Q 2020 Facts and figures, Communication and multimedia,' 2020, https://www.mcmc.gov.my/skmmgovmy/media/General/pdf/1Q-2020-C-M-Facts-and-Figures.PDF.

[51] Ibid.

[52] Kaiping Zhang and Rene F. Kizilcec, 'Anonymity in social media: Effects of content controversiality and social endorsement on sharing behavior', *Conference: Eighth International AAAI Conference on Weblogs and Social Media, 2014*, https://rene.kizilcec.com/wp-content/uploads/2014/03/zhang_kizilcec_anonymity_icwsm2014.pdf.

[53] Shakuntala Banaji and Ram Bhat, 'WhatsApp Vigilantes: An exploration of citizen reception and circulation of WhatsApp misinformation linked to mob violence in India,' 2019, http://eprints.lse.ac.uk/104316/1/Banaji_whatsapp_vigilantes_exploration_of_citizen_reception_published.pdf

Figure 3: Left: Shafie Apdal's unity poster used in the 2020 state elections, said to be inspired by Obama's Hope campaign of 2008. *Right*: A controversial version of the same poster that circulated in social media several days before the polling day with the words 'Vote for Warisan is akin to vote for Abu Sayyaf and a vote for terrorists', with the hashtag '#UnitedforDignity'. Juxtaposed into the poster is also the image of Mahathir Mohamad, Lim Kit Siang and Anwar Ibrahim. At the very bottom of the poster is a picture of members of the Islamic State.

The rampant allegation of Warisan as a party of migrants escalated until members of BN instigated whether Shafie Apdal was one himself. The party president took to clarifying that his ancestors were buried in Semporna to prove his indigeneity[54] and warned that legal action would be taken if the rumours did not cease.[55] This was already played up in the 14th General Election of 2018. Previously, the mood of the elections was far more intense than it was in 2020, and Warisan's pledge to uphold all native rights, specifically the Malaysia Agreement 1963, was able to carry more weight. Changing in this election, however, was the push for a more united Sabah, a spirit of oneness that differed from West Malaysia. Messages of unity were seen as important in countering the divisive campaign strategy from the opponent. 'In God we trust. Unite we must', 'We are here to build a nation. Not a particular race or religion', 'Sabahans unite not divide' were some of Warisan's taglines. These messages aimed at highlighting Sabah's multiracial society in combating racism and even xenophobia.

---

54 M. Fakhrull Halim, 'Campaign takes "grave" turn – Shafie says grandmothers buried in Semporna, not Japan', *Malaysiakini*, 14 September 2020, https://www.malaysiakini.com/news/542569.

55 'Shafie warns those making false claims', *Daily Express*, 23 August 2020, http://www.dailyexpress.com.my/news/157410/shafie-warns-those-making-false-claims/.

Figure 4: In areas in the east like Tawau, messages were non-xenophobic as shown here in the town roundabout, which only showcased billboards and flags promoting unity and togetherness.

This was not, however, solely a problem associated with BN. The following poster (Figure 5) perfectly summarises the blame game when it comes to the influx of irregular migrants in Sabah, politicising the issue further. In truth, Warisan and BN had a difficult time addressing the migrant problem and could not commit to policies without angering Sabahans. The irony is that Shafie, like many others in Warisan, treated the migrant problem as an issue they were new to, when this had been political fodder for many years of his career. The accusation of Shafie hosting phantom voters in his constituency of Semporna was not new to him nor to many others in Warisan who have had illustrious political careers in political parties such as UMNO. In this election, Shafie was quick to shift the blame solely to BN and argued that the attacks he received were for always standing up to the truth and representing his Sabahan heritage.

Warisan Plus only won 32 seats while Gabungan Rakyat Sabah (GRS)[56] secured 38 seats, enabling them to form the government. Many analysts and Sabahans believe that anti-migrant messages were much stronger than Warisan Plus had understood. The KDM community felt that Sabah has been physically, culturally and economically infiltrated by irregular migrants who have been part of the Bajau and Suluk communities of the East Coast

[56] GRS comprises of BN, Perikatan Nasional, Parti Bersatu Sabah, STAR, Parti Bersatu Rakyat Sabah, Sabah Progressive Party and PAS.

and were protected by Warisan. This was further complicated by the fact that Warisan were allies of Mahathir Mohamad, thought to be responsible for Sabah's demographic engineering which exacerbated the growing resentment. GRS managed to utilise this anxiety to fuel a total rejection of Warisan Plus, as harbouring PATI would further diminish what little was left of their native rights. While Warisan Plus performed well on the east coast, it was the KDM heartland that cost them the state government.

Figure 5: An image that made its way around through mobile application WhatsApp. The content is translated as: 'Who has actually been breeding PATIs? For 57 years, from 1963 until 2018, there were 1.2 million PATI under the administration of the BN government. For 26 months, from 2018 until 2020, there was no known record of PATIs under the administration of the Warisan government.'

Conclusion

As highlighted in this chapter, anti-migrant messaging as an explicit form of xenophobia is an important political tool that has been able to influence and shape local governance and power. The systematic racism in Malaysia between Bumiputeras and non-Bumiputeras has long been tolerated in Malaysia, with the Federal Constitution clearly providing special privileges to members, shaping the status quo. On the contrary, blatant racism towards migrants has also become an accepted norm, turning them into scapegoats and building on the political currency that xenophobia offers to a vulnerable Sabah. The year 2020 saw Malaysia as a whole enduring various levels of a Movement Control Order (MCO) resulting from the Covid-19 pandemic. During this time of great social and economic turbulence, anti-immigrant sentiments grew even stronger. For example, Rohingya refugees became the target of xenophobic attacks stemming from the belief that they had demanded naturalisation. Later, the media and other scholars revealed that political alliances (or lack thereof) had led to their demonisation, an indication of how anti-migrant sentiments are constantly used to propagate a nationalistic agenda on the pretext of saving the country from the unknown.[57]

While these decisions can be seen as problematic, Sabah voters' reactions towards the dangers of migrants also reveals a position that many living on the periphery are faced with. The nature of survival means oppressed Sabahans must consider how, and if, their votes can keep the undesirable at bay. Anti-migrant political messages have been increasingly accompanied by a pro-migrant movement in Sabah in recent years. The pro-migrant movement is slowly gaining traction in Sabah, reminding locals of the importance of tolerance and inclusivity. And so, what is important to remember is that those who vote to support anti-migrant politics do not necessarily choose to be xenophobic but must consider this option for the sake of protecting and keeping identities alive, necessities and ideals that are believed to be at risk of disappearing. Thus, the decision to vote along anti-migrant lines is actually usually done for reasons of survival.

In the end, Warisan failed to recapture the state in the elections, and this was due to several reasons: money politics and the buying of loyalties, the loss of support for the Pakatan Harapan coalition and the rise of state nationalism, to name a few.[58] Adding to this is of course, the migrant issue that ultimately bled into racial politics. Just a month before the elections, Philippine Foreign Secretary Teodoro Locsin, Jr tweeted: 'Sabah is not in Malaysia,' in reply to a tweet from the American Embassy in Manila about donations for Filipinos repatriated from Sabah.[59] This reignited negative feelings about the local migrant population for many Sabahans, whilst

---

57 Aslam Abd Jalil, 'Malaysian Malaysia': the rise of xenophobia', *Strengthening Human Rights and Peace Research Education in ASEAN*, 4 May 2020, https://shapesea.com/op-ed/malaysian-malaysia-the-rise-of-xenophobia/.

58 Bridget Welsh, 'Why Warisan Plus lost'.

59 Francesca Regalado, 'Malaysia's spat with Philippines over Sabah: Five things to know', *Nikkei Asia*, 29 September 2020, https://asia.nikkei.com/Politics/International-relations/Malaysia-s-spat-with-Philippines-over-Sabah-Five-things-to-know.

exacerbating the complex realities for many migrant communities. With so many unresolved migrant-related problems in the state, the anti-migrant narrative used during the campaign proved to carry more weight than the unity politics of Warisan.

Many Sabahans who were initially undecided chose to give their vote to BN simply because they felt it was the safer route to choose. One voter from Kepayan of Dusun descent expressed that he had previously voted for Warisan, buying into their message of peace and togetherness. But for this election, he felt as if the migrant presence at the west coast had caused him to feel '*nda sadap ati*' (uneasy) as he felt that '*Shapie kasi pam durang sini gayanya*' (Shafie Apdal pumped them over here). He said that while he had no problem with migrants residing in the east coast, as they were '*bangsa sama bah*' (of the same ethnic group), the BN was able to '*simpan syak durang di sana*' (able to keep them there) in the past, and still offered his community a semblance of order.

Post-elections, the Covid-19 pandemic reached worrying heights in Sabah, as a third wave began to cripple the east coast, later spreading to the rest of Sabah, leading to the state's lockdown. As newly appointed members of the state government were forced to take up an enforced 14-day self-quarantine from being in close contact with Covid-positive individuals, the growing resentment towards migrants continued. Amidst this, local civil society groups took to social media to express anger and disappointment at the way Covid-positive migrants, most of whom contracted it in detention centres, were treated. Their efforts have helped bring focus to the ways younger Sabahans view these archaic reactions to, and utilisations of, foreignness. The demands that many have made is for transparency and open communication between stakeholders who actively engage with migrant populations (state agencies, civil society, religious bodies, community leaders) in hopes of building supportive, inclusive and progressive narratives of unity: ironically, an ambition of Warisan that was not successfully delivered.

In this case, the most pressing issue is to address how irregular migrants can be granted ethical and legal recourse to remain in Sabah without further offending and apprehending the indigenous and local population of the west coast. Furthermore, open discourse is important in helping to separate the identities and realities of east coasters from their migrant neighbours. To do this, there is a pressing need for local politics to acknowledge the complex ethnic composition of the state, which draws from both mainland and coastal communities and also a diverse population of biracial Sabahans. It is important to realise from this article that xenophobic narratives have aided in Sabah's political polarisation and has only benefitted those most detached from the problem. Unfortunately, victimised in this process are residents who are both local and foreign, all attempting to survive in already arduous conditions, with little to no assistance from those in power.

Chapter 6

Sabah's Youth Talk Politics: Ethnic Identity, Illegal Migrants & Religious Freedom

Trixie Tangit

Introduction

As the drive home began, the traffic jam towards Donggongon town in the district of Penampang, east of the city of Kota Kinabalu, felt more congested than ever. I could not help but wonder whether the next day's election had anything to do with it. It all became clear at the main roundabout where a huge concrete monument in the shape of a *sigah* (Kadazan male headgear) stood in tribute to the area's predominant indigenous group. Young people encircled the roundabout armed with banners, flags and posters of Warisan, the party touted to win. Amid their jubilant cheers, drivers honked either in support or as a reaction to the inconvenience. Unbeknown to them at that point, this political party would fail to retain the Sabah government in the coming days. To the less politically motivated, this turn of events may not have meant much. However, if the recent election in Sabah proved anything, it was that Sabah's youth were visibly part and parcel of Sabah's political scenery.

The 2020 Sabah state election (PRN2020) saw a growing number of youth-led initiatives come to the fore, such as *Sabah Peka* (Sabah [is] Aware), which aimed to educate young (and senior) voters to assess their candidates.[1] The Undi Sabah (Vote Sabah) movement also sought to

1 Dhesegaan Bala Krishnan, 'Sabah 2020: Grade Them Before You Vote Them

mobilise youth.[2] In time, Malaysian and Sabahan youths can be expected to become more poll-friendly and savvy. Young voters in Malaysia were supposed to be eligible to cast their first ballot by 2021 after the government of Malaysia lowered the voting age to 18 years old (from 21 years old) on 16 June 2019.[3] The new proposed date is September 2022, but it is not clear when this will happen.[4]

In the meantime, some may assume that youth are still generally dependent on the philosophy and leadership of their parents and elders in the matter of politics. However, this perceived acquiescence should not be fully assumed. On the contrary, Sabah's youth are becoming aware of their agency and collective strength. Thus, what is crucial at this point is to understand how they engage socio-politically with others as a way to learn what meaning they take from the recent general election and the Sabahan political landscape overall.

To know and understand what youths' perspectives were or are before and after PRN2020, I spoke with seven Sabahan youths in a series of interviews for their thoughts on several intertwining topics that often become politicised during election campaigns. Their responses on their ethnic identity, on illegal immigrants (*Pendatang Asing Tanpa Izin* or PATI) and (the threat to) religious freedom in Sabah basically showed that while informants were ethnically conscious and aware of anti-PATI sentiments, they were open to migrants and the idea of an inclusive society. Further, if asked to choose between the two issues, they would rather safeguard Sabah from becoming too conservative. Such a mindset reflects youths' wish for a cohesive Sabahan society: one that would demand more equitable outcomes for all irrespective of ethnic background and religious preference.

As the first of many future conversations with Sabah's youths, this

---

In'. *New Straits Times*, 26 September 2020, https://www.nst.com.my/news/politics/2020/09/626206/sabah-2020-grade-them-you-vote-them. See also Sabah Peka on Facebook, https://www.facebook.com/sabahpekaorg.

2 Their story on how they did so can be found in this volume. See Chapter 10, 'Undi Sabah and Youth Mobilization' by Mahirah Marzuki, Fiqah Roslan and Auzellea Kristin Mozihim.

3 'EC: Voting for 18 year olds not yet implemented', *New Straits Times*, 7 June 2020.

4 Afiq Aziz, 'Undi 18 will only be implemented in September 2022', *The Malaysian Reserve*, 26 March 2021, https://themalaysianreserve.com/2021/03/26/undi-18-will-only-be-implemented-in-sept-2022/

chapter is a report from the ground surrounding the election and thus not exhaustive about the topics discussed. To further support the data at hand, I draw on my experiences researching these topics for my PhD study on the fluid ethnicity of the Kadazan people in Penampang, Sabah. Throughout this chapter, I refer to youth participants as 'informants' to prevent confusion for the reader. This chapter begins with informant perspectives on the current political scenario in Sabah followed by their discussions on the key topics above.

Seven informants form the base of this analysis. The author met the informants through several means (through work contacts; through Facebook; introduced by someone; invited by another informant). Informants voluntarily offered data (they are unpaid) in a series of in-depth interviews that were conducted online (as is the current norm with Covid 19) from 29 September to 11 October 2020. To protect their identities, all informants are described through pseudonyms. The participants by name, gender, age, ethnicity and occupation are as follows:

> 1) Alexander Iha, male, 24, KDMR,[5] logistics executive, 2) Aqmar Z, male, 21, Brunei Malay, student, 3) Catherine, female, 26, Kadazan, programme officer, 4) Genevieve, female, 23, Murut, student, 5) Latif, male, 29, Kadazan-Suluk, civil servant, 6) Lydia, female, 25, Murut, student and 7) Rick, female, 27, Sino-Kadazan, unemployed.

Sabah Politics from a Youth Perspective

Whenever Sabah politics is discussed, whether on the news or by a small group of friends, the consensus easily points to how it is characterised by instability. Politicians can betray their loyalists and switch, or rather hop to a rival party (the phrase '*katak*' [frog in the Malay language] is used aplenty by locals). In PRN2020, Sabahans further saw the trend of 'loose' coalitions forming between new and old political parties; and between individual and

[5] The acronym KDMR refers to the first initial of some of the primary Indigenous ethnic groups found in Sabah, i.e., Kadazan, Dusun, Murut and Rungus. Note that in Sabah, the historical indeterminate use of ethnonyms means that local frames of reference on the ground can be more varied and complex than government categories. Typically seen in censuses, textbooks or government brochures, such categories tend to be conflations of more than one ethnic groups or groupings.

independent politicians as well. Informants started by talking about the campaigning strategies of politicians; they brought up the issue of 'money politics' and what they perceive to be the unbecoming antics of would-be leaders. In this, elders' criticisms of politicians appear useful for youth to get a sense of the politics in their area. Questioning the morality of would-be politicians involved in cock-fighting, an illegal activity, Genevieve said:[6]

> *Kalau macam pemimpin, (kalau) kepimpinan dia tidak bagus memang itu rakyat pun mana mau ikut. Ada orang tua cakap 'Eh, dia (wakil calon) ni macam alim, tapi dia sabung ayam begitu. Orang kampung pun pandang serong sama dia. Bila dia dipandang serong, itu yang buat dia tidak kena undi.*
>
> . . . *Kalau silap-silap polis datang sana, sama-sama YB kena angkat. Macam mana mau jadi contoh sama orang kampung kau. Macam mana buat orang kampung kau bagus? Kalau ciri-ciri kepimpinan pun belum bagus.*
>
> . . . *Tidak perlu jauh-jauh, parents saya sendiri pun cakap macam tu. Terus saya pun, okay, bila parents saya cakap macam tu terus saya pun terdominasi sudah, macam 'Iya betul juga. Kenapa mau pilih orang macam tu?'*
>
> [If, for instance, a leader's leadership isn't good then surely the people will not follow. Some elders said, 'Oh, this person (representing the candidate) seems to be pious, but he's into cock-fighting [*sabung ayam*]' So people will look at him sideways (negatively). When he is viewed negatively, that's what makes him lose the vote.
>
> . . . If you are unlucky and the police come (to raid since cock-fighting is illegal in Sabah and Malaysia), even the YB (initials for 'Yang Berhormat' (Honorable Sir/Madam), an honorific term for members of parliament or state assemblymen/women) will be arrested along (with the cock-fighters). How can you be an example in your village? How can you make your village good? If your leadership traits are not yet good.
>
> . . . We don't have to compare too far (with another place/case), as my parents say the same thing. Straightaway I go, okay, when my parents say this, I immediately feel dominated (in thoughts) and think, 'Yes, that's true. Why would I choose someone like that?']

---

6 All interview excerpts in the Malay language are transcribed verbatim and expressed by informants in the Sabah Malay dialect.

Informants then talked about the differing experiences between urban and rural youths when it came to Sabah politics. Some informants felt that in Sabah's remote villages and districts, more than in the urban areas, blatant politicking through money and gifts is rampant because of 'traditional politicians'. Such politicians, informants say, are seen to work based on a 'tit-for-tat' basis, and will pander to the wishes or wants of citizens by getting prominent families in the area to push their agendas. Such politicians then gather votes, and when they win, none are too surprised. In her area, towards the middle of Sabah, Lydia says that there have been families (usually the same ones) who become flush with money during election season. These, said Lydia, are those that drive around the village in their new 'double cab',[7] a symbol of their political gain. In the disparity of development between urban and rural therefore, a good and stable infrastructure (or at the very least the promise of) can also become the currency in dealing with would-be voters. The tongue-in-cheek sayings '*Ada Jalan, Ada Undi*' ('Give us roads, and we will give you our vote') and '*Ada Aspal* [asphalt], *Ada Undi*' heard during campaigns act doubly as the proverbial weapons for seemingly powerless voters.[8] On the one hand, they help voters to bargain for their share in the world of money politics; on the other, such maxims are put in place to warn off the disingenuous politician.

Would-be voters, say informants, are also scrutinising politicians' intents in their speeches. To be endearing, politicians would often attempt to use a local word or phrase in an area not their own and may even try to find a blood connection with their constituents. For instance, the term *onsoi* (meaning '[all] good' in the Murut language) typically rouses a

---

7 The expression typically refers to Sabah's ubiquitous four-wheel drive vehicles of whatever make. A necessity for long journeys, the 'double cab' ('Hilux' [a popular Toyota model among Sabahans] is often used interchangeably) can better handle Sabah's infamous road conditions. This, and other poor infrastructure (roads, buildings and bridges) are often cited by Sabahans as evidence of corruption. Many informants that I have engaged with in the past (both young and old) feel that politicians are passing their projects from one sub-contractor to another, making full completion unattainable. When the projects go past their due date and issues of corruption come to light, the public's eye are diverted from the pertinent topics of development and underdevelopment in Sabah.

8 James C. Scott, *Weapons of the Weak: Everyday Forms of Peasant Resistance* (New Haven: Yale University Press, 1985).

sense of camaraderie. The ex-Prime Minister Najib Razak used it in his last campaign.[9] However, when Shafie Apdal (the president of Warisan) attempted this in Nabawan, he did not receive the same reception. Although he claimed in his speeches that he had Murut roots, people were not convinced since his Suluk identity was already widely publicised by the media. Informants say that nowadays Sabahans can tend to feel belittled, if treated to stunts and gimmicks instead of being engaged in political debates.

Meanwhile, many informants acknowledged that the marked difference between urban and rural youths is in how they respond to political campaigns. Admittedly, some informants felt that they still had too little information in this area and needed to explore. In suburban Penampang, Alexander Iha said that people were more discerning compared with the 'closed minds that still dominate in the rural areas'. Penampang voters, it seemed, didn't fall for propaganda that blamed all of Sabah's problems (usually the ongoing illegal migrant issue is mentioned) on the past Warisan-led government. This is evident, according to Alexander Iha, in how in the recent election, Darrell Leiking, a local Warisan leader, led by over 5,000 votes and managed to keep his seat in the Moyog constituency. Other informants, however, say that many Sabahans are 'racists' and 'egoists' and tend to lump all migrants unfairly as being 'illegal'.

While the category of 'Non-Citizens' in the Sabahan and Malaysian censuses should logically refer to temporary and permanent migrants, it also alludes to illegal migrants. For instance, in the 2010 census, the category of 'Non-Citizens' (then stated as '*Pendatang Tanpa Izin* (PTI) [Illegal immigrant]') listed 889,779 Sabahans as non-citizens while 568,575 comprised Kadazandusuns. The 2019 statistics show that in the Sabahan

---

9 Olivia Miwil, 'Malaysia to remain "onsoi" under BN rule, says Najib,' *New Straits Times*, 7 May 2018, https://www.nst.com.my/news/politics/2018/05/366752/malaysia-remain-onsoi-under-bn-rule-says-najib. Note that Najib Razak would go further to exploit familiar Sabahan expressions, such as '*bossku*' [my boss] and '*malu apa bossku*' [No need to feel ashamed, my boss]. Najib's use of such terms is largely seen as cultural misappropriation. Sabahans may only use these expressions to elicit camaraderie between friends and family. Najib, on the other hand, used it as a slogan to bolster his fan base during his highly publicised trial for embezzlement of public funds. See Trixie Kinajil, 'The Daily Digest: Ini kalilah, bossku', (podcast), *BFM 89.9 (The Business Station)*, 21 February 2019, https://www.bfm.my/podcast/the-bigger-picture/the-daily-digest/dd-ini-kalilah-bossku.

Figure 1: Warisan supporters at the Sigah roundabout in Penampang, one day before PRN2020 on 26 September 2020.
Source: https://www.youtube.com/watch?v=14TsdQhu3VE&ab_channel=CarlNicholas Marvel

population of 3.9 million, there are 1,127,100 non-citizens against the 'Bumiputera' category represented by 2,329,800 people. The superordinate category of Bumiputera (with the literal meaning 'Sons of the Soil') comprises Kadazan, Dusun, Bajau, Malay, Murut and Other Indigenous numbers. These ethnic categories are thus removed altogether in the census data.[10]

'Illegal Immigrants' or *Pendatang Asing Tanpa Izin* (PATI)[11]

Although the controversial topic of PATI has been covered extensively by researchers and the media, a solid policy to fully resolve the issue of the entry to Sabah by non-citizens and the subsequent stays of such individuals has not been forthcoming. Prior to the election, Warisan proposed a

---

10 See, for example, Department of Statistics, 'Current Population Estimates, Malaysia, 2020' (Kuala Lumpur: Department of Statistics, Malaysia, 2020), Table 4, https://newss.statistics.gov.my/newss-portalx/.

11 Following my informants' preference, I use the term 'PATI' (*Pendatang Asing Tanpa Izin*) meaning 'foreign illegal immigrant' over 'PTI' (*Pendatang Tanpa Izin*) or 'illegal immigrant'. The word 'foreign' places the emphasis on non-citizens as opposed to non-Sabahans (Malaysians from other parts of Malaysia). Note that older generations tend to use 'PTI' since that was the first term coined by the authorities in the 1990s. See, Trixie Tangit, *Ethnic labels and identity among Kadazans in Penampang, Sabah (Malaysian Borneo)*, PhD thesis, Australian National University (ANU), 2017.

single system of documentation for migrants to distinguish between those migrants who were illegally in Sabah and those with legal status (refugees who came in the 1970s from the Philippines, for instance). However, a backlash from sovereign rights' groups prevented the plan from coming to fruition. 'A shame', said some of my informants, who felt that none of the politicians involved had the courage to realise the idea. Warisan and Shafie Apdal were labelled '*penternak PATI*' (PATI breeders) on social media for their openness to the reconstruction of identity papers for migrants.

It is unclear how PATIs may figure numerically under the category of 'Non-Citizen' in the census, for the nature of a PATI's identity is largely unknown until the time of their being apprehended by the relevant authorities (police, immigration officers, doctors/nurses). In other cases, a PATI's identity may be 'invisibly legal'[12] to others until they are found in possession of a fake Malaysian identity card (IC). Informants say that 'illegal' migrants are susceptible to the temptation to purchase ICs on the black market. While being costly, the IC racket is competitive, and informants claim that one IC can be bought at RM7,000 while special offers of RM5,000 could get someone two to three ICs. Because of the indeterminate statuses of migrants and 'illegal' migrants, and the ease with which the black market can provide ICs, there is a blanket view among locals that all migrants, even those with temporary visas and work-passes, are 'PATI', and hence 'undesirable' among the Sabahan population.

When informants were asked how they felt about the PATI situation in Sabah, many said that it was unfair for those migrants who have been in Sabah for a long time to experience the stigma of being unfairly perceived as 'PATI'. Some said that it was simply a racist and egotistical thing for Sabahans to do, and that they want Sabah to be an open society and welcoming of outsiders. However, other informants said that locals now have to compete with migrants in the workplace. That is, when certain migrant ethnic groups outnumber any one local ethnic group, local Sabahans sense animosity brewing and can feel threatened. One informant cited PATIs in this context. Yet, some other participants say that not all migrants are good people, and one cannot be biased towards them.[13]

---

12 Trixie Tangit, 'Broader Identities in the Sabahan Ethnic Landscape: 'Indigenous' and 'Sabahan'', *Borneo Research Bulletin* 49, (2018): 246.

13 Some Kadazan informants from Penampang have said that they are now vying for the

There was overwhelming sympathy for migrants, especially PATIs, among informants, indicating that Sabah's society is perhaps becoming more open, caring and compassionate. Informants realise that not only have many Sabahans intermarried with migrants; children of mixed local-migrant marriages can suffer the stigma of suspected PATI descent. For instance, while stateless children cannot go to public schools due to their lack of birth papers and/or Malaysian documentation, children of mixed local-migrant background may also suffer from the loss of opportunities owing to the same situation. Or when their migrant parents cannot go far in life (vie for job promotions, for example) given the prejudice of colleagues and employers. Latif said:

> Because I am half Kadazan and half Pinoy … I know the treatment given to me when I say that I am half Pinoy. I know how it feels like to be called a *Pilak*.[14] I know how it feels like for my uncles and aunties, because they tell me, 'Don't tell people that you are half Pinoy, *nanti diarang minta kau punya IC tu* [or else they will ask for your IC] … *nanti kau punya IC kana tarik balik* [or else your IC will be taken back] … I know how it feels like to be scared in grabbing opportunities because *tidak mau orang tau yang half of me* [I don't want people to know that half of me] is Pinoy … but that's not fair at all … my dad was a great worker at Company X in Kota Kinabalu … he was doing so well that he was supposed to go to Japan to attend a conference but he couldn't because he had a red IC [for permanent/ temporary residents]. Imagine how bad my family had to take all this discrimination *yang* [which is] legalised discrimination … and also cultural discrimination.

The image of a seemingly harmonious society in Sabah owing to intermarriages among ethnic groups belie the double standard that has gone on for too long when it comes to the treatment of migrants and PATIs in Sabahan society. Local employers are known to use migrants for dangerous,

---

same public sector jobs along with migrants who have ascended in society, See Trixie Tangit, *Ethnic labels and identity among Kadazans in Penampang, Sabah (Malaysian Borneo).*

14 New Filipino migrants in the 1970s, who would sell seafood along the sidewalks of the fish market in Kota Kinabalu town, were said to use this term to call out to or attract their potential customers. However, locals came to associate '*pilak*' [lit. silver in Tagalog to mean 'a coin'; '*perak*' in the Malay language also means 'silver'] with 'PATI'. In the 1980s, the UNCHR built Filipino asylum seekers an outdoor market in the then Kota Kinabalu town, referred locally as 'Filipino Market' [*Pasar Pilipin*].

demeaning and low paying work at a lower wage, compared to local workers. At the same time, locals may entertain ideas about migrant adults and children being violent terrorists.[15] Informants basically feel that given the bad treatment and negativity surrounding the PATIs and migrants, locals should consider humanitarian rights and give migrants the opportunity to prove themselves worthy as Sabahans.

Figure 2: #Tackle the PTI (issue), who can do it? The individual on the left, holding a campaign poster, says that he has heard a rumour that Chong Kah Kiat ('CKK'), an ex-Chief Minister, might contest for the role of Chief Minister again The individual on the right, selling what could be smuggled cigarettes from a tray, shaking in fear, says, 'Really? We're done for, if he comes back as chief minister...' Both individuals are depicted as PATIs. Cigarette smuggling and other vices such as drug pushing and prostitution are often blamed on migrants rather than locals. This cartoon is published by the Liberal Democratic Party (LDP), a local Chinese-based political party, led by ex-Chief Minister, Chong Kah Kiat. LDP has a hard-line stance against PATIs, and this was reflected in their party slogans throughout their campaigns in the recent election.

The sentiment of youths for a more open, inclusive, society thus clashed with the inflammatory remarks of politicians in the last election. Some politicians incited indigenous sentiments and told would-be supporters, '*Jangan sampai kita yang jadi PTI*' ('Don't let us become the PTI [the minority]'). Elsewhere, indigenes were warned against an imminent land grab by PATIs. Apart from the native title, Sabah's indigenes have been

15 Vilashini Somiah, 'We Can't Talk About The Terrorists: An Ethnography of Silence In The East Coast of Sabah', *Iman Research*, 20 December 2017.

concerned with a shift in their status. In 2013, the Sabah Native status was formally extended to the Bugis community who affiliate as 'Sabah Bugis'. This was seen as an effort by them to distance themselves from the migrant Bugis community at large, which is believed to comprise Bugis PATIs from Sulawesi.[16]

Religious Freedom

After the election, the ruling government under the coalition Gabungan Rakyat Sabah (GRS, Sabah People's Coalition) allowed Parti Islam Se-Malaysia (PAS, Malaysian Islamic Party) to send a representative (Dr Aliakbar Gulasan, secretary of PAS) to the state assembly. Although PAS (previously a party dominant in the north-east of Peninsular Malaysia) had been present in the Sabahan political arena for more than 30 years, this caused several politicians to raise concerns as to why PAS could have special representation when it neither contested nor won seats in the recent Sabah election. Other politicians said that PAS's ideologies go against the shared value of moderation in Sabahan society.[17] PAS has since then employed a special officer in charge of inter-racial relations, Herman Obi, a Christian Sabahan, as an effort to soften their image.[18]

When asked about this latest development, some informants did not actually find the PAS movement something to worry about, because they were confident that Sabahans already practised a strong tolerant culture that could withstand religious sentiments. It can be said that it is deeply rooted among Sabahans to view ethnic identity as something profound and that boundaries are not fixed to a single marker.[19] For instance, one may have a sense of belonging to a place and village; or to the icons of their group, where the *tagung* (brass gong) and its booming melody, for many indigenes,

---

[16] See Trixie Tangit 'Broader Identities in the Sabahan Landscape'.

[17] Stephanie Lee, 'PAS representation in Sabah assembly unacceptable, says PKR's Christina Liew', *The Star*, 3 October 2020, https://www.thestar.com.my/news/nation/2020/10/03/pas-representation-in-sabah-assembly-unacceptable-says-pkrs-christina-liew

[18] Avila Geraldine, 'Controversial Pas rep appoints Christian as special officer', *New Straits Times*, 11 October 2020, https://www.nst.com.my/news/politics/2020/10/631363/controversial-sabah-pas-rep-appoints-christian-special-officer

[19] Victor T. King, 'The Peoples of Borneo' in Paul Bellwood and Ian Glover (eds.) *The Peoples of South-East Asia and the Pacific* (Oxford: Basil Blackwell, 1993).

can evoke a primordial connection. Language as a key cultural ethnic feature is also salient even though many of Sabah's ethnic languages are becoming subsumed through the extensive use of Malay, English and also Mandarin. Further, the ease with which Sabahans can eat and drink with each other, irrespective of ethnic and religious membership, is also an overt display of Sabahan identity.

At first, some informants like Catherine said that cross-cultural contact with Malaysians on the Malaysian Peninsula causes them to reflect and cherish their unique identities. But eventually, for some other informants, they sense that they cannot truly fit into mainstream Peninsular Malaysian society, because their cultural distinctions are not more commonly shared. Rick said:

> Sometimes I get pressured when people ask me to classify my ethnicity, because when I say that I am Sino-Kadazan during my university days in Kedah (a Malaysian state in West Malaysia), I can't really fit any group. I thought that because there were fewer or no Sino-Kadazan people there that I might easily fit in with the Chinese. But my Mandarin isn't *champin* ('champion', meaning fluent), and I can't really follow the Malay group either. So in the end, I identify myself as 'Malaysian'.

Then Christian informants, as students in Peninsular Malaysian universities, saw that the disconnect became apparent through religious confrontation. They said that they had bad experiences with Muslim students there, who feared coming into close contact with them. One informant shared, 'In my first semester, I was told, "Don't touch me, you are *haram*. You touch pigs/eat pork." I really felt so bad and wanted to cry, but thankfully I had two Sabahan friends there, who were Muslims but they did not behave that way towards me'. Meanwhile, Sabahan Muslims' more relaxed attitude surrounding religion can also make Peninsular Malays become sensitive. Aqmar Z said:

> *Bukan juga kita mau kasi tinggalkan itu solat bah. Baru tinggal asar tadi kan (sebab temuramah ini). (Lepas itu, Aqmar Z cakap berloghat Semenanjung Melayu:) 'Aqmar, kamu tak biasa ke sembayang?' Eh, kenapa kau question ni? Kau question sia punya iman bah tu. Kau ni... Kalau kita di sini tiada lah kita, yang Muslim kah atau non-Muslim kah, tanya, 'Aqmar, kau ada sembayang lima waktu kah hari ni?' Ya lah, mungkin kadang-kadang for certain time yang main-main (kita tertanya yang ini tapi) kita tau (hanya) main-main. Kalau yang serious ni kan, lahhhh! Bikin lain mood bah gitu.*

> [It's not that we want to leave behind our solat prayers. See, we just missed asar prayers (due to this interview). (Then, Aqmar Z speaks in a Peninsular Malay accent:) 'Aqmar, aren't you used to performing prayers?' Hey, what's with the question? You are questioning my faith, you know. You're too much… For us here, we don't, whether we are Sabah Muslim or non-Muslim, ask, 'Aqmar, did you pray five times today?'. I know sometimes we say this to joke around, and then again, you know when someone is joking. But this, when asked in all seriousness, arghhh! That really turns me off.]

When they say that they feel protective towards their religious freedom, it is because of their response to being rejected on account of religious differences. This need to defend the Sabahan way of life is also to counter their sense of being pressured to conform to prescribed religious practices. One informant who has lived in Kuala Lumpur for the past nine years said that he has sensed how more and more Muslims around him are getting quite conservative and feels that he should try to return to Sabah to be more at peace. Many informants did say that Malaysia as a whole was still quite intolerant to cultural and religious differences. For instance, a piece by Joshua Neoh debates whether it is possible in Malaysia to obtain the freedom to profess and practise one's religion as well as the right to convert out of a religion.[20]

Perhaps informants are still grappling with the idea of religious freedom. Alternating between the two expressions, 'religious freedom' and 'freedom of religion', informants state that they refer to the absolute freedom to practice one's own religion without being forced or monitored by others, although informants did not bring up topics of apostasy or changes to constitutional law. When asked however, what religious freedom/freedom of religion truly meant to them, informants could only refer to it as an innate privilege that they have taken for granted, and perhaps only through its loss, may they come to truly appreciate it. In this respect, informants' main concerns, should the Sabahan government move towards applying a more religious form of governance, are Sabahans' inability to preserve their current shared values, which has made practicing a multicultural and inter-religious way of life possible. 'In time, we will find out whether the PAS inclusion into the

---

[20] Joshua Neoh. 'Apostasy and Freedom of Religion in Malaysia' in Paul Babie, Neville Rochow and Brett Scharffs (eds.), *Freedom of Religion or Belief: Creating the Constitutional Space for Fundamental Freedoms* (Edward Elgar Press, 2020), 363-385.

state government will be good or bad in the long run', say informants.

To this end, when asked to consider a hypothetical situation, where they have to choose between the PATI issue or lack of religious freedom, almost all informants said that they would rather accept the intractable PATI situation than have Sabahan society become a conservative one. They acknowledge that the PATI situation, while deeply controversial, is somewhat tenable because it implores on the other to respect human rights. Whereas, religious sentiments felt harder to contain and could easily spill over into outright violence and destablisation.

Conclusion

In this paper, I have attempted to describe the perspectives of seven Sabah youths, who had first-hand experience of the recent general election in Sabah. While they may echo some of the thoughts and opinions already in the Sabahan mainstream, such as the concern over the instability of the Sabah government, it is worth noting that informants are not relying on hearsay, but base their feedback on their own lived realities, life experiences and keen observations of the world around them. We saw how these youths were as much concerned by the topics being argued by their elders, such as the illegal migrant situation in Sabah, which for some hit closer to home. The words of informants, 'don't be too egoistical' and 'we all have a right to be here', echo the desire to promote inclusion for all migrants. Therefore, while youths' vision for a genuinely peaceful Sabahan society is to first and foremost preserve religious tolerance, this can only be met if they protect the openness to the unique cultural milieu in Sabah. That is, if Sabahan identities continue to remain fluid and are not forced to conform to a single identity trait, then they will continue to be more open to appreciating cultural and religious differences. As for future Sabah elections, it is clear that Sabah politicians would do well to continue reaching out to this demographic and find ways to allow youth voices to be heard. Barring this, politicians may find that Sabah's emerging politically savvy youth are only too eager to remove those leaders who are slow in appreciating their concerns.

Figure 3: The view from Gaya Island. Taken from Pulau Gaya (Gaya Island), where locals say PATIs can be found, the two iconic government buildings, the Sabah Foundation or Tun Mustapha Tower and the Sabah State Administrative Centre can be seen in the distance. Locals refer to them as 'battery' (cell) and 'charger', respectively, in reference to their uncanny shapes. 'I keep this photo around, because some day, I want to work there', said Aqmar Z, when asked what in the landscape caught his attention during the recent political season.

Part 3

Campaigning

Chapter 7

Key Players in Sabah's '*Keroyok*' Politics

Philip Golingai

Introduction

Sabah's politics is shaped by the players, their roles and narratives. This chapter is based on interviews with leading politicians and observations on the ground during the 2020 Sabah state election and tells their stories.

Before the 2020 Sabah state election, the Musa Aman v. Shafie Apdal rivalry dominated the state's politics. Their UMNO rivalry spilled over into Sabah state politics when suspended Vice President Shafie quit the party on 4 July 2016 to take on Musa, the Sabah chief minister and Sabah UMNO chief. Shafie formed Parti Warisan Sabah (Warisan) in October that year to bring down the Barisan Nasional (BN) government in Sabah.

Their antagonism culminated in a tied state election during Malaysia's 14th General Election (GE14) in 2018. Sabah BN, headed by Musa, and the Warisan/Pakatan Harapan (PH) alliance, led by Shafie, received 29 state seats each. STAR Sabah (Parti Solidariti Tanah Airku or Homeland Solidarity Party), which contested against both blocks, won the two remaining seats. With STAR Sabah's support, Musa was appointed chief minister, a post he had held for 15 years. Two days later, his government fell when Shafie persuaded four UMNO and two United Progressive Kinabalu Organisation (UPKO) assemblymen to ditch BN and support the opposition.

In a move which was disputed in court, Sabah Governor Juhar Mahiruddin appointed Shafie as chief minister, replacing Musa, who insisted that he had not resigned and had not been sacked from the post. The Shafie v. Musa saga continued. Musa attempted to take back the chief minister post via court cases and by encouraging government assemblymen to switch sides. With the fall of the PH government at the federal level in February 2020, of which Warisan was an ally, and the rise of Perikatan Nasional (PN), Musa had the federal government's backing to bring down Shafie's government.

Musa succeeded on 30 July 2020. He received the support of 33 out of 65 assemblymen in the Sabah State Assembly. The next day, having lost his majority, Shafie requested the governor's consent to dissolve the assembly. The 2020 Sabah state election was set for 26 September, in the midst of the Covid-19 pandemic. It was supposed to be round two of Musa v. Shafie in the state polls. However, the fight between the two nemeses fizzled out when UMNO did not field Musa as a candidate.

The 2020 Sabah state election was instead a *keroyok* (a Sabah slang for 'ganging up' on or 'ganged up on') politics. Shafie's Warisan Plus, consisting of Warisan, the Democratic Action Party (DAP), Parti Keadilan Rakyat (PKR or People's Justice Party), Parti Amanah Negara (Amanah) and UPKO, was pitted against leaders of Gabungan Rakyat Sabah (GRS), comprising BN (UMNO, MCA and Parti Bersatu Rakyat Sabah), PN (Parti Pribumi Bersatu Malaysia or Bersatu, STAR Sabah and Sabah Progressive Party or SAPP) and Parti Bersatu Sabah (PBS).

More specifically, the 2020 Sabah state election was a *keroyok* between Shafie and Sabah UMNO chief Bung Moktar Radin, Sabah Bersatu chief Hajiji Noor and STAR Sabah president Dr Jeffrey Kitingan, all backed by the might of the PN federal government, with Musa in the shadows. Sabah's *keroyok* players are outlined below.

Shafie Apdal

Shafie was the Sabah chief minister and the leader of Warisan Plus, which formed the state government. The 63-year-old Bajau politician is the Bajau and Suluk communities' paramount leader, especially on the east coast of Sabah. The Chinese overwhelmingly supported the Semporna MP and Senallang assemblyman. Yet most of the Kadazan, Dusun and Murut (KDM) communities, especially in semi-rural and rural seats, had yet to accept him as a Sabahan leader.

Sabah DAP secretary Chan Foong Hin described Shafie's role in the 2020

Sabah state election as 'too big and we overemphasised him.'[1] Shafie travelled to almost all the 73 state seats in the second largest state in Malaysia. Geographically, Sabah is a big state. There are state seats the size of West Malaysian states such as Perlis and Malacca. The Kota Kinabalu MP said the Sabah chief minister campaigned from a central point where he could deliver his speech to voters in two or three seats.

'He would say that he covered the area. He could only come to the area once in the 14 days of campaigning. But because of Covid-19, those who came to listen were mostly our supporters. It was also touch and go – you arrive, you touch base with the voters, you talk, and then you go,' Chan said. Throughout the campaign, it was only Shafie, and not Warisan leaders such as deputy president Darell Leiking or youth chief Azis Jamman, who campaigned statewide. 'Warisan has good speakers, but they relied on Shafie too much. We hoped he could carry us to win the state election. But this strategy had weaknesses. We over-relied on him to carry us to victory. If your candidate or machinery is not strong enough, how can you expect the boss to carry you? No way,' said the Sabah DAP secretary.

'Shafie was the key player on the other side. He was the only one,' said Yong Teck Lee, the SAPP president.[2] '[Dr Mahathir Mohamad] was not allowed to campaign in Sabah. [PKR president] Anwar Ibrahim had no impact. He was [busier] with his numbers game in KL,' he said. Yong pointed out that the local leaders within Warisan Plus such as Leiking, Warisan vice-president Peter Anthony, UPKO president Wilfred Madius Tangau and Sabah PKR chief Christina Liew were almost invisible in the statewide campaign.

'It was one man, Shafie with his slogans "In God We Trust" and "Unity". He was the only key player for Warisan Plus because it had only one image – Shafie Apdal. He overestimated that. He forgot that Sabah is a big and diverse state. In some areas you need local flavour,' said Yong, a former Sabah chief minister.[3]

According to the SAPP president, the strategy was both good and

---

1 Chan Foong Hin (Sabah DAP secretary), personal communication, 13 November 2020.

2 Yong Teck Lee (Sabah Progressive Party president), personal communication, 19 November 2020.

3 Editor's Note: Yong Teck Lee served as chief minister from 1996 to 1998.

bad. Good, he said, in areas like the east coast of Sabah, and in Chinese-majority and mixed seats. 'The Chinese were fed up with the racial politics in Peninsular Malaysia, and here you have a Malay leader who speaks like a liberal. He is not, but he speaks like one'. Bad, he said, as in some areas, especially in the rural seats, Shafie and Warisan's branding as pro-PTI (*pendatang tanpa izin* or undocumented persons) worked against Warisan Plus. 'Leiking and Tangau were not able to take away the image that Warisan Plus was PTI-friendly,' he said.

UPKO president Tangau agreed that Shafie, being the incumbent chief minister, dominated and led Warisan Plus. 'He set the agenda,' he said. 'Shafie was the major communicator for our coalition. Throughout the elections, 80 per cent of the Warisan Plus's communications came from Shafie. The media focussed on him whenever he went. He got his strength in communication. He got his aura.'

Shafie was the poster boy of the Warisan Plus campaign. 'About 80 per cent of the Warisan Plus campaign was about Shafie. The 20 per cent was on the candidate's strength,' said Chan. On billboards and posters, where Shafie's portrait was stylised in a manner inspired by Barack Obama's 'Hope' poster in his 2008 presidential campaign. Warisan Plus had catchy slogans such as 'In God we trust, unite we must,' and 'We are here to build a nation, not a particular race or religion.'

'Warisan Plus harped on unity. It matched with Shafie's role in unifying Sabahans to move forward,' said Chan. The Kota Kinabalu MP contended that Warisan Plus ran a better campaign than its opponents. 'We have clarity, we have a chief minister candidate [Shafie], and we did not have much argument on seat allocation'. In contrast, GRS did not have a singular message (as the PN, BN and PBS did not synchronise their campaign strategy), a single chief ministerial candidate (it was a toss-up between Bung Moktar or Hajiji) and its parties clashed in 17 seats. 'Our unity message was much better than our counterpart. They did not run a good campaign. But why did we still lose?' Chan asked.

The unity campaign won the hearts of the urban and semi-urban voters. Warisan Plus, especially the DAP, won most of the urban seats in Kota Kinabalu, Tawau and Sandakan. A majority of their opponents lost their deposit. But the unity campaign did not resonate with many of the voters from semi-rural and rural seats, especially among the KDM communities. 'The narrative of unity did not relate to voters who are only concerned about earning a decent living. Unity is a good message, but it is a very urban-driven message. *Kampung* folks talk about: what development [did] you bring?' Chan said. 'On our part, Warisan Plus seldom talked on development even though we were the state government. We overemphasised unity.'

According to UPKO president Tangau, the unity message promoted by Shafie was a good idea. However, for UPKO, it backfired. 'For our constituents [the KDM voters] the story is *misompuro* (unite). When they talk about unity, it is among the KDM,' he said. Tangau pointed out that UPKO did not have enough time to explain to the voters the unity message. 'At this eleventh hour, you want us to communicate this? How is it going to reach the KDM community?' he said. Yong explained that the unity message and Shafie as the poster boy for Warisan Plus did not resonate in marginal KDM and mixed seats because the rural voters were not impressed with his claim to unite everybody. 'He was not seen as a unifying factor'.

Many KDM, according to the SAPP president, saw Shafie as a politician involved in PSS (Pas Sementara Sabah or Sabah Temporary Pass),[4] which the opposition alleged was the Warisan Plus government's plot to legalise the undocumented persons in the state, and in the burning-down of squatter colonies (which the opposition claimed was a black operation to give legal documents to what is perceived as illegal immigration).[5]

On the ground, Tangau[6] said the PBS and STAR Sabah message that Warisan Plus was pro-PTI was much more effective than the unity message. Shafie, he said, was a minus for many of the KDM voters in the seats UPKO was contesting. 'They saw him as a Suluk and the chief architect of the influx of PTI, and UPKO being associated with him and Warisan worked against us,' said Tangau who ditched BN two days after GE14 for UPKO to form the Sabah government with Warisan and PH. The Tuaran MP said a significant

---

4 Editor's Note: The Shafie government introduced the PSS in 2019, which would have provided official documentation for over 100,000 undocumented persons. The proposal was to take effect in June 2020 but was scrapped in January 2020 after it became a contentious issue in the Kimanis by-election.

5 Editor's Note: This issue was raised during the campaign. See: 'What's going on with illegal immigrant issue in Sabah, asks opposition leader', *Free Malaysia Today*, 7 May 2019, https://www.freemalaysiatoday.com/category/nation/2019/05/07/whats-going-on-with-illegal-immigrant-issue-in-sabah-asks-opposition-leader/.

6 Wilfred Madius Tangau (UPKO President), personal communication, 16 December 2020.

part of PBS's and STAR Sabah's campaign against UPKO was that Shafie was a PTI, a Suluk and a promoter of PTI, and that UPKO and Madius were part of the game.

'It is rubbish. There's no proof that the Warisan Plus government, which did not have the power to do so, was involved in the accusation. It is the federal government which had the power. It was a very successful smearing campaign by our opponents,' he said.

'It is unfortunate that the KDM did not see the unity message of Shafie in spite of the various initiatives that he has taken to make the government more inclusive such as the declaration of Christmas Eve, December 24th, as additional public holiday, increased allocation to churches and his liberal approaches to interfaith relations.'

UMNO supreme council member Abdul Rahman Dahlan[7] loved Warisan Plus's unity campaign. 'But it only worked in urban seats but not in rural seats. It has a long way to go'. Rahman argued that the problem was that the narrative Warisan Plus was pushing revolved around Shafie's personality. 'Everywhere you go, it was about Shafie. He should have learned from history. You can't sustain your political popularity centred on a personality,' he said. The former Kota Belud MP argued that when a campaign revolved around a personality, every weakness the politician had was amplified many times over. 'His approach was very much presidential, and in a presidential election, you choose the person and not the party. Unfortunately, in Sabah, it is a parliamentary democracy. The danger of putting all your eggs in the basket i.e. banking on the popularity of one person, is very dangerous in politics'.

Rahman noted that he believed Shafie made unguarded moves in his 26 months as chief minister. He argued that the Warisan president made a tactical mistake when he supported Mahathir instead of Muhyiddin Yassin for the prime ministership after the 'Sheraton Move' brought down the PH federal government in February 2020. 'That caused him [to lose] some positions in the Federal government – three ministers and several deputy ministers,' he said. 'Look at Sarawak, they [Gabungan Parti Sarawak][8] did

---

7 Abdul Rahman Dahlan (UMNO Supreme Council member) in discussion with the author, 18 November 2020.

8 Editor's Note: This coalition consists of Parti Pesaka Bumiputera Bersatu, Sarawak United Peoples' Party, Parti Rakyat Sarawak and Progressive Democratic Party,

not say whether they will go with Mahathir or Muhyiddin as they wanted to see where the scale tipped. Shafie was bold but misplaced. He openly declared support for Mahathir not knowing that Mahathir was losing support in Peninsular Malaysia.'

Musa Aman

The 69-year-old former Sabah chief minister was instrumental in the downfall of the 26-month Warisan Plus government. 'Without his initiative to bring down Shafie's government by enticing assemblymen to hop, this poll wouldn't have happened,' said Chan of the DAP. However, Musa was not on the ballot paper to defend his Sungai Sibuga seat. Sabah BN chairman and Sabah UMNO chief Bung Moktar was adamant that he shouldn't be nominated as a candidate.

Musa did not contest in the 2020 Sabah state election, but Yong was convinced that he posed a psychological threat to Shafie. 'Hanging over Shafie's head is Musa. Although Musa was not Sabah BN chairman or GRS chairman, the fact that during the campaign Shafie attacked Musa, Anifah (Musa's brother who is Parti Cinta Sabah [PCS] president) and their family showed that in the back of Shafie's mind he was scared of Musa,' he said.

Musa's family members contested in the 2020 Sabah state election. His son-in-law Mohd Arifin Arif, of Bersatu, and the father-in-law of his daughter, Ghulam Haider Khan, both of Bersatu, defended their Membakut and Kawang seats respectively. His nephew, Anuar Ayub of STAR Sabah, contested in Liawan, whilst his brother, Anifah, the former foreign minister and ex-Kimanis MP, is president of PCS, which branded itself as a third force, contested in Bongawan.

Rahman noted that Musa played a significant role in calming politicians from UMNO and Bersatu who were at odds over seat allocation. 'There was a lot of anger between the two parties. He told them this is the reality and deal with it. You can't deny Bersatu seats as the PM is from Bersatu. And you can't also deny UMNO as it is still very strong in Sabah,' he said.

'He advised UMNO not to be too greedy and for Bersatu to give face to UMNO. So UMNO got a slightly bigger chunk of the seats compared with

---

chaired by Sarawak Chief Minister Abang Abdul Rahman Johari governs the state of Sarawak, with the parties elected into office in 2018 in the state elections and the coalition formed in 2018 after GE14.

Bersatu.' Rahman conceded that GRS would have had a more challenging time if Musa had become a third force. 'In this battle of giants where you have Shafie on the other side, you want the likes of Musa on your side,' he said. 'Musa has been chief minister for 15 years, and his political network is incredible and [goes] deep into many layers. He knows the *ketua kampung* [village heads], the big families, the influential family in a seat. And he gets first-hand information. Musa is a consummate politician. Before you talk, he knows your background,' he said. 'One way or the other, Musa helped the candidates who are his friends who have been with him for ages. He helped them with advice and strategies. Musa rekindled his network. It is still there although he was out of sight for two years. He still has many people in every division. He can make one call and ask a local leader to support a candidate.'

Musa, according to Rahman, played a role in GRS's victory. 'But he was not the only reason. The pushback against Warisan Plus was huge just like the tsunami against BN in 2018'. According to Chan, Musa was a shadow figure in the 2020 Sabah state election who wanted to take revenge on Shafie for deposing him as chief minister. 'Don't underestimate him. Who can talk to two parties – UMNO and Bersatu? He is the one. He couldn't settle the seat allocation among the GRS parties. But perhaps that was his strategy. He wanted a multi-cornered fight to dilute the votes so that only a strong local warlord can win,' he said. 'If you have two opponents – Warisan Plus v. GRS – a straight fight is too clear. But if you supply a long list of candidates, somehow the voters will choose a candidate they are familiar with. These players are somehow linked to Musa as he held the position of CM for 15 years.'

Semporna Bersatu leader Nixon Habi[9] elaborated that some of the Bersatu-linked independents helped GRS to win seats. For example, if independent candidate Musbah Jamli did not defend his Tempasuk seat, his votes could have gone to the PKR candidate. Chan pointed out that Musa did not need a party platform to campaign for his candidates. 'He is just Musa Aman, and that was enough. He did not have to be Musa Aman of UMNO or Musa Aman of Bersatu. Musa is not a paramount leader to any ethnic group in Sabah. He is like a corporate leader'.

As Chan noted, Musa has been in power for a long time and has many

---

9 Nixon Habi (Parti Pribumi Bersatu Malaysia politician), personal communication, 23 November 2020.

friends in political and economic circles. 'He is connected to the elite circle and small warlords. In an election, you need to raise money, and he can tap on his elite friends and distribute the fund[s] to the small warlords'.

Bung Moktar Radin

When almost all the UMNO MPs and assemblymen in Sabah abandoned the party to join parties like Bersatu, Warisan and UPKO, the 62-year-old Kinabatangan MP remained loyal to the party. 'His *radu tatap radu* [to plough on regardless of the obstacles] slogan galvanised UMNO which was down in Sabah. Most of the party's big guns had crossed over to other parties. Bung Moktar himself is the embodiment of *radu tatap radu*. He just *radu* and *lawan* [fight],' said a Warisan Plus leader, who did not want to be identified.

But it was not Bung Moktar alone who was responsible for UMNO winning 14 out of the 32 seats it contested in the 2020 Sabah state elections. He had the backing of UMNO's machinery and funding from Peninsular Malaysia. UMNO maximised its resources. For example, its national party leaders each adopted a seat in the 32 constituencies UMNO contested.

The Sabah UMNO chief contested in the new seat of Lamag within his parliamentary seat of Kinabatangan. Bung Moktar saw winning the seat as a step to becoming the Sabah chief minister. He envisioned himself as a Duterte-style Sabah chief minister with his 'no protocol' style of leadership. Even though Bung Moktar was a controversial figure, he saw himself as chief minister material, since previous Sabah chief ministers like Shafie and Musa were linked to corruption charges.

However, his critics claimed that many in GRS did not take Bung Moktar's dream of becoming chief minister seriously. 'How can you have a chief minister candidate who will be going up and down the courts for his corruption cases hearings?' said a Sabah UMNO insider.[10] UMNO lost in 18 of the seats it contested. 'The party did badly because of his choice of candidates. It was based on his self-interest,' the UMNO insider said.

Bung Moktar was, however, the only GRS leader who travelled all over the state to campaign. 'Bung was flying in a helicopter like a de facto CM,' observed a Warisan Plus politician. The media loved Bung Moktar as he

---

[10] Anonymous (Sabah UMNO politician), personal communication, 14 December 2020.

was accessible, and he loved the press in return. He also gave quotable statements and did not avoid controversial questions. According to Chan, the Kinabatangan MP was more visible than Hajiji, the other GRS candidate for the chief minister post. 'Bung Moktar visited the constituencies which BN contested. He was more influential in the polls than Hajiji. Hajiji was too concerned about his constituency'.

Hajiji Noor, backed by Muhyiddin Yassin and Hamzah Zainudin

The 65-year-old Sulaman assemblyman campaigned mainly in the seat which he has held since 1990. At the start of the election, there was a *gelombang* (wave) against Hajiji in Sulaman. The Sulaman incumbent was facing a popular Warisan candidate Aliasgar Basri.

He was also not confident that the UMNO grassroots would support him this time as he had left the party. The Sabah Bersatu chief won the seat under UMNO but switched to Bersatu in 2018. 'That is why he was stuck there. He was fighting for his political survival in Sulaman. He did not contribute to Bersatu and GRS's overall victory,' said a Warisan Plus leader.[11]

Yong, the president of SAPP, which joined the PN coalition days before the Sabah polls, maintained that being a core player was not only about a politician going around the state to campaign. According to him, Hajiji was the possible incoming chief minister if GRS won. 'Although he did not travel widely in Sabah to campaign, he was a viable choice as CM without which Perikatan Nasional/GRS did not have a selling point,' he said.

Yong explained the key issue among the voters was the question of who would be GRS's chief minister if they won. 'If Hajiji was not named, people assumed it would be Bung Moktar who, I think, BN admitted was not a viable option. Bung Moktar might be a good chief minister, but that the public's negative perception of him did not make him a marketable CM candidate,' he said. Hajiji's significant role, Yong argued was to offer himself as a viable chief minister, 'I repeat, there is no other name (in GRS) which is viable than his'.

An UMNO insider noted that Hajiji's strategy in being seen to be in the running to be a chief minister was to be as decent as possible. 'He is Mr

[11] Anonymous (Warisan Plus politician), personal communication 16 December 2020.

Nice Guy. He tried not to step on anyone's toes as much as possible. But the flip side is you have a mundane politician,' he said. The UMNO insider said Hajiji never waded into controversy, unlike the controversial Bung Moktar. 'By nature, he doesn't like to do things outside a familiar situation. He doesn't like to make comments on issues'.

Nixon, a Semporna Bersatu leader, pointed out that Hajiji was instrumental in the seat negotiation between UMNO and Bersatu. The two parties were in conflict, especially after Bersatu pinched most of UMNO's assemblymen and MPs. 'He sacrificed a few seats such as Lumadan and Tempasuk to appease UMNO, to ensure seats such as Klias, Kuala Penyu, Kawang, Apas and Membakut remained with Bersatu,' he said. The significance of Bersatu getting Klias, Kuala Penyu, Kawang, Apas and Membakut was that those seats (except for Kuala Penyu) were won by UMNO politicians who had jumped to Bersatu. And Bersatu wanted those seats so that the incumbents (who had left UMNO, or UPKO in the case of Kuala Penyu) could defend the seats.

The Warisan Plus politician contended that Hajiji was not the type of leader who could lead Bersatu statewide. He argued that Bersatu president Muhyiddin Yassin and its secretary-general Hamzah Zainudin were instrumental in their party's success. Being a popular prime minister, Yong said PN widely used Muhyiddin's posters in its campaign. 'The personal assurances of [the] prime minister to support Sabah's economic recovery and security and counter to the Philippines' claim to Sabah were key to convincing voters to back PN/GRS,' he said.

Nixon noted that Muhyiddin was popular among the rural voters because of his management of the Covid-19 pandemic and the Bantuan Prihatin Nasional cash aid. 'His *Abah* (father) personality went well with the kampung people'. Chan also acknowledged that the Prime Minister's popularity won votes for PN. 'He is *Abah* (father). Perikatan Nasional and Bersatu harped more on Muhyiddin than Hajiji. You can see Muhyiddin's face in Luyang (a state seat in the Kota Kinabalu parliamentary constituency), but you won't see Hajiji's face,' he said. The Kota Kinabalu MP noted that voters wanted stability in the state and in Sabah's federal relationship. They saw that GRS was *sehaluan* (on the same page) with the federal government because of Muhyiddin, he said. 'They were tired of non-stop politicking, and they voted for stability. Some of the voters might not agree with *katak* politicians (lit. frogs, who jump parties). Still, they liked stability and development (which the federal government can bring) which we talk less about as we talked more on *katak* and unity,' he said.

A PBS insider[12] said the prime minister reminded Sabahans that their state must be on good terms with the Federal Government to get socioeconomic and infrastructure development funding. 'GRS also mined extensively the nationwide approval rating of the prime minister which reaped intuitive counter-returns'. The PBS insider noted that Muhyiddin campaigned in many of the constituencies in which GRS contested. 'In some areas, the candidate made use of the PM's banner instead of the candidates themselves as if the candidates are not important compared to the association with the prime minister,' he said.

Muhyiddin had a consensus-based approach in political disputes and relations. 'He did not push the issue. For instance, PBS did not use the Perikatan Nasional or Barisan Nasional symbol. But Muhyiddin did not demand that it use either one of them. He went along with PBS,' Yong said.

Bersatu secretary-general Hamzah also held together the newly announced and disparate GRS. 'He spent most of the campaign time in Sabah. He had a strong and disciplined team based at the Bersatu headquarters in Kota Kinabalu. As PN and GRS were very new, that team under Hamzah played a key role in the PN campaign,' Yong said. According to the SAPP president, Hamzah was a peacemaker in the hostility between PBS and STAR Sabah when the former placed candidates in six seats allocated to the latter. 'If Hamzah was not there, there would have been an all-out war between PBS and STAR Sabah.'

Hamzah also minimised conflict between GRS members, and he kept UMNO in check by talking to its leaders at the federal level. 'He did not entirely manage to put out the fire, but there was enough peace between the GRS members to make sure that they were able to win seats,' Yong said. A PBS insider confirmed that Hamzah played a significant role in the withdrawal of the party's candidates from Tambunan and Bingkor to avoid clashes with STAR Sabah. 'It was in exchange for the withdrawal of STAR Sabah-sponsored independents in Api-Api and Bengkoka,' he said.[13]

---

12 Anonymous (PBS insider), personal communication, 18 December 2020.

13 Editor's Note: Three days before polling, on 23 September 2020, GRS announced that an agreement had been reached between STAR and PBS over four of the seats where they clashed.

According to the same PBS insider, as the home minister, Hamzah's statement on the permanent solution of undocumented persons in Sabah was crucial. To a large extent it was able to influence the voting preference of the Sabahans especially among the non-Muslim natives, he said. 'They viewed Hamzah's assurance to the solution of PTI in Sabah as promising and therefore had positive hope for the PN government as compared with Warisan, whose leader was seen as PTI friendly,' he said.

Jeffrey Kitingan

Last, but not least, in the *keroyok* was Jeffrey. In the 2020 Sabah state election, the 72-year-old STAR Sabah president came out of the shadow of his older brother Joseph Pairin Kitingan, who was Sabah's chief minister from 1985 to 1994. After GE14, the PBS founder Pairin retired from politics when Jeffrey defeated him in his Tambunan state seat, which he had held since 1976.

'With Pairin out of the picture, people speculated whether Dr Jeffrey would come up as a prominent leader from the KDM base in the 2020 Sabah election. The results showed that the KDM has no problem with him,' said Yong. STAR Sabah won six out of the eight state seats it contested. You can drive continuously through all the six seats – Paginatan, Tambunan, Bingkor, Liawan, Sook and Tulid – which the party won without exiting their border, highlighting the regional strength of the party. The seats in the Ranau, Keningau and Pensiangan parliamentary constituencies are in the heartland of the KDM communities.

The negative labelling of Jeffrey as a *katak*, who jumped from PBS to Akar, back to PBS, then to PBRS, before turning Independent, trying to join UMNO, then joining PKR, forming United Borneo Front (an NGO fighting for Sabah rights) and finally establishing STAR Sabah, however, did not stick. 'Some say that he jumps from one party to another. But when Dr Jeffrey jumped, he brought his struggle with him. When he could not push for his struggle, he changed parties. He was also not a president of a party before STAR Sabah was established,' said STAR Sabah Secretary-general Guandee Kohoi.[14]

---

[14] Guandee Kohoi (STAR Sabah Secretary-general), personal communication, 20 November 2020.

Jeffrey's party grew in strength. It got one seat in the state polls in 2013 when Jeffrey won the Bingkor seat. It doubled its state seats in 2018 when Jeffrey took Tambunan and Robert Tawik won Bingkor. In 2020, the KDM-based party tripled its state seat count. Yong pointed out that Sabahans, mostly the KDM, did not forget about Jeffrey's fight for Sabah rights. 'The cumulative effect of his fight of several decades is that he has emerged as the single most prominent KDM leader,' he said.

'I did not see a catchy slogan or striking posters by STAR Sabah in the election. It was sheer hard work built up through the decades. In rural seats, it is about accumulating support over the years through the core message – Sabah rights – for which he was jailed for under the ISA [Internal Security Act] in the 1990s.' Yong explained that with Pairin retired and PBS president Dr Maximus Ongkili unwell, Jeffrey was the leading voice and face of GRS's KDM campaign.

Chan acknowledged that Jeffrey was another *Huguan Siou* (the Kadazan-Dusun paramount leader) to succeed his brother, Pairin. 'STAR Sabah is the radical voice of the KDM to demand their rights in the name of Sabahans,' he said. Pensiangan Warisan leader Martin Tommy[15] knows about Jeffrey's fight. Martin was with him from 2004 until the middle of 2016 before leaving to join Warisan, which was in the process of being established. In 2004, Martin contested in Pensiangan as part of an independent alliance headed by Jeffrey, who stood in Sook under the same umbrella symbol. In 2013, Martin contested as a STAR Sabah candidate in the state seat of Sook in the Pensiangan parliamentary constituency. Back then, he said, Jeffrey spoke consistently about the same issue – Malaya (Peninsular Malaysia) has short-changed Sabahans and Sabah should be getting much more, according to the Malaysia Agreement 1963. He would also highlight the state's perennial illegal immigrant problem.

'The first time Dr Jeffrey contested on his own he lost, the second time, he lost, but the third time he won because of the new voters,' he said. Martin recalled when he was with Jeffrey 15 years ago, youths would gather to listen to their talks on Sabah rights. 'They were also helping us to put up our flags and posters. At that time, these kids could not vote. When they were eligible to vote, the issues were entrenched in their head. Dr Jeffrey managed to indoctrinate them with his ideology,' he said.

---

15 Martin Tommy (Parti Warisan Sabah politician), personal communication, 4 December 2020.

Fast forward to 2020, Martin was now with Warisan. He campaigned for Warisan Plus against GRS, including STAR Sabah, in the state seats in the Pensiangan parliament constituency. 'Dr Jeffrey has played a big role in changing the mind of the people in the interior. Since 2018, his party's campaign against us was that Shafie was PTI and Warisan was PTI. It got stuck in the minds of the people in the interior,' he said.

'We have gone on the ground to help the people, especially during the Covid-19 pandemic. As the state government, we have also delivered projects such as building small bridges and gravel roads. But STAR Sabah won against us [Warisan Plus] because the people believed the fake news they were spreading. ... Despite being with Warisan, I still love this guy [Shafie] as we go back a long way,' Martin added.

Rahman of UMNO pointed out that Jeffrey got his timing right. 'He was in the right place at the right time. UPKO [a KDM-based party with Warisan Plus] was on the other side and [was] bashed by the people, especially the Kadazan-Dusun, because it was linked to Warisan. 'PBS [which is a KDM-based party with GRS] is seen as a grand old party in Sabah. Unfortunately, its president Maximus Ongkili was not well during the state elections. The KDM were looking for a loud and strong voice to represent them. And then you have a firebrand like Dr Jeffrey. People like him because he is seen as very straightforward and forthcoming.'

Rahman noted that Jeffrey's decision to align STAR Sabah with the PN coalition was the right tactic. 'The prime minister is from Perikatan Nasional, so naturally he [Jeffrey] was inclined to Perikatan Nasional. He wanted to be with the powers that be,' he said. A STAR Sabah leader admitted that his party joined the PN coalition because it needed resources to campaign. 'In an election, you need money. It is not to buy votes but to pay for the machinery, transportation – everything.'

Shafie Apdal v. Musa Aman, Bung Moktar Radin, Hajiji Noor, Jeffrey Kitingan and Independents

The big surprise in the 2020 Sabah state election was that the three independent candidates who were backed by Bersatu won. Masiung Banah retained Kuamut, Rubin Balang won Kemabong and Rudy Awah secured Pitas.

But it was no surprise for those who went on the ground in the rural seats. The chatter among locals was that they would pick a candidate and not a party in a confusing multi-cornered fight as they preferred a politician who they knew would serve them. The winning independents were politicians well connected to the grassroots. 'In warlord politics, if you pick the right independent candidate, they can win regardless if it is a multi-cornered fight even against their pact,' Chan said.

Take the example of Rubin, the independent who won in Kemabong, a state seat in the Tenom parliamentary constituency. It was an open secret that Rubin was a Bersatu-backed candidate. During the campaign, the mood was *manggis* (mangosteen) would win against BN's Raime Unggi of UMNO and UPKO's Dr Lucas Umbul in the six-cornered fight. Rubin won the seat as PBS candidate in 1994 but jumped to UMNO and held the seat until 2018 when the party picked him as a candidate for the Tenom seat.

Personality overshadowed issues in the rural seat of Kemabong. Manggis defeated Barisan Nasional's *dacing* (scale) symbol as most of the Murut voters were drawn to the *mesra rakyat* (people-friendly) politician. A politician's likeability goes a long way as voters expect them to attend weddings, funerals and to mingle and spend time with the people. Rubin is known to be more *mesra rakyat* than former Tenom MP Raime and former senator Lucas.

Conclusion

In the 2020 Sabah state election we can say that GRS's *keroyok* politics worked against Shafie – the alliance won 38 seats, Bersatu-backed independents three and Warisan Plus 32.

Despite GRS not having a clear message, a single chief ministerial candidate or a coordinated campaign strategy like Warisan Plus, GRS won the state elections. GRS component parties even contested against each other in 17 seats. Yet it was the combined success of UMNO, Bersatu, STAR Sabah and PBS in winning enough seats, plus the three independents, who were small warlords in their constituencies, which were key in GRS defeating Warisan Plus.

They, together with the mighty federal government, ganged up against a common enemy, Warisan Plus and Shafie. The combination of Musa, Bung Moktar, Hajiji, Jeffrey and the independents, plus national leaders like Muhyiddin and Hamzah, were greater than the sum of their parts.

Chapter 8

'Don't Jump, Time to Work': The Political Maturity of Sabahan Digital Spaces Through the 2020 State Election

Benjamin YH Loh and Yi Jian Ho

Introduction

In the wider Malaysian context, political campaigning in cyberspace has become dominated by 'cybertroopers', political agents who blend into online spaces to subversively promote, defend, or attack political figures and parties.[1] There was recognition of this from the Barisan Nasional (BN) government as early as 1996 (when the opposition *Reformasi* movement was gathering steam in early digital spaces such as bulletin boards and newsgroup forums). However, the term 'cybertrooper' came into currency in the late 2000s, when the opposition coalition Pakatan Rakyat managed to wrestle away the BN's two-thirds majority in Parliament in the 2008 General Elections – causing the UMNO leadership to rethink their approach to cyberspace. Adopting martial language and metaphors against a hitherto opposition-dominant cyberspace, the ruling government saw their activities

1 There are many different names for cybertroopers depending on locality, for example, 'troll farms': 'state-sponsored agents who control a set of pseudonymous user accounts and personas (sock puppets) which disseminate misinformation and propaganda in order to sway opinions, destabilise the society, and even influence elections'. See Darren L. Linvill and Patrick L. Warren. 'Troll Factories: Manufacturing Specialized Disinformation on Twitter', *Political Communication* 37, no. 4 (3 July 2020): 447–67.

as a form of re-occupation in a 'cyberwar'[2] – now further expanding not only from websites and blogs but also into social media, with greater formal coordination and monitoring capacities.[3] In 2010, UMNO's Youth Wing claimed that 27 bloggers and another 1,800 members were trained for digital operations under their New Media Unit.[4]

By the 2013 General Elections, the opposition could no longer claim dominance in Malaysian cyberspace: there was an overt and dedicated new media presence of UMNO and its component parties in BN (94-7)[5] – with the potential to increase the sophistication of their cyberspace operations through big data.[6] These same built-up capacities were brought to bear in the Sabah state election, which Peninsular Malaysian parties saw as a litmus test of their legitimacy, especially given that a 'backdoor' government came into power.

Thus, the Sabah state election in 2020 was a unique political phenomenon: typically, it takes place concurrently with a general election, in step with the rest of Malaysia. Now *out* of step with the general election process, it provided a rare opportunity to examine the discursive dynamics created by political machinery and organic campaigning at work for a state-wide election without distractions or divided focus from the rest of Malaysia. This chapter examines the combined arms of political campaigning using social media for the 2020 Sabah election. Despite the pressure exerted by the Peninsular Malaysian political machinery, we find that Sabahan social media discourse demonstrates a form of centripetal, democratic maturity that resists the dynamics of divide-and-conquer politics. Themes that emerged from the social media space include an overarching anti-

2 Julian Hopkins, 'Cybertroopers and Tea Parties: Government Use of the Internet in Malaysia', *Asian Journal of Communication*, (2014): 5-24.

3 Claudia Theophilus, 'Malaysia Poll Battle Goes Online', *AlJazeera, 9 March 2008,* https://www.aljazeera.com/news/2008/3/9/malaysia-poll-battle-goens-online.

4 Nigel Aw, 'Umno Can't Control Papagomo, Parpukari', *Malaysiakini*, 20 January 2012, https://www.malaysiakini.com/news/187158.

5 Pauline Leong, *Malaysian Politics in the New Media Age: Implications on the Political Communication Process* (Singapore: Springer, 2019).

6 BN was purported to have been pitched by Cambridge Analytica, a dubious but extensive data gathering and analytics firm. In 'Kaiser Expose: Cambridge Analytica Pitched Plan to Umno on Retaining 40 Seats in GE14', *The Star*, 3 January 2020, https://www.thestar.com.my/news/nation/2020/01/03/kaiser-expose-cambridge-analytica-pitched-plan-to-umno-on-retaining-40-seats-in-ge14.

federalism/Peninsular Malaysian sentiment that made many sceptical of all Sabah political parties and their true allegiances, a more muted impact of cybertroopers in this state election as opposed to Peninsular Malaysia and a generally increased maturity from all sides, being able to think beyond partisanship once the election was over.

Monitoring the Sabah Election Campaigns

We examined the Sabah online media spaces using a social media discourse analysis methodology.[7] This approach involves targeting a series of public social media spaces where a large number of Sabahans would be participating in political discussions and monitoring the types of posts and comments being made. Due to the possible presence of cybertroopers and non-disclosed political agents, quantitative approaches would neither be effective nor accurate in measuring voter sentiments and election predictions. Through discourse analysis, we instead found important topics and values that Sabahans would highlight and discuss in these online spaces.

The Sabah online spaces consist of two main platforms: WhatsApp groups and Facebook groups/pages. WhatsApp groups would be the dominant discursive space, but they are impenetrable to our chosen methodology. Thus, we focused on Facebook groups and pages. There are numerous public or open groups and pages which have a strong Sabahan membership. These groups can be based around certain state identities (e.g. 'Sayang Sabah'), localities (e.g. 'The Real Politik Penampang') or politics (e.g. 'Tatap UMNO/BN [Sabah]'). The composition of these groups tended to be quite diverse, with members having varying political affiliations and viewpoints. Since the dissolution of the state assembly, these sites have been highly active with dozens of posts made every hour, growing in intensity as major developments occur.

We present here an aggregation of the sentiments, views and comments from Sabahans in these public online spaces. We have focused primarily on the comments for this analysis as we can observe discussions that are taking place. The criteria of selection for analysis were posts that featured at least 20 comments that would yield some semblance of a discussion. From these

---

7 We would like to thank Mahirah Marzuki, another author in this book, for her assistance with the social media monitoring.

discussions, we focused our analysis on the following within comments: (1) topics that attract attention; (2) kinds of comments posted; (3) debates that occur between commenters; (4) the presence of cybertroopers and their tactics; and (5) commenter approaches to contrasting or opposing views.

Through these analytical lenses, we examined hundreds of posts and thousands of comments from an assortment of twenty Facebook groups and pages from early August (about a week after the dissolution of the state assembly) all through the end of September (a week after the election ended). Over this period, the energy and engagement within these posts and comment threads were quite consistent all the way until election day: Strong partisanship was present amongst commenters, showing support and condemnation across the political spectrum.

We found that after the chief minister had been appointed, there was a very distinct shift in energy as Sabahans almost unilaterally contained their partisan views and instead focused on engaging with the ruling government of the day; the elections were over and it was time to get to work. Thus, we present these sentiments in two different periods: (1) during the campaign and (2) after the campaign.

During the Campaign: Cybertrooper Activity

Despite the fact that campaigning officially began on nomination day on September 12, the political discussions began dominating Sabah social media from the moment the initial takeover attempt by Musa Aman had begun. The political machinery from every involved party then started to engage in campaigning in full force the moment Shafie Apdal announced the dissolution of the state assembly. While these elections were unprecedented with a massive 447 candidates vying for 73 seats, ultimately, the discourse mainly viewed the election as a two-horse race between the incumbent coalition of Warisan Plus against the newly formed opposition Gabungan Rakyat Sabah (GRS).

It was clear to most commenters of the digital spaces we monitored that cybertroopers and '*macai*' were present. While cybertroopers are formally organised and potentially paid, *macai* are *digital ideologues*: highly spirited and dogmatic political supporters who dominate online discussions with continuous posting and engage often with other commenters.[8] This term is unique to Malaysia but not as a form of political support and it has been documented by social media analysts through other terms, such as 'keyboard armies'[9] and 'diehard supporters.'[10] Typically, they do not hide their political affiliations and wear them like a badge of honour. However, they may not be formally coordinated or paid like cybertroopers. Their impact on discussions may create a 'spiral of silence' effect: due to their perseverance in posting frequency and in discussion, they can create the impression that they represent the majority view where they might just be a highly vocal minority and in turn cause others who do not share their views to disengage or falsely believe that they are actually part of the minority.[11] Thus, the activities of both cybertroopers and *macais* both distort and

---

8 '*Macai*' is a slang term that entered the wider Malaysian lexicon circa 2013-2015, with very few Google search entries occurring prior to that, and has not been formally recognised by Dewan Bahasa dan Pustaka. There exists some academic work that analyses political social media discourse which translate it as "accomplice and supporters", "sycophants": it has a derogatory connotation. See Isma Noornisa Ismail, Thilagavathi Shanmuganathan, and Azianura Hani Shaari, 'Defying Out-Group Impoliteness: An Analysis of Users' Defensive Strategies in Disputing Online Criticisms'. *GEMA Online® Journal of Language Studies* 20, no. 1 (28 February 2020). An online source traces its etymological roots back to a Chinese term, "馬仔" (*ma chai*), an impolite way to refer to Malay people. 仔 (*chai*) is translated as boy, but 馬 (*Ma*) can both mean a contraction of Malay/Malaysia as well as horse, with the combination taking on an informal meaning of a subordinate whom you can ride on/do as you please. See Azlan Halim, 'Asal-Usul Perkataan MACAI', Facebook, 8 September 2013, https://www.facebook.com/notes/azlan-halim/asal-usul-perkataan-macai/10151833351666445/.

9 Aim Sinpeng, Dimitar Gueorguiev, and Aries A. Arugay, 'Strong Fans, Weak Campaigns: Social Media And Duterte In The 2016 Philippine Election', *Journal of East Asian Studies* (27 July 2020): 1–22.

10 Jeremy A. Frimer and Linda J. Skitka, 'The Montagu Principle: Incivility Decreases Politicians' Public Approval, Even with Their Political Base', *Journal of Personality and Social Psychology* 115, no. 5 (2018): 845–66.

11 Elisabeth Noelle-Neumann, 'The Spiral of Silence a Theory of Public Opinion', *Journal of Communication* 24, no. 2 (1 June 1974): 43–51; Sherice Gearhart and Weiwu Zhang, 'Gay Bullying and Online Opinion Expression: Testing Spiral of Silence in the Social Media Environment', *Social Science Computer Review*, (23 September 2013); Amelia Johns and Niki Cheong, 'Feeling the Chill: Bersih 2.0, State Censorship, and "Networked Affect" on Malaysian Social Media 2012–2018', *Social Media + Society* 5, no. 2 (1 April 2019): 1-12.

extinguish vibrant political discourse as they both create false impressions of representing the majority view and suppress less vocal voices.

The discourse engaged by cybertroopers and *macai* on both political sides was highly partisan and crude, built around typical political mudslinging as the most common form of political engagement. While there were some posts that attempted to laud the successes of their respective political parties, commenters would often counter these positive points based on negative actions and their associations with that party. Provocative political assassination-type posts and posts on certain trending issues were made quite frequently (several times a day). As a result, many such comment threads here devolve into shouting matches where *macais* on both sides end up just repeating political hyperbole without meaningful engagement. Topics that are discussed at length provide an implicit indication of the campaign strategies that are employed by these political parties to shift public opinion in their favour and away from their opponents.

Opposition Cybertrooper Operations

The dominant rhetoric levied against Warisan Plus was its association with being a 'Parti PATI' (pro-illegal migrant party), an old label that has been applied to the party since it took state office in 2018. This can be attributed to its popularity in the east coast of Sabah (away from the hegemonic centre of Kota Kinabalu on the west coast), and the party has often been accused of having strong ties with the southern Philippines. This becomes contentious in Sabah due to a fraught history of federal interventions resulting in migrants (assumed to be mostly Southern Filipinos, Indonesians and other regional identities) being given citizenship in an attempt to distort the demographics of the state.[12] The pro-migrant rhetoric for Warisan Plus reached a critical point when the party sought to establish a rationalised way of documenting migrants called the Sabah Temporary Pass or Pas Sementara Sabah (PSS).[13]

---

[12] On Project IC, see James Chin, 'Exporting the BN/UMNO Model: Politics in Sabah and Sarawak', in Meredith Weiss (ed.) *Routledge Handbook of Contemporary Malaysia*, (London: Routledge, 2014), 83–92.

[13] The Sabah Temporary Pass was a proposal made in September 2019 to standardise three different immigration documents issued by different government agencies to foreigners residing in the state: the IMM13 (issued to refugees from the 1970s.

The opposition took the opportunity to frame it as a smoking gun to highlight that this was part of Warisan's plan to legalise these migrants and further distort Sabah's population. This rhetoric was especially resonant amongst the KDMs (an aggregate term combining the largest three indigenous ethnic groups of Sabah: the Kadazan, Dusun and Murut) of Sabah who saw this as a way for locals native to the east coast (Bajau, Suluk etc.) to increase their numbers (as most irregular migrants from the Philippines are from similar indigenous groups). Thus, social media political attacks in 2020 against Warisan Plus often focused on highlighting the PSS policy, disputes over Shafie's real allegiances, negative image associations with the party logo and a senior Warisan politician making a poor joke late in the campaign, detailed below.

Shafie himself has been the target of an elaborate political assassination campaign that paints him as a duplicitous Filipino agent meant to bring Sabah back to the Philippines. This includes claims disputing his place of birth and his prominent Bajau heritage (which shares similarities to other ethnicities which hail from the southern Philippines). When placed together with a renewed claim from the Philippines over Sabah in August,[14] which Shafie himself refused to reject,[15] this further entrenched the pro-migrant rhetoric amongst Warisan Plus opponents. He has also been blamed for relaxing restrictions of entry into Sabah and for creating a more inviting atmosphere for more migrants to enter Sabah.[16]

Many posts would reinterpret any action by Warisan that could be remotely seen as being sympathetic towards undocumented migrants as

---

They were issued after this period). Kad Burung-Burung (issued by the Sabah Chief Minister's Department in the 1980s) and the Census Certificate (issued by Federal Special Task Force in the 1990s). See Kirsty Inus, '136,055 Eligible for Proposed Sabah Temporary Pass', *The Star*, 21 November 2019, https://www.thestar.com.my/news/nation/2019/11/21/136055-eligible-for-proposed-sabah-temporary-pass.

14 See Basilio Sepe and Hadi Azmi, 'Malaysia, Philippines Take Row over Sabah to the UN', *BenarNews*, 3 September 2020, https://www.benarnews.org/english/news/malaysian/Sabah-dispute-09032020141241.html.

15 'Shafie Demands Wisma Putra Protest Manila's Plan to Include Sabah in Map on Its Passports', *The Star Online*, 24 August 2020, https://www.thestar.com.my/news/nation/2020/08/24/shafie-demands-wisma-putra-protest-manilas-plan-to-include-sabah-in-map-on-its-passports.

16 Haspaizi Zain, 'Warisan Pro-Illegal Immigrants in Sabah, Says Abdul Aziz', *Malaysiakini*, 7 December 2019, https://www.malaysiakini.com/news/502752.

providing a gateway for these migrants to becoming citizens. The Warisan party logo, which is a sailboat, is often referred to as a '*kapal lanun*' or pirate boat. This creates an association with pirate groups which mainly hail from the Philippines and have been involved in various kidnapping or terror activities on the Sabah east coast. While posts that use this language were rather sparse, it was mainly used as a simple comment (calling Warisan a '*parti lanun*', or a pirate party) as a means to distract or diffuse ongoing discussions.

The unfortunate joke, which was argued to have cost Warisan Plus the election, was made by the Warisan Plus candidate for Segama, Mohammadin Ketapi. In a speech to local voters, he cracked a joke regarding the Malaysian armed forces in their handling of the Lahad Datu standoff in 2013.[17] Mohammadin's remarks were seen as callous, disrespectful and highly untimely. More importantly, these remarks fit in perfectly into the migrant narrative against Warisan Plus: they were denying the severity of the Lahad Datu incursion because they secretly support the claim to Sabah: to rejoin the Philippines.

Incumbent Cybertrooper Operations

Turning our attention to the incumbent Warisan Plus, their rhetoric focussed on the failures and shortfalls of BN/Perikatan Nasional (PN) during their tenure as the state government. This idea was supported through the use of terms such as '*perompak*', '*penyamun*' and other synonyms for thieves or robbers. One common cybertrooper post template consisted of before-and-after pictures, which compared the stark differences in development in the same location; where there was either little to no development, huge improvements were shown after Warisan had taken over (as shown in Figure 1).

Most discussions around BN/PN/GRS (these terms were often used interchangeably) referenced the generally poor economic conditions in Sabah that is attributed to the decades of purported plundering from the federal-focused BN coalition.[18] Sabah, a state that is rich in natural resources

---

17 This event occurred when militants representing the defunct Sulu Sultanate invaded Sabah in a bid to reclaim the state and engaged with the Malaysian police and armed forces. The exchange that lasted more than a month, resulted in 10 fatalities amongst Malaysian forces, including one police officer.

18 BN, PN and GRS can be used interchangeably in these contexts because at this

Figure 1: Image highlighting the differences in development under BN for 26 years versus Warisan's 26 months. The image indicates that under BN there was nothing but a makeshift bridge using a collapsed communication tower with people crossing precariously while under Warisan, a proper bridge was created. (n.d.). Source: https://www.facebook.com/photo/?fbid=154294486240775.

is somehow lagging far behind many other Malaysian states in terms of overall development.[19] Many regions in Sabah still lack basic infrastructure or even access to roads.[20]

Commenters lay all this blame on their politicians who have sold their state over to the federal government: for them, it was a one-sided exchange that benefitted only those who associated themselves with the ruling political coalition, against the interests of Sabah as a whole. Many commenters suggest that voting GRS would be akin to inviting back the same criminals

stage, they were different configuration of coalitions partners. PN is a federal-level coalition comprising BERSATU, PAS, SAPP and STAR, with BN itself a coalition of three parties. GRS is another formally registered coalition specifically set up to contest the 2020 Sabah state election between PN, BN and another Sabahan party, Parti Bersatu Sabah (PBS).

19 Avila Geraldine, 'Sabah Ranks as Malaysia's Poorest State, Again', *New Straits Times Online*, 19 September 2020, https://www.nst.com.my/news/nation/2020/09/625711/sabah-ranks-malaysias-poorest-state-again.

20 Bung Moktar Radin made an electoral promise to focus on water and roads. 'Sabah's Basic Amenities, Infrastructure Will Be Upgraded, Says Bung Moktar'. *Bernama*, 30 September 2020, http://www.theedgemarkets.com/article/sabahs-basic-amenities-infrastructure-will-be-upgraded-says-bung-moktar.

to rob your house a second time. This particular line of thinking sheds some light on the deep-seated mistrust and resentment of Sabahans against Peninsular Malaysia.

Dissecting Cybertrooper Effectiveness

Similar to Peninsular Malaysian social media, the social media spaces in Sabah contain a highly noticeable cybertrooper or *macai* presence, and many Sabah political groups have openly admitted to recently deploying and utilising cybertroopers.[21] However, their effectiveness is not nearly as devastating as in Peninsular Malaysia in creating a spiral-of-silence effect because Sabahan online users can quickly identify and isolate cybertroopers and *macai*.

First, a cybertrooper/*macai* can be identified through the quality of their content, which varies greatly. Some will often make dozens of comments at a time with little thought for participating in a discussion or focus on debating or attacking opposing views. The latter action happens more frequently and these commenters behave like aggressive trolls where they attack opposing views to ensure that only supporting views are expressed in the comments. As the presence of obvious cybertroopers in comments is usually no more than a dozen, their attempts to overwhelm and distort discussions are not very effective and do not appear to do much to quell discussion – regular Sabahans simply ignore these comments to focus on others.

Secondly, cybertroopers stand out so much in the Sabah online space based on language usage. Sabahans make use of a local dialect of Bahasa Melayu called Bahasa Sabah. It is common to all Sabahans and differs in terms of vocabulary, pronunciation and unorthodox sentence structures. As a result, the written form of Bahasa Sabah is used throughout all Sabah social media spaces; to the average Sabahan, seeing its correct (or incorrect) usage in posts or comments is a signpost of credibility and authenticity worth the effort of meaningful engagement.

Considering the significance of this state election, there were expectations that Peninsular Malaysian cybertroopers would attempt to

---

21 'Warisan Hires RM500k Cybertroopers, Says GRS Man', *Daily Express Online*, https://www.dailyexpress.com.my/news/158872/warisan-hires-rm500k-cybertroopers/; 'BN Wasted Funds, Did Nothing, Opposition Cyber Troopers Told', *Borneo Today*, https://www.borneotoday.net/bn-wasted-funds-did-nothing-opposition-cyber-troopers-told/.

operate in these Sabah spaces. Indeed, their presence can be clearly seen as many commenters or posters would pretend to be Sabahan by inserting the ubiquitous Sabah colloquialism 'bah' randomly in sentences. Sabahans often see through this quite clearly as these Peninsular Malaysian cybertroopers have yet to adapt to the unique spelling and sentence structures that are second nature to any Sabahan. This severely limits the influence of non-Sabahan actors in these online spaces and makes Sabahans feel more comfortable: Anyone who passes the test of being a Sabahan online, whether a *macai* or not, is often treated with respect and engaged in conversation, which elevates these digital spaces closer to the ideals of a democratically deliberative discursive space.

Despite this positive outlook for Sabahans, we exercise caution in taking this at face value. We cannot ignore the possibility of the presence of highly trained and coordinated cybertroopers in these discussions, using more covert and subtle means to direct and nudge discussions without drawing attention to themselves. Throughout our analysis, we could very well be mistaking cybertroopers as regular Sabahans as well and that is of course the fundamental caveat – our research cannot be fully used as a barometer for public opinion. There is a possibility that these 'obvious' cybertroopers are used strategically as a bait-and-switch tactic to lull Sabahans into a false sense of security over posts or comments from anyone that isn't an obvious cybertrooper. Nevertheless, unlike Peninsular Malaysians, who have allowed their worldviews to be poisoned by the knowledge of cybertroopers so as to shut down any form of critical and healthy debate, we find Sabahans are still somewhat open to opposing views and still capable of listening to negative comments.

Organic Anti-federalist Discourse

An example of the interplay between cybertrooper/*macai*-injected discourse and organic local deliberative engagement is the formal relationship between Sabah as a 'state' and the Federal government's prerogatives. Despite the bitter partisanship that was raging between Warisan Plus and GRS, there was an overarching, common sentiment that was brought up in almost all discussions – the ongoing issue of Sabah's poor development and its continued subservience to the federal Malaysian government. In many comment sections, most issues affecting Sabah would often include several commenters highlighting that the root cause has and continues to be Sabah's servant role in relation to the federal government. Since the formation of Malaysia, Sabah has never had the full autonomy to govern itself and as such many of Sabah's issues and woes can be traced back to some form of lackadaisical governance, high corruption and a one-way exploitative relationship.[22]

When applied to political campaigns, this sentiment was so pervasive that it had a negative impact on *all* political parties. The main focus was often centred on GRS/PN/BN; particularly because PN is the current government and BN was in charge of the federal government since the formation of Malaysia. BN was essentially seen as a colonial power which had been exploiting all of Sabah's natural resources to enrich Peninsular Malaysia with visibly little return for Sabahans. Many commenters argue that parties which worked or aligned with the BN were selfish and corrupt individuals who provided everything that BN requested for without question as long as they could enrich themselves in the process. The long list of failures attributed to BN include: poor or failing infrastructure; dilapidated public facilities; and even the lack of basic access to paved roads within the interior of Sabah.

The focus of anti-federalism against Warisan Plus is not as straightforward as GRS, but many of its campaign materials and rhetoric are viewed through a similar cynical worldview. While the Warisan Plus campaign boasts many accomplishments within its short two-year tenure, commenters are quick to highlight other campaign promises that have failed to materialise, inclusive of greater autonomy and development. The historical connections of many of its leaders with BN[23] are also raised to highlight that the promises of Warisan being a 'Sabah First' party were merely a facade; like many other Sabah-based parties, it too played second fiddle to Putrajaya's hegemony. The longstanding allies of Warisan, the Peninsular Malaysia-based Democratic Action Party (DAP) and National Trust Party (Amanah), are also seen as extensions of Peninsular Malaysian influence that further dilute Warisan's authority and credibility within the state.

---

22 See James Chin, 'The 1963 Malaysia Agreement (MA63): Sabah And Sarawak and the Politics of Historical Grievances', in Sophie Lemiere (ed.) *Minorities Matter: Malaysian Politics and People* (Singapore: ISEAS–Yusof Ishak Institute: 2019).

23 Even the chief minister and leader of Warisan of Shafie Apdal himself was an UMNO vice president before he was sacked from UMNO in 2016.

Two major events that occurred in the run-up to these elections provided clear examples of Peninsular Malaysia's disrespectful attitudes towards the state of Sabah: the unexpected and vicious attacks from representatives of the federal government on a young, intrepid Sabahan university student and a Peninsular Malaysian MP making unrepentant derogatory remarks against Christianity.

For the former, Veveonah Mosibin, a University Malaysia Sabah student, became an overnight sensation across Malaysia in June 2020 because she livestreamed herself camping overnight in a tree to get better Internet reception to take her university exams online. She was forced to do so due to her home in the interior of Sabah having poor Internet connection and the university exams were now online due to Covid-19 restrictions. By July, this issue was raised in the Dewan Negara. However, the deputy communications and media minister, Zahidi Zainul Abidin, accused her of lying and ultimately claimed that there were no Internet connectivity issues in Sabah.[24] This caused an outpouring of public support for Veveonah as more evidence in her favour surfaced. Nevertheless, Vevonah became subject to vicious cyberbullying, forcing her to take her account offline.[25]

The Veveonah episode laid bare what many Sabahans have felt all this while; the federal government felt they have done a great job in developing Sabah, without reservations. The rebuke from the deputy minister was coached in this idea that many Peninsular Malaysians probably believed – that Sabah is as developed as the rest of the country and problematic infrastructure and poor Internet access cannot possibly be true. It is this tone of denial and ignorance that makes Sabahans feel like strangers in their own country as the federal government, whose job it is to ensure equal and balanced development for all states, has been derelict in its duties since the formation of Malaysia.

The second incident was when a federal MP, Nik Muhammad Zawawi

24 Sira Habibu, 'Zahidi Says Kudat MP Told Him Veveonah Did Not Have Exams on Day She Uploaded Video', *The Star*, 9 July 2020, https://www.thestar.com.my/news/nation/2020/09/07/zahidi-says-kudat-mp-told-him-veveonah-did-not-have-exams-on-day-she-uploaded-video.

25 Stephanie Lee, '"Treetop Girl" Veveonah Goes off the Grid Following Negative Comments on Social Media', *The Star*, 6 July 2020, https://www.thestar.com.my/news/nation/2020/09/06/039treetop-girl039-veveonah-goes-off-the-grid-following-negative-comments-on-social-media.

Salleh, from the conservative Malaysian Islamic Party (PAS) stated that the Bible was 'deviant' and thus all Christians are following a lost faith. This statement was made during a Parliamentary debate on drink-driving and this MP argued that the 'true Bible' did in fact ban the consumption of alcohol but it has since become deviant over centuries of people altering the text. This action was widely condemned by Christian groups from across Malaysia as an incredibly incendiary and disrespectful remark meant to insult and disrupt religious harmony, and his subsequent apology was not fully accepted by Christian leaders.[26]

Figure 2: Infographic image describing reactions of Sabah-based parties in GRS who did not respond to the insult of the Bible from PAS. (n.d.).
Source: https://www.facebook.com/photo?fbid=339712240801901

[26] Julian Leow, 'Religious Harmony — Bedrock for Nation's Prosperity, Development', *Herald Malaysia Online*, http://www.heraldmalaysia.com/index.php; Olivia Miwil, 'Sabahan Leaders Unhappy with Pas MP's Bible Remark', *NST Online*, 30 August 2020, https://www.nst.com.my/news/nation/2020/08/620700/sabahan-leaders-unhappy-pas-mps-bible-remark; Julia Chan, 'Sabah Churches Call for PAS MP to Be Investigated for Sedition after Bible Remarks', *Malay Mail*, 1 September 2020, https://www.malaymail.com/news/malaysia/2020/09/01/sabah-churches-call-for-pas-mp-to-be-investigated-for-sedition-after-bible/1899048; 'Christian Group Does Not Accept Zawawi's "Apology"', *Malaysiakini*, https://www.malaysiakini.com/news/550127.

For Sabahans, this incident is just one of many similar incidents which suggests the slow and subtle encroachment of Peninsular Malaysian-based politics into Sabah, potentially poisoning local culture. This tension between Islam and other religions is practically absent throughout Sabah as many commenters often highlight that Sabahans live a truly multicultural life where people of all beliefs can coexist in the same spaces. They consider that the religious rhetoric in Peninsular Malaysia has become incredibly fractious and toxic where Islam is seen as trying to embed itself throughout all aspects of the country with little respect given to those from other faiths.[27] Thus, many commenters express a great deal of fear about Peninsular Malaysian Islamic parties gaining a foothold in Sabah. This event was used to rebuke the entry of PAS into Sabah and to condemn any Sabah coalitions associated with them, most notably STAR and PBS from GRS, which includes PAS as a member.

All these arguments were raised consistently in most comment threads throughout the campaign period, to serve as a reminder to all Sabahans to carefully consider who they would be voting into government – your chosen elected representative should prioritise Sabah first, instead of Peninsular Malaysia. The common arguments used were highlighting past behaviours of candidates which favoured Peninsular Malaysia over Sabah cautioning against candidates who have ties with Peninsular Malaysian political entities.

Post-Elections: It was a Good Fight, But Let's Move On

Election day proceeded with little incident, but the real drama began as the results came out showing GRS having a clear majority. Political engagement remained high within social media spaces, although there was a distinct reduction in some forms of cybertrooper activity. Despite the obvious winner, rumours started to circulate that certain parties might change allegiances and Warisan Plus refused to accept the loss but instead sought to form the government through defections from GRS. Combined with some uncertainty within GRS over who would be the chief minister of Sabah, this resulted in a tense environment for several days where there was no

[27] This is also in consideration of the sentiment that Peninsular Malaysia has attempted to engineer a demographic shift towards a Muslim majority in Sabah through Project IC. Kamal Sadiq, 'When states prefer non-citizens over citizens: Conflict over illegal immigration into Malaysia', *International Studies Quarterly* 49, no. 1 (2005): 101-122.

Figure 3: Image in style of a news report, highlighting Shafie Apdal's refusal to admit defeat. (n.d.). Source: https://www.facebook.com/photo?fbid=125503235959253

Figure 4: Meme image in style of Shafie Apdal's 'Unity' poster with Bung Moktar and the caption 'Pakiu' referencing a vulgar word he uttered in Parliament in 2018 and the hashtag #SepaEndaMau (Nobody wants you). This image was created as a rejection of Moktar when he was mooted to be chief minister of Sabah. (n.d.). Source: https://www.facebook.com/photo?fbid=221404209406648

certainty over who would hold the post. Only on 29th September, three days after the election, Hajiji Mohd Noor was finally sworn in as chief minister.[28]

Within these three days, the Sabah social media space was fiery with activity as Sabahans deeply speculated over who would be taking office. Strong partisan comments and posts were made by both GRS and Warisan Plus supporters, fiercely advocating for why their politician deserved to become chief minister. Cybertroopers were highly involved in making both posts and comments through the heavy use of memes and simple

---

28 Hajiji was only sworn in as a state assemblyman a month later because he contracted Covid-19. Stephanie Lee, 'Hajiji Finally Sworn in as Rep after Covid-19 Recovery', *The Star*, 27 October 2020, https://www.thestar.com.my/news/nation/2020/10/27/hajiji-finally-sworn-in-as-rep-after-covid-10-recovery.

infographics (which are easily shared outside of Facebook). Posts supporting GRS highlighted the need for Warisan Plus to respect the election results and not to entice elected representatives or parties to switch sides. On the other hand, posts supporting Warisan Plus were focused on technicalities such as highlighting the illegitimacy of GRS as an unregistered coalition and that Warisan Plus was the single coalition with the highest number of seats, and thus deserved the chief minister seat.

Once the dust had settled with Hajiji and GRS as the new government of Sabah, these social media spaces took on a very different air. As Covid-19 cases started to rise rapidly in the state (exacerbated by the election) people were more focused on addressing this health crisis (and other issues in Sabah) than dwelling on the election. Cybertrooper activity was noticeably reduced, with the primary activity being the posting of a couple of politically charged posts a day, with little to no activity within comments sections. These posts tended to follow the same partisan style of posting during the elections, with routine attacks against parties, and politicians using common political rhetoric.

However, in a positive twist, despite the attempts by cybertroopers to continue the bitter cycle of polarising political rhetoric, many Sabahan commenters were quick to disengage from this line of discourse. Commenters commonly ignored many of these posts or asked these instigators to stop petty political infighting, and posited that since the elections were now over, and they should focus on supporting the new government in working on their electoral promises. These fair-minded commenters would be critical of both GRS and Warisan Plus supporters; they would regularly chastise Warisan Plus to accept the election loss while also being critical of GRS for not delivering on their campaign promises or for showing poor governance.

The first promise that was ostensibly broken by GRS was the appointment of a PAS assemblyman to the Sabah State Assembly, the first for the Peninsular Malaysian conservative Islamic party. Commenters were quick to press the Sabah parties within GRS, particularly STAR and PBS, who were adamant that PAS would not be part of the GRS government should they win. As political promises and manifestos are treated as the performance indicators for winning parties, this was seen as a reneging of a clear promise and is viewed as Sabah parties kowtowing to Peninsular Malaysian interests.

On the aspect of poor governance, GRS was seen as a glacial and lackadaisical government, reacting slowly to emerging crises and not responding effectively. Flash floods hit parts of Sabah within a week of the election and the GRS's government's weak response was heavily criticised on social media. The almost exponential increase in Covid-19 cases overwhelmed Sabah's healthcare system and resulted in the country's highest number of deaths.[29] Sabah commenters attributed this failure to GRS, who failed to appoint a health minister, which led to unclear leadership over the handling of the growing crisis. Another major failure was a publicity stunt by GRS to highlight the millions spent in care packages that were prepared to be distributed to families affected by the crisis, which did not include a well-thought through distribution plan.[30]

Figure 5 & 6: Screenshots of a post questioning the missing presence of opposition politicians; Screenshot of comments from the same post criticising the original poster and asking instead for the government to do its job and stop attacking the opposition. Source: https://www.facebook.com/groups/368703623956969/permalink/866930824134244

[29] Ashswita Ravindran, 'Sabah Pushed to the Brink in Covid-19 Fight', *CodeBlue* (blog), 12 October 2020, https://codeblue.galencentre.org/2020/10/12/sabah-pushed-to-the-brink-in-covid-19-fight/.

[30] 'Sabahans Call on State Govt to Improve Covid-19 Food Aid Programme', *Malay Mail*, 28 October 2020, https://www.malaymail.com/news/malaysia/2020/10/28/sabahans-call-on-state-govt-to-improve-covid-19-food-aid-programme/1917213.

Due to the government's embattled state, there were significant attempts by GRS cybertroopers to deflect attention from their issues. The misdirection involved blaming many of the current issues on the previous administration under Warisan Plus and to point out how many representatives of Warisan Plus were 'missing' during this crisis. Many of these posts were made quite regularly but were often ignored, gathering zero comments. For those with comments, Sabahans responded negatively by calling these claims ridiculous since Warisan Plus was no longer in power and the incumbent government needed to be more present and accountable. As far as cybertrooper activities go, these attempts were incredibly transparent and appeared as feeble acts of desperation from a government that was grasping at straws to correct their public image.

Conclusion: Lessons from the East

We are mindful that while these Facebook groups/pages are occupied by Sabahans, we are hesitant to suggest that these views and comments are fully representative of Sabah as a whole. From our observations, many of these commenters appear to be urban Sabahans from across the state, with many hailing from the Kota Kinabalu metropolitan area. Sabahans from the interiors and rural areas are likely to engage through WhatsApp groups rather than Facebook, as the latter consumes more Internet data – a limited and unreliable resource in rural Sabah.

Despite Sabahan digital platforms being incredibly fractured, divisive and polarised during the campaign period, Sabahan social media users did not forget the promises and impasses that were made by politicians and parties, but were also willing to work with the democratically elected government regardless of their own political affiliations. They also applied the same critical assessment towards the opposition, arguing that they should focus on playing their role as an effective opposition rather than reactionarily and divisively attacking any and all government actions (merit notwithstanding) to gain political mileage.

Peninsular Malaysian politics is a perfect representation of a highly polarised, divisive political environment.[31] Since GE14, the losing side of

---

[31] Bridget Welsh, 'Malaysia's Political Polarization: Race, Religion, and Reform', in *Political Polarization in South and Southeast Asia: Old Divisions, New Danger*, Carnegie Endowment for International Peace, https://carnegieendowment.

BN has used all manner of arguments and schemes to villainise and attack the government of the day. It has argued that the elections were won due to lies and slander, grossly misinterpreted and misrepresented all government policies and they then opposed any action by the government without merit. Of course, the PH government was also very quick to capitalise on their win and did not seek any sort of reconciliation with the opposition, which was entrenched in government for more than half a century. The end result – Peninsular Malaysia was more divided than ever as racial tensions were at an all-time high and bipartisan cooperation was virtually non-existent. This situation was further exacerbated and compounded by venomous and devastating cybertrooper and *macai* activity. The culmination of this tension was the collapse of the PH government as the racial rhetoric that was sown by BN dominated the discourse and led to a restoration of old race and religion-based values.

In contrast, the Sabah digital publics offer positive signs that Malaysian society can compartmentalise their politics to unite and work together for the betterment of their own society, independent of the political dynamics that a larger federal state brings to bear. Here, the unifying, centripetal impulse could come from several factors: there is a strong element of anti-Peninsular Malaysian sentiment, demonstrated in commenters challenging the new GRS to really stand by its promise that it will work to return more autonomy and wealth to Sabah. Another factor we suggest could be that cybertroopers are ineffective in masquerading as Sabahan publics and by exposing themselves as inauthentic actors, they inadvertently strengthen in-group sentiment amongst Sabahans. Overall, the greater pluralism that exists in Sabah (*vis-à-vis* the 'racial silos' of Peninsular Malaysian politics) corresponds with the idea that the 'ethnic cross-cuttingness' can decrease conflict likelihood and resist divisive rhetoric.[32]

The Sabah digital publics are exemplary of a society that can see beyond partisan borders and come together through a bitter and questionable election. Instead of arguing on the semantics and technicalities of the election, the new government is given a chance to prove itself, which was

org/2020/08/18/malaysia-s-political-polarization-race-religion-and-reform-pub-82436.

32 Joel Sawat Selway, 'Cross-Cuttingness, Cleavage Structures and Civil War Onset', *British Journal of Political Science* 41, no. 1 (2011): 111–38.

never afforded by the opposition in Peninsular Malaysia. Time will tell if cybertroopers will eventually overwhelm the more optimistic democratic values displayed in Sabah, which is why it's imperative that the positive values espoused by the people of Sabah are studied and understood. Peninsular Malaysia sorely needs to take a page from Sabah to refresh its democratic norms and take more steps towards overcoming its tribal tendencies in spite of the negative influence of social media in public sphere deliberations.

Chapter 9

Sabah Style amidst Uncertainty: Campaigning in the 2020 Sabah State Polls[1]

Bridget Welsh

Introduction

The campaign in Sabah's 2020 state election (PRN2020) began officially after nominations were announced on 12 September, but they had de facto been in the works after the state assembly was dissolved at the end of July. Unevenly, with difficult seat negotiations within parties and between political alliances hampering on-the-ground campaigning, candidates slowly began battling for 73 different constituencies. The two-week official campaign was intense, in a contest where 78 per cent of the seats were seen to be competitive.[2] Ultimately, the election was won by the Perikatan Nasional (PN) federal government-linked new alliance Gabungan Rakyat Sabah (GRS), which defeated the Pakatan Harapan (PH)-aligned Warisan Plus and all the other smaller parties to secure a victory of 38 to 32 seats. Three independent candidates also won, allying themselves with GRS, giving the GRS alliance a larger majority in the state assembly.

1 The author would like to thank Philip Golingai and my fellow editors for their comments on the chapter and Jillian Simon and Mahirah Marzuki for their assistance with background research. Errors are the responsibility of the author.

2 Competitiveness was assessed based on interviews, candidate slates and previous voting patterns.

Election Campaigns in Context

Campaigns in Malaysia have been important in shaping electoral outcomes. Foremost, election campaigns are widely publicised and participatory, framed as a period for ordinary citizens to engage in 'politics'. Arguably, this is the most intense time of political engagement between the electorate and politicians. Given the large number of Malaysians, including Sabahans, who disengage from the contentious ongoing everyday political discourse but tune in during campaigns, this period is essential in how citizens participate (or do not participate) in the democratic process. Second, campaigns have mattered in shaping results, decisively so. The 14th General Election (GE14) is perhaps the most recent example, where the opposition PH went into the campaign as the underdog and emerged the winner. This also occurred in Sabah in 2018, when Warisan became a political force, winning 29 seats with its political allies to position itself to take control of the state. The campaign messaging that parties adopt and how they mobilise supporters shape their electoral fortunes. Third, the effects of the campaigns are impactful because every election involves a different electorate, with large numbers of young voters coming of voting age. We also see more swing voters who change their political allegiances and large numbers of 'undecided' voters waiting to be wooed by contenders. In 2020 Sabah had 18.3 per cent new voters, a history of voters changing their loyalties in GE14 (where then newcomer Warisan captured 32.5 per cent of the vote) and, based on focus group interviews in early September, large numbers who were undecided about who to support in the 2020 campaign when it started. The fact that the polls occurred suddenly, as a result of pressures to remove the Warisan government in July, only served to make the campaign even more important.

This chapter looks in-depth at the Sabah PRN2020 campaign. Rather than laying out a description of the high (and low) points of the campaign, the focus is on how campaigning in Sabah differs from the rest of Malaysia, and how PRN2020 compared with other Sabah campaigns. The argument developed is that there is indeed a 'Sabah style' tied to the unique socio-political demographic realities of the state. Much of this is tied to the challenges of survival that many Sabahans face in their everyday lives. At the same time, Sabah reflects broader trends that are taking place in the changing practices of Malaysian election campaigning, where campaigns are becoming more multi-faceted, targeted and modern.

Below, I lay out four features of the Sabah campaign – messaging, mobilisation, allegiances and divisions. I argue that while Warisan Plus campaigned hard and adopted many innovative 'modern' techniques, it was at a disadvantage when the federal government applied its resource advantage in the state election and supported its allies in a 'full-on' campaign. GRS was ultimately more effective in harnessing different techniques and using local conditions in Sabah to its advantage, particularly tapping into heightened insecurities in a period of political and economic uncertainty. It would seem that 'traditional' politics beat out 'modern' politics, but in fact both campaigns used both forms of campaigning. In the final analysis, victory came to the parties that were able to better adapt 'old' politics to the new conditions. In PRN2020 this was GRS. The chapter is based on field research conducted from August through September 2020 in Sabah and draws from interviews with candidates and voters across the state. This includes visits to all of the districts in Sabah, and focus-group interviews in 'hot seats' during the campaign period. These findings are complemented by an in-depth analysis of social media – Facebook and WhatsApp groups – during and after the campaign.

Politics of Appropriation: Messaging and Message

Despite the Sabah campaign arising from a snap poll, the varied campaigns were quite sophisticated and targeted. Both campaigns adopted slick modern professional messaging techniques, tying their campaigns around leadership and calculated messages about identity and Sabah itself.

The most prominent poster of the Sabah campaign was arguably the Warisan Plus 'Unity' billboards fashioned in Obama-esque 'Hope'-like colors and style.[3] Warisan centered its campaign on its chief minister, Shafie Apdal and tied his leadership to messages of 'unity' and 'dignity'. The phrase 'we are here to build a nation, not a particular race or religion' resonated with liberal supporters nationwide. It was reinforced by calls to recognise religion across faiths, 'In God we trust, unite we must,' while promoting a stronger 'united' Sabah with dignity: *#BerpaduDemiMaruah*. These ideals tapped into the imagination of voters, of a Sabah that led Malaysia through ethnic harmony

---

3 This chapter extends from an article written in the field; Bridget Welsh, 'Old and New Politics Blend in Sabah', *Malaysiakini*, 18 September 2020, https://www.malaysiakini.com/columns/543140

and its combined strength. It hit head-on against the divisive messages of race and religion that typified traditional Barisan Nasional (BN) campaigns and extended the notion of a 'special' Sabah led by Warisan among its supporters. Shafie Apdal was portrayed as a 'modern' leader, representing Sabah for all Sabahans. By extension from the peninsula, Shafie was seen as a Malay leader representing all Malaysians.

GRS, on its part, organised its campaign around Prime Minister Muhyiddin Yassin, tapping into his popularity in allocating Covid-19 relief (known as Bantuan Prihatin Nasional [National Relief Aid]) and attention to the economy. GRS recognised that economic issues – unemployment, low wages, slow growth – were the most salient concerns among Sabahans.[4] GRS posters featured a more traditional paternalistic message: '*#abahkitabah*' (our father) with a token Sabah 'bah' linguistic flavor. The GRS campaign appropriated the phrase '*#kitajagakita*' from the civil society campaign, aiming to build solidarity while reinforcing the protector image typical of BN campaigning. Muhyiddin was portrayed as '*#abahtetapsayangsabah*' (a father that deeply loves Sabah). He was thus showcased as a loving protective father for Sabah, a father that would take care of their wellbeing.

Not to be left out in the narratives were the messages of UMNO, campaigning strategically under the rubric of BN and loosely tied to GRS. Here, Sabah party chief Bung Moktar Radin was featured as the leader for the state, in a fighting stance with his fist raised. The fighting theme was replicated across the young slate of UMNO candidates fielded. The main theme revolved around a battle, with candidates regularly signaling the need to fight with their body language. Messaging spoke for the need to work hard for victory for party survival. The label '*radu tetap radu*' (fight to the end) signaled that the fight must continue despite obstacles. Campaigning focused on rallying the party faithful to protect UMNO's presence in Sabah, to continue to fight for Malay (Muslim) rights and the return to national leadership. Sabah was portrayed as the arena for the renewal of the party,

---

4 Three different organisations conducted and reported their surveys conducted the campaign – Society Empowerment and Economic Development of Sabah (SEEDS), Ilham Center and Merdeka Center, with one common theme. See, for example, Tarrence Tan, 'Economic Issues will Influence How Young Sabahans vote says think tank', *The Star*, 6 September 2020, https://www.thestar.com.my/news/nation/2020/09/06/economic-issues-will-influence-how-young-sabahans-vote-says-think-tank.

building indirectly on the party's success in the January 2020 Kimanis by-election.[5] As with GRS, BN attacked Warisan's economic performance and implied that their fight would be a fight for their supporters.

These contrasting portrayals of leadership, of unifier, protector and fighter, were targeted at the party's core base and potential supporters, but simultaneously involved different assumptions about the ideological orientations of their voters. Warisan's appeal spoke particularly to non-Muslims and liberals, while GRS led by Muhyiddin and UMNO spoke to more conservative paternalistic voters, reinforcing old feudal models of governance.[6] All the campaigns were 'masculine' campaigns, with UMNO's 'fight' message the most so. While Bung's image was tied to his personality, both Muhyiddin's and Shafie's portrayals were tied to their personas – with all of these messages clearly aimed at winning/empowering their base and widening their appeal. In all of the messages, Sabah was centre stage – a role model, a place to protect or a place for renewal. In all of the messages, there was a sense of strengthening in the face of adversity.

While campaign messages are regularly analysed for what is portrayed, in PRN2020 – and arguably other Malaysian campaigns as well – the equally impactful messages were those unspoken or framed in the responses to public messages, particularly those circulated on social media and messaging applications, notably Facebook and WhatsApp. Other chapters in this collection focus more specifically on these messages, but it is worth integrating these more hidden narratives with the public campaigns.

Warisan's 'unity' campaign, for example, was in part a response to the effective attacks on the party within Sabah as predominantly representing the Bajau-Suluk community (to the exclusion of other communities) and supporting the 'irregular' immigrant communities *Pendatang Asing Tanpa Izin* (PATI).The call for unity was an attempt to bridge this race-based attack, which especially targeted Warisan's ally United Progressive Kinabalu Organisation (UPKO) which has traditionally been a Kadazan, Dusun and Murut (KDM) party. For many, KDM calls for 'unity' were reminders of

---

5 For more details see: Bridget Welsh, 'Kimanis: An UMNO Revival?' *Malaysiakini*, 20 January 2020, https://www.malaysiakini.com/columns/507936

6 Chandra Muzaffar, *Protector? An Analysis of Leader-Led Political Relationships in Malay Society* (Penang: Aliran Press, 1979) and Shaharuddin Maaruf, *Concept of a Hero in Malay Society*, (Petaling Jaya: SIRD, 2014).

'disunity' the party was believed to facilitate.[7] At the same time, for other minorities, such as Chinese Sabahans, the unity message was about their inclusion, messages the other parties ignored. Chinese Sabahans have been disempowered over the years from their traditional 'kingmaker' role and the respectful calls for inclusion resonated.[8] For some Malays/Muslims, the unity call was quietly attacked as an effort to displace their prominent political role, and Islam as the dominant national faith. 'Unity' was seen as an attempt to divide their 'unity', the *ummah*. Most of these counter-campaigns however were less overt, using WhatsApp messages through trusted networks and quiet signaling. For the Malay/Muslim community, Telegram was also an important medium. The disunity calls played an integral part on the ground, tapping into insecurities and fears of displacement. They reflect the continued salience of divisions among ethnic communities and different views of place within Sabah and Malaysia. Unity calls ironically heightened attention to the category of race among the different communities, in ways not directly implied in Warisan's unity message.

A similar contradictory reaction was provoked by Muhyiddin's 'protector' father role. Rather than being seen positively, in contrast it was one of a predator. He and his close allies in the PN government such as Azmin Ali and Hamzah Zainuddin (who was targeted for his perceived role, together with former Chief Minister/Shafie's predecessor Musa Aman, in instigating the downfall of the Warisan Plus government) were portrayed as using Sabah's election for their political ambitions. Senior opposition leaders such as former chief minister Bernard Dompok and former Malaysian Chief Justice Richard Malanjum spoke about Peninsular leaders using the state for their advantage, with the referent of the PN government implicitly clear. Sabah was a 'victim of a power play' by federal leaders, it was argued.[9]

---

7 See Benjamin YH Loh and Kevin Zhang, 'Sabah 2020 Elections: Sentiments Trending on Social Media', *ISEAS Perspective* no, 106, 23 September 2020, https://www.iseas.edu.sg/wp-content/uploads/2020/09/ISEAS_Perspective_2020_106.pdf.

8 Danny Wong Tze Ken, 'Weaker Kingmakers? Chinese Politics in Sabah under Mahathir,' in Bridget Welsh (ed.) *Reflections: The Mahathir Years* (Washington DC: Johns Hopkins SAIS, 2004), 199-209.

9 See, for example, 'Sabah Victim of Federal Power Play Says Ex CM Dompok,' *Malay Mail*, 23 September 2020, https://www.malaymail.com/news/malaysia/2020/09/23/sabah-victim-of-federal-power-play-says-ex-cm-dompok/1905810.

Not to be left out, Bung's image as a fighter was also disputed, even panned. One widely circulated video involved him childishly sitting on an escalator, aimed to portray Bung as a fool, and not capable of state leadership. He was attacked personally for his perceived crass style, labeled '*Pakiu*' for how he used expletive language in Parliament. The same contradictory portrayal was used to showcase failure in how he fights and behaves. The views resonated differently, with the attacks on Bung actually adding fire to his supporters as they confirmed the need to 'fight on'.

These messages and the counter-messages shared common threads – calculated appeals to emotion and ideas of place within, about and 'for' Sabah. The campaign lacked meaningful discussion of policies, programmes to address Sabah's challenges or the real economic and social problems Sabahans were facing. While leaders were featured, their records in government were largely generalised and simplified around Covid-19 governance or last-minute land distribution by Warisan Plus. Records featured as fodder for attacks, not for laying out a vision for Sabah moving forward. The form of messaging may have been modern, with sophistication in the messaging and signaling on par with professional advertising campaigns, but the types of messages were in substance less sophisticated, touching on traditional insecurities.

Politics of Promise: Mobilisation and Money Politics

Beyond messages, Malaysian campaigns have been about the ability to mobilise the electorate, to use and oil party machinery, often with money and government resources. These factors were prominent in PRN2020.[10] As with the messaging, the mobilisation took on a Sabah character, distinct from both Peninsular Malaysia and Sarawak. Political parties going into Sabah polls were comparatively weaker/weakened; many lacked the same membership foundation, with many of the parties such as Bersatu new, others such as UMNO rebuilding and others working to recover from party

---

10 See, for example, Arnold Puyok, 'Kota Marudu and Keningau, Sabah: Personality, Patronage and Parochial Politics,' in Meredith Weiss (ed.), *Electoral Dynamics in Malaysia* (Petaling Jaya/Singapore: SIRD/ISEAS, 2014), 181-196. The broader impact of party machinery is made by Meredith Weiss, *The Roots of Resilience: Party Machines and Grassroots Politics in Singapore and Malaysia* (Singapore: NUS Press, 2020).

defections/splits, notably UPKO and PKR. This made PRN2020 a critical window to reconnect with the electorate, and ultimately (re)shape party fortunes. This also made for intensity in the contest, which was compounded by the singular national political focus on Sabah and the high stakes connected to the outcome at both federal and state levels.

Studies of mobilisation in Sabah have regularly pointed to federal advantage centred around greater control and access to resources.[11] This contest was unique in that Warisan Plus had its own resources as the state incumbent. At the same time, with the election occurring during the Covid-19 period and an economic downturn, the role that the federal government could play in mobilisation was especially salient. Throughout, money – or rather the promise of money – played a major role in shaping campaign mobilisation on the ground.

Understanding the role that money plays in Sabah begins with who enters the fray. Arguably more than in other parts of Malaysia, campaigns in Sabah at the individual level have been about making money – or rather the dream of making money. Individual financial gains usually involve pocketing shares of the funds distributed for campaigning and ultimately winning office to secure contracts – both of which are as common in Sabah as they are in the rest of Malaysia. Yet in Sabah, campaigns inject opportunities for potential candidates. Traditionally, independent candidates have been 'bought' out with a sizable quick sum given to the lucky individual, whose name remains on the ballot but does not campaign. This practice is less common now as more candidates are contesting, thus reducing the effect of removing a potential challenger. In fact, in Sabah's polls more independents were encouraged to enter, with many believed to have been sponsored to do so. A total of 56 independent candidates contested, along with 228 from smaller parties – the largest number of candidates in any state campaign, resulting in an unprecedented number of multi-cornered contests.

During the campaign, I interviewed many of these independent and

---

[11] See, for example, Mohamad Nawab Mohamad Osman, 'A transitioning Sabah in a changing Malaysia,' *Kajian Malaysia* 35, no. 1 (2017): 23-40; Faisal S. Hazis, 'Domination, contestation, and accommodation: 54 years of Sabah and Sarawak in Malaysia,' *Southeast Asian Studies* 7, no. 3 (2018): 341-361 and James Chin, 'Exporting the BN/UMNO model: Politics in Sabah and Sarawak,' in Meredith Weiss (ed.) *Routledge Handbook of Contemporary Malaysia*, (London: Routledge, 2014), 83-92.

smaller party candidates, asking the reasons why they ran for office and their perceived electoral prospects. While answers differed, there were two important consistencies. First, independents and candidates from smaller parties run in Sabah because they (genuinely) think they can win. Part of this is an inherent Sabah optimism, but most of this is driven by an appreciation of how individual factors such as personality, family and ethnic appeals can win support. Partisan loyalties are comparatively not as strong among the electorate as in Peninsular Malaysia. Not surprisingly, repeatedly, candidates had a logic of how they could secure victory, connecting their campaigns with representing their ethnic community, local networks or particular grievances or causes.

At the same time, elections in Sabah are seen as personal 'opportunities' for social advancement. Losing did not necessarily mean a loss, as a person's standing within the community could rise. For many candidates, participating was about reinforcing their local networks. Almost all the candidates that were fielded were from local areas or had family roots in the constituencies. Often, competing was not about the individual alone, but the family's fortunes as a whole. Disproportionately, most of the independent (and many smaller party) candidates actually lost money in the campaign. Nevertheless, many pledged to return for the next round.

Sabah's PRN2020 offered a particularly promising path for political opportunities for Bersatu. Generally, Malaysian elections reflect a broader trend in seeing more diversity among candidates. Many of Sabah's entrenched elites had been dislodged in 2018, with the 2020 contest seen as highly competitive. The entrance of a new party – as Warisan itself had been two years earlier in GE14 – offered different elites and individuals a new vehicle for advancement. Not surprisingly, there was intensive jockeying to become a Bersatu candidate, in part because there was a potential for 'secure' federal income attached. In multiple seats, especially where Bersatu did not have an established leader, lobbying and mobilisation of members began in earnest. The party's elections in June contributed to this mobilisation, as new local alignments in support occurred, fueled by access to funds and the promise of future funds. Bersatu would capture 11 seats in the election and expand its party membership. While most elected were incumbents (7), new local mobilisation and money tied to that mobilisation was part of the party's success. Bersatu Sabah became the strongest political base in any state for the party (more than Johor), making Sabah an integral part of Prime

Minister Muhyiddin's political fortunes and in the process tying Sabah even more closely to trajectories for Malaysia. At the same time, Sabah became an arena for even greater political opportunism.

While a new federal party was embraced locally, the pledging of federal funds for Sabah was sorely lacking in PRN2020. Traditionally, Sabah politics (along with that of Sarawak) has been understood to be the product of developmentalism, tied to the promise of specific projects and allocations.[12] Sarawak elections – usually timed separately from national polls – have been especially full of promised projects.[13] What was striking is how completely devoid the PRN2020 campaign was of meaningful spending commitments on both sides of the divide. Development – or rather the lack thereof – was a major campaign issue, from poor Internet infrastructure to persistent poverty. Rather than offer concrete solutions, the campaigns engaged in a blame game, accusing each other of neglect and failure. Jeffrey Kitingan, for example, blamed Shafie Apdal for failing to develop the state when he was rural development minister, while Warisan Plus continued to lay blame on UMNO.[14]

What accounted for this rhetorical rather than concrete discussion of resources? The contest's competitiveness and associated political uncertainty were certainly contributing factors, as neither side was assured of victory or of remaining in office. Usually, this greater insecurity would yield more commitments to secure political security, especially at the federal level, rather than less. In this case, both sides opted for a strategy of displacement of responsibility. GRS opted to shift its spending focus to centre on Covid-19 relief money, with Bantuan Prihatin Nasional signs peppering constituencies,

---

12 Francis Loh Kok-Wah, 'A 'New Sabah' and the Spell of Development: Resolving Federal-State Relations in Malaysia,' *South East Asia Research* 4, no. 1 (1996): 63-83; 'Understanding politics in Sabah and Sarawak: an overview,' *Kajian Malaysia XV*, no. 1/2 (1997). For a broader discussion of the developmentalism concept, see Francis Loh Kok Wah. 'Developmentalism and the limits of democratic discourse,' in Francis Loh Kok Wah and Khoo Boo Teik (eds.), *Democracy in Malaysia*, (London: Routledge, 2014), 33-64.

13 Faisal S. Hazis, *Domination and Contestation: Muslim Bumiputera Politics in Sarawak* (Singapore: Institute of Southeast Asian Studies, 2012).

14 'Shafie did nothing for Sabah as Federal Minister says Jeffrey,' *Free Malaysia Today*, 25 September 2020, https://www.freemalaysiatoday.com/category/nation/2020/09/25/shafie-did-nothing-for-sabah-as-federal-minister-says-jeffrey/.

thus targeting its allocations at the individual rather than the community level. With the prospect of Warisan Plus winning Sabah, the PN federal government was reluctant to make any promises to support development projects at the state level. They had done comparatively little to support the state when PN assumed office from March, due to the state being held by the opposing political camp. Instead, PN regularly alluded to an ambiguous promise of greater federal spending if they won power.

Warisan was also reluctant to make concrete promises. Warisan had won considerable support in GE14 by making promises at the local level – bridges, roads and infrastructure projects, appropriating the use of promised spending to its advantage. Its success was tied to differentiating itself from UMNO/BN.[15] The inability of Warisan Plus to deliver on these promises, its over-promising, was one of the underlying reasons for its drop in support in some constituencies, such as Nabawan and Sook. One prominent failed promise repeatedly mentioned by voters was the RM300 state Covid-19 assistance which they claimed did not arrive, which was often contrasted with federal Bantuan Prihatin Nasional delivery. Both campaigns moved from specific spending promises to the promise of spending. Throughout, many Sabahans expressed scepticism about delivery from the government as they are used to surviving on their own, but at the same time holding out hope for better conditions – as the reality of persistent neglect of development of the state is stark.

Money played a third role in the campaign: to woo voters. This is the 'money' feature most associated with Borneo campaigns. Local election watchdog, Bersih 2.0, for example, documented widespread use of 'incentives' in exchange for votes during the Sabah campaign.[16] Voters reported receiving anywhere from RM300-RM900 for their support,

---

15 James Chin, 'Sabah and Sarawak in the 14th General Election 2018 (GE14): local factors and state nationalism,' *Journal of Current Southeast Asian Affairs* 37, no. 3 (2018): 173-192.

16 Bersih 2.0, *Laporan Pemerhatian Pilihan Raya Umum Negeri Kali Ke-16*, October 2020, http://www.bersih.org/wp-content/uploads/2020/10/Laporan-Pemerhatian-Pilihan-Raya-Umum-Negeri-Sabah-Kali-Ke-16.pdf. See also Ainaa Aman, 'Widespread Vote Buying in Villages during Sabah Polls Claims Bersih 2.0,' *Free Malaysia Today*, 12 October 2020, https://www.freemalaysiatoday.com/category/highlight/2020/10/12/widespread-vote-buying-in-villages-during-sabah-polls-claims-bersih-2-0/.

although the majority of voters bemoaned a lack of funds distributed to the ground. The amounts distributed varied by the seat, the parties contesting and competitiveness. In seats like Bongawan and Karambunai, amounts increased as the campaign evolved. Importantly, what distinguished PRN2020 is that this practice of distributing money occurred across the political divide.

This feature helps us understand that the money advantage associated with traditional campaigning no longer exclusively favored the PN/BN, nor was the practice concentrated in rural areas. Based on interviews, there were three different categories of seats – those that did not distribute funds to voters but involved campaign expenses (limited), seats where modest levels of funds were used, largely allocations from parties (moderate), and finally, a third group of seats where party and personal funds flowed, often by multiple contesting parties (significant). This third group of seats involved spending over RM1 million, with some seats extending into the multiple millions. The findings show that significant 'money' seats – across different geographic areas – were the most competitive, while those seats involving moderate or limited money spent were the least competitive and were won by larger margins. While in specific seats the financial advantage did contribute to the victory of candidates, PRN2020 suggests a needed rethink of the role of money generally – it was not a guarantee of victory. In fact, seats involving less spending of money – and more modern campaigning – were more secure.

Table 1: Money Politics Advantage in Sabah Polls

Role of Money	Urban	Semi-Rural/ Urban	Rural	Total Seats	Spending Range	Share Majority
Significant	4	28	12	44	Above RM1,000,0000	19%
Moderate	8	8	3	19	>RM500-RM1,000,000	30%
Limited	2	6	2	10	<RM500	39%

The distribution of money on the ground also varied. While the focus is on vote-buying, this was arguably the least common expense, occurring only in seats where there were intensive slush competitions such as Bongawan, Sook and Karambunai. It also remains unclear how much vote-buying shapes outcomes, as the candidate often perceived to be spending the most funds in many seats ultimately lost. In GE14, vote-buying similarly did not yield the results expected, suggesting that the mode of 'buying and supporting' is not as stable in shaping outcomes as believed.

What is not often understood is that the most money spent in Sabah elections have to do with conditions in Sabah itself. Large shares of funds are spent on the mobilisation of voters, with high costs to bring voters to the polls. *Duit tambang* (travel fare) can be costly as it involves ferrying in voters living on islands to the polling station and bringing voters in hired vans/ four-wheel-drive vehicles from remote areas without roads. Transportation outside of the major towns is poor, and the inadequate infrastructural conditions are well-known. Sabah's large number of outstation voters – estimated at 18 per cent of the electorate – also add to the costs. A similar payment is the *duit rugi* (compensation money) – the funds to cover the loss of income foregone to vote. Many Sabahans subsist on daily wages and the loss of a day's pay can affect a family's well-being. Finally, there is the social obligation of support for vulnerable families in need – for a child's school uniform, for medication or for food. Candidates are asked to provide local social services in financial allocations to families. Sabah's high poverty rate– estimated at 19.5 per cent of households – contributes to these demands, along with the inadequacy of the social safety net.[17] These practices – *duit tambang, duit rugi* and 'donations' – are expected and expensive, regularly promised and delivered expenses. Mobilisation of voters at the local level in Sabah requires investment, and these contributions are regularly seen by winners and losers alike as leading to victory, as was the case in PRN2020 as well.

Politics of the Familiar: Incumbency and Personality

From the promise of rewards, failed promises of development to local promises of support, money was an integral part of the PRN2020 campaign. A key element of this was the person making these promises and engaging

[17] Malaysia Department of Statistics, *Household Income and Basic Amenities Survey Report*, 2020, https://www.dosm.gov.my/v1/index.php?r=column/cthemeByCat&cat=323&bul_id=c3JpRzRqeTNPamMxL1FpTkNBNUVBQT09&menu_id=amVoWU54UTl0a21NWmdhMjFMMWcyZz09#:~:text=In%20terms%20of%20value%2C%20the,%2C402%20to%20RM4%2C916.

in their distribution. Studies of Sabah elections have regularly highlighted the personality and personal dimensions – themes addressed in other parts of this collection.[18]

In the campaign on the ground, the talk is often about the person, not the policies. Sabah politics is highly localised and personalised, similar to dynamics in Sarawak. Almost all of the candidates contesting are locals, with family ties, sometimes through marriage. While some candidates live (and work) outstation in the urban centers, social connections and standing in localities matter. Churches and *surau* are often the first arena where candidates are assessed, as schoolmates and work colleagues share personal stories about the candidates and their families.

For many voters, especially the more vulnerable voters, an important part of a candidate's character was whether they were generous. Candidates are assessed as either 'Santa Claus' or 'Scrooge' – with expectations higher for those who have held positions and garnered contracts.[19] Candidates who have benefitted from the system but do not deliver financially are resented. Along with support is the issue of access. Voters, especially those in semi-rural and rural areas, want to be able to connect to their representative, to be able to know he (or she) is there and can be trusted to be generous when needed, not just during the election campaign. This factor helps us understand why well-known personalities that had lost in GE14, such as former Chief Minister Salleh Said Keruak and victorious independent candidate Rubin Balang were returned to office. It also helps us understand why candidates such as Peter Anthony of Warisan and Ewon Benedick of UPKO won support, as they were both seen to have brought changes to their communities in a short period of time and were accessible, and were rewarded for doing so.

This politics of the familiar is part of Sabah campaigns, and particularly salient in PRN2020. The election occurred in a period of high uncertainty, under the Covid-19 shadow, an economic downturn and the reality of

[18] See, for example, Arnold Puyok, 'Kota Marudu and Keningau, Sabah: Personality, Patronage and Parochial Politics,' in Meredith Weiss, *Electoral Dynamics in Malaysia* (Petaling Jaya: SIRD/ISEAS, 2014), 181-196.

[19] The term 'Santa Claus' was first coined here for the Sabah PRN2020: 'Manggis is the talk of Kemabong', *The Star*, 21 September 2020, https://www.thestar.com.my/news/nation/2020/09/21/manggis-is-the-talk-of-kemabong

political instability ever-present at the state and federal levels. A general argument runs that in difficult conditions, voters engage in a 'flight to safety'. In Sabah, they flocked to the familiar – a flight to candidates (and parties developed below) who made them feel safe, or at least did not contribute to further unknowns and uncertainties.

If there was one predominant finding in the election results it is the return of incumbents. Based on assessing seats from GE14, 40 incumbents, or 55 per cent, were returned to office.[20] This does not include new candidates who won seats they had held in some capacity before, or winners of new seats that were carved out from the areas where they previously represented, which would increase this figure. Generally, despite the change in government, Sabah's polls were about sticking with what was known to voters. Incumbents won by a comfortable 30 per cent margin on average, and despite perceptions that this was common in more rural areas, margins were higher in more urban areas. Only five seats changed parties across political alliances, with a contrasting average majority of 9 per cent.[21] Even shifts to different parties within alliances (where there was a choice between the GRS parties) occurred with a low average majority of 13 per cent. Independents only won with an average 8 per cent majority. In contrast, staying with the party that won the seat before – even with a new candidate – the average majority was 28 per cent, on par with the level of support for incumbents. Voters stayed with what they knew, the candidates and parties they were comfortable with. DAP incumbents performed the strongest, while Warisan incumbents won with less secure average majorities.

---

[20] Incumbency is assessed based on winning the same seat by a candidate that held the seat from GE14, not necessarily a new seat that might cover the same area or a return from an earlier term as assemblyperson for a seat, which would make the number higher. The seats with incumbents are: Banggi, Tanjong Kapor, Matunggong, Kadamaian, Sulaman, Tamparuli, Kiulu, Likas, Api-Api, Luyang, Tanjung Aru, Petagas, Kapayan, Kawang, Bongawan, Membakut, Klias, Kuala Penyu, Sindumin, Kundasang, Karanaan, Tambunan, Bingkor, Melalap, Sugut, Gun-Gum, Karamunting, Elopura, Tanjong Papat, Tungku, Silam, Kunak, Sulabayan, Seballang, Bugaya, Merotai, Kuamut, Sook, Paginatan, and Apas.

[21] A total of 19 seats changed their affiliation to another party or to independent status. For details see Andrew Ong, 'Eight Takeaways from Sabah Polls,' *Malaysiakini*, 29 September 2020, https://www.malaysiakini.com/news/544494. My focus is on change of political alliances, excluding independents that jumped to the other side and still won their seats in Kuala Penyu and Paginatan.

Table 2: Changes in Support: Incumbency and Party

Shifts in Support	Seats	Average Majority Share	Incumbents by Party	Incumbent Seats	Average Majority Share
Changed Party	5	9%	Bebas	1	14%
Changed Party w/in Alliance	3	13%	Bersatu	7	35%
Changed to Independent	2	8%	PBS	4	19%
Incumbents	40	30%	STAR	4	33%
New Seats	13	16%	UMNO	1	22%
New Candidate, Same Party	10	28%	DAP	5	65%
Rural Incumbents	10	17%	PKR	1	46%
Semi-rural Incumbents	20	34%	UPKO	1	22%
Urban Incumbents	10	37%	Warisan	16	20%

My other chapter (Chapter 11) in this collection looks at other factors shaping voting behavior, but this discussion of familiarity is part of the campaign discussion because it shows how central the emotions of insecurity and trust were in the election, and became integral parts of campaign messaging, patterns of mobilisations and frames for understanding voter engagement. Snap polls – 28 months after an earlier election – held at a time of heightened insecurity was not a period for risk or 'change', but for remaining with the person or party that was known, even, for many, when the person and party was (often far) less than perfect.

Politics of Division: Pragmatism and Persistence

If insecurity and trust made up the politics of the familiar, the emotions of anger and resentment could be found in the politics of division. Traditionally, scholars have pointed to personal and family feuds driving Sabah campaigns.[22] For many years, ethnic divisions were the paramount

[22] See Bruce Gale, 'Politics at the Periphery: A Study of the 1981 and 1982 Election Campaigns in Sabah,' *Contemporary Southeast Asia*, 6, no. 1 (1984): 26-49; Francis Loh Kok Wah, 'Strongmen and federal politics in Sabah,' in *Elections and Democracy in Malaysia*, (Bangi: Penerbit Universiti Kebangsaan Malaysia, 2005), 71-117.

explanation, underscoring the repeated returns of UMNO to power from 1986 to 2018.[23] More recently, state nationalism – opposing federal power – has taken centre stage.[24] In PRN2020 we saw all of these, but in Sabah style and in response to the new conditions of the campaign. Despite the prominence of 'divide and rule' tactics, these divisions were not as salient mobilisers of new support, but they continued to reflect standing divisions among a highly divided electorate.

The role that family plays in Sabah's highly personalised politics has long been recognised, especially the competition and power of elite political families. As candidates were announced, it became clear that family dynamics would play a role.[25] In Senallang, the seat of former Chief Minister Shafie Apdal, he was challenged by his nephew, Norozman Utoh Nain. Another type of family feud took place in Sungai Sibuga where Armani Mahiruddin, who is the sister of the current Sabah state governor, defended family honour over the attempt to take over the state in July in the heartland base of former Chief Minister Musa Aman. Both challengers lost. The most significant family squabble involved the Kitingan brothers and party leaders, Joseph Pairin and Jeffrey, of the parties PBS and STAR respectively, who went head-to-head against each other in six seats.[26] In Tambunan – the heartland of the indigenous rights movement – and neighboring Bingkor they were able to make peace during the campaign.[27] Even as PRN2020 proved more competitive, elite families – many represented by incumbents

---

[23] Arnold Puyok, 'Ethnic Factor in the 2008 Malaysian General Election: The Case of The Kadazan Dusun (KD) In Sabah,' *Jebat: Malaysian Journal of History, Politics & Strategic Studies* 35 (2020): 1-16.

[24] Arnold Puyok and Piya Raj Sukhani, 'Sabah: breakthrough in the fixed deposit state,' *The Round Table* 109, no. 2 (2020): 209-224; Arnold Puyok, 'The Appeal and Future of the "Borneo Agenda" in Sabah,' in Johan Savaranamuttu, Hock Guan Lee and Mohamed Nawab Mohamed Osman (eds.) *Coalitions in Collision: Malaysia's 13th General Elections, KL & Singapore* (Singapore: ISEAS, 2016) 173-92; James Chin, 'Sabah and Sarawak in the 14th General Election 2018 (GE14): local factors and state nationalism,' *Journal of Current Southeast Asian Affairs* 37, no. 3 (2018): 173-192.

[25] Bridget Welsh, 'All in the Family: Candidates and Contests in Sabah Polls,' *Malaysiakini*, 14 September 2020, https://www.malaysiakini.com/columns/542581.

[26] These seats were Moyog, Liawan, Tambunan, Bingkor, Paginatan and Tulid.

[27] The truce was actually only in two seats where they contested against each other. Kow Gah Chie, 'Partial truce between PBS and Star achieved,' *Malaysiakini*, 22 September 2020, https://www.malaysiakini.com/news/543582.

– continued to remain powerful, even those not contesting, such as former Chief Minister Musa Aman, with his family members winning seats in Membakut, Kawang and Liawan. While feuds may have captured the headlines, traditional elite families captured and held onto power.

Differences extended into political alliances. PKR had tensions with Warisan over seats, and the decision by Anwar Ibrahim to announce his claim that he 'had the numbers' to retake the federal government a few days before polling day in Sabah turned attention away from Warisan Plus's state campaign and created tensions. Nevertheless, these conflicts did not spill into contestation as was the case for GRS, which competed against each other in 17 seats.[28] Of these, GRS still managed to win 12, mostly new seats and where the parties have established political standing in constituencies. The efforts among PBS and STAR was not officially extended beyond PBS's two seats, but what happened on the ground was that voters responded by choosing among the GRS alternatives that they thought would serve them best. The intra-alliance competition resulted in voters pragmatically prioritising, and ultimately did not hurt GRS as badly as expected. The more serious alliance divisions came to a head after the election, over the choice of chief minister between UMNO and Bersatu. While the issue was accommodated in Sabah – after some reported colourful exchanges and portfolio switches – the impact on the federal alliance between the two Malay parties has been more lasting, fueling resentments within UMNO against Bersatu.

Persistent resentments over UMNO's legacy in Sabah – notably irregular immigration – remained salient in the campaign and heightened ethnic differences among Sabahans. Other chapters in the collection explore the participation of ethnic communities in more depth, but any attention to division cannot ignore how different ethnic views of citizenship and displacement affected support for parties and candidates. UPKO's losses (11 out of 12 seats) in particular were tied to how Warisan was seen as a 'PATI party'. Yet, what was evident in the vote was more consistency in support than change. The only exception was the win of Ewon Benedick in Kadamaian where there was a sizeable shift in support in UPKO's favor.

[28] These seats include Bengkoka, Matunggong, Tandek, Kadamaian, Tanjung Aru, Kapayan, Moyog, Lumadan, Paginatan, Tambunan, Bingkor, Liawan, Melalap, Tulid, Sook, Telupid and Karamunting.

Repeatedly, studies of Sabah politics speak to the different mobilisation of KDM, Chinese and Muslim communities.[29] The PRN2020 pattern of support geographically – with Warisan winning the majority of its seats along the east coast and in urban areas and voting along ethnic lines – gives credence to the persistence of differences between the larger ethnic groups, despite calls for unity. Closer attention to the PRN2020 results, with a polarised electorate in the popular vote being repeated from GE14, highlights consistency in divided ethnic loyalties (a theme developed in my other chapter, Chapter 11).

Viewing the PRN2020 campaign from the ground, however, points to the centrality of other, less recognised ethnic identities. One dimension is about empowerment – as regularly happens with the election of representatives from local ethnic communities such as the Iranun in Pintasan or the Kedayan in Sindumin. Attempts at the local level to split the vote by appealing to other minority identities to divide the vote, as occurred in both of these seats, did not displace the loyalties toward the local majority community. A similar failed attempt at splitting the vote happened in Kuala Penyu, where the Malay candidate only secured 23 per cent of the vote based on ethnic appeal, but did not displace the incumbent. Campaigns tapped into these local sentiments strategically, and while splits were evident, they did not necessarily affect the outcome.

Perhaps the most prominent division involved the ties to the federal government. In the last two Sabah campaigns, rising state nationalism had shaped the outcome, with the emergence of an indigenous rights movement and push for state-based parties. In PRN2020 Warisan Plus and GRS openly tapped into different views of the federal government, pushing autonomy and greater cooperation respectively. For voters, the party's positions were more muddied, even contradictory. Warisan faced greater attention on its record in (inadequately) promoting the state when allied with the PH government, where it was not able to deliver many of the promises on the oil royalty and recognition in the wording of the MA63 agreement. While anger towards the PN federal government and the 'frogs' they pulled over to attempt to change the state government in 2020 was real among many, especially more educated and urban voters, some voters were not convinced

[29] Faisal S. Hazis, 'Domination, contestation, and accommodation: 54 years of Sabah and Sarawak in Malaysia,' *Southeast Asian Studies* 7, no. 3 (2018): 341-361.

that being in the federal opposition would necessarily help the state, in part due to the lack of resources to develop the economy and the potential threat of political destabilisation. At the same time, the indigenous rights movement led by Jeffrey Kitingan was now allied with federal authorities, following PBS's earlier pattern. The traditional pro-autonomy leaders who had been on the forefront of mobilising grievances were now part of the federal government, arguing that this would bring more resources to Sabah. Here too, voters looked with scepticism at how state rights were being fought.

The tendency is to see PRN2020 results as a vote for greater federal cooperation. This is what the outcome appears to show. Yet this is not necessarily the case from the ground. For most voters, especially those not among the elites and in the urban areas, the issues of MA63, and who is in and working (or not) with Putrajaya had very little to do with their daily lives and were not consequential in shaping their votes. Repeatedly, voters expressed the view that it would make little difference in how the federal government engaged Sabah, highlighting that neither greater autonomy nor an alliance had made a difference. The fight for state rights was seen as an elite battle at a time when ordinary voters were struggling with their own battles for survival. In the final analysis, voters largely stayed with the loyalties of GE14, despite the mixed records and new positioning of political players on state rights. Those that did change their loyalties highlighted the need for greater security in a period of uncertainty: a pragmatic vote tapping into insecurity. State nationalism as a mobiliser was thus not as decisive as it was in recent campaigns. As with the ethnic divisions, the past persisted, but leading to a different outcome favoring PN because conditions had changed.

Sabah's Campaign Style: Concluding Reflections

PRN2020 brought unprecedented attention to Sabah and its local socio-economic realities. Messaging, mobilisation, strategies to tap allegiances and divisions were shaped to respond to conditions on the ground and how they were responded to also reflected local conditions. From reactions to unity and paternalism, to the promises and delivery of money and the reaffirmation of the familiar and persistence of divisions, all of these were uniquely Sabahan, showcasing its complexity and a more diverse, sophisticated and sceptical electorate.

Among the most prominent of the conditions of PRN2020 was heightened insecurity. Covid-19, political instability and a sluggish economy set the context for the campaign. The insecurities took different forms, from ethnic displacement to economic precarity. Voters stayed with what they were more comfortable with in a period of uncertainty, largely opting for the known rather than the risks of the unknown, with the embrace of Bersatu as the exception. The focus for many voters was on surviving.

Throughout PRN2020, emotions played a pivotal role; not only did voters express a range of reactions from hope to anxiety, but campaigns worked to harness these emotions, to make voters more aware of their power and their powerlessness. The mobilisation of emotions was prominent due in part to the greater adoption of modern campaigning methods, but also because of the weakness in organisation needed for effective traditional campaigning.

GRS's campaign was more effective overall as it best harnessed insecurity in a period of political uncertainty. While both sides used modern and traditional forms of campaigning, GRS used a wider range of measures and better adapted during the campaign itself, through peacemaking initiatives and ratcheting up the rhetoric and mobilisation. Warisan's momentum was diverted because of Anwar's 'numbers' announcement, ironically reinforcing the uncertainties that advantaged GRS.

Sabah's PRN2020 campaign offers lessons for trajectories ahead as parties across Malaysia weaken through the loss of memberships, decreased patronage to members and continued factionalism. Voters remain loyal to the parties which tap into the emotions that they know and the candidates who are familiar to them. In this period of uncertainty, winning new political support, especially if parties themselves do not fundamentally change their engagement with voters or address the underlying factors contributing to insecurities, will remain a challenge, even remaining elusive.

Chapter 10

Undi Sabah: Igniting Youth Participation in Sabah's Democracy

Mahirah Marzuki, Auzellea Kristin Mozihim and Fiqah Roslan

Introduction

From Greta Thunberg to the Hong Kong protests in 2019, to the call for reforms in Thailand in 2020, youths have taken the lead in initiating change and altering the current political narrative. The call to lower the voting age to 18 and the amendment to the University and University Colleges Act 1971, now allowing university students to participate actively in politics, have paved the way for youths to amplify their voice in politics.[1] This wave is evident in Peninsular Malaysia where youth organisations are slowly emerging. However, in Borneo, and Sabah in particular, youth voices usually go unheard due to a lack of engagement and exclusion. Youth organisations like Undi Sabah have thus emerged as an important platform for youths to make their voices heard and to localise political issues through a Sabahan lens.

This chapter draws on conversations and research about Sabah youths in PRN2020 as well as participant observation through our involvement in the Undi Sabah movement. We were among the movement's founders and argue that the organisation is reshaping the political landscape in Sabah. While youth registration in Sabah's election remained low, Undi Sabah served to educate, mobilise and empower youth – bringing our issues into the public domain and bringing more informed and engaged younger voters to the polls.

---

1 The University and University Colleges Act 1971 was amended in December 2018 by the Pakatan Harapan government allowing students to participate in politics.

Youth Awakening in Sabah's 2020 State Election

When Chief Minister Shafie Apdal announced the dissolution of the State Assembly, triggering a snap election, there was public uproar.[2] People may not have taken to the streets in protest, but the dissent and frustration in the air was palpable. The frustration was not so much channeled towards the dissolution, but rather the events that led up to the decision. For many Sabahans, it was considered a 'bold' move by Shafie to go to polls, foiling what seemed to be another 'Sheraton Move' inflicted on the people of Sabah.[3]

People were agitated by leaders who were more concerned with self-preservation than the wellbeing of the *rakyat* (people). The frustration for many we knew, however inadvertently, led to political apathy. What was the point, they would ask, of participating in the democratic process and exercising the right to vote, if the vote counted for nothing at the end of the day? Despite this, there was also a unique contrast among youths, who seemed to be ignited by the ongoing political drama and wanted better leadership for Sabah, and Malaysia as a whole. In the age of social media, youths took to their personal profiles to voice their concerns and dissatisfaction. Some even started movements to galvanise Sabahans and demand accountability from leaders, with Undi Sabah being one of them. However unfortunate the catalyst, youths began taking part in the political conversation.

The weeks following the dissolution of the Sabah State Assembly, and leading up to the state election, went by in a whirlwind of activities. In the constant stream of news, updates and content circulating online, it was challenging for youths to keep abreast of the rapid political developments. At the same time, there was a growing thirst for information among young Sabahans who wanted to see better political practices and wanted to be part

---

2 Then Chief Minister Shafie announced the dissolution of the 15th Sabah State Legislative Assembly on 30 July 2020. The decision was made following an announcement by former Chief Minister Musa Aman claiming that he had the majority to form a new state government.

3 In February 2020, the ruling Pakatan Harapan coalition was ousted when several Members left the coalition leading to the resignation of Prime Minister Mahathir after which a new government was formed without going through a general election. The plan was believed to have been hatched at the Sheraton Hotel, Petaling Jaya, hence the power grab was dubbed the 'Sheraton Move'.

of the solution towards achieving that aspiration. Recognising the rise of youth investment in the affairs of the state, Undi Sabah sought to provide a platform for youths to amplify their voices.

Finding A Place: Youth Belonging in Sabah's Poll

A study conducted by Society Empowerment and Economic Development of Sabah (SEEDS)[4] argued that PRN2020 belonged to the youths. The study found that throughout Sabah, more than 40 per cent of registered voters were youth voters aged between 21 and 40. Later, an article by *The Borneo Post* titled 'Politicians urged to connect with young people' further illustrated the call for alternative methods to be employed to connect with young people. They highlighted the particular need for specific programmes with which to address economic and employment issues, as those were most pertinent among Sabahan youths.[5]

Our own research found that the economy was the paramount concern among young Sabahans. Leading up to the state election, Undi Sabah conducted a survey online titled '*Manifesto Anak Muda*' (Youth Manifesto), with the objective to collect feedback from Sabahan youths on their aspirations for the state.[6] Results of the survey showed that concern about employment opportunities was in the top three policy areas of focus at 19.4 per cent, alongside education at 19.4 per cent and political reform at 17.5 per cent. Sabahan youths lamented the lack of employment opportunities in Sabah that offered competitive, livable wages. Many agreed there were indeed jobs in Sabah, but that the pay was too low compared with that in Peninsular Malaysia, especially since the cost of living in Sabah was higher in many areas. Food and transportation, for example, are more expensive, as public transport in Sabah is not reliable and often out of service.

---

4 SEEDS conducted a study titled 'SEEDS Sabah Electoral Project 2020' (#SEEDSEP2020) to examine the key realities that would most likely influence the state election. Information about the survey is available on their Facebook page: https://www.facebook.com/pg/seedssabah1/posts/

5 'Politicians urged to connect with young people,' *The Borneo Post*, 7 September 2020, https://www.pressreader.com/malaysia/the-borneo-post-sabah/20200907/281547998294087.

6 Undi Sabah, 'Manifesto Anak Muda Sabah (online survey),' Manifesto Anak Muda Sabah, 21 August 2020, https://docs.google.com/forms/d/1ZomZL2DlpZl--VAKJ0Al88ivlPbqD3_cXa20bETyYHk/viewform.

Some youths also urged for more industries to be developed in Sabah so as not to depend heavily on the tourism industry alone. Youths argued for greater expansion of both the manufacturing and agriculture sectors. Many downstream opportunities could stem from the manufacturing industry, they argued, while industries such as farming, livestock rearing and fisheries could improve the economy in rural areas to be more on par with that in urban areas. Many believed this would stimulate economic growth in Sabah, which would then result in better wages and even spur infrastructure development, such as improved Internet connectivity and public transportation.

One such example provided by a Sabahan youth was in the state constituency of Liawan in Keningau. Keningau was one of the towns receiving public attention during the election and is a strategic economic business partner for nearby developing districts. However, whilst the town has a lot of untapped resources, job opportunities in the area are limited and not increasing. Youths believe Liawan should have already been developed, but its potential has been unrealised due to a lack of focus from leaders and infrastructural support.

Another concern for Sabahan youths was the culture of nepotism in securing jobs in the government sector. Many respondents urged to do away with the use of 'cables' or connections to obtain jobs as civil servants, insisting that positions should instead be granted fairly based on merit, and that equal opportunities should be given to fresh graduates. One such response conveyed that many Sabahan youths desired to contribute to the state and cultivate the economy of their homeland, but limited and unfairly distributed opportunities and low wages hindered their intentions.

Education was also a pressure point for many Sabahan youths who were largely passionate about its improvement in the state, especially in terms of infrastructure within rural communities. Recurring concerns were Internet accessibility to facilitate learning, as well as infrastructure such as good roads and modes of transport to ease travel to schools, the conditions of school buildings and basic student necessities such as learning materials and stationery. The reality is that education is still a 'privilege' as many students in rural areas face immense challenges to simply attend school. This is due to poor connectivity as many villages still do not have accessible roads. The condition of schools in rural areas was also a cause for concern, as dilapidated buildings do not provide a conducive or safe environment for learning. Respondents also brought up the fact that students from lower income families could not afford learning materials and urged the state government to provide allocations or aid in such instances. Sabah's high poverty rate remains a serious obstacle for youths born and raised in difficult circumstances.

Internet connectivity in rural areas was also a major cause for concern, with the Covid-19 pandemic making open distance learning (ODL) the new norm. Both students and teachers were expected to conduct teaching and learning online, but many found this to be a great challenge due to poor network strength and abysmal infrastructure. Some students were forced to resort to 'creative' measures, such as the well-known case of the university student Veveonah Mosibin, who built herself a makeshift treehouse to take her online exams.[7] Worse still, after the elections, were three secondary school students from Sekolah Menengah Kebangsaan (SMK) Ulu Sugut in Ranau, who suffered severe injuries when the suspended bridge they were on collapsed, while they were trying to secure an Internet connection.[8]

Youths also hoped to see a more engaging and hands-on curriculum that encouraged critical thinking and challenged conventional concepts. This was to do away with the 'spoon-feeding' and indoctrinating nature of the Malaysian education syllabus. Sabahan youths especially desire a more comprehensive syllabuses on Sabahan and Sarawakian history, with greater attention to the experience and diversity of the Borneo states. Youths strongly believe in the importance of better representation for Sabah and Sarawak here, which can inculcate a more patriotic Malaysian identity stemming from a broader knowledge of the territories that formed Malaysia. Equal opportunity and access to education were similarly emphasised, regardless of socioeconomic standing. This is achievable through an increase in available scholarships to young Sabahans, which youths urged to be awarded based on merit. Youths strongly believed in the importance of education and hoped all Sabahans would have the opportunity to pursue international-standard, high-quality tertiary education.

---

7 'Malaysian student sits exam in tree to ensure good wifi', *BBC News*, 18 June 2020, https://www.bbc.com/news/blogs-news-from-elsewhere-53079907.

8 May Vin Ong, '8 students badly injured after suspension bridge they gathered on for internet collapses,' *SAYS*, 27 November 2020, https://says.com/my/news/8-students-badly-injured-after-suspension-bridge-they-gathered-on-for-internet-collapses.

Unsurprisingly, Sabahan youths harboured concerns about autonomy and the treatment of Sabah as an equal partner of Peninsular Malaysia. This was reflected in the persistence of the 'Sabah for Sabahans'[9] narrative, which translated into greater political independence (local parties governing the state) and more respect for the rights of Sabah as promised in the Malaysia Agreement 1963 (MA63), particularly where the distribution of oil royalties and taxes are concerned.

Youths also felt strongly about anti-hopping laws to prevent elected representatives from shifting alliances from one party to another in the middle of a term, which caused the political instability that plagued the country in 2020 and set the conditions PRN2020. Youths were very vocal and insistent on this. Recurring concerns were to hold politicians accountable for their actions and ensure they delivered what was promised in election campaigns. A sense of betrayal was felt by not only by youths but Sabahans at large by the events that led to the snap polls. As much as politicians have the right to freedom of association, Sabahans also have the right to choose their leaders.

Sabahan youths also wanted local-based parties to unite and govern without the intervention of politicians from Peninsular Malaysia. They felt this was pertinent as issues faced in Sabah were unique to the state and its people, believing that local politicians would best understand the sentiments on the ground, as well as the realities of Sabah's diverse demography, and could result in policies that better reflected the needs of the people. Youths also believed politicians from local parties would have the best interests of the state and its people at heart.

Decentralisation of power therefore played a vital role in realising the desire to see Sabah progress. Youths highlighted the importance of having autonomy in the state, especially in the education and healthcare sectors. This would enable the state government to act swiftly in making decisions especially in times of crisis, such as during the Covid-19 pandemic. One such example was how many Sabahan students were stranded outside the state at the height of the pandemic, without the resources to travel home.[10]

---

9 This sentiment, which has existed long before the 2020 state election, was meant as a 'claim' for Sabahan autonomy as an equal partner in Malaysia.

10 'Sarawak, Sabah students still in peninsula need to wait,' *The Borneo Post*, 12 April 2020, https://www.theborneopost.com/2020/04/12/sarawak-sabah-students-still-in-

State sanctions, independent of the federal government, would enable matters to be resolved more efficiently in the interest of Sabahans.

In addition, Sabahan youths want to see more young politicians and women elected as representatives. They believe youthful and youth-friendly leaders would have a better grasp of struggles faced by youths of the day, especially in terms of economic and employment prospects. The same was true for women representatives, whom youths believed were crucial in voicing the concerns of an under-represented group that made up half of Sabah's population. Youths believed that younger representatives and women leaders could bring progress and reforms which would translate into more inclusive policies.

Despite the circumstances bringing it about, the snap election offered hope for young Sabahans as it presented them with the opportunity to choose, instead of having to tolerate the actions and consequences of existing politicians. However, no reform or change is actually possible without the enactment of anti-hopping laws or rules regarding electoral recall.

The survey found that in contrast to stereotypes of uninformed and disengaged youths, many young Sabahans had clear ideas about how to improve the state. Across political parties, there were common threads of inclusion and commitment to improving the well-being of fellow Sabahans.

Undi Sabah: Channeling Protest and Embracing Pluralism

This shared desire was also an integral part of how Undi Sabah started. In the midst of a global pandemic, there was a common hope that politicians would put aside their ambitions and focus on the welfare of the *rakyat*. When the Warisan-led government fell, many of us felt disappointed but not surprised by the turn of events; sadly, it seemed to be a familiar political pattern. Through a WhatsApp group chat, a group of 17 youths in Sabah felt that it was time for the younger generation to be part of the change.[11] Rather than stand by and watch, we believed we should coalesce, demand youth voices to be heard and work together towards the changes they desperately

peninsula-need-to-wait/.

11 The group consisted of Arrif Adi Putera, Audrey Lim, Afiqah Izzati S., Auzellea Kristin, Fiqah Roslan, Hiew Wen Tian, Irdina Jailani, Khairizal Naim, Khairul S, Zamzaini, Kieran Luke Lamudin, Clerie Olivia Fadrick, Mohd Safizzul Abdul Wahap, Timothy Wong, Willbryan Lee Reyes, Shaan Gom, Wilson Gan and Mahirah Marzuki.

wanted to happen. Undi Sabah became a movement for this group of youths to channel their dissent against the ongoing political upheaval. In the process of working together, we managed to harness the different voices of Sabahans.

From the start, Undi Sabah aimed to increase Sabahan youths' active political involvement and was committed to being the agents of change. Undi Sabah emerged from a broader movement for youth empowerment in Peninsular Malaysia, #Undi18. This was a Malaysia-wide youth movement that successfully lobbied the Pakatan Harapan government and Parliament of Malaysia to amend Article 119(1)(a) of the Federal Constitution to reduce the minimum voting age in Malaysia from 21 to 18 years old in July 2019. #Undi18 became a powerhouse in galvanising and inspiring Malaysian youth. Having committed to nation-building programmes and established campaigns before Undi Sabah, they became part of the main support structure to help forward the Sabahan agenda in organising and mobilising for youth empowerment.

Despite members of Undi Sabah having different political leanings and backgrounds, they all shared the spirit of bipartisanship. Thrilled with the prospect of creating meaningful change for all, members were unified in the aim to achieve higher, and more meaningful, participation from Sabahan youths within the democratic process. With our shared goal, it was easy to mobilise as a group despite political differences, as most members were already friends even before the conception of Undi Sabah.

Having shared daily interactions and late nights discussing policies before, most met when they became Members of Parliament (MPs) in the Digital Parliament initiated by Challenger Malaysia, #Undi18, Liga Demokratik Malaysia and UNAM Youth during the Covid-19 Movement Control Order (MCO) in Malaysia.[12] In fact, the Program Coordinators of Undi Sabah were the MPs of Digital Parliament Penampang and one of the facilitators for the Sabah division respectively.[13] Through Digital Parliament, the group bonded, shared aspirations to change Malaysia and felt that Undi Sabah could be the starting point to spark those conversations. Considering that most of the members of Undi Sabah were representing their respective constituencies in the Digital Parliament, the team composition not only

---

[12] Everyone above except Fiqah Roslan, Timothy Wong and Kieran Luke Lamudin.

[13] Shaan Gom and Mahirah Marzuki.

represented urban districts like Kota Kinabalu, Sandakan and Tawau but also smaller towns and rural areas in Sabah.

With that being said, members were from different ethnic and socio-economic backgrounds as well, from students to young professionals. Members of the movement found commonality in their passion for empowering and assisting the communities around them whether in their private capacity or through the local activism scene and participation in non-governmental organisations (NGOs)/civil society organisations (CSOs) prior to their involvement in Undi Sabah. While understanding that politics can easily divide people, this group of Sabahan youths acknowledged their differences in political ideologies, and still found a way to share the same vision for a meaningful and stronger democracy. Our diversity was our strength.

Cognisant of the feudal structure of political parties, Undi Sabah sought to be an organisation that was less hierarchical in structure. Whilst Program Coordinators were selected to keep things in check, each of the members played a vital role in the mobilisation of this movement. The members were divided into three main teams: the Research Team, Content Creation Team and the Events and Logistics Team. We reached out to other youth organisations. #Undi18 shared their knowledge and assisted Undi Sabah in mobilising their programme efficiently, whenever needed.

#UndiSabah's Programmes and Activities

Our connections and support underscored our commitment to nation-building and the inclusion of youths towards this goal. Our efforts were focused on the coming election. The looming threat of the pandemic made members feel that they needed to first address the implementation of postal voting for the state election. This first message from Undi Sabah was picked up by the press and released in most news portals, demanding that the Election Commission revise their decision with regard to postal voting.[14] Since most Sabahans stuck in Peninsular Malaysia were students and young professionals, Undi Sabah wanted them to still be able to participate in the democratic process despite the obstacles posed by the pandemic and costly

[14] On 16 August 2020, a press statement by Undi Sabah was picked up by *Free Malaysia Today*, *The Malaysian Insight* and *Astro Awani* who released it on their news portals, whilst *Daily Express* and *New Sabah Times* did the same on 17 August 2020.

travel expenses. Unfortunately, this message was not enough to convince the Election Commission.

However, this did not stop Undi Sabah from continuing to spread this message via social media, which has become increasingly popular amongst Sabahan youths. Most of Undi Sabah's advocacy happened online, across social media platforms like Facebook, Twitter, Instagram, Zoom and WhatsApp. Through infographics, explainers and videos about political awareness and developments, Undi Sabah engaged with Sabahan youths and was able to share their sentiments. Information sharing was instrumental in building the solidarity of the movement.

We also organised webinars. By being bipartisan, Undi Sabah programmes invited individuals across the political spectrum to encourage inclusivity. For the first webinar, Undi Sabah discussed party-hopping in Sabah, an extremely common occurrence with long historical roots. Activists and scholars were invited to speak about the issue. The second webinar addressed the involvement of youths in politics and invited young politicians from the Democratic Action Party (DAP), ARMADA Sabah (Bersatu Youth Wing) and Parti Cinta Sabah (PCS) to give their insights. The last engagement was the Undi Sabah Summit, a two-day event limited to 50 in-person participants, with others joining via livestream on Undi Sabah's and #Undi18's Facebook pages. The Summit discussed Sabah's political direction and a Sabahan youth manifesto based on feedback received. Despite only beginning less than two months before the state election, Undi Sabah received a positive reception from people. At its peak, the Undi Sabah page received more than ten thousand views during the Summit, which motivated members to develop more content and carry out more events in the future.

The team was also invited to speak for Undi Sabah on platforms in local or national media and invited to webinars organised by various NGOs and causes to forward the message. Undi Sabah, for example, spoke on Astro (the satellite television provider)[15] and over radio (BFM 89.9[16] and KK12FM 89.5),

[15] 'PRN Sabah: Perkembangan PRN Sabah Bersama Wakil Penampang Parlimen Digital, Shaan Gom,' *Astro Awani*, 26 September 2020, https://www.astroawani.com/video-malaysia/prn-sabah-perkembangan-prn-sabah-bersama-wakil-penampang-parlimen-digital-shaan-gom-1868850.

[16] Dashran Yohan, Juliet Jacobs & Tee Shiao Eek, 'The Daily Digest: #UndiSabah: Promoting Youth-Centric Agenda and Democratic Reforms,' *BFM 89.9*, 4 August 2020, https://www.bfm.my/podcast/the-bigger-picture/the-daily-digest/undisabah-

on youth empowerment.[17] From a small initiative bred of frustration and hope, Undi Sabah had gained more traction than its members had imagined. Through these invitations, members felt that they were empowered to disseminate the movement's messages and initiatives on a larger scale. Seeing how other youths in Sabah became generally more engaged with the same message gave reassurances that Undi Sabah was on the right track. After the state election, Undi Sabah continues to release content and organise activities, focusing on Sabahan concerns and nation-building.

Youth Mobilisation: Engagement and Broader Issues

Considering that Undi Sabah only came into fruition in the midst of a pandemic and so close to the election, there were definitely some challenges faced by the movement. Based on data by the Election Commission of Malaysia, the share of registered young voters between 21-39 in PRN2020 was 41 per cent, while the share of voters between the age of 21 to 29 remained low at 14 per cent.[18] It is also clear that youths were not registering to vote, as the share of youths in Sabah is higher than their share on the electoral role. Based on a comparison of the electoral roll and census numbers, Bridget Welsh, as outlined in Chapter 11 in this volume, estimated that 22.3 per cent of potential voters under 30 did not register – more than a fifth of young people.

The voter turnout for PRN2020 was roughly 66 per cent.[19] This number comprises normal voters, early voters and postal voters. It is assumed that among the 41 per cent that comprised younger voters, their turnout was lower than that. The most likely reason for low youth voter turnout is because most are working or studying outside of Sabah. For many, the lack of financial resources means they have to opt to remain in the Peninsula or Sarawak rather than return to vote. The surge of Covid-19 cases in Sabah

---

promoting-youth-centric-agenda-and-democratic-reforms.

[17] 'KK12FM (89.5) Podcast,' KK12FM (89.5), 23 September 2020, https://podcasts. google.com/feed/aHR0cHM6Ly9hbmNob3IuZm0vcy8xZmFhNjI2MC9wb2RjYXN0L3Jzcw==.

[18] 'Pengundi muda jadi penentu di Sabah,' *Sinar Harian*, 18 September 2020, https://www.sinarharian.com.my/article/101535/ANALISIS-SEMASA/Pengundi-muda-jadi-penentu-di-Sabah.

[19] 'EC: Voter Turnout for Sabah Poll at 66.61pc,' *Malay Mail*, 27 September 2020, https://www.malaymail.com/news/malaysia/2020/09/27/ec-voter-turnout-for-sabah-poll-at-66.61pc/1907116.

around the election was also a cause for concern. Prior to the election, these spiked, especially on the east coast of Sabah. Voters from that area who were residing elsewhere expressed fear of contracting the disease if they decided to go back to their voting constituencies.

Drawing from the preliminary estimates of youth voter turnout by Bridget Welsh in this volume, young Sabahans followed low turnout expectations. Welsh estimates that only 56.1 per cent of young voters turned out to vote, a significant decline of 19.4 per cent from 2018. Voters under 30 contrasted sharply with voters from 30-50 years of age, with an estimated average turnout of 62.9 per cent of voters in this age group. While many students had returned home by voting day (in part due to Covid-19), importantly, many did not come out to vote. We believe Undi Sabah made an impact, offsetting an even higher decline in turnout. We do know, however, from Welsh's turnout estimates, that a majority of young Sabahans are still vested in the political future of their state. They are not apathetic – at least not those who are registered to vote.

Beyond voting, many were also able to indirectly participate in the election by engaging in political discourse. This indicated a political awakening of sorts among youths, particularly in this election. Media and surrounding support structures, like friends and family, enabled the democratisation of information and allowed issues to be discussed and debated. Undi Sabah became that enabling structure for Sabahan youths to engage in politics. Youths participated in politics through talking to people close to them – friends, family and even strangers online. Youths we spoke to would engage family members on which political parties to vote for and later brought those discussions out in the open once they felt more informed and passionate about them. More often than not, family members have an influence on our political views. The pandemic played a role in reinforcing youth engagement – fostering discussion among trusted groups and youth networks. Most Undi Sabah members had contacts who had decided not to return to their constituencies to vote due to fears of Covid-19, but members continued to discuss the political situation in Sabah with them by exchanging opinions and sharing political information on Twitter and Facebook, which usually shifts narratives. Many later supported the Undi Sabah movement despite not being able to go back.

One unique experience related to us was from a teacher who, days after the election, had overheard her secondary school students – who would be eligible to vote by 2021 – openly talking about politics. These youths were still under the voting age but had already started to get into political discussions even before they turned 18. This shows that even if they were not yet eligible to vote, they had gained some political consciousness through their casual discourse among peers, which is a sign of early political participation. This gives hope to a future where youths are more involved in politics, whether directly or indirectly. In fact, in the Undi Sabah team itself, we have team members who were not able to vote in the recent election, but already have their own views on politics. This goes to show that not being able to vote or having a lower voter turnout in Sabah does not mean that local political apathy is the case.

We at Undi Sabah asked ourselves: why are youths now interested in participating in politics, be it directly or indirectly? As reflected in the survey undertaken by Undi Sabah, issues such as education and social and economic issues are the main reasons why youths engaged in active political discourse. Many of these issues are shaped by policies decided upon by politicians. In fact, policies do not exist in isolation but form part of a broader political, economic and social context. Furthermore, it is hard to separate politicians and policy-making processes that will definitely have an impact on youths in the long run. There are policies that have been enacted (or have been recommended) that concern the youth, apart from the ones gathered by the survey from Undi Sabah.

As we noted earlier, education is a priority. School-going youths and university students were among the groups affected during the MCO. When 'distance learning' was implemented, flaws in the education system were magnified, especially the lack of Internet access in many areas in Sabah. According to statistics released by the Sabah State Education Department, 52 per cent of students in Sabah lack Internet access, impeding their education.[20] This statistic could easily extend to university students who returned to Sabah during the MCO as well, where many of them live in areas that make it difficult to obtain Internet connections. We already mentioned the well-known example of Veveonah Mosibin above, but her example represents the struggle of most rural Sabahans.

---

20 '52% of students in Sabah have no internet access, gadgets,' *The Borneo Post*, 9 May 2020, https://www.theborneopost.com/2020/05/09/52-sabah-students-have-no-internet-access-gadgets/.

As for social issues, one of the broader issues highlighted was the decriminalisation of suicide. According to the 2017 National Health and Morbidity Study,[21] there was a rising trend in suicide among Malaysian youths aged 13 to 17, which totaled about 10 per cent of reported cases. This was an increase from the 7.9 per cent measured back in 2012. Criminalisation of suicide comes under Section 309 of the Penal Code. By decriminalising suicide, youths can be more open about their mental health problems and seek help. As of 2021, the law is still in effect, which is why the stigmatisation of mental illness is still prevalent. In Sabah, the first youth-friendly mental health care line was introduced: '*Kawan Bah*'.[22] It is a 24-hour care line communication channel, accessible via phone call or WhatsApp, that aims to provide a safe space for youths to express their feelings and opinions. Only youths who use it are able to comment on the programme's effectiveness, but as the stigma of suffering from mental health problems still exists at large, it is difficult to gauge any success as of yet.

The economy remains the most important concern for youths in Sabah as there are a lot of young local entrepreneurs looking for opportunities and many seeking employment. Since the MCO was imposed in March 2020, there has been a significant drop in the number of jobs available in Sabah, with job listings in Sabah having dropped by about 70 per cent in 2020 and Sabah's GDP dropping from 8.1 per cent in 2017 to 0.5 per cent in 2019.[23] Malaysia saw its GDP plunge by 17.1 per cent in the second quarter of 2020, greatly impacting the Malaysian economy as a whole.[24] In light of the Covid-19 pandemic, with the government having introduced the Bantuan Prihatin Nasional (National Relief Aid) SME Economic Stimulus Package 2020, small and medium enterprises received modest assistance. In addition, young entrepreneurs have also applied for business loans in order to kick start their businesses. However, there have been concerns with loan

---

21 Ministry of Health, *National Health and Morbidity Survey (NHMS) 2017: Adolescent Health* (Malaysia: Institute for Public Health, 2017).

22 Introduced by YouthPREP Centre, launched on 16 July 2020 by the then Sabah Minister of Youths and Sports YB Phoong Jin Zhe.

23 Bridget Welsh and Calvin Cheng, 'Emerging Humanitarian Covid-19 Crisis in Sabah,' *Malaysiakini*, 25 October 2020, https://www.malaysiakini.com/columns/548026.

24 Ng Min Shen, "BNM: Malaysia GDP contracted 17.1% in 2020, worst decline since 4Q98,' *The Malaysian Reserve*, 14 August 2020, https://themalaysianreserve.com/2020/08/14/malaysias-gdp-falls-17-1-in-2q20-lowest-since-1998/.

applications as some youths have suggested that banks have taken a long time for loan approvals. This has demotivated young entrepreneurs from starting their own businesses.

The three aforementioned issues often dominate the conversations of youths in Sabah. With the increasing ease of accessing information, youths have become increasingly conscious and have begun to hold politicians and the government to account for policies that will affect them in the long run. These engaged youths can serve as a check-and-balance for the government as they are at the receiving end of the policies, as well as having the intellectual capacity to evaluate them. Since they are active users of social media platforms, they often express their opinions openly and politicians who are social media savvy may encounter these opinions and take note of what they have said.

Sabah youths today are more engaged with the world around them. Youth-led anti-establishment protests in neighbouring countries such as Thailand are an inspiration for Sabahan youths.[25] This is not a call to hold protests against the government, but rather it shows that youths have the responsibility, the power and the voice to advance a democracy. We know that youths are vital in determining the direction of a country and the voices of youths can no longer be excluded from political conversations and policy-making decisions. Such discourses are no longer limited to the previous generation of leaders. We believe that everyone, at all levels of society, must provide an avenue for youths to speak up and be listened to regarding their concerns.

The Way Forward: Taking Charge

Those in power have yet to fully appreciate the role that youths can play. Undi Sabah is part of a broader movement for change that lays the foundation for other Sabah-based youth organisations to propel narratives that can develop Sabah's potential forward, be they political, economic

25 Demonstrations began on university campuses in Thailand at the start of 2020 when the court decided to dissolve Future Forward, a prominent opposition party. Popular among young people during last year's election, the party ran with hopes to return Thailand to democracy following a 2014 military coup, but was deemed to be unconstitutional. Youth protests expanded over the year to call for more systemic change.

or social. It is part of a broader national Malaysian movement of youth empowerment.

Political parties are being left behind and are out of touch. There is reluctance to field younger candidates. Only 69 out of 447 candidates (15.4 per cent) in the Sabah elections were below 39.[26] Political parties still need to embrace the idea of allowing youths to take charge. Many political parties still do not have a youth-centric view in letting them manage their constituents.

We believe that with Undi Sabah contributing to the larger narrative, we can see the share of youth candidates increasing in the coming elections. Seeing that this election did not address many youth concerns, and other issues were amplified by all sides of the political divide, it is imperative for Undi Sabah to keep mobilising and demanding that future election candidates address these issues in the next election. While this state election has come to an end, Sabahans still have a responsibility in continuously evaluating our elected leaders. Voting is only one of the many responsibilities we have as citizens.

However, there is no denying that among youths, there are still those who do not see the importance of voting and the relevance of politics in their lives. The change in youth registration and lowering of the voting age expected in July 2021 will bring in new voters who have not been engaged. Undi Sabah sees it as our mission to help inform them about the goings-on in our state. This process of educating each other on politics and policies is vital because voters should be able to make informed decisions before going to the polls. Platforms such as Undi Sabah act as a vehicle to encourage more Sabahan youths to be aware of the political situation in Sabah and Malaysia as a whole. This quote by Pericles, a Greek statesman, resonates with the process of raising the political awareness among youths: 'Just because you are not interested in politics, does not mean politics does not take an interest in you.'[27]

In the aftermath of PRN2020, it was observed that youths had indeed developed an understanding and interest in politics, spurring participation

---

[26] Bernama, 'Call for More Youths to Represent Sabah,' *Malaysiakini*, 25 September 2020, https://www.malaysiakini.com/news/544133.

[27] Scotty Hendricks, '10 Quotes from Great Minds on Why You Should Vote,' *Big Think*, 26 October 2020, https://bigthink.com/politics-current-affairs/quotes-voting-thinkers.

in political conversation. Ultimately, most youths want to move away from political dynasties, nepotism and tribalistic mentalities when it comes to politics. It does not matter to youths if a political leader or party had a longstanding history in the state or not. What youths want to see is action being taken in of meeting the concerns of the people.

Youths today are more interested in holding politicians to account and ensuring they deliver on their word. With Internet connectivity and social media, youths are more empowered to exercise their democratic rights in demanding a better future not only for them, but for generations to come. The turbulent political events of 2020 were impossible to ignore, because the ramifications of those events impacted the lives of everyone residing in Malaysia. Youths are now more empowered and emboldened to name and speak out against the injustices they face and are more motivated to demand better policies. Today, if youths are not satisfied, they want to change things themselves.

This perhaps indicates a paradigm shift and therefore a new direction in Malaysia's politics. What was certain in the Sabah polls is that youths were no longer willing to settle for less. As the future generation and heirs of this nation, we acknowledge the need to claim our space, voice our concerns and aspirations, and to turn our visions into reality. Undi Sabah has started the change but there remains lots of work to do.

Part 4

Results

Chapter 11

A Holistic Society-Centred Analysis of the Sabah Election 2020 Results: Voters, Voting and Trajectories of Survival and Change

Bridget Welsh

Vignette 1

In Sulaman, the seat of the current Chief Minister Hajiji Noor, a conversation with *Pak* (a Malay man over 50).

BW: Good morning. Are you heading to vote?

Pak: Yes. I always vote.

BW: What do you think will happen in this seat?

Pak: It will be blue. I always vote for blue. (Hajiji won the seat contesting for Bersatu, red color. He was a long-time leader in UMNO and Barisan Nasional, dark blue color, before defecting to Bersatu).

Vignette 2

In Tandek, the seat won by United Sabah Party (PBS) Hendrus Anding, defeated the challenge of the female incumbent Anita Baranting running initially as an independent then as a STAR candidate, with Julia a 35-year old women of Dusun Kimaragang origin.

BW: What do you think about voting for a woman in this election?

Julia: I like Anita. She did a good job.

BW: Will you vote for her?

Julia: Not this time.

BW: Why?

Julia: I want to vote for the winner. This is a PBS seat, and I will stick to the party. Hendrus is good. He is part of my family.

BW: Do you not think that voting for a woman would help women?

Julia: We need to help ourselves. We can't vote for a woman because she is a woman. We need to vote for the person that is best for us. Our family is the one who helps us most when we are struggling.

On Sabah's election day, 26 September 2020, I drove from Kota Kinabalu north to Pitas, stopping to discuss the election with voters. For two weeks voters had been bombarded by political campaigning and in some places bombed with funds. Even those who opted not to vote could not escape. In Sulaman, Pak was choosing to stay loyal to the blue BN with a vote for Bersatu, while Julia in Tandek supported women in office but prioritised putting an extended family member into office. These vignettes point to the complexity in understanding voting in Sabah – how the varied ties to party, candidate, the broader social and political conditions and perceived self-interest shape voting.

When the results came in on election night in Sabah, it was clear that a new government had secured victory. Muhyiddin Yassin's Perikatan Nasional's (PN) coalition partners had a majority. As the winners battled (and shouted) among themselves for positions, questions began to be asked as to why Warisan Plus lost power and whether the new Gabungan Rakyat Sabah (GRS) alliance would be stable. Warisan supporters initially refused to accept defeat, arguing that they were the largest party and should have the right to form the government. Within days, the dust had settled and Sabah had installed a new chief minister and cabinet. Attention turned to the challenges of governing, including the devastating impact of Covid-19 from the election itself.

There is a tendency in Sabah not to look back, to move on, to wrestle with the everyday realities of survival and political jockeying. If one does look back, it is to focus on the unfairness of the 1963 Malaysia Agreement (MA63) or the heyday of politics in the 1980s and 1990s which witnessed

Sabah's first transfers of power and the entry of UMNO into the state.[1] Sabah's electoral history is rarely explored or discussed in depth, especially outside of Sabah, and there is even less exploration of the underlying shifts in voting and society at large. More fundamentally, there is little appreciation of how Sabah is changing, and how those changes are in fact altering its political landscape. Sabah is mistakenly seen as static, even stagnant, acted upon from the outside, either by Peninsular Malaysia or by immigrants from neighboring Indonesia and the Philippines.

The agency of ordinary Sabahans, everyday voters, is largely missing. This chapter aims to work to correct this deficit and to enrich our understanding of how voters have changed their political support over time. I argue that not only are different lenses required to understand voting in Sabah, there needs to be more appreciation of how choices are made by voters based on their own needs, rationally and in response to more systemic patterns of political engagement rather than solely responding to political narratives and campaign tactics, including financial inducements. This chapter adopts a society-driven analysis to look at how voters themselves shaped Sabah's election outcome.

While interviews enrich the discussion, this analysis is primarily data-driven. I draw from three primary sources – available demographic statistics,[2] the 2020 electoral roll[3] and polling station results of the Sabah 2020 elections,[4] and build on a longitudinal assessment of different localities at the polling station level based on interviews and visits to the different

1 Sabah had its first major political turnover in 1985, when Parti Bersatu Sabah (PBS) won a majority of seats. UMNO entered Sabah politics in 1990. See James Chin, 'Going east: UMNO's entry into Sabah politics', *Asian Journal of Political Science* 7, no. 1 (1999): 20-40.

2 Material is from the Department of Statistics Malaysia. The main report is *Household and Basic Amenities and Survey Report by State and Administrative District Sabah 2019*, Department of Statistics Malaysia, 2020, https://www.dosm.gov.my/v1/uploads/files/1_Articles_By_Themes/Prices/HIES/HIS-Report/HIS_Sabah.pdf.

3 Electoral roll data by the Election Commission (Suruhanjaya Pilihan Raya, SPR) released quarterly. The data are based on the 2020 roll in PRN2020.

4 This data are provided to political parties and candidates by the Election Commission. Sometimes this data are published on their website, but generally this data are only available through the kind sharing of those who contested in the election. Thanks to a number of political parties and individuals, the complete data set was shared for the analysis and builds on data collected in Sabah from earlier elections.

areas.[5] The polling station data are the smallest units of the results and details them according to different streams, when voters are included in the electoral roll. Combining data at the polling station level allows for statistical assessments of voting by ethnicity, urbanisation, gender, class and generation based on ecological inference, a method that allows inferences of individual behavior based on group data.[6] The findings should, however, be understood to be estimates, rough indicators of patterns rather than exact measures. The main comparison detailed below is the September 2020 Sabah polls with the May 2018 (GE14) election results at the state level,[7] but in some cases the analysis stretches back to 2013 (GE13) when the most recent, and important, shifts in voting in Sabah intensified. The data analysis is complemented by ethnographic field interviews and conversations conducted throughout Sabah from August through September 2020.

Below, I first look at the electorate. Then I examine voting behavior – turnout and support – along different socio-economic cleavages. Rather than only adopting the dominant paradigm for understanding voting behavior – ethnicity – the analysis expands to include gender, generation, geographic (urbanisation and regionalism) and, importantly, class dynamics. It aims to clearly show that to understand Sabah's electoral results one has to adopt multiple analytical lenses and bring the changing complex society into the analysis. Finally, I turn to examine how the context of the campaign affected the outcome – a change in government and deep political divisions. Here I explore the impact of specific issues associated with the results, postal voting, the new seats and, importantly, who changed (and did not change) their support. The empirical findings help us understand broader social

---

5 Over the past two decades I have assessed and reviewed the geographic areas for their level of urbanisation and the predominant income level, supplementing this data with government figures on poverty/income levels, housing and urbanisation. This has been done through visits to localities and interviews with local leaders. The figures are weighted to reflect government measures of urbanisation and income levels per the 2020 DOSM data noted above.

6 For more background on ecological inference see: Gary King, Martin A. Tanner, and Ori Rosen, eds. *Ecological inference: New methodological strategies* (Cambridge University Press, 2004).

7 In many cases there is split voting, where Sabahans vote for different parties in the federal parliament than for their representatives at the state level. To keep the analysis consistent, the focus in on the state level throughout.

and political divides in Sabah – the political impact of persistent poverty, increasingly entrenched political polarisation and the challenges of bringing about reform. Sabah is indeed changing, but as argued below, it is the things that are not changing which are predominantly shaping its current political trajectory.

A Transforming Electorate

An electorate of 1.2 million Sabahans were eligible to vote in the 2020 state election. This is slightly more than a third of those living in Sabah, a population of 3.2 million. Of the registered voters, 66.6 per cent went out to vote in September, a large share given the realities of Covid-19, but a drop in turnout of 9.3 per cent from GE14. The data from the electoral roll and that released by the Election Commission show that Sabah's electorate is diverse. Over time it has evolved with the demographic, generational and ethnic shifts in the state, largely driven by new settlements and different birth rates between communities.

The most prominent lens used to differentiate voters is their ethnicity. Sabah joins Sarawak as being among the most ethnically diverse states in the country. My earlier chapter on the campaign (see Chapter 9) points to the role these diverse ethnicities play at the local level in shaping outcomes. In order to understand ethnic differences in Sabah as a whole, there is need for some amalgamation. This analysis groups ethnic communities into five different categories – Chinese, Bajau-Suluk, Kadazan-Dusun, Murut, Malay and others, building on the largest groups.[8] Chinese voters comprised 15.2 per cent of the electorate, Bajau-Suluks[9] comprised 15.4 per cent, Kadazan-Dusun communities 21.8 per cent, Malays 13.8 per cent, Murut 3.5 per cent and others 30.3 per cent – including a range of communities often concentrated in different areas, from Rungus and Orang Sungai to Bugis and Kedayan. Over time the share of voters from the Chinese, and to a lesser extent the Kadazan, Dusun and Murut (KDM) communities, have declined, largely due to lower birth rates and the waves of migration and settlement

---

8 The decision to separate Murut voters stemmed from the observation of different voting patterns from the other KDM ethnic communities.

9 This includes all Bajau and Suluk. The Bajau community is seen to have both sea and land Bajau, Bajau-Suluk and Bajau Sama, with the latter communities living on both the west and east coasts of Sabah. Bajau-Suluk are primarily on the east coast.

– a challenging issue involving undocumented persons well-covered in the collection due to the political saliency of these resentments.[10]

Table 1: Registered Voters 2013, 2018 and 2020 by Ethnicity

Election	CHINESE	BAJAU-SULUK	KADAZAN-DUSUN	MURUT	MALAY	OTHERS
2013	16.8%	13.5%	21.9%	3.3%	16.4%	28.1%
2018	15.3%	13.7%	23.5%	3.5%	12.5%	31.6%
2020	15.2%	15.4%	21.8%	3.5%	13.8%	30.3%

Sabah also has a young population. Drawing on the electoral roll, an estimated 43.8 per cent of the population is 40 years or below, with 17.8 per cent under 30. Younger voters, however, have not been registering. This means that while they are decisive in shaping electoral outcomes, at nearly one-fifth of the electorate, they are less powerful than they can be if they opted to register. This is why the Undi Sabah movement, described in Chapter 10 in this collection, is so important, since it encourages participation. Table 2, comparing registered voters with 2020 census population numbers, shows that 22.3 per cent of younger voters were not registered in 2020. The gap closes as voters age, but even among those in their 30s, an estimated 7.9 per cent of voters are not registered.

Table 2: Registered and Disenfranchised Sabah Voters 2020 by Age Cohort

Age (Years)	Share Registered Voters	Share Population Disenfranchised
21-30	17.8%	22.3%
31-40	26%	7.9%
41-50	20.7%	3.9%
51-60	17.7%	1.7%
Above 60	17.8%	.2%

One reason why voters are not registered is the sheer size of the state and, based on where they live, the geography. Sabah is the second largest

[10] Catherine Allerton, 'Contested statelessness in Sabah, Malaysia: Irregularity and the politics of recognition,' *Journal of Immigrant & Refugee Studies* 15, no. 3 (2017): 250-268.

state in the country, with many of the state constituencies larger than the states of Melaka and Perlis in Peninsular Malaysia. A large share of Sabahans live in rural, semi-rural and remote areas. Using data from Malaysia's Department of Statistics (DOSM) and an analysis of the 2020 Electoral Roll, over half (50.9 per cent) of Sabah voters reside in rural areas, another 33 per cent in semi-rural areas and only 16.1 per cent in urban centres such as Kota Kinabalu, Sandakan, Keningau and Tawau. There is often limited access to actually register to vote in many remote areas, with the process tightening after the 2013 election. With party representatives no longer allowed to register voters, it is even harder for rural voters to register outside of the appointed village headmen.

Geography also affects the interface with politics. Many rural areas lack basic amenities, which contributes to a lack of access to information and limited political engagement. There has been migration to the urban areas, especially for work, but in contrast to other parts of Malaysia the overwhelming majority of Sabahans still live outside of the towns and cities, many deriving their livelihood from agriculture. Yet, despite different livelihoods, the urban-rural divide is less a marker of support than it once was. Changes in access to information in rural areas, as well as different forms of mobilisation by political parties, which have won over rural areas at different points of time (especially in the KDM areas), have blurred a clear distinction between rural and urban support.

Place also plays a different role politically, in the form of regionalism within Sabah. In Peninsular Malaysia, for example, there is attention to the Malay heartland and particular patterns of political support for the Islamist party PAS, for example, along the east coast. In Chapter 5, Vilashini Somiah and Aslam Abd Jalil discussed regional tensions between the east and west coasts of Sabah, tied to long-standing contentions of belonging and perceived threats. We will see similar coastal patterns of political support in Sabah as well, as described below, with Warisan's support concentrated along the east coast. This intertwines with ethnicity (and as suggested below class) but is yet another political divide tied to social conditions.

Arguably the most underestimated divide in Sabah society relates to economic status. There are stark differences in living conditions among Sabahans. It is the state in the country with the most poverty, with 19.5 per cent of households, or an estimated 615,000 persons, living on an income of less than RM2,208 ($552) a month.[11] This is not a new development, as inequality and hardship have been common features in Sabah, but the awareness of these differences has changed with increased communication and as demands for improvements in infrastructure and equitable allocation of Sabah's resources from the federal government have intensified. Living conditions and economic status, I argue below, play an important role in influencing voting, with political support among wealthier, more educated voters in the cities quite different from many parts of the less economically advantaged rural areas. Class, along with gender in an almost evenly divided electorate of 50.1 per cent men and 49.9 per cent women, are the underappreciated lenses that enrich our understanding of voting trends, as will be developed below.

Understanding Voting Behavior

In-depth public studies of voting behavior in Sabah are scarce. Political parties do conduct post-mortems after elections, but scholars have not looked deeply into the results. There are obstacles to doing so. With ethnicity being the dominant paradigm to look at voting behavior, Sabah in its diversity often gets left out. Sabah is not part of the dominant Malay-Chinese-Indian-Other (MCIO) rubric. There are misguided efforts to force it into this framing. This is further enhanced by the Election Commission's simplistic labelling of voters as Muslim or non-Muslim Bumiputera, a division that can divide families in Sabah and explains little (except what people want others to see). Second, electoral data are not available and shared. Parties in Sabah are more fragmented so they often do not have access to large comparative samples, and often the lack of party machinery for smaller parties means that data are not collected when the poll results are announced. Finally, there is little interest in looking beyond the surface, to understand the outcome. The answers are often assumed. Moreover, it is argued, a new election will come along with new opportunities yet, alas, minimal lessons are learnt.

---

11 Department of Statistics Malaysia, *Household and Basic Amenities and Survey Report by State and Administrative District Sabah 2019*. Department of Statistics Malaysia, 2020, https://www.dosm.gov.my/v1/uploads/files/1_Articles_By_Themes/Prices/HIES/HIS-Report/HIS_Sabah.pdf

With the exceptions of some important local studies,[12] the study of Sabah voting behavior still focuses primarily on the macro explanations. Our introduction laid out some of these dominant macro paradigms for understanding Sabah elections – state nationalism in federal-state relations, patronage, personality, party machinery, developmentalism and ethnic identity, as the dominant socio-economic cleavage. Our book, and this chapter, brings attention to other dimensions – generation, gender and class differences in a society-centred analysis of voting. We see the emergence of what we are calling a 'survival' narrative, in which Sabahans adopt rational strategies to navigate the difficult circumstances they face. Below the findings from the polling station are detailed and analysed.

Voting by Ethnicity in PRN2020

Data over the last three elections show that there are sharp ethnic differences in voting among Sabahans, especially with regard to the parties they support. It was only in the 2020 state election that ethnic differences extended into turnout as well. Table 3 outlines estimates of voting behavior along ethnic lines.[13]

Table 3: Estimates of Voting in Sabah by Ethnicity, 2013, 2018 and 2020

2013	CHINESE	BAJAU-SULUK	KADAZAN-DUSUN	MURUT	MALAY	OTHERS
Turnout	71.8%	78.5%	83.1%	81.6%	86.2%	74.1%
BN	12.1%	81.8%	39.5%	54.2%	76.9%	69.5%
PR	82.3%	7.9%	34.4%	25.8%	19.2%	20.6%
Others	5.6%	10.4%	26.2%	19.9%	3.9%	10.0%

12 See, for example, Arnold Puyok, 'What issues matter to local voters, and Why?: Electoral politics in Ranau, Sabah', *Journal of Borneo-Kalimantan* 4, no. 1 (2018): 20-27 and Anantha Raman Govindasamy and Yew Meng Lai, 'GE14: The Urban Voting Pattern In P172 Kota Kinabalu and P186 Sandakan, Sabah,' *Jebat: Malaysian Journal of History, Politics & Strategic Studies*, 45, no. 2 (2018): 298-318.

13 This is a more comprehensive analysis of ethnic data first presented in Bridget Welsh, 'Why Warisan Lost – a preliminary analysis,' *Malaysiakini*, 28 September 2020, https://www.malaysiakini.com/columns/544346.

2018	CHINESE	BAJAU-SULUK	KADAZAN-DUSUN	MURUT	MALAY	OTHERS
Turnout	73.9%	78.1%	82.4%	80.4%	75.1%	76.1%
BN	6.0%	39.0%	44.4%	61.8%	59.7%	49.9%
Warisan/PH	92.7%	60.7%	26.7%	36.0%	40.2%	38.5%
Others	1.3%	0.3%	28.9%	2.2%	0.1%	11.6%
2020	**CHINESE**	**BAJAU-SULUK**	**KADAZAN-DUSUN**	**MURUT**	**MALAY**	**OTHERS**
Turnout	60.7%	71.8%	74.9%	79.8%	53.2%	65.6%
Turnout Change from GE14	-13.2%	-6.3%	-7.5%	-0.6%	-21.9%	-10.6%
GRS	3.6%	43.7%	55.4%	57.8%	57.5%	44.1%
Warisan Plus	92.9%	55.9%	28.2%	29.8%	35.0%	29.9%
Warisan Plus Support Change from GE14	0.2%	-4.8%	1.4%	-6.2%	-5.2%	-8.6%
Others	3.5%	0.3%	16.5%	12.4%	7.5%	26.1%

The focal point of ethnic analyses of the Sabah 2020 polls has been on the KDM communities[14] – their lack of support is blamed for the Warisan

[14] This community has been the main focus of ethnicity analyses. See, Arnold Puyok, 'Ethnic Factor in the 2008 Malaysian General Election: The Case of The Kadazan Dusun (KD) In Sabah,' *Jebat: Malaysian Journal of History, Politics & Strategic Studies* 35 (2020): 1-16; Arnold Puyok and Tony Paridi Bagang, 'Ethnicity, Culture and Indigenous Leadership in Modern Politics: The Case of the KadazanDusun in Sabah, East Malaysia,' *Kajian Malaysia: Journal of Malaysian Studies* 29 (2011): 177-97. This focus was established early in Sabah political analyses, with attention to developments from the 1980s. See Robert S. Milne, and K. J. Ratnam, 'Patterns and Peculiarities of Voting in Sabah, 1967,' *Asian Survey* 9, no. 5 (1969): 373-381 and James Chin, 'The Sabah State election of 1994: end of Kadazan unity,' *Asian Survey* 34, no. 10 (1994): 904-915.

Plus defeat.[15] The data show that KDM never substantively supported Warisan (or Pakatan Rakyat/Harapan in earlier elections), as only an estimated 26.7 per cent of Kadazan-Dusuns and an estimated 36 per cent Muruts voted for Warisan and Pakatan Harapan in GE14. In 2020 there was almost no change in support for Warisan Plus among Kadazans and Dusuns (an estimated small 1.4 per cent increase) while there was an estimated 6.2 per cent drop in support among Muruts. This latter shift needs to be understood through a class lens, as Muruts are disproportionately less economically advantaged compared with the other two KDM groups, especially Kadazans, whilst another factor was the popularity of independent Murut candidates such as Rubin Balang, president of Persatuan Murut Sabah (Sabah Murut Association) and victor in the Kemabong seat.

What the earlier ethnic voting patterns suggest is that in both the earlier 2013 and 2018 elections KDM voters were divided, splitting their support for the rising STAR Sabah rights movement led by Jeffrey Kitingan, BN parties and their Pakatan/Warisan challengers. The plurality of KDM voted for BN-related parties which extended into support for GRS in the 2020 Sabah polls. The biggest difference among KDM in 2020 is not a change in support for Warisan Plus, rather it is the impact of Kitingan's STAR move into the UMNO/BN GRS alliance, increasing support among Kadazan-Dusuns for the alliance by an estimated 22.4 per cent. Kitingan's 'star' power is sizeable based on the data. Change can also be seen among Muruts, who increasingly opted for independent candidates like Balang.

The KDM-based United Progressive Kinabalu Organisation (UPKO) in the Warisan Plus alliance has been blamed for 'failing to deliver' KDM votes,[16] but the ethnic voting patterns show that their core KDM support came from their time in BN. In all of the 12 seats UPKO contested, they needed large swings of support among the KDM to win and the party was lucky to win the one seat it did, Kadamaian, retained by Ewon Benedick.

15 James Chin, 'Commentary: Sabah's Surprise Results and how Warisan Lost Big in Sabah's State Elections,' *Channel News Asia*, 28 September 2020, https://www.channelnewsasia.com/news/commentary/sabah-election-results-how-warisan-lost-big-grs-won-huge-13156026.

16 Hisommudin Bakar, 'Indifference, KDM rebellion, and Weak Allies Cost Shafie his Sabah Prize,' *Malaysia Now*, 27 September 2020, https://www.malaysianow.com/news/2020/09/27/indifference-kdm-rebellion-and-weak-allies-cost-shafie-his-sabah-prize/.

Support levels among KDM remained the same as they did 26 months earlier; UPKO was not able to bring BN-allied KDM support with them.

When we look at turnout results, we see that fewer among the Kadazan-Dusun communities opted to come out to vote (a 7.5 per cent estimated drop) while the Murut voted in higher numbers, with a marginal estimated drop in turnout (0.6 per cent). These numbers are above the average drop in turnout across communities for the election, suggesting that KDM loyalties and political engagement remain strong, as do the political divisions in the communities.

Chinese Sabahans have also shown consistency in their voting recently, but this consistency did not yield the kingmaker role that was projected.[17] Traditionally, Chinese Sabahans have been important kingmakers in state politics, but their influence in shaping final outcomes has waned with greater demographic diversity in Sabah.[18] Among Chinese Sabahans there is more unity as the overwhelming majority have voted for non-BN related parties in recent elections. In 2020, support levels among Chinese Sabahans marginally increased, reaching an estimated 92.9 per cent in favor of Warisan Plus – in line with earlier levels. There was, however, a sharp drop in turnout among Chinese Sabahans, an estimated drop of 13.2 per cent. Some of this was tied to Covid-19, but interviews from the ground suggest there was greater cynicism about the electoral process among Chinese Sabahans, especially after the February 'Sheraton Move' and persistent 'frogging' (defections from parties), and for some, disappointment with Pakatan Harapan and Warisan Plus, especially in their economic performance.

The community that was expected to continue to support Warisan Plus was the Bajau-Suluk, especially those located on the east coast.[19] Interviews in Sekong (located near Sandakan on the east coast), with young Bajau-Suluk voters, yielded a consistent answer in explaining their support for

---

17 Bridget Welsh, 'Chinese Sabahan Kingmaker Factor,' *Sin Chew Daily*, 23 September 2020, https://www.sinchew.com.my/content/content_2346917.html.

18 Henry Robert Glick, 'The Chinese Community in Sabah and the 1963 Election,' *Asian Survey* 5, no. 3 (1965): 144-151 and Danny Wong Tze Ken, 'Weaker Kingmakers? Chinese Politics in Sabah under Mahathir,' in Bridget Welsh (ed.) *Reflections: The Mahathir Years* (Washington, DC: Johns Hopkins University-SAIS, 2004) 199-209.

19 James Chin, 'Sabah and Sarawak in the 14th General Election 2018 (GE14): local factors and state nationalism,' *Journal of Current Southeast Asian Affairs* 37, no. 3 (2018): 173-192.

Warisan – '*bangsa*' or nation, support along ethnic lines. Warisan Plus's leader Shafie Apdal is Bajau and this appeal was a factor in shaping support from GE14 onwards. In fact, his coalition did secure a majority of this community, winning an estimated 55.9 per cent of these groups. This however was a drop of an estimated 4.8 per cent from GE14, with a drop in turnout of an estimated 6.3 per cent. Collectively, this is a noticeable decline in support among these groups, but also speaks to the diversity among the Bajau-Suluk communities and, importantly, the limits of ethnic appeals. At the same time, many in the Bajau-Suluk communities had high expectations of Shafie's government, leading to expected gaps in realising these expectations.

A parallel decline of support was found among Malays in Sabah, disproportionately among Brunei Malays. This community is also diverse and included Malays from the Peninsula. Modestly fewer Malays supported Warisan Plus, an estimated drop of 5.2 per cent from an estimated 35 per cent in GE14. Malays have traditionally supported BN, especially UMNO. The opposition across Malaysia has struggled hard to win over this community, not only in Sabah but in Malaysia as a whole. In comparison to Pakatan Harapan in Peninsular Malaysia (with an estimated 24 per cent support in GE14) Warisan did well in GE14, securing an estimated 40 per cent of Malay support. GRS gains in 2020 reflect modest shifting loyalties, as GRS worked hard to project an image of a 'Malay' government. Yet, the most important finding among Malays is greater political disengagement, with an estimated 21.9 per cent opting not to vote. Interviews suggest this was tied to dissatisfaction with UMNO and its leadership, as well as its comparatively weaker machinery as it was decimated after GE14 in Sabah and suffered defections to Bersatu. Another factor which also swayed the low turnout was inter-Malay party competition.[20] There was unhappiness with

[20] For a discussion of inter-Malay party competition in Sabah see Mohamad Shaukhi Mohd Radzi, Syahruddin Awang Ahmad, and Nordin Sakke, 'Penyertaan Parti Islam Se-Malaysia (PAS) dalam Pilihan Raya Umum 14 (PRU-14) di Sabah: Penelitian ke atas Pola Pengudian, Pendekatan Berkempen dan Persepsi Masyarakat (The Malaysian Islamic Party (PAS) in the 14th General Elections (GE-14) in Sabah: A Study on Voting Patterns, Campaign Approaches and Society's Perceptions),' *Jurnal Kinabalu* (2018): 437-437. Party loyalties did sway support in areas where these loyalties were strong in 2020. See Bridget Welsh, 'The PAS Factor in Sabah Polls,' *Malaysiakini*, 2 October 2020, https://www.malaysiakini.com/columns/545038.

the party that was chosen to compete in different contests and in some areas disgruntlement among some PAS supporters about the party not contesting. Many party loyalists stayed home. More Malays were disappointed with all the options on offer.

The final 'others' grouping – comprised of a wide range of indigenous communities often locally concentrated in specific seats – is a large share of the electorate, nearly a third, at 30.3 per cent. With the creation of more seats geared around specific communities, the 'other' communities are in fact quite different from each other, except that they are all smaller minorities in a plural ethnic mosaic. We see changes in the support of these minorities for Warisan at an estimated 8.6 per cent and an estimated drop in turnout of 10.6 per cent. The diversity in this grouping cautions overinterpreting this data, but generally the declines in support point to dissatisfaction and limited engagement among smaller ethnic communities with Warisan Plus. The estimated support levels from 'others' at 29.9 per cent are in line with support levels from KDM communities and highlight that while a plurality of 'others' support GRS, many also voted for independent candidates as well, as many of these independents were from the 'other' communities. This suggests that for many 'other' voters, ethnicity is a factor in voting.

Overall, the data show that Warisan Plus was not able to fundamentally change long-standing ethnic support patterns from GE14 while in office for 26 months. Declines in turnout along ethnic lines also affected the core support base of both Warisan Plus and UMNO, especially Chinese and Malay voters respectively. The entrance of Bersatu and realignment of STAR shaped new ethnic voting patterns, with Kitingan's new political alignment decisive in changing ethnic voting patterns.

By-generation Voting in PRN2020

Another way to understand voting is to look at different age cohorts. While Sabah's youth are a large share of the electorate, all of the different age cohorts can make a difference in the outcome as they each comprise a large share of the electorate.

Table 4 details shifts by age cohort in the last three elections. The table shows that in GE14 there was a swing away from BN across age cohorts, with Warisan/PH particularly gaining among younger voters, capturing an estimated 50.4 per cent of them. In the 2020 polls Warisan Plus experienced a phenomenon similar to that of Pakatan Harapan – erosion of support among younger voters. Warisan Plus lost an estimated 8.2 per cent of voters in their 20s and an estimated 8.1 per cent of voters in their 30s. Sabah's then incumbent government did not retain the support of the young. Parallel to this was greater disengagement among younger voters. Nearly a fifth, an estimated 19.4 per cent of registered voters under 30, opted not to vote – some of these due to Covid-19 and the costs of travel. An estimated 13.8 per cent of voters in their 30s also stayed home, also likely impacted by Covid-19 conditions. Even with the circumstances of the election, the drop in turnout is sizeable and shows youth disengagement, even some displeasure with elections. Those in their 50s – the *Reformasi* generation (those that were socialised into politics around the 1999 election) – also opted not to come out in high numbers, an estimated 19.1 per cent drop. Voters in their 40s were the most engaged politically, with only a modest estimated turnout drop of 1.6 per cent.

Table 4: Estimates of Voting in Sabah by Age Cohort, 2013, 2018 and 2020

2013	**21-30**	**31-40**	**41-50**	**51-60**	**> 60**
Voters	23.0%	24.1%	21.9%	16.5%	14.5%
Turnout	77.3%	79.6%	80.7%	81.2%	72.4%
BN	58.4%	56.8%	54.2%	53.3%	54.0%
PR	29.8%	30.6%	32.0%	36.7%	33.8%
Others	11.8%	12.6%	13.8%	10.0%	12.2%
2018	**21-30**	**31-40**	**41-50**	**51-60**	**> 60**
Voters	20.6%	25.5%	20.4%	17.3%	16.3%
Turnout	73.5%	76.7%	81.1%	82.8%	74.1%
BN	38.6%	40.9%	44.1%	41.9%	45.7%
Warisan/PH	50.4%	48.3%	43.5%	49.2%	43.9%
Others	11.0%	10.8%	12.5%	9.0%	10.4%
2020	**21-30**	**31-40**	**41-50**	**51-60**	**> 60**
Voters	14.2%	27.1%	20.9%	18.2%	19.6%
Turnout	54.1%	62.9%	82.7%	63.7%	66.3%
Change Turnout GE14	19.4%	-13.8%	1.6%	-19.1%	-7.8%
GRS	44.4%	45.3%	45.1%	40.1%	40.0%
Warisan Plus	42.3%	40.2%	40.5%	47.6%	46.8%
Others	13.3%	14.5%	14.5%	12.3%	13.1%
Change Warisan+ GE14	-8.2%	-8.1%	-3.0%	-1.5%	3.0%

One way to interpret the data are that the erosion of youth support and drop in turnout affected the electoral outcome negatively for Warisan Plus. Given the competitiveness of the outcome, this generation swing is important as part of our understanding of why Shafie's government was not returned to power. At the same time, the data suggest that there is an ongoing battle for support across cohorts, including the young. The support among younger voters was evenly divided, with GRS having more of an advantage among those in their 30s and 40s and Warisan Plus winning over the *Reformasi* generation. Independents also won more support in the Sabah 2020 poll across age cohorts. Overall, there is no clear generational vote bank for different alliances in Sabah. Parties can no longer take different age cohorts for granted.

Geography at Play: The Urban-Rural Divide and Regionalism

If there is another paradigm that is used to interpret the election, it is based on geography. Repeatedly, analysis draws attention to the urban-rural divide as a frame to understand voting.[21] The assumptions are that those in the rural areas have less access to information and are seen as being potentially more susceptible to the persuasions of incumbent narratives and financial inducements. Implicitly, rural folk are seen as captured by the BN, often through pejorative lenses.

Table 5 below details voting by levels of urbanisation, using polling stations as the unit of analysis. As noted above, the majority of voters live in rural areas, most without access to regular Internet access and amenities. A small share of voters, 16.1 per cent, live in urban areas. This is in stark contrast with Peninsular Malaysia and differs from Sarawak in the larger share of voters in rural areas.

---

21 See, for example, Anantha Raman Govindasamy and Yew Meng Lai. 'GE14: The Urban Voting Pattern In P172 Kota Kinabalu and P186 Sandakan, Sabah.' *Jebat: Malaysian Journal of History, Politics & Strategic Studies* 45, no. 2 (2018): 298-318 and Arnold Puyok and Piya Raj Sukhani. 'Sabah: breakthrough in the fixed deposit state.' *The Round Table* 109, no. 2 (2020): 209-224.

Table 5: Estimates of Voting in Sabah by Urbanisation, 2013, 2018 and 2020

2013	RURAL	SEMI-RURAL	URBAN
Estimated Voters	48.8%	35.8%	15.3%
Turnout	79.8%	79.7%	77.5%
BN	57.9%	61.0%	35.2%
PR	28.0%	27.4%	57.4%
Others	14.0%	11.6%	7.4%
2018	**RURAL**	**SEMI-RURAL**	**URBAN**
Estimated Voters	50.9%	33.0%	16.1%
Turnout	77.5%	74.4%	74.2%
BN	49.8%	38.8%	23.3%
Warisan/PH	35.7%	53.2%	72.4%
Others	14.5%	8.0%	4.3%
2020	**RURAL**	**SEMI-RURAL**	**URBAN**
Estimated Voters	50.9%	33.0%	16.1%
Turnout	69.7%	63.7%	62.9%
Change Turnout GE14	-7.8%	-10.7%	-11.3%
GRS	51.5%	41.1%	18.5%
Warisan Plus (W+)	31.5%	47.6%	74.2%
Others	17.0%	11.3%	7.4%
Change W+ GE14	-4.2%	-5.6%	1.8%

The data show a clear urban-rural divide in voting. Urban areas – areas where the dominant narratives about politics are often shaped, including on social media – vote for non-BN aligned parties. Urban support for BN-aligned GRS eroded further in the 2020 polls, by an estimated 4.8 per cent, reaching only an estimated 18.5 per cent. Interestingly some of this erosion of support went to other candidates, as Warisan Plus was only able to capture half of the change in the urban vote, an estimated 2.2 per cent. Independent candidates appealing to issues of justice and good governance, such as well-known local activist Jan Chow Fan who contested in the Tanjung Aru seat as part of the Independent Candidate Alliance (ICA), which contested in Kota Kinabalu, were only able to capture a small share of the vote. Rural and semi-rural support did not go to Warisan Plus, with GRS capturing an estimated 51.5 per cent and 41.1 per cent respectively. It is important to recognise that rural and semi-rural areas disproportionately favored the BN even before the 2020 polls. Yet, large shares of rural and semi-rural support continue to go to others, notably independent candidates – an estimated 17 per cent and 11.3 per cent respectively in 2020. These findings regarding the support for 'other' candidates point to the relevance of local personalities and social networks in rural and semi-rural areas, a traditional explanation for understanding the urban-rural divide.[22] This is a demonstration of the politics of the familiar noted in my earlier chapter. The findings also highlight that the BN – having been in power for decades – still retains a considerable hold on the rural and remote areas. The urban-rural factor maintains relevance in voting patterns, even as the divide narrows with improvements in communication and greater access to remote areas. The continued relevance of this difference highlights how sharp it remains in Sabah – as development has not extended to the rural areas to the same extent as in parts of Peninsular Malaysia, and these differences in living conditions remain relevant for ordinary Sabahans.

Regionalism: Another Geographic Divide

Sabah's vast size and unique geography calls for further reinterpretation of the role of place in voting. Fellow co-editor Vilashini Somiah and her chapter co-author Aslam Abd Jalil concentrate on the east-west divide, pointing to the different regional narratives around place among Sabahans. In their analysis of voting, Ilham Centre also pointed to different regional clusters.[23] Regions are shaped by Sabah's geography, the rivers and mountain ranges in particular, and reflect different patterns of settlement, and to a lesser extent, different livelihoods. Those involved in the lush agriculture around Kundasang have greater access to vegetables compared with those living near the oil palm plantations outside of Lahad Datu, for example. Drawing from these differences, I identify four regions – North, Central, East and West – and find that the electoral data reinforces the saliency of looking at regionalism within Sabah.[24]

---

[22] The pivotal role of personality was emphasised early on in research on Sabah. See Robert S. Milne, 'Patrons, clients and ethnicity: The case of Sarawak and Sabah in Malaysia', *Asian Survey* 13, no. 10 (1973): 891-907.

[23] See their Facebook post: https://ilhamcentre.info/persaingan-sengit-warisan-plus-di-hadapan/.

[24] North is comprised of Banggi, Benkoka, Pitas, Tanjong Kapor, Matunggong, Bandau and Tandek seats, while Central refers to Kundasang, Karanaan, Paginatan,

Table 6 below shows important political shifts taking place. The GE14 outcome reflected changes in voting across the state, but especially concentrated in the East where the BN lost 23.8 per cent of its support. There were, however, sizeable erosions of political support in the North and West as well, 10.2 per cent and 10.4 per cent respectively. Warisan may have its base in the East, but its appeal extended across Sabah in GE14.

Table 6: Shifts in Voting by Region 2018, 2020

2018	TURNOUT	BN	Warisan/PH	IND	BN Change
Central	78.5%	47.4%	33.3%	19.3%	-3.9%
East	73.7%	40.6%	54.4%	5.1%	-23.8%
North	74.0%	43.4%	37.5%	19.1%	-10.2%
West	81.1%	40.8%	49.1%	10.1%	-10.4%
2020	**TURNOUT**	**GRS**	**Warisan Plus**	**IND**	**W+ Change**
Central	70.4%	58.7%	27.6%	13.7%	-5.7%
East	59.9%	36.9%	52.8%	10.2%	-1.5%
North	66.5%	47.3%	27.7%	25.0%	-9.8%
West	70.5%	40.5%	45.7%	13.8%	-3.4%

The North was, interestingly, the area that changed most in PRN2020, with an estimated 9.8 per cent shift away from Warisan Plus in places such as Tanjung Kapor in Kudat and Julia's (from Vignette 2) district Tandek near Kota Marudu in the region as whole. By comparison, the East and West stayed more consistent in their support in 2020. The East, however, showed the most significant drop in turnout: 13.8 per cent. In part this could have been affected by Covid-19 cases, which at that time was concentrated on the east coast, but this pattern reflects the more general pattern of Warisan Plus losing support amongst its political base.

Tambunan, Bingkor, Liawan, Melalap, Kemabong, Tulid, Sook, Nabawan, Telupid, Sugut and Labuk. West includes Pintasan, Tempasuk, Usukan, Kadamaian, Sulaman, Pantai Dalit, Tamparuli, Kiulu, Karambunai, Darau, Inanam, Likas, Api-Api, Luyang, Tanjung Aru, Petagas, Tanjung Keramat. Kapayan, Moyog, Limbahau, Kawang, Pantai Manis, Bongawan, Membakut, Klias, Kuala Penyu, Lumadin and Sindumin. East includes Gum-Gum, Sungai Manila, Sungai Sibuga, Sekong, Karamunting, Elopura, Tanjong Papat, Kuamut, Lamag, Sukau, Tungku, Segama, Silam, Kunak, Sulabayan, Senallang, Bugaya, Balung, Apas, Sri Tanjong, Kukusan, Tanjong Batu, Merotai and Sebatik. Thanks to Vilashini Somiah for her assistance with these categories.

Regionalism offers new insights into voting patterns. It allows us to understand how connected areas shape outcomes, particularly given the vast size of Sabah and the fact that constituency lines often do not correspond to clear divisions in engagement of daily life. We see that the east-west narrative, while politically salient, does not correspond to clear cut differences in voting. Both regions are split in their political loyalties. The East is as politically competitive as the West. In fact, more so in 2020 given the drop in turnout in the East. We also see the ability of parties to expand their machinery in particular areas, as was the case in the Centre with the expansion of Kitingan's support around his base in Tambunan.

Gender Swing: Male Mobilisation and Engagement

If the regional lens adds further understanding to patterns of support, a gender lens offers even more necessary new insights. In the election campaign Sabah women's organisations such as Sabah Women's Action Resource Group (SAWO), as well as Rakyat is Bos and other activists raised concerns about the exclusion of women by political parties. Only 43 out of 447 candidates in PRN2020 were women, fielded in 32 constituencies.[25] Neither Warisan Plus nor GRS worked to include women – fielding only 13 women between them. Only seven women won seats. Warisan's Kalabakan Women Chief Rina Jainal won in a very close contest (10 votes) in Kukusan – a real victory given the sizeable number of postal votes in this seat. Flovia Ng also won in an uphill contest, beating six others in the new seat of Tulid. Female incumbents Christina Liew, Julita Mojungki, Norazlinah Arif, Manis Muka Mohd Darah and Jannie Lasimbang were returned in Api Api, Matunggong, Kunak, Bugaya and Kapayan respectively. Manis Muka passed away after the election, with her seat still unfilled. Jannie Lasimbang secured the second highest majority of all the (female and male) candidates. Female candidates not part of the political parties performed poorly, with 29 women losing their deposits. To worsen the exclusion of women further, the GRS government refused to appoint any women to cabinet and only appointed one woman, Amisah Yassin, among the six nominated assemblypersons

[25] See SAWO and Rakyat is Bos, 'Appoint women as assemblypersons to remedy gender imbalance,' *Malaysiakini*, 20 September 2020, https://www.malaysiakini.com/letters/543279 and Majidah Hashim, 'Women's issues are political issues,' *Malaysiakini*, 24 September 2020, https://www.malaysiakini.com/columns/543913.

that the winning government is able to appoint under Sabah's Constitution, despite calls to do so by civil society.[26]

Sabah's low female political representation in the state assembly is illustrative of a broader pattern of female participation in Sabah. While women make up almost half the electorate, there is a deficit in their political engagement and, importantly, how they are engaged. Table 7 estimates voting behavior by gender in Sabah since the 2013 election. Consistently, women turned out less than men, with this gap widest in GE14 (an estimated turnout gender gap of 12.3 per cent). This narrowed in the 2020 polls to an estimated 3.3 per cent difference as overall turnout dropped. Nevertheless, through the last three elections, Sabahan women have not participated to the same degree as men. This is despite the fact that a larger number of women are registered to vote than men. When comparing the 2020 electoral roll with the census, 306,675 men were estimated to not be registered compared to 295,747 women.

There are reasons for this gender gap in female political participation, which the data on voting helps us understand. Scholars regularly explain a gender gap in voting as a product of women being expected to perform traditional family roles and the 'double' or 'triple' demands on their time: earning a living, taking care of housework and often caring for others.[27] With political parties in Sabah not empowering women, this reinforces traditional values of family roles which are already seen to be quite entrenched in Sabah society.[28] As the vignette from Tandek above showed, women also do not necessarily support women. Yet the answers also lie in other practices by parties. Campaigns in Sabah (and arguably Malaysia as a whole) are geared towards men. My earlier chapter on campaigns highlighted the 'masculinity' of the 2020 campaign – the 'fighting' rhetoric and toxic masculinity. On the ground observations of campaigns showed that many of the campaign workers are disproportionately men, with considerably fewer women than found in Peninsular Malaysia. Political

26 Stephanie Lee, 'No Women in New Sabah Cabinet a Backward Move,' *The Star*, 10 October 2020, https://www.thestar.com.my/news/nation/2020/10/10/no-women-in-new-sabah-cabinet-a-backward-move.

27 Ronald Inglehart and Pippa Norris, 'The developmental theory of the gender gap: Women's and men's voting behavior in global perspective,' *International Political Science Review* 21, no. 4 (2000): 441-463.

28 Interviews with women's empowerment activists in Kota Kinabalu, September 2020.

parties in Sabah lack strong female foundations in their party machinery. It is thus not surprising to see that men change their political support more than women. As shown in Table 7, in GE14 an estimated 19.5 per cent of men abandoned BN (UMNO), compared to an estimated 7.2 per cent of women. In the Sabah 2020 polls an estimated 7.3 per cent of men opted not to support Warisan Plus, compared to an estimated 0.3 per cent of women. Sabah men are the swing, even 'emotional' voters.

Another interpretation of these results is that women are more loyal, that they do not change their support as easily. Clearly some of this is steadfastness and risk-adverse behavior. As the main primary caregivers in families, women do not want to risk changing political loyalties in a system tied to political patronage at the local level.

At the same time, a large part of lower female political participation has to do with the fact that Sabah campaigns ignore women – in the messages, the issues addressed, in the mobilisation and as noted above, in who they field and appoint. Women do not change their vote to the same extent because they are given no reason to do so.

Table 7: Estimates of Voting in Sabah by Gender, 2013, 2018 and 2020

2013	MALE	FEMALE	Gender Gap	Change Male	Change Female
Voters	50.4%	49.6%	0.9%	N/A	N/A
Turnout	81.5%	75.5%	6.0%	N/A	N/A
BN	63.2%	47.3%	16.0%	N/A	N/A
PR	29.7%	34.9%	-5.2%	N/A	N/A
Others	7.0%	17.8%	-10.8%	N/A	N/A
2018	**MALE**	**FEMALE**	**Gender Gap**	**Change Male**	**Change Female**
Voters	50.2%	49.8%	0.4%	-0.2%	0.2%
Turnout	83.7%	71.4%	12.3%	2.2%	-4.1%
BN	43.8%	40.0%	3.8%	-19.5%	-7.2%
Warisan/PH	45.7%	48.9%	-3.2%	15.9%	14.0%
Others	10.6%	11.1%	-0.5%	3.5%	-6.7%
2020	**MALE**	**FEMALE**	**Gender Gap**	**Change Male**	**Change Female**
Voters	50.1%	49.9%	0.2%	-0.1%	0.1%
Turnout	68.2%	65.0%	3.3%	-15.5%	-6.4%
GRS	49.9%	36.2%	13.8%	6.1%	-3.9%
Warisan Plus	38.4%	48.1%	-9.7%	-7.3%	-0.8%
Others	11.7%	15.8%	-4.0%	1.2%	4.7%

The lack of engagement comes at a party's own peril. Even with lower turnout, women are a large share of the electorate and have made an important difference in outcomes. From 2013 onwards, women have opted to vote for the opposition and independent candidates more than men – the latter shaped by close ties that independent candidates have within local social networks. In GE14 as well women were more likely to support Warisan/PH than men, although the scope of the swing to Warisan/PH by men was larger. Women continued to vote in larger numbers for Warisan Plus by an estimated 9.7 per cent more compared to men in 2020. Interviews from the ground in 2020 suggest that men in particular are more mobilised by Kitingan's STAR, UMNO and Bersatu. While electoral outcomes may be shaped by the swing voters in the close contests in Sabah, who are largely men, women have through their support over the last three elections assured that Sabah elections remain competitive.

Class Voting: Capitalising on Disadvantage

Last, and definitely not least, is the role that socio-economic or 'class' status, based narrowly on income differentials, plays in underscoring voting. I argue elsewhere that class is an essential lens to understanding voting in Malaysia – and this was clearly the case in Sabah 2020.[29] The poorer you are, the more you vote and the more you vote for the alliance that controlled Sabah for decades – BN/UMNO. GRS is at its core these same BN parties, and also relied on lower income support to secure its victory in 2020.

Table 8 details class patterns of voting in Sabah since 2013. The categories are differentiated by income, drawn from assessments of areas at the polling station and weighted for representativeness based on the latest 2019 DOSM survey data. Lower income voters are households earning less than RM2000 monthly, lower middle income RM2000-5000, middle income RM5000-10,000, upper middle RM10,000-20,000 and upper above RM20,000 monthly.[30]

Consistently, through the last three elections, although not by large

---

29 Bridget Welsh, 'Warisan Swing: How it helped "win" Sabah in GE14,' *Malaysiakini*, 24 September 2020, https://www.malaysiakini.com/columns/543711.

30 As noted earlier, these classifications are done for polling station areas through field visits and interviews with local elites familiar with the different localities. The income classification is based on perceived average income in a locality.

margins, lower income voters turn out more than middle or upper income voters. The common explanation for this is that lower income voters come out due to the financial incentives provided during elections. I argue that this explanation is too simplistic and dismissive of the broader context faced by poorer Sabahans, who disproportionately comprise at least a third of the electorate. The funds and food-in-kind given in campaigns are impactful, but the ties to state patronage and access to local representatives extend well beyond election day. Poorer voters need to know their representatives more than richer voters do, they are more dependent in a personalised patronage system where social and political networks are important. This is especially the case in a peripheral state such as Sabah where the bureaucracy and government infrastructure is less developed and citizens have to rely on personal ties for access to social services, even in some cases this happens in the urban areas.

Table 8: Estimates of Voting in Sabah by Class (Income-Based), 2013, 2018 and 2020

2013	LOWER	LOWER MIDDLE	MIDDLE	UPPER MIDDLE	UPPER
Turnout	81.1%	80.6%	78.4%	78.8%	76.0%
BN	72.9%	63.7%	50.7%	38.9%	38.6%
PR	16.0%	26.9%	35.3%	48.3%	41.4%
Others	11.1%	9.5%	14.0%	12.8%	20.0%
2018	**LOWER**	**LOWER MIDDLE**	**MIDDLE**	**UPPER MIDDLE**	**UPPER**
Turnout	78.6%	75.3%	76.1%	76.1%	73.0%
BN	61.5%	44.5%	37.7%	34.0%	29.0%
Warisan/PH	23.0%	44.1%	53.3%	57.5%	58.0%
Others	15.5%	11.4%	9.0%	8.5%	13.0%
2020	**LOWER**	**LOWER MIDDLE**	**MIDDLE**	**UPPER MIDDLE**	**UPPER**
Turnout	71.3%	66.0%	66.2%	66.0%	64.4%
GRS	67.1%	50.3%	36.0%	26.6%	29.0%
Warisan Plus	17.5%	34.9%	51.6%	61.2%	56.7%
Others	15.4%	14.8%	12.3%	12.2%	14.3%
Change GRS	5.6%	5.8%	-1.7%	-7.4%	0.0%

The data also show that BN traditionally (and GRS in 2020) get their core support from the lower income voters, winning an estimated 61.5 per cent of lower income voters in GE14 and an estimated 67.1 per cent of this group in 2020 – a gain of an estimated 5.6 per cent. This reinforces the point made in my campaign chapter on the saliency of Bantuan Prihatin Rakyat aid from the federal government for those struggling during the pandemic. Warisan Plus was not able to maintain their support among lower income voters, especially as the economy did not grow significantly, with high unemployment and Covid-19. Lower middle class voters were more divided among Warisan Plus and GRS. Wealthier voters supported non-BN alternatives, from Pakatan Rakyat and Warisan/PH to Warisan Plus, to a greater extent. In 2020 an estimated 56.7 per cent of upper class voters voted for Warisan Plus compared with only an estimated 29% supporting GRS. The findings along class lines suggest that class lines in Sabah politics are as decisive as ethnic ones and the urban-rural divide. Historically, the BN/UMNO has relied on poorer voters to keep itself in office and looked to this group to put it back into office – which happened in 2020 as well.

Assessing PRN2020's New Context

The 2020 polls were a different contest than earlier elections, however. Non-BN parties were the incumbent fighting to stay in power. The BN/UMNO, after a devastating defeat in GE14 and mass party defections, had to rely on its coalition partners to get back into power. When it did, UMNO was a secondary partner to Bersatu which now helms the state. Warisan/PH, after ousting UMNO, was itself ousted.

The status of different parties was not the only difference in the Sabah polls.[31] An important change was the addition of 13 new seats – a decision initiated in 2016 that Musa Aman had resisted supporting when in power and which Warisan/PH had pushed and received legislative approval for in June 2019. Warisan Plus lost the majority of these 13 new seats, only winning four – Darau, Limbahau, Segama and Kukusan. Arguments were

[31] This extends a discussion on the new seats. See Bridget Welsh, 'Sabah's new seats- a reassessment' *Malaysiakini*, 9 September 2020, https://www.malaysiakini.com/news/538790 and Ng Xiang Yi and Andrew Ong, 'How 13 new seats tilts the balance for BN, Warisan,' *Malaysiakini*, 15 August 2020, https://www.malaysiakini.com/columns/541922.

made that the decision to go ahead with the recommendations of a BN-initiated delineation worked against Warisan/PH.[32] A closer look, drawing from all of the seats impacted by the delineation at the polling station levels, suggests Warisan/PH did in fact lose out in the delineation process, one that was stacked against them from the start.

A total of 39 state seats were affected, either through a new seat being created or the removal of polling stations from other seats, which made the original seat safer for the incumbent party or packed votes into another seat. Traditionally, these practices of cracking and packing have benefited UMNO, and sometimes specific individuals in UMNO. The Sabah delineation exercise, however, also followed the pattern set in Sarawak to create seats for smaller minorities – as was the case in the new Pintasan seat, empowering the Iranun community with greater representation. This logic assumed that smaller ethnic groups would opt to be part of the BN-allied alliance, as was the case in Sarawak after their delineation in 2016. On the ground, this combination of cracking, packing and minority empowerment was more complicated.

I examine the seats affected by the delineation and the outcome of the polls. The findings show that the creation of new seats advantaged GRS. Assessing voting patterns from GE14 at the polling station levels, they retained 20 of their seats,[33] while Warisan retained 13.[34] Warisan Plus lost the most seats – four – affected by the delineation (Pantai Manis, Kuamut, Tanjung Keramat and Karambunai) while GRS only lost two (Sebatik and Pitas). When one looks at the entire range of seats impacted, the outcome is less decisive – a two-seat difference in shaping outcomes – but the structural advantage that UMNO/BN built in through the delineation exercise is evident.

---

[32] Andrew Ong, 'Eight takeaways from Sabah polls,' *Malaysiakini*, 29 September 2020, https://www.malaysiakini.com/news/544494.

[33] Seats are assessed by looking at the polling stations results that made up the seat in GE14 and comparing them to PRN2020. GRS retained Bengkoka, Bandau, Pintasan, Tempasuk, Pantai Dalit, Tamparuli, Tulid, Sungai Manila, Lamag, Tanjung Batu, Sungai Manila, Sulaman, Usukan, Labuk, Mantunggong, Tandek, Kiulu, Kawang and Sook.

[34] Warisan Plus retained Darau, Inanam, Luyang, Tanjung Aru, Petagas, Limbahau, Segama, Silam, Kukusan, Merotai, Kapayan, Tungku and Banggi.

In fact, my analysis of the results suggests that two other features of the campaign were also impactful in shaping outcomes. The first of these were changes in the military and police vote. Former Minister of Tourism, Arts and Culture and current Silam Member of Parliament and Segama state assemblyman Mohamaddin Ketapi made remarks regarding the 2013 Lahad Datu standoff that went viral and were seen to insult security forces.[35] While an apology was subsequently issued, the findings show that these inappropriate comments lost Warisan its support. Interviews on the ground with police and military personnel evoked strong negative reactions regarding Mohamaddin, and the electoral results do point to a shift in support. Yet, the shift was concentrated in the military, and only impacted the final results in two seats – Karambunai and Tanjung Keramat.[36]

Chart 1 below, drawing from the specific streams detailing the postal votes of police and military over time from all of the seats, shows that support for GRS among military personnel increased by 20 per cent as Warisan's support was cut almost in half, reaching only 33 per cent. The shift was not as significant among police, which unlike the military in GE14 had not dropped their support for the BN/UMNO in Sabah. This is not surprising as the GE14 campaign in Sabah was about states' rights, and many of the police stationed in Sabah are from Peninsular Malaysia and all of them work for the federal government. That said, after Mohamaddin's comments support among police personnel dropped by 5 per cent for Warisan Plus, with more police personnel opting for independent candidates.

The electoral impact of changes in the vote of security forces was assessed on a seat-by-seat basis, as this vote is concentrated and can affect the outcome in seats where the outcome is close or there are a large number of security forces voters. The security forces only comprised more than 500 votes cast in five seats – Tanjung Keramat, Karambunai, Karamunting, Kukusan and Kawang. Table 9 lists the seats where the security forces' votes were over 200 and the respective increased share of the personnel vote received by GRS in 2020. It was only in two seats that the margin of change

[35] 'Mohamaddin apologies over remarks on Ops Daulat,' *Malaysiakini*, 21 September 2020, https://www.malaysiakini.com/news/543491.

[36] Zainal Epi, 'Warisan Lost Military Votes over Lahad Datu Comments,' *Malay Mail*, 22 September 2020, https://www.malaymail.com/news/malaysia/2020/09/22/warisan-lost-military-votes-over-lahad-datu-comments/1905580.

Chart 1: Military and Police Voting in Sabah by Party, 2018 and 2020

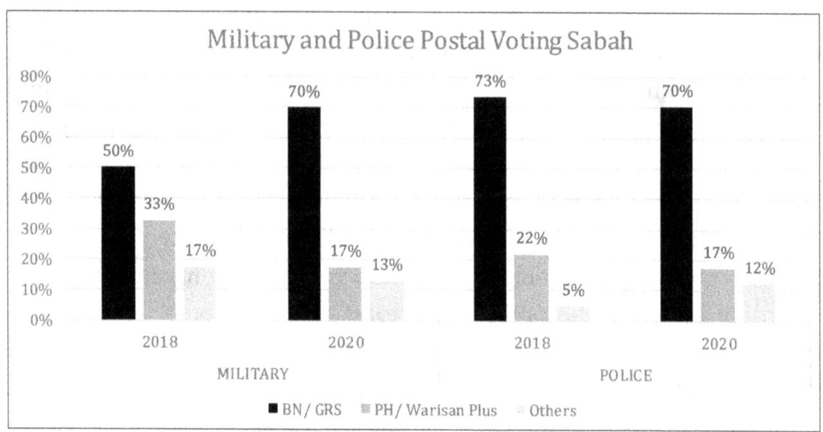

impacted the final outcome – Tanjung Keramat and Karambunai. It came close in other seats, especially Kukusan, which was only won by a margin of 10 votes. Two seats may not seem large given the overall decline in support, but the two-seat difference assured that Warisan Plus would not be able to form a government, as the final outcome was 38 versus 32 seats for the two alliances: GRS and Warisan Plus. No question: Warisan Plus needs to recognise the self-inflicted electoral damage caused by one of its leaders.

Table 9: Vote Share Security Forces BN % GRS in 2018, 2020 and 2020 Gain in 2020, Selected Seats

State Seat	BN Postal Vote 2018	GRS Postal Vote 2020	GRS Share Gain
Tanjung Keramat	54.7%	68.0%	13.4%
Karambunai	33.8%	60.8%	27.0%
Karamunting	47.2%	55.8%	8.6%
Kukusan	45.1%	50.7%	5.7%
Kawang	61.3%	77.6%	16.2%
Silam	44.5%	70.3%	25.8%
Apas	34.7%	92.2%	57.5%
Sebatik	55.6%	71.0%	15.4%
Merotai	50.0%	57.3%	7.3%
Sungai Sibuga	77.0%	87.9%	10.9%

A second contextual factor affecting the outcome was voter turnout. Based on interviews on the ground, four factors were seen to shape turnout levels: Covid-19 affecting the return and movement of voters, with many afraid to go out to vote due to the risks of the pandemic; disengagement/disenchantment with politics/political parties; disgruntlement with the party selected by party elites to contest in a seat; and ineffective mobilisation by political parties. Earlier, I suggested that voter turnout along ethnic lines affected Warisan Plus and UMNO in 2020. Voter turnout by gender and the urban-rural divide also influenced the results. Others have suggested that voter turnout did not impact the results at all.[37] A closer look at the data by polling station suggests otherwise. Assessing turnout and support patterns, Warisan Plus was most negatively affected by lower turnout.

Table 10 details turnout levels in polling stations with a pattern of voting for Warisan Plus and GRS, comparing turnout levels to GE14. The results show that Warisan Plus was more negatively impacted by the decline in turnout, with an estimated larger drop of 4.1 per cent, compared with GRS. Looking at the impact of lower turnout on the results, Warisan Plus lost two seats tied to lower turnout – Karambunai and Pantai Manis, both won by close margins of 0.1 per cent and 6.6 per cent of the overall vote respectively to UMNO. Better mobilisation of Warisan support in these areas could have affected the outcome.

Table 10: Estimated Turnout Levels by Political Support Overall and Selected Seats 2018, 2020

Turnout	GE14 2018	2020 Polls	Diff (2020 - 2018)
Overall (Actual)	76.0%	66.6%	-9.3%
BN / GRS Turnout	80.3%	72.4%	-7.9%
Warisan Plus Turnout	71.3%	59.0%	**-12.3%**
Independent Turnout	80.1%	72.3%	-7.7%
Karambunai (Actual)	77.2%	63.7%	-13.5%
BN / GRS Turnout	78.0%	67.8%	-10.2%
Warisan Plus Turnout	76.4%	59.6%	**-16.8%**
Independent Turnout	81.0%	63.7%	-17.3%

[37] Andrew Ong, 'Eight takeaways from Sabah polls,' *Malaysiakini*, 29 September 2020, https://www.malaysiakini.com/news/544494.

Turnout	GE14 2018	2020 Polls	Diff (2020 - 2018)
Pantai Manis (Actual)	81.8%	73.3%	-8.5%
BN / GRS Turnout	83.9%	77.0%	-6.9%
Warisan Plus Turnout	80.1%	69.1%	**-11.0%**
Independent Turnout	73.6%	73.1%	-0.5%

Consistency of Political Polarisation

While contextual factors did influence the electoral outcome, arguably one of the most significant findings from the data analysis is the persistence of voting patterns from previous elections. Earlier lenses allow a picture to emerge of changes in voting behavior – turnout drops among Chinese and Malays, modest changes in support across ethnic, generation, class and geographical lines and larger shifts by gender. We also see patterns of support for Warisan Plus and GRS along ethnic, regional, urban-rural, gender and class cleavages. These patterns point to the consistency in voting. Both BN-allied and non-BN allied political coalitions draw from familiar – and arguably politically divided – social foundations. Sabah's electoral results reflect the same polarisation of Peninsular Malaysia, not just in the closeness of the results (38 versus 32 and 10 seats or 14 per cent of all seats with less than 5 per cent majority [with 2 seats less than 1 per cent]), but in the underlying political loyalties.

In assessing the data from the 740 different polling stations, the polarisation is evident. 82 per cent of the polling stations stayed loyal to GRS, while 77 per cent did so for Warisan Plus. Only 10 per cent of polling stations moved from BN to Warisan Plus, while 17 per cent of Warisan/PH polling stations moved to GRS. Among 'Others/Independents' that changed support, the overwhelming majority of 96 per cent of these moved to GRS were the result of the Kitingan factor, while 'Others/Independents' drew from both BN and Warisan Plus. The overall takeaway is that nearly 80 per cent of support patterns stayed the same, and they are almost evenly split. The other 20 per cent that moved disproportionately reflected the Kitingan/STAR alliance with BN-allied GRS and moved toward the more competitive independents contesting these polls.

Table 11: Consistency in Support 2018 v. 2020

GE14	GRS (2020)	Warisan Plus (2020)	Others/Independents (2020)
BN	82%	10%	9%
Warisan/PH	17%	77%	6%
Others/Independents	96%	4%	0%

Traditionally, Sabah is understood to have political shifts, with more changes of state governments than any other state in Malaysia. Weighting for voters as opposed to the number of polling stations of seats, an estimated 12 per cent of the electorate changed their support, which is a significant share reflecting the competitiveness of the state. This also, however, simultaneously points to the consistency in support patterns in the past two elections. There is a politically divided Sabah – as there is a politically divided Malaysia.

In understanding political polarisation in Peninsular Malaysia, arguments rely on four pillars – ethnicity, forms of political socialisation (information source/education), different values and party loyalties/patronage.[38] The first explanation – ethnicity – predominates, with the other interconnected dimensions less developed. Sabah provides insights that help us understand polarisation in Malaysia as it does not conform to Peninsular patterns along ethnicity; different communities comprise support for both poles. Sabah's 2020 results suggest the need to move our analysis further.

When one accounts for areas where there are swings, i.e. gender or partisan loyalties to Kitingan/STAR, and consistencies in support along class, urban-rural and regional lines, additional insights emerge. Partisan loyalties and machineries do matter.[39] But given the comparative weakness of party machinery and limited political patronage in Sabah compared to Peninsular Malaysia or even Sarawak, the answers lie less with the parties themselves than with the voters, with the conditions they live in. Political

---

[38] Bridget Welsh, 'Malaysia's Political Polarization: Race, Religion, and Reform' in Thomas Carothers & Andrew O'Donohue (ed.) *Political Polarization in South and Southeast Asia: Old Divisions, New Dangers* (Carnegie Endowment for International Peace, 2020) 41-52.

[39] Meredith L. Weiss, *The Roots of Resilience: Party Machines and Grassroots Politics in Southeast Asia* (Cornell University Press, 2020).

polarisation emerges, in part, from the inequalities in Sabah society and political representation – the class divisions, gender engagement gaps and urban-rural/regional divides. Poorer voters opt for the party/alliance that best offers them survival, men politically engage because they are engaged by parties and rural and urban voters stick with what they can relate to, with rural areas relying on known social connections and urbanites, where political networks are less personalised, attracted to the messages that they connect to through the lens of their different value outlooks.

Grappling with Change and Survival

To understand Sabah's contemporary politics, it is necessary to bring a better understanding of the society into the analysis. The chapter has illustrated that looking at voting behavior with attention to different social cleavages offers richer insights into what happened in the election. The findings show that geography, gender and class were especially illuminating in underscoring patterns of voting in the Sabah polls, suggesting the need to go beyond ethnic and even generational frames. The lesson, however, lies in not prioritising one lens over another but in adopting a more holistic approach to interpreting voting behavior.

Among the implications of a society-oriented approach to understanding Sabah politics is the need to recognise the different possible drivers of politics. While attention has centred on the youths in Sabah's election, voting behavior of youths suggests considerable disengagement. Sabah's youth remain an untapped reservoir for political change. Demographic pressures alone – even when voters above 18 are registered – will not bring about political change without greater political engagement by and with younger voters.

Gender matters in Sabah politics. Campaigns that have engaged men bring them into the political process. At the same time, exclusion has moved more women toward the opposition, underscoring unappreciated pressures for political change.

Urbanisation has strengthened the non-BN parties/alliances' chances. Sabah, however, remains a rural society. Even as Internet and social media usage expand – which they have done extensively in the last few years – the shifts in voting are not changing to the same degree. This can be understood in part as the result of slow development in the rural areas as well as greater reliance on personalised social and patronage networks in these areas.

This is being shaped by the features in society that are not changing – poverty and economic exclusion. Development and higher incomes have led to decreased support for a BN status quo. It is thus not a surprise that BN-allied parties and elites have been slow in how they address the economic exclusion in Sabah society. The focus for many Sabahan voters remains on trying to survive. A clear trajectory of survival mode is to vote for candidates and parties that strengthen the capacity to survive by providing access to state resources or other forms of assistance. The social networks and ties – often reinforced by ethnicity, geography, generation cohort, and gender – are an integral part of the survival tactics evident in voting.

In the PRN2020 polls, a new alliance took office in Kota Kinabalu – it got into office by more effectively actualising its traditional social base and as described above, better capitalising on local Sabah conditions – a strategic alliance with Jeffrey Kitingan/STAR, fanning anger over remarks about Lahad Datu and its base turning out to a greater extent than Warisan Plus's. The contest was tight, however, as victories in a few seats would have led to a different victor. The electorate in Sabah remains polarised, suggesting that when the next election comes around the chances of change remain alive.

Chapter 12

Chinese Sabahans in the 2020 Sabah State Election

Oh Ei Sun and Amanda Yeo Yan Yin

Introduction

In the 2020 Sabah state election (PRN2020), Chinese Sabahan voters can be said to have opted overwhelmingly for the Warisan Plus coalition. The nine state constituencies which saw contests between Chinese candidates were all won by Warisan Plus candidates – five by the Democratic Action Party (DAP), three by Warisan (although DAP contested under the Warisan Plus ticket) and one by Parti Keadilan Rakyat (PKR). The largest majority among all Sabah state constituencies was found in the Luyang constituency, where DAP's 'Ginger' Phoong Jin Zhe beat his closest rival by 14,521 votes,[1] having obtained 91 per cent of the votes cast.[2] Warisan Plus won three such constituencies with 60 to 70 per cent of the votes cast, two each in the 50 to 60 per cent and 70 to 80 per cent ranges, and one in the 80 to 90 per cent range.[3]

This strong support from Chinese Sabahans for Warisan Plus is at least commensurate with, if not surpassing, their level of support in the 2018 General Election. Nevertheless, this rather one-sided support stands in contrast to that of many other Sabah communities which have been divided

---

1 'Sabah 2020: Razor thin, huge majority differentiates winners and losers,' *New Straits Times*, 26 September 2020, https://www.nst.com.my/news/politics/2020/09/627537/sabah-2020-razor-thin-huge-majority-differentiates-winners-and-losers.

2 'LIVE: Battle for Sabah – GRS 38, Warisan Plus 32, Independent 3,' *Malaysiakini*, 26 September 2020, https://www.malaysiakini.com/news/541008.

3 'Sabah Election Result,' *The Borneo Post*, 26 September 2020, https://sabah2020.theborneopost.com/

between support for Warisan Plus and Gabungan Rakyat Sabah (GRS). It is also contrary to the electoral trend in Peninsular Malaysia, which has seen a significant drop in Chinese support for the Pakatan Harapan (PH) government in a string of by-elections.[4]

Conversations with and ethnographic observations of Chinese Sabahan voters and other related stakeholders from the time of former Sabah Chief Minister Musa Aman's attempted change of government to the state election, as well as shortly after polling day, provide insights into the sentiments that propelled Chinese Sabahans' overwhelming support for Warisan Plus during PRN2020.[5]

This is supplemented by the authors' own personal experiences growing up as Chinese Sabahans on the western and eastern coasts of the state and their later exposure to Peninsular and Sarawakian politics. Further insights were gleaned from on-the-ground observations and general perusals of online postings during the two months before polling day. Based on the data we collected, we have a strong sense of Chinese Sabahan voters across Sabah and their sentiments in this election.

Divergent Sociopolitical Perspectives

From the outset, it is crucial to distinguish between the general socioeconomic and political conditions of Chinese Sabahans, and those of Peninsular Chinese and Chinese Sarawakians. Many Chinese Sabahans may be said to be of a different socioeconomic and hence political outlook when compared to their Peninsular and Sarawakian counterparts, at least since the Second World War. It is thus instructive to first summarise the longstanding socioeconomic and political positions of the Peninsular Chinese and Chinese Sarawakians, in order to lay the foundation for meaningful comparison with Chinese Sabahans, so as to more fully comprehend the latter's one-sided electoral support for Warisan Plus. It is equally pertinent to briefly delve into the historical perspective of Chinese Sabahans from the Second World War onwards, in order to arrive at a more complete picture of their contemporary political outlook.

---

4 Nigel Aw, 'Chinese voters abandon Harapan at more than double the rate of Malay areas,' *Malaysiakini*, 17 November 2019, https://www.malaysiakini.com/news/500113.

5 Bridget Welsh, 'Chinese Sabahan kingmaker factor,' *Sin Chew Daily*, 23 September 2020, https://www.sinchew.com.my/content/content_2346917.html.

In Peninsular Malaysia (then known as Malaya), many rural Chinese, who were essentially subsistence farmers or estate workers, were required by the British to relocate to New Villages in an effort to battle the spread of communism.[6] Although the movement restrictions in and around these New Villages relaxed over the years, the Chinese who emerged from these villages would have had to quickly adjust to rapid urbanisation with often limited means. The livelihoods of the Chinese urban workers and small business owners in the towns and cities of Malaya also came under increasing stress as the nation came to adopt a more Bumiputera-centric socioeconomic policy.[7]

In short, a socioeconomic-turned-political gap was thus engendered between the Peninsular Chinese and the governmental authorities. In came the Malaysian Chinese Association (MCA), a welfare organisation-turned-political party, to partially bridge this gap, having continued to claim to represent the interests of the Chinese community in a decidedly racialised political setup. For many years, the MCA was the de facto main Chinese political representative in the Barisan Nasional (BN) ruling coalition, so whether they liked it or not, many Peninsular Chinese would have to depend on the MCA as the go-between in order to address many issues which affected them. These ranged from places in Chinese public schools, provisions of government scholarships and (preferred) placements in public universities, to licenses and government loans for business operations as well as public allocations and permits for schools and places of worship. The MCA-supported Tunku Abdul Rahman University College (TARUC) and Universiti Tunku Abdul Rahman (UTAR) have also been crucial as further education channels for many Peninsular Chinese students. A general argument is that the Chinese-based, but supposedly multiracial, Gerakan party played a similar role within BN, especially in Penang where MCA's presence was not as significant as in other parts of Peninsular Malaysia.

---

6 Kernial Singh Sandhu, 'Introduction: Emergency Settlement in Malaya,' in Shirley Gordon (ed.) *Chinese New Villages in Malaya: A Community Study*, (Singapore: Malayan Sociological Research Institute [MSRI], 1973) xxix-lxv.

7 Muhammed Abdul Khalid and Li Yang, 'Income Inequality and Ethnic Cleavages in Malaysia: Evidence from Distributional National Accounts (1984- 2014),' *World Inequality Database*, Working Paper no. 2019/09 (April 2019), https://wid.world/document/9231/.

On the other hand, by historical circumstances, in Sarawak the socioeconomic challenges of the Chinese are geographically and structurally diverse. Though many Chinese Sarawakians live in large towns such as Kuching and Sibu, a significant number of them are scattered across various remote settlements throughout the country's largest state, where infrastructural amenities remain poor if not non-existent. New Villages, though fewer in number than in Peninsular Malaysia, were also set up in Sarawak for the similar purpose of defeating the then communist threat in Sarawak. Many of these Chinese Sarawakians would have possessed few if any parcels of land, with land ownership in Sarawak becoming highly concentrated in the hands of a few well-linked conglomerates. As such, a similar socioeconomic-turned-political void was created in Sarawak, with the Sarawak United People's Party (SUPP), a formerly socialist and multi-racial party of the Sarawak state ruling coalition becoming Chinese-based and assuming a similar mediating role as the MCA or Gerakan.

Of Expectations and Dependence

Over the years, it might be said that the Chinese communities in Peninsular Malaysia and Sarawak developed a sort of a dependence-expectation mentality with regard to Chinese-based parties.[8] The MCA and SUPP, and to a lesser extent Gerakan, were depended upon and expected to not only deliver those 'essential' facilitating services enumerated above, but also to champion the broader political and socioeconomic aspirations of their respective Chinese communities.[9] When these Chinese-based parties were perceived to be effective in either the delivery of services or the championing of issues, or both, they would be rewarded with Chinese votes, enabling them to win many Chinese-majority or Chinese-significant seats, such as throughout the 1990s and early 2000s.[10]

---

8 James Chin, 'Malaysian Chinese Politics in the 21st Century: Fear, Service and Marginalisation,' *Asian Journal of Political Science* 9, no. 2 (December 2001): 87-88.

9 Mohamed Mustafa bin Ishak, 'From Plural Society to *Bangsa Malaysia*: Ethnicity and Nationalism in the Politics of Nation-Building in Malaysia,' (PhD diss., University of Leeds, 1999), 200.

10 MCA won 30 parliamentary seats in the 1995 General Election; 28 in 1999 and 31 in 2004. SUPP won 7 parliamentary seats in the 1995 General Election; 7 in 1999 and 6 in 2004. Gerakan won 7 parliamentary seats in the 1995 General Election, 7 in 1999 and 10 in 2004.

However, when these Peninsular and Sarawakian Chinese-based parties were perceived to be ineffective, especially in their championing of issues of great concern to the Chinese communities such as rampant corruption, racial inequality or religious extremism, they would also be roundly punished in the polls, such as in successive general elections since 2008, where the Chinese voted overwhelmingly for the opposition.[11] When the MCA and Gerakan were removed from the federal government, their replacements – the DAP, with most of its elected representatives being Chinese and Indians, and to a lesser extent the Malay-based but supposedly multiracial PKR – were expected by the Peninsular Chinese to replace, and perhaps even magnify, the role played by MCA and Gerakan, especially on the issue-championing front.

Unfulfilled Roles Punished

Once in government, DAP and PKR decided to emphasise the interests of all races and not focus on a particular one. In their eager efforts to court conservative Malay votes in future elections, issues such as the long-awaited recognition of the Chinese independent school Unified Examination Certificate (UEC) certificates, as well as the teaching of *khat* and the Jawi script in vernacular schools, were rather clumsily handled, causing increasing displeasure amongst the Peninsular Chinese community within a short period of two years. This was compounded by the PH government's refusal to subsidise Tunku Abdul Rahman University College (TARUC) through the traditional MCA channel,[12] but instead through the TARUC alumni association. This matter was successfully twisted by a barrage of MCA propaganda into alleged but widely believed persecution of Chinese higher education, something which struck at the deepest fears of the Peninsular Chinese community. The results of such dissatisfaction could be discerned by Peninsular Chinese voters' swing back to MCA and even

---

11 MCA won 15 parliamentary seats in the 2008 General Election, 7 in 2013 and 1 in 2018. Gerakan won 2 parliamentary seats in the 2008 General Election, 1 in 2013 and none in 2018.

12 'Cut ties with UTAR and TAR UC for more funds, MCA told,' *The Star*, 22 November 2018, https://www.thestar.com.my/news/nation/2018/11/22/cut-ties-with-utar-and-taruc-for-more-funds-mca-told/.

UMNO during a series of by-elections,[13] to the extent that it is doubtful if the DAP could repeat its all-time-best electoral results in 2018.

In Sarawak, SUPP has over the years been perceived by Chinese Sarawakians as having subtly but significantly changed the colour of its spots,[14] from a party that was somewhat adequate in upholding the rights of Chinese Sarawakians to one that became a vehicle for patronage through its place in the state's ruling coalition. They were roundly punished by the voters in the 2011 state election, losing almost all of their seats to DAP and PKR. But when the latter two, still in the state opposition, could not deliver on services, and when an iconic, relatively incorruptible figure in the person of the late Adenan Satem assumed the chief ministership, SUPP was able to recover many of its state seats in the 2016 state election.[15] The pattern for Chinese voters' electoral preferences in Peninsular Malaysia and Sarawak may thus be said to be broadly similar.

Nuanced Chinese Sabahan Outlook

The Chinese Sabahan community presents a somewhat different socioeconomic and, by extension, political outlook to their Peninsular Malaysian and Sarawakian counterparts. To start with, only 10 to 11 per cent of Sabahans identify themselves as Chinese[16] (although they make up roughly 15 per cent of the total voters), as opposed to up to around 25 and 24 per cent in Peninsular Malaysia[17] and Sarawak[18] respectively. But Chinese Sabahans' comparatively lower percentage of Sabah's population is somewhat

---

13 Arfa Yunus and Hana Naz Harun, 'Tg Piai by-election: Msians realizing the power of the vote,' *New Straits Times*, 18 November 2019, https://www.nst.com.my/news/exclusive/2019/11/539738/tg-piai-election-msians-realising-power-vote.

14 James Chin, 'The Sarawak Chinese Voters and Their Support for the Democratic Action Party (DAP),' *Southeast Asian Studies* 34, no. 2 (September 1996): 399-400, https://kyoto-seas.org/pdf/34/2/340203.pdf.

15 SUPP won 6 state seats in 2011 Sarawak State Election, 7 in 2016.

16 Robert Hirschmann, 'Population distribution in Sabah Malaysia 2019-2020, by ethnicity,' *Statista*, 25 September 2020, https://www.statista.com/statistics/1041537/malaysia-population-distribution-ethnicity-sabah/.

17 'People: Peninsular Malaysia,' *Britannica*, https://www.britannica.com/place/Malaysia/People#ref279151.

18 'Malaysia: Indigenous peoples and ethnic minorities in Sarawak,' Minority Rights Group International, https://minorityrights.org/minorities/indigenous-peoples-and-ethnic-minorities-in-sarawak/.

misleading and doesn't give the whole picture. At least two other somewhat similarly predisposed cohorts in Sabah's population can be associated with the Chinese. One is the Sino, and especially Sino-Kadazan, community, with members who are of mixed Chinese and Sabah Bumiputera, especially Kadazan, ancestries. The other are the groups of Sabah Bumiputera who are Chinese-educated up to at least the primary if not secondary level; there are many Chinese schools throughout both urban and rural regions of Sabah, with Bumiputera student populations of up to 70 to 90 per cent in some of the more remote ones.[19] The Chinese 'Plus' population in Sabah may thus be significantly higher than that traditionally represented. Of course, these three cohorts of Chinese 'Plus' Sabahans would have similarities and differences of political sentiments, but it is equally important to note that there is an almost inevitable degree of mutual influence among them, as most extended Chinese families in Sabah would typically consist of non-Chinese or Chinese 'Plus' members.[20]

Better Off Than Some

Chinese Sabahans may be said to be at least marginally better off than their Peninsular Malaysian and Sarawakian counterparts, so much so that since at least the 1960s, when socioeconomic conditions in Peninsular Malaysia and Sarawak became more difficult, there have been waves of Chinese who migrated to Sabah from Malaya and Sarawak in search of better livelihoods.[21] Most Chinese Sabahans live in towns and suburbs, large and small, dotting the coasts and the major rivers of Sabah. A number of them are businessmen and professionals, others being mainly shopkeepers and, in general, office workers. Some have inherited wealth mainly in the form of shophouses, residences or parcels of land in towns or on their outskirts, or even swaths of small- and medium-sized agricultural plots, now mainly

---

19 'Children Out of School: The Sabah Context,' UNICEF Malaysia, https://www.unicef.org/malaysia/media/921/file/Out%20of%20School%20children%20%20(OOSCI)%20Accessible%20version.pdf.

20 Trinna Leong, 'Who are Malaysia's bumiputera?' *The Straits Times*, 3 August 2017, https://www.straitstimes.com/asia/se-asia/who-are-malaysias-bumiputera.

21 'Growth rates of Chinese and Malay Populations in Malaysia,' Central Intelligence Agency, 27 April 2001, https://www.cia.gov/library/readingroom/docs/CIA-RDP79T01019A000200320001-3.pdf

used for oil palm plantations, in the interior of Sabah. This is in stark contrast to the concentration of land ownership in Sarawak, and land-generated wealth may thus be said to be more evenly distributed among the Chinese Sabahan community, despite the increasing presence of some large, conglomerate-owned plantations in Sabah. In fact, there was never any significant communist threat in Sabah, and no New Village system was ever established, testifying to the comparatively better socioeconomic conditions of the Chinese community in Sabah. The timber boom in previous years, the oil palm fad since the 1990s and the burgeoning tourism industry (before the onset of the Covid-19 pandemic) all contributed to the relative socioeconomic well-being of the Chinese Sabahan community.

Cosmopolitanism All Along

Many Chinese Sabahans have traditionally acquired a somewhat more cosmopolitan social outlook than their Sarawakian and Peninsular Malaysian counterparts (with the exceptions of perhaps Kuala Lumpur and Penang) due to their cultural interactions with immigrants from different parts of the world. For example, Sandakan, a timber boom town since shortly after the Second World War, was dubbed 'Little Hong Kong' as it welcomed waves of Hong Kong and Shanghai immigrants seeking new lives and ventures as communism swept across mainland China. Some senior citizens in Sandakan recalled that at least a fraction of the glitz and glamour of high society from Hong Kong was also present, with the most renowned Cantonese opera troupes making frequent port calls at Sandakan. A sense of cultural confidence, if not superiority, thus descended upon many Chinese in Sandakan. They also took to speaking Cantonese, instead of the more prevalent Hakka dialect in the rest of Sabah, as their lingua franca.

This sense of cosmopolitanism was certainly not limited to Sandakan and overlapped with the timber boom starting in the 1950s, as Japan undertook domestic reconstruction after the devastation of the Second World War, requiring a lot of wooden construction materials in the process. Japanese trading houses set up representative offices in towns across Sabah, from Sandakan and Tawau on the east coast, to Kota Kinabalu and Keningau on the west coast and in the interior. Most of the timber merchants, as well as their workers dealing with the Japanese traders, were Chinese Sabahans, and, when interviewed, some of them claimed to have learned first-hand the meticulousness and the quest for perfection famous of the Japanese. They not only interacted with the Japanese locally but also made frequent trips to Japan. Kota Kinabalu, for example, boasted some of the first Japanese restaurants in the whole of Malaysia, as they catered to the entertainment needs of the Japanese and their local counterparts. The famed efficiency of the Japanese was not lost on Chinese Sabahans, and stood in stark contrast to their having to navigate the increasingly rough political waters of Sabah.

Differing Educational Options

Many Chinese Sabahans, perhaps unlike their Peninsular Malaysian and Sarawakian counterparts, have long given up on the Malaysian public and (local) private university systems as the primary destinations for their children's higher education. Chinese in Sabah tend to aim to send their children overseas for further studies, with the United Kingdom, Australia, New Zealand, Singapore, and even the United States and Canada as preferred locations.[22] It should be noted that these Chinese Sabahan students, across a few generations, are thus more exposed to the good governance and democratic ideals in their countries of study. Some even settled more or less overseas after graduation, but still retain their Malaysian citizenship, allowing them to, among other things, vote in Sabah often, of course for more progressive political parties.

The TARUC subsidy issue was alleged to have hurt Peninsular Chinese support for the DAP (as its secretary-general Lim Guan Eng was the finance minister) and by extension PH,[23] as many Peninsular Chinese parents were either TARUC graduates themselves or saw TARUC as an indispensable channel for their children's further studies. But TARUC graduates in Sabah

---

22 There is no adequate data on the numbers of Chinese Sabahans abroad. These observations are drawn from interviews and authors' networks. Those studying abroad represent the broader national trend of going overseas for studies with the expansion of the New Economic Policy. See Robert C. Thornett, 'Chinese Malaysian university students discover a world of opportunities venturing abroad, transcending affirmative action quotas at home,' *The Solutions Journal* 10, no. 4 (November 2019), https://www.thesolutionsjournal.com/article/chinese-malaysian-university-students-discover-world-opportunities-venturing-abroad-transcending-affirmative-action-quotas-home/.

23 Ho Wah Foon, 'Politicising education hurts the Chinese,' *The Star*, 27 November 2018, https://www.thestar.com.my/news/nation/2018/11/27/politicising-education-hurts-the-chinese-as-malaysia-tackles-a-rm1-trillion-national-debt-it-may-be.

are few and far between,[24] and most Chinese Sabahan parents typically do not see their children furthering studies in TARUC, despite TARUC having erected a Sabah campus recently. So a 'punish DAP' (and by extension, Warisan Plus) sentiment was effectively absent in Sabah, unlike in Peninsular Malaysia.

And while Chinese Sabahan parents may wish for their children, upon graduation overseas, to come back to Sabah, it is primarily to participate in the family business, to work in lucrative professions or to take up other jobs in the private sector. Seldom do Chinese Sabahan parents encourage their children to take up public sector employment as the chances for Chinese civil servants to be fairly and meritocratically promoted are perceived to be rather low.

UEC Certificates: A Matter of Solidarity but not Necessity

That is mainly why the perennial call for official recognition of the Chinese independent school UEC certificate, while certainly an important concern for Peninsular Chinese and Chinese Sarawakians – who still harbour dreams of landing civil service jobs with UEC qualifications – is arguably less of a concern for Chinese Sabahans. Chinese Sabahans extend empathy to the UEC cause more in the sense of solidarity with their Peninsular Chinese compatriots, despite the fact that Sabah hosts nine out of the sixty Chinese independent schools in the whole of Malaysia.

In fact, the UEC examinations in Sabah are conducted in English as opposed to Mandarin in most parts of Peninsular Malaysia and Sarawak, as the Chinese independent schools in Sabah are effectively considered premier preparatory schools for further studies overseas or at most in local private universities, but certainly not in local public universities. Their student enrollments consist of not only the Chinese community, but increasingly other communities as well. In recent years, a trend was also observed whereby Chinese Sabahan parents, at least those who could afford to do so, gradually shifted their children away from Chinese independent schools into other types of private and international schools, so that their children could allegedly be even better prepared for higher education overseas.[25]

---

[24] Leonard Alaza, 'Few takers – for fear of English,' *Daily Express*, 27 May 2019, https://www.dailyexpress.com.my/news/135791/few-takers-for-fear-of-english/.

[25] Ho Wah Foon, 'Can Dong Zong survive?' *The Star*, 12 July 2015, https://www.thestar.

So the Shafie Apdal government's recognition of UEC as a qualification for state civil service employment was indeed widely welcomed by the Sabahan Chinese community, which we believe was more of an abstract indication of his inclusiveness and open-mindedness as a leader, and less of a fulfillment of a much yearned for necessity, as would have been the case for at least a number of their Peninsular Malaysian and Sarawakian counterparts.

Tourism Opens More Eyes

There is also the explosive growth of tourism in Sabah over the last two decades, as Japanese and European, followed by Korean and Chinese tourists flocked to Sabah for vacations and tourism-related business.[26] With this phenomenal growth, many Chinese Sabahans take up the core or the periphery of the tourism industry. Based on conversations with Sabahans in the tourism industry, tourism entrepreneurs revealed that most of the tour agencies and activities centres are operated by Chinese Sabahans, sometimes with Bumiputera partners. Hotels and souvenir shops spring up ubiquitously, often with Chinese Sabahan owners and their foreign partners. Korean, mainland Chinese and European restaurants also appear, operated mostly by their respective expatriates. While tourism and hospitality add to the variety and vitality of the Sabah economy (at least before the Covid-19 pandemic), it also imbues a further dose of cosmopolitanism to major towns such as Kota Kinabalu with a large Chinese population.

Based on conversations with Chinese Sabahan tour operators, the tourism boom reinforces their economic, and by extension, political 'autonomy', which affords independence from public sector largesse. In admiring the diligence and efficiency of their foreign partners and competitors (originally the Japanese and then the mainland Chinese and Koreans), they are provided with a stark contrast to the perceived inadequacies of the administrative capabilities of Malaysia as a whole.

com.my/news/nation/2015/07/12/can-dong-zong-survive.

26 Sabah Tourism Board, 'Sabah: Visitors arrival by nationality 2019,' https://www.sabahtourism.com/assets/uploads/visitor-2019.pdf.

Resilience v. Dependence

Therefore, a subtle sense of self-sufficiency and resilience in the face of adversity permeates a large part of the Chinese Sabahan community, at least more than their Peninsular and Sarawakian counterparts. In Peninsular Malaysia, a typical middle- or low-income Chinese family blessed with one or more academically gifted children who score exceptionally well in public examinations would usually hope to receive either a government scholarship to study overseas or a placement in a preferred faculty in local public universities. The expectation is for the Chinese-based incumbent party, such as the MCA or DAP, to engage with the relevant authorities if the scholarship or preferred placement application is initially rejected. If the MCA or DAP is not able to effectuate such expected public gratuities, then they are to be blamed for political ineffectiveness, and sometimes press conferences would even be called separately by the rival Chinese-based parties, together with the parents and the students, in order to highlight the entrenched inequity and their rival's inefficacy.

If a similar case were to take place in Sabah, however, the Chinese parents are unlikely to even contemplate availing themselves of public assistance in sending their children overseas to study. We have been told that they would scrape together their meagre savings, sell properties or even borrow from friends and extended families – even quietly seeking donations from tycoons – in order to send their children to their overseas universities of choice. This does not mean that their children would not apply for public scholarships. They still do so, but more as a means to attain recognition for their academic achievements if granted scholarships, and there is no painful disappointment if they do not receive it. The scholarship is considered more as a 'bonus', and not something of a necessity, and certainly not a right. So, MCA's traditional pitch of being the reliable 'community service' provider proved to be a hard sell to Chinese Sabahans, as was vividly demonstrated by their recent poor electoral performance.

Indeed, there was never such an 'anchor' Chinese-based party that was comparable to MCA or SUPP in Sabah's political history that could be depended upon by Chinese Sabahans to deliver 'essential' services, at least not over a sustained period of time. This is partly due to the less race-centric political environment in Sabah, where local-based parties of substance tend to be multiracial to a much greater degree. BERJAYA, Parti Bersatu Sabah

(PBS) and Warisan, which were all ruling parties in Sabah, paid more than lip service to their multiracial setups, with genuinely senior party leaders from the various major communities of Sabah, including the Chinese. So, there was no specific need for local or Peninsular-based Chinese parties to emphasise their capabilities for delivering community-related services. The alleged service provision is not generally requested nor required by most Chinese Sabahans.

Sense of Entitlement

When Chinese Sabahan leaders did clinch the top executive job in the state (chief minister), such as Yong Teck Lee of Sabah Progressive Party (SAPP) and Chong Kah Kiat of Liberal Democratic Party (LDP), their 'extra' service and contribution to, or special but official appropriations for the Chinese Sabahan community were often taken for granted or as 'something which is only to be expected of them'. During their tenures, both Yong and Chong either granted permits for the building of new Chinese schools or even ceded public lands for the same, something that should have been much valued by the Chinese community, which prizes the importance of Chinese education. PBS's Yee Moh Chai, a former deputy chief minister of Sabah, was also responsible for using his parliamentary funds to erect municipal beautification amenities in Kota Kinabalu. Yet both Chong and Yee were roundly defeated in the 2020 state election, and Yong decided not to contest, only to be appointed as a nominated assemblyman by the new GRS state government.

This sense of entitlement is not necessarily reciprocal in elections. Chinese Sabahans' sense of entitlement emboldens them to not reciprocate the aforementioned largesse of the government by votes, as they have long observed that the government could not afford to 'punish' them for voting or not voting for one party or another.[27] This is because most Chinese live in town areas or the suburbs, and if the government of the day were to halt infrastructural development in these locations, the Sabah economy would be gravely affected, as the Chinese could not smoothly carry out their business activities which are the mainstay of the state economy.

[27] James Chin and Arnold Puyok, 'Going against the tide: Sabah and the 2008 Malaysian general election,' *Asian Politics & Policy* 2, no. 2 (2010): 219-235.

Of 'Affordability' and Electoral Punishment

In other words, Chinese Sabahans can 'afford' to vote as their political predilections dictate, in stark contrast to voters of other, especially more rural, communities, where the acute need for basic amenities and the determination of which party is most 'resourceful' casts a long shadow over their voting decisions. And when the powers that be intended to 'punish' the Chinese for not voting a certain way, as BERJAYA did in the 1980s, by ordering blackouts in Sandakan, the Chinese voters tended to effectuate even bigger electoral victories for their opponents.[28]

There is also a common perception among many Chinese Sabahans that they could actually spend away their aforementioned inherited wealth gradually, or at least maintain their family businesses big and small, while 'indulging' in attempting to 'implement' the more abstract political ideals as espoused by some of the more progressive political parties. There is a certain grain of truth to this, as Chinese Sabahans could 'afford' to look at the bigger sociopolitical picture for the state and the nation and be defiant of various forms of political persecution or reprisal. There is a Chinese saying which was frequently used to describe this phenomenon, that the Chinese Sabahans 'swallow only the soft and not the tough stuff',[29] which is to say their hearts and minds may only be won with sincere entreaties, and not be threatened into submission.

So, whereas Peninsular Chinese voters decided to punish the DAP and by extension PH by lowering their level of electoral support in a string of by-elections in 2019 and 2020, for allegedly not fulfilling some of PH's 2018 General Election manifesto promises, such as the aforementioned UEC recognition, the Chinese Sabahan voters would see this as a relatively minor issue, of less concern to them.[30] They would stick with the DAP and also the similarly reformist PKR and by extension Warisan Plus to empower

---

[28] Arnold Puyok, 'Political Development in Sabah, 1985-2010: Challenges in Malaysian Federalism and Ethnic Politics,' *Irasec's Discussion Papers* #9, February 2011, 8, http://www.irasec.com/documents/fichiers/44.pdf.

[29] '吃软不吃硬' in Mandarin.

[30] Muguntan Vanar and Stephanie Lee, 'En bloc Chinese voting pattern unlikely in Sabah polls, say analyst,' *The Star*, 22 September 2020, https://www.thestar.com.my/news/nation/2020/09/22/en-bloc-chinese-voting-pattern-unlikely-in-sabah-polls-says-analyst.

what they perceive as the longer-term goals of greater equity and better governance for Sabah, which they simply could not see from the motley crew of parties and old faces which hastily made up GRS.

Dearth of Chinese Sabahan Leadership

Although Shafie's comparatively down-to-earth demeanor and willingness to listen to challenges faced by all Sabah communities appeared to be refreshing,[31] part of Chinese Sabahans' seeming infatuation with Shafie was also due to the lack of genuine and effective Chinese Sabahan leadership. The aforementioned Yong and Chong had long passed the prime of their political careers, and in any case were perceived as still associating themselves 'too closely for comfort' with the much-disfavored BN regime, despite their parties having officially left the former ruling coalition. Yee was also rejected by the voters in the Chinese-majority Api-Api constituency at state polls since 2013.

Yet the Sabahan Chinese leadership vacuum is as glaring on the Warisan Plus side. Junz Wong, the Chinese vice president of Warisan, was viewed by many as too young to fill those shoes. The vacuum was also not shored up by Christina Liew of PKR who, though a veteran politician in the state, could have done a more proactive job with her tourist ministry portfolio. Frankie Poon Ming Fung, who heads the state DAP, was similarly perceived to be lacklustre, and the rest of the DAP lineup was considered to be either too showy or too junior. As such, due credit must be given to the Chinese Sabahans, who apparently did not think twice in crossing racial and religious lines to embrace Shafie, a non-Chinese leader, as a symbol not only of their own aspirations, but also those of the state and the nation as a whole.[32] The aforementioned Chinese leaders in Warisan Plus all won their respective seats in the recent state election, some by even higher vote margins than two years ago, albeit somewhat holding onto the coattails of Chinese support for Shafie.

---

31 Julia Chan, 'As clock ticks down to Sabah election, a laser-focused Shafie Apdal keeps calm and campaigns on for Warisan,' *Malay Mail*, 25 September 2020, https://www.malaymail.com/news/malaysia/2020/09/25/as-clock-ticks-down-to-sabah-election-a-laser-focused-shafie-apdal-keeps-ca/1906409.

32 Bridget Welsh, 'Chinese Sabahans can make and break Warisan,' *The Straits Times*, 23 September, 2020, https://www.straitstimes.com/asia/chinese-sabahans-can-make-and-break-warisan-sin-chew-daily-contributor.

Indeed, Shafie's electoral message of unity also chimed with Chinese Sabahans' abstract and 'affordable' yearning for a more equitable sociopolitical framework for the state and for the nation. The slogan 'We are here to build a nation, not a particular race or religion', which was emblazoned next to Shafie's Obama-esque portrait on various billboards at major traffic junctions, echoed Chinese Sabahans' sense of propriety for 'what Malaysia should have been'. The outpourings of sympathy from Chinese Sabahans for Shafie, as Musa instigated a takeover attempt, were tremendous. They felt that Shafie's reform agenda was cut short by Musa's ruthless coup attempt, and that Shafie thus deserved at least another full term to 'put the state back on the right track' after nearly a quarter century of what they perceived as rampantly corrupt BN rule.

Not Quite Economic Blues?

Much has been said about the continuously weak economy in Sabah as having an impact on the recent state election.[33] What is perhaps more accurate is that economic problems had a disproportionate effect on the non-Chinese in Sabah. The Chinese oil palm plantation owners and smallholders would cyclically complain about low palm oil prices, but they usually keep quiet when prices soared, and in any case the prices never dived below their production costs.[34] The hospitality owners would complain about low or zero occupancy in their premises, but often choose to omit the exorbitant prices they previously charged foreign tourists at some of the tourism hotspots.[35] The empty rows of housing and shop lots dotting the suburbs of Kota Kinabalu are not necessarily unsold. Many of them are actually owned by the same oil palm planters above, often in bulk but left unoccupied.[36]

---

33 Durie Rainer Fong, 'As Sabah election looms, a host of issues take centre stage,' *Free Malaysia Today*, 6 September 2020, https://www.freemalaysiatoday.com/category/nation/2020/09/06/as-sabah-election-looms-a-host-of-issues-take-centre-stage/.

34 Ganeshwaran Kana, 'Confidence in PN government lifts palm oil prices,' *The Star*, 30 November 2020, https://www.thestar.com.my/business/business-news/2020/11/30/confidence-in-pn-government-lifts-palm-oil-prices.

35 Ethel Khoo, 'Growing demand for good-quality hotels in Kota Kinabalu,' *The Edge Malaysia*, 11 July 2019, https://www.theedgemarkets.com/article/cover-story-growing-demand-goodquality-hotels-kota-kinabalu.

36 Kristy Inus, 'Lack of China, South Korea tourists taking a toll on KK businesses,' *The*

Some sources revealed that at least for the Chinese community, the state is still so abundant that some of those younger Chinese who previously emigrated overseas decided to come back as the economy shrank even more drastically in their new homes, sometimes rendering them suddenly unemployed abroad. At least back in Sabah, the parents could still support them with a shop lot or two where they could operate many of the trendy cafés springing up all over Kota Kinabalu and Sandakan. Never mind that many of these food and beverage outlets do not last long, for they are just temporary occupations for privileged youths who would soon leave again for their adopted overseas homes, such as Melbourne or Perth.

The Chinese Sabahans did not expect Shafie to deliver economic wonders, especially not over just two years; they just wanted him to provide a fairer platform where they could conduct business with relative ease.[37] There is a perception that the Chinese, in general, are more resilient in adjusting livelihood expectations and challenges, as they always believe that every crisis would also bring about opportunity. Due to Chinese Sabahans' flexibility in adapting to changes, tour operators hit hard by dwindling tourism, for example, could easily become private-hire drivers. Restaurants closed for on-site dining during the Movement Control Orders but quickly went online and offered food deliveries, some reporting even double business earnings compared to pre-pandemic times.[38] And the Shafie government did provide some assistance to the small and medium enterprises, which included many Chinese businesses in the state.[39]

In any case, even if drops in business volumes were perceived, the criticism was squarely laid at the door of the federal instead of the state

Star, 4 March 2020, https://www.thestar.com.my/news/nation/2020/03/04/lack-of-china-south-korea-tourists-taking-a-toll-on-kk-businesses.

37 Durie Rainer Fong, 'RM240 mil stimulus package inadequate, says Sabah bosses' group,' *Free Malaysia Today*, 19 June 2020, https://www.freemalaysiatoday.com/category/nation/2020/06/19/rm240-mil-stimulus-package-inadequate-says-sabah-bosses-group/.

38 Jotham Lim, 'MCO a big win for online food deliveries and cloud kitchens,' *The Edge Markets*, 19 June 2020, https://www.theedgemarkets.com/article/mco-big-win-online-food-deliveries-and-cloud-kitchens.

39 'Sabah unveils second Covid-19 aid package worth RM240m,' *Malay Mail*, 18 June 2020, https://www.malaymail.com/news/malaysia/2020/06/18/sabah-unveils-second-covid-19-aid-package-worth-rm240m/1876757.

government. The much-despised federal cabotage policy, requiring goods to be carried by Malaysian-flagged merchant ships between Malaysian ports, though suspended for the past few years,[40] was blamed for having choked Sabah's industrial development over the years, rendering it a bit too late to pick up the slack. As such, it could be argued that the slow-chugging economy did not quite reduce Chinese Sabahans' support for Warisan Plus. If anything, it strengthened their animosity towards those in power at the federal level.

Seeing through the Autonomy Charade

Similarly, while the Sabah autonomy movement and sentiment may be quite prominent in some of Sabah's many communities, it received at best a lukewarm response from the Chinese Sabahan community. This is because those who champion such causes both within (such as Yong and his SAPP) and outside (such as Jeffrey Kitingan and his STAR party) the Chinese community are seen as being curiously chummy with BN or Perikatan Nasional (PN, the federal ruling coalition), both decidedly Peninsular Malaysian coalitions, which makes their otherwise ardent support for Sabah's autonomy illogical, or at least less than convincing.

The Chinese Sabahans could, again, 'afford' to see through these charades as nothing more than political gambits to win or split votes on BN's or PN's behalf. By the same token, it did not quite matter for the Chinese Sabahan voters that both the DAP and PKR in Warisan Plus were as much Malayan parties as UMNO, Bersatu and MCA in GRS. But it did matter that they were perceived as relatively 'clean' and progressive.[41] So for the purposes of the recent state election, DAP candidates were subsumed under Warisan Plus tickets. The Chinese Sabahan voters did not mind and still returned them with thumping majorities. And Warisan Plus also adopted at most a moderate level of appeals for autonomy, having crafted their electoral message with what may be deemed as more national themes such as unity.

---

40 'Gov't to revisit cabotage policy liberalisation in Sabah, Sarawak – Loke,' *Malaysiakini*, 10 December 2019, https://www.malaysiakini.com/news/503056.

41 Azril Annuar, 'Pakatan's "full mandate" to Anwar for political talks to reclaim Putrajaya has limits, says PKR official,' *Malay Mail*, 22 July 2020, https://www.malaymail.com/news/malaysia/2020/07/22/pakatans-full-mandate-to-anwar-for-political-talks-to-reclaim-putrajaya-has/1886773.

Persona v. Party

The crossing over or 'frogging' by a few Chinese state assemblypersons during Musa's attempted putsch engendered a degree of political cynicism among the Chinese Sabahans, such that some expressed a hapless wish to base their votes more on the persona and character of the various candidates than the ideologies of the parties the latter represented.[42] The saying went around that 'even if you vote in Warisan Plus candidates, they might later "frog"! Better to vote for somebody you trust!'

This sentiment was seized upon and magnified by GRS as somewhat of a 'godsend', as GRS was aware from the outset that it would be difficult to promote GRS among the Chinese Sabahan community. Thus, for example, a 'presentable' candidate was found in the person of Dr Chan Kee Ying, a dentist from the MCA who represented BN in the Likas constituency. But at the end most Likas voters apparently still subscribed to the 'greater' (progressive) cause and voted overwhelmingly for the DAP incumbent Tan Lee Fatt, and Dr Chan lost her candidacy deposit.[43]

Independents' Fates and Influences on the Young

The same 'personality not party' sentiment was also picked up by a number of Chinese independent candidates, harping on their professional or community-service credentials. An informal league of five Chinese independent candidates was even formed, led by Melanie Chia, a former SAPP senior leader and state assistant minister. But at the end, voters saw many of these independent candidates as being either too close to the GRS side for comfort, or relatively unknown before the election. Most independent candidates similarly lost their deposits. It would appear that while Chinese Sabahan voters did care a lot about the character of the candidates, most of them still pinned their hopes on a party or coalition such as Warisan Plus to drive through a progressive agenda.

Sources also indicated that many among the younger (below 40 years

---

42 Arnold Puyok, 'Political Turmoil in Sabah: Attack of the Kataks,' *ISEAS Commentary*, 2020/113, 5 August 2020, https://www.iseas.edu.sg/media/commentaries/political-turmoil-in-sabah-attack-of-the-kataks/.

43 According to election regulations, candidates who fail to get at least one-eighth of the total votes would lose their election deposit.

old) generation of Chinese Sabahans, Sino-Kadazan and even Chinese-educated Bumiputeras were quite susceptible to online propaganda or influence. They derived political information mainly from Facebook, messaging platforms, and news portals not only in Chinese, but in English and Malay as well. It was pointed out that DAP and Warisan were the best at handling Chinese and English online political news respectively, eliciting electoral support for their candidates effectively.[44]

Conclusion

The Chinese Sabahan community may thus be said to have set themselves socio-economically and, by extension, politically apart from many other communities in Sabah, as well as from the Peninsular and Sarawakian Chinese communities. They have greater exposure to the more lofty and progressive ideals of some of the more democratically advanced societies, where good governance is the order of the day. They are more resilient and less reliant upon government largesse as they carry on their livelihoods compared with other communities, as well as Peninsular Chinese and Chinese Sarawakians. Issues which may affect Peninsular and Sarawakian Chinese support for the more progressive parties do not quite affect Chinese Sabahans. They are less susceptible to political innuendos and machinations. In short, they could 'afford' to vote undauntedly, almost irregardless of the turns of the political tides. Chinese Sabahans are not to be mollycoddled with short-term promises of cosmetic and often unfulfilled reforms or material gains. They expect nothing less than long-term but drastic and equitable change, not only for Sabah, but for the nation as well.

[44] Samsudin A. Rahim, 'Social Media and Political Marketing: A Case Study of Malaysia During the 2018 General Election,' *Advances in Social Science, Education and Humanities Research* 241 (2018).

Chapter 13

Kadazan-Dusun Politics: The Persistence of Personality Politics, Patronage and Ethnonationalism

Tony Paridi Bagang and Arnold Puyok

Introduction

Kadazan-Dusun politics has always impacted the broader development of politics in Sabah. Even though the Kadazan-Dusun people are the largest indigenous community in Sabah, their political representation does not reflect this reality.[1] The Kadazan-Dusun are disproportionately represented, and this is especially obvious in how fragmented they are politically. Before Warisan's ascent to power, the Kadazan-Dusun were represented by the Sabah United Party (Parti Bersatu Sabah or PBS), United Progressive Kinabalu Organisation (UPKO, formerly known as Pasok Momogun National Organisation) and Sabah People's United Party (Parti Bersatu Rakyat Sabah) under the Barisan Nasional (BN) coalition. Joseph Pairin Kitingan – also known as the *Huguan Siou* (Paramount Leader)[2] of the Kadazan-Dusun – was the president of PBS before he was replaced

---

1 James Chin, '"Malay Muslim First": The Politics of Bumiputeraism in East Malaysia,' Sophie Lemiere (ed.) *Illusions of Democracy: Malaysian Politics and People* (Petaling Jaya: SIRD, 2017), 201-220.

2 This title is conferred to a Kadazan-Dusun leader for their contributions to the community in various affairs. So far, there have only been two *Huguan Siou* in the Kadazan-Dusun community – Donald Stephens and Joseph Pairin Kitingan. See Herman Luping, 'The Making of a Kadazan *Huguan Siou* (Great Leader),' *Sarawak Museum Journal*, 21 no. 54 (1984): 83-87.

by Maximus Ongkili. Other Kadazan-Dusun leaders, Madius Tangau and Joseph Kurup, were heads of UPKO and PBRS respectively. UPKO's withdrawal from BN in 2018 had left the coalition in disarray.

The break-up of BN continued to polarise Kadazan-Dusun politics. Upcoming young Kadazan-Dusun leaders such as Darell Leiking and Peter Anthony decided to support Warisan and became the key leaders in the party. Joseph Pairin's brother Jeffrey Kitingan remained the leader of STAR Sabah (Parti Solidariti Tanah Airku or Homeland Solidarity Party). Other small parties with a strong Kadazan-Dusun presence were Parti Cinta Sabah (Love Sabah Party or PCS) and Parti Anak Negeri (the Native Party or AN). The PCS was headed by Wilfred Bumburing and AN by Henrynus Amin. PCS, AN and another local-based party, Gagasan (Parti Gagasan Rakyat Sabah or Sabah People's Vision Party), were supposed to merge and be led by the former Minister of Foreign Affairs Anifah Aman, but this plan never took off. Wilfred later relinquished his post to Anifah while AN and Gagasan decided to go their separate ways.

In the 2020 Sabah state election (PRN2020), PBS decided to contest using its own party symbol as it was no longer part of BN. The move was also seen as PBS's attempt to field their candidates in most of the seats they contested in previous elections before the party rejoined BN in 2002. Furthermore, by contesting using its own symbol, PBS hoped to relive the spirit of 1985, which catapulted the party into power.

UPKO and PKR (Parti Keadilan Rakyat or People's Justice Party) remained Warisan's allies but chose to contest using their own party symbols, except for the DAP, which decided to contest using Warisan's logo. The responsibility to win Kadazan-Dusun support in Warisan seemed to weigh heavily on Madius's shoulders even though Warisan and DAP fielded candidates in Kadazan-Dusun areas too. Madius aimed to prove that UPKO was more popular than PBS and STAR Sabah in the Kadazan-Dusun areas.

PBRS contested using BN's logo while STAR Sabah and Bersatu (Parti Pribumi Bersatu Malaysia or Malaysian United Indigenous Party) chose to contest under PN (Perikatan Nasional). PBRS and STAR Sabah contested mostly in the interior where they already had loyal supporters. BN, PN and PBS were collectively known as the Gabungan Rakyat Sabah (Sabah People's Coalition or GRS).

The battleground for Kadazan-Dusun votes in PRN2020 is illustrated in Table 1.

Table 1: Parties/Number of Seats Contested in 24 Predominantly Kadazan-Dusun Seats

Party	No. of Seats Contested
Warisan Plus	9
PKR	4
UPKO	11
STAR Sabah/PN	7
Bersatu/PN	3
PBRS/BN	5
UMNO/BN	5
PBS	16
PCS	24
LDP	17
AN	2
USNO	9
Gagasan	8

Source: Authors' calculations from the Election Commission of Malaysia. Accessed at https://dashboard.spr.gov.my/#!/home.

In PRN2020, many had predicted a victory for Warisan, albeit with reduced seats and popular votes. Attention was focused on the Muslim Bumiputera and non-Muslim Bumiputera voters and how they could tilt the balance of power either in GRS's or Warisan's favour.[3]

In 2018, Warisan was able to break UMNO's dominance in the Muslim Bumiputera areas, particularly in the Tawau/East Coast Division, where Shafie remained a central figure.[4] In the Kadazan-Dusun constituencies, however, BN was more popular than Warisan, gaining more than 40 per

[3] Some of the KDM seats are categorised as Muslim Bumiputera (MB) due to their religious affiliation. However, in terms of their ethnicity, they are either Kadazan-Dusun, Murut or Rungus. We determined that the total number of predominantly KDM seats are 24, based on the demographic profile of the voters and their ethnicity. Therefore, we defined Kadazan-Dusun seats as one predominantly occupied (more than 51 per cent) by the Kadazan-Dusun as an ethnic entity. There is no official definition that refers to KDM seats.

[4] Arnold Puyok and R. Piya Sukhani, 'Sabah: Breakthrough in the Fixed Deposit State,' *The Round Table*, no. 2 (2020): 209-224.

cent of the popular votes.[5] PBS alone garnered more than 40 per cent of the popular support – more than what UPKO and Warisan obtained.[6] Warisan, therefore, needed to increase its Kadazan-Dusun support in PRN2020 in order to stay in power. Was Warisan able to pull through in the Kadazan-Dusun constituencies? Did Warisan manage to win the support of the Kadazan-Dusun voters? What were the factors that determined voting in the Kadazan-Dusun areas? These are among the questions that this chapter aims to unpack.

In this chapter, we analyse the voting pattern of the Kadazan-Dusun. Our analysis is based on our observations of the selected 'competitive' Kadazan-Dusun seats of Kiulu, Moyog and Tambunan. These constituencies were the battlegrounds for key Kadazan-Dusun leaders such as Madius Tangau, Darell Leiking and Jeffrey Kitingan.[7] We employed an ethnographic approach to gather detailed qualitative data on campaign strategies and issues during our fieldwork in Matunggong, Tenom, Keningau, Pensiangan, Tambunan, Penampang and Kiulu from 22 to 25 September 2020. We obtained our data primarily through observations of the campaign process, interviews and casual conversations with local Sabahans. Data was then transcribed and categorised according to the key themes and research questions formulated earlier.

We argue that voting in the Kadazan-Dusun areas is influenced by the politics of personality, patronage and ethnonationalism, which are shaped by the leaders' past legacies, contributions and the cultural roles they play in society. The Kitingan brothers are still influential among the Kadazan-Dusun in the interior. There are no similar personalities in Warisan and UPKO who can arouse sentiments and mobilise political support. Patronage politics in the Kadazan-Dusun areas are strengthened through the various monetary assistance and development pledges made by GRS.

Similarly, the Covid-19 pandemic and the enforcement of the Movement

---

5 Ibid.

6 Tony Paridi Bagang and Arnold Puyok, 'Sabah: the End of BN and a New Order?' in *The Defeat of Barisan Nasional: Missed Signs or Late Surge?* ed. Francis E. Hutchinson and Lee Hwok Aun, (Singapore: ISEAS, 2019), 402-422.

7 The president of UPKO, Madius Tangau, contested in Kiulu to challenge the incumbent Janiston Bingkuai of PBS. Darell Leiking is the deputy president of Warisan party and contested in Moyog; Jeffrey Kitingan, the president of STAR Sabah contested in Tambunan.

Control Order (MCO) severely affected the people's economic well-being. Warisan's 'Pakej Bantuan Covid-19 Sabah' (Sabah Covid-19 Special Aid Package) was regarded as inadequate compared to the federal government's 'Bantuan Prihatin Nasional' (BPN, or National Relief Aid). By accusing Warisan of harbouring illegal immigrants and being an 'outside' party, the Kadazan-Dusun ethnonationalists were relatively successful in rallying support for GRS. UPKO and its leaders were victims of collateral damage after choosing to support Warisan. Warisan's inability to manage the perception that it was pro-illegal immigrant or to come up with a workable plan to address the issue of illegal immigration into Sabah had made the party less popular in the Kadazan-Dusun areas, and eventually cost them the election.

Personality Politics, Patronage and Ethnonationalism in Kadazan-Dusun Politics

Personality politics, patronage and ethnonationalism are among the dominant themes in studies of Kadazan-Dusun politics.[8] Personality politics are seen here in the context of the psycho-cultural aspect of political culture.[9] They relate to a person's personal attributes such as their charisma, legacy and contributions to society. In the context of Kadazan-Dusun politics, personality politics are accentuated by the leader's cultural role in the community. This is where the Kadazan-Dusun case study is important. In the history of the Kadazan-Dusun, the *Huguan Siou* title has been only conferred upon two persons – Donald Stephens in 1960s and Joseph Pairin Kitingan in 1980s. Stephens' and Pairin's conferments as the indisputable leaders of the Kadazan-Dusun coincided with the community's desire to be culturally recognised within the context of the Malay-Muslim-dominated federal government.[10] For most of the older Kadazan-Dusun, the role of the *Huguan Siou* is still pertinent even though the younger Kadazan-Dusun

---

8 See, for instance, Arnold Puyok, 'Kota Marudu and Keningau, Sabah: Personality, Patronage and Parochial Politics,' Meredith L. Weiss (ed.) *Electoral Dynamics in Malaysia: Findings from the Grassroots* (Petaling Jaya: SIRD & ISEAS, 2014), 181-196.

9 Lucian Pye, *Politics, Personality and Nation-Building: Burma's Search for Identity* (New Haven: Yale University Press. 1962).

10 Herman Luping, *Sabah's Dilemma: The Political History of Sabah (1960-1994)* (Kuala Lumpur: Magnus Books).

have a somewhat indifferent view about the function and contribution of their indigenous leader.

Patronage politics involve a reciprocal relationship between a patron (a person of higher status) and a client (a person of lower status). This relationship is characterised by a patron using his influence, position and social status to protect another person who becomes a 'client'. When applied in the political context, the role of the patron is assumed by the party leader or elected official and the client by party workers, volunteers, supporters and even voters.[11] In the Kadazan-Dusun areas, patronage politics are pursued under the guise of 'development'. Throughout BN's over 22 years in power, for instance, the Kadazan-Dusun voters were told to support the ruling coalition as only BN had the capability and resources to develop them. They continued to support the ruling coalition due to the lures of development promises, cash distribution, government aid, not to mention threats of being excluded from mainstream development.[12] Even after the rise of opposition politics in 2008 that promised to promote programmatic rather than clientelistic politics, patronage politics are still pervasive in most of the rural areas in Peninsular Malaysia, Sabah and Sarawak. The fact that most of the Kadazan-Dusun areas in Sabah are still underdeveloped and that the Kadazan-Dusun are living in poverty means that infrastructure development and direct economic aid from the government are considered a necessity rather than a choice.

Ethnonationalism or ethnic nationalism looks at the notion of nation and nationality in ethnic terms.[13] Ethnonationalists debate issues and policies along the lines of ethnicity, believing that nations exist due to shared identities, a common language and culture. The influx of undocumented immigrants from the southern Philippines into Sabah in the late 1960s and mid-1970s changed Sabah's demography substantially, posing a threat to the

---

11 Alex Weingrod, 'Patrons, Patronage and Political Parties', *Comparative Studies in Society and History* 10, no. 4 (1968): 377-400; James Scott, 'Patron-Client Politics and Political Change in Southeast Asia', *The American Political Science Review* 66, no. 1 (1972): 91-113.

12 Arnold Puyok, 'Voting Pattern and Issues in the 2006 Sarawak State Assembly Election in the Ba' Kelalan Constituency', *Asian Journal of Political Science* 14, no. 2 (2006): 212-228.

13 Anthony D. Smith, *Nationalism: Theory, Ideology, History* (Cambridge: Polity Press, 2001).

Kadazan-Dusun, who represented the largest ethnic group in Sabah. The Kadazan-Dusun leaders believed that this was a deliberate move backed by the Malay-Muslim federal government to weaken Kadazan-Dusun political and cultural influence.[14] Similarly, some Kadazan-Dusun leaders accused Warisan of trying to bring in 'foreign elements' through the party in order to further dilute the cultural identity of the Kadazan-Dusun and to change Sabah's unique cultural make-up. Others went to the extent of questioning the ethnic origins of some Warisan leaders. This us-versus-them attitude had cultivated fear and hatred towards Warisan, which the ethnonationalists considered an outside party.

Factors Influencing the Kadazan-Dusun Voters

The Personality Factor

Politics in the Kadazan-Dusun areas are still largely personality-based. The Kadazan-Dusun are following the leaders whom they are familiar with.[15] Pairin may no longer be active in politics but he is still the *Huguan Siou* of the Kadazan-Dusun and is still respected by most older Kadazan-Dusun. The *Huguan Siou* institution remains an integral part of the political life of the Kadazan-Dusun: traditionally, the title is conferred to one for their contributions to the community.[16] Some young Kadazan-Dusun have a jaundiced view about Pairin, arguing that he has not done much to develop the Kadazan-Dusun.[17] Jeffrey Kitingan's (Pairin's brother) checkered record is not much of a help but he is overall seen as the 'consistent' leader who has fought for Sabah's rights such as enforcing MA63, the oil royalty and the PTI issue. Despite being labelled as the 'King of the Frogs' due to his penchant of jumping from one party to another, Jeffrey still has many loyal

---

14 Luping, *Sabah's Dilemma*.

15 Bridget Welsh, 'Why Warisan Plus lost – a preliminary analysis,' *Malaysiakini*, 28 September 2020, https://www.malaysiakini.com/columns/544346.

16 See Herman Luping, *Sabah's Dilemma*; Arnold Puyok, and Tony Paridi Bagang, 'Ethnicity, Culture and Indigenous Leadership in Modern Politics: The Case of the Kadazandusun in Sabah, East Malaysia,' *Kajian Malaysia* 29, Supp. 1 (2011): 177-97; Fausto Barlocco, 'An Inconvenient Birth. The Formation of a Modern Kadazan Culture and Its Marginalisation within the Making of the Malaysian Nation (1951-2007),' *Indonesia and the Malay World*, 41 (2013): 116-4.

17 Anonymous (newspaper journalist), personal communication, 27 September 2020.

supporters. He is regarded as leading the contemporary fight when it comes to the MA63, which is a pertinent issue among the Kadazan-Dusun. The young Kadazan-Dusun see this as Jeffrey's 'plus point', which also makes him slightly more popular than Pairin, particularly among the more educated Kadazan-Dusun. Furthermore, he is regarded as more outspoken compared with his older brother. Like Pairin, Jeffrey also holds the traditional title *Huguan Siou Lundu Mirongod* (Brave Paramount Thinker) by the Keeper of the *Adat* (custom) and Traditions of the Kadazan-Dusun.[18]

Despite Warisan's attempt to promote Peter and Darell, both are seen as newcomers who do not hold any 'traditional positions', unlike Jeffrey and Pairin. Peter is the president of Kadazan-Dusun Malaysia (KDM Malaysia), a non-governmental association seen as a rival to KDCA (Kadazan-Dusun Cultural Association), but support for KDM Malaysia is not as widespread, especially so in the interior. There was an accusation that Peter was using KDM Malaysia as a tool to mobilise support – for example, during the Kimanis by-election, a Christmas celebration was held by KDM Malaysia, purportedly to woo the Kadazan-Dusun voters.[19] Darell, on the other hand, is regarded as the 'Penampang boy', whose influence can only be felt among the young Kadazan-Dusun in Penampang. Darell's popularity rose at the national level when he was appointed as Minister of International Trade and Industry under the PH-led government. Another personality, Madius, who lost his presidential bid in KDCA, widely seen as a bastion of Kadazan-Dusun support for Jeffrey and Pairin, found himself caught in the long-standing rivalry between PBS and UPKO, once headed by Bernard Dompok. He left PBS to form PDS (Parti Demokratik Sabah or Sabah Democratic Party, which was renamed UPKO in 1999). Since taking over as president of UPKO, Madius has been relentless in pursuing the Sabah IC (identification card) in order to solve the issue of fake Malaysian ICs allegedly held by illegal immigrants. Prior to the election, protests against Madius's leadership led to the resignations of key party leaders such as Ewon Ebin and Marcus Mojigoh. UPKO has its own key supporters but the absence of key figures

---

18 'Humbled Jeffrey Kitingan Installed "*Huguan Siou Lundu Mirongod*"', *Borneo Today*, 17 December 2016, https://www.borneotoday.net/humbled-and-honoured-jeffrey-installed-huguan-siou-lundu-mirongod/.

19 'KDM leader denies Christmas function linked to Warisan's campaign,' *Malaysiakini*, 5 January 2020, https://www.malaysiakini.com/news/505984.

who can command the respect of the Kadazan-Dusun makes the party less attractive.

Warisan and UPKO went to the extent of roping in Richard Malanjum, former chief Justice of Malaysia, to campaign for them. In one of his many appearances on social media, Malanjum said:

> It is our responsibility to protect our state, [sic] our identity, [sic] our integrity. Do not allow ourselves to be easily convinced by the so-called leaders who are merely puppets of the Malayan politicians. Do not allow them to tell us what to do. We decide [as] the power is in our hands [and] votes. Vote wisely. Vote for Warisan Plus.[20]

Undoubtedly, Malanjum's appearance was a big deal to the middle-class and urban Kadazan-Dusun voters. Malanjum is an icon to many Sabahans, especially the Kadazan-Dusun, as he is the first Sabahan and Kadazan to be appointed as chief justice of Malaysia. However, despite his credentials, he is largely an unfamiliar figure among most Kadazan-Dusun in the rural areas. The rural Kadazan-Dusun only see him in the media rather than in person. The voters in urban areas may be more concerned about the ability of their representative to raise issues and solve problems. But for those in rural areas, a 'personal touch' is also equally important. A simple act, like a politician making a donation to a constituent in need or routinely attending social functions, can have a lot of impact.[21] The Kadazan-Dusun in the rural areas are closer to their local leaders than the technocrats and elites living in the urban areas.

Another Kadazan-Dusun-based party, PBRS, had failed to make an impact in PRN2020 except in areas where its founder Joseph Kurup had a loyal following. PBRS is still led by the septuagenarian Kurup, who like Dompok is a founding member of PBS. PBRS contested in five seats – Matunggong, Tandek, Kadamaian, Tulid and Sook – but was not able to win any of them. Without widespread support and influential personalities, PBRS struggled to remain relevant among the Kadazan-Dusun electorate.

---

[20] KiniTV, 'Beri Warisan Plus Peluang Untuk Lima Tahun Lagi – Bekas Ketua Hakim Negara (YouTube Video),' 4:01, 23 September 2020, https://www.youtube.com/watch?v=jMPBv5GkHZU.

[21] Tony Paridi Bagang, 'Beaufort, Sabah: Whither Lajim's popularity?' in *Electoral Dynamics in Malaysia*, 223-233.

The Patronage Factor

The Kadazan-Dusun feel more secure with PBS and STAR Sabah. Even though PBS is not a member of PN, it established a partnership with PN, the current ruling coalition at the federal level. In what was seen as PBS's attempt to convince its supporters that it was an independent entity, it signed an agreement with PN on 19 September 2020. The party said:

> PBS will uphold cooperation and partnership with all component parties of PN, as constituted in the party's registration [sic] ... we are on our own, fully autonomous, not dictated by any party or parties, and yet part of the bigger family of PN, to jointly develop and make Malaysia greater.[22]

STAR Sabah took a different path, becoming a member of PN with Jeffrey as the coalition's deputy chairman. PN's logos and Muhyiddin's pictures could be conspicuously seen in PBS's and STAR Sabah's strongholds in the Kadazan-Dusun areas. A Kadazan-Dusun petty trader said she supported STAR Sabah because it was part of a ruling coalition whom she credited for distributing various forms of financial aid to the needy during this current Covid-19 pandemic.[23] Warisan, on the other hand, was blamed for its failure in making sure that financial aid reached the rural people when it was needed. Chin observed that

> Many KDM villagers are angry that Warisan did not fulfill its promise of monetary aid. Warisan representatives had promised some villagers RM300 [sic] each but the money never arrived.[24]

Support for PN was not because of the distribution of financial aid alone. Poverty and under-development were among the key issues raised by many Kadazan-Dusun, apart from state rights and cultural autonomy. A Kadazan-Dusun girl who was studying at a local university stated that PN was in a

---

22 'PBS Seals Formal Political Partnership With PN', *Borneo Post Online*, 19 September 2020, https://www.theborneopost.com/2020/09/19/pbs-seals-formal-political-partnership-with-pn/.

23 Anonymous, personal communication, 23 September 2020.

24 James Chin, 'Commentary: Sabah's surprise results – and how Warisan lost big in state elections,' *Channel News Asia*, 28 September 2020, https://www.channelnewsasia.com/news/commentary/sabah-election-results-how-warisan-lost-big-grs-won-huge-13156026.

better position to bring the much-needed development to her district.[25] A candidate contesting as an independent in the predominantly Kadazan-Dusun area of Matunggong noted how the people in his constituency struggled to commute to the nearby town areas as the road access was bad. He openly supported STAR Sabah with the hope that the party could make use of its affiliation with PN to develop his area.[26] While making our observations in Keningau, we saw a banner that reads: '*Ada aspal/jambatan, ada undi*' (Our vote is guaranteed if our road is paved and a bridge is built).

The Ethnonationalist Factor

Warisan, founded by Shafie in 2016, attempted to emerge as a party for all including the Kadazan-Dusun. Warisan was able to secure support among the Bugis, Suluk and Bajau communities living along Sabah's east coast areas. Still, it was less popular in the Kadazan-Dusun areas in the west coast and the interior. Some Kadazan-Dusun were skeptical of Warisan due to Shafie's ethnicity. This was where the roles of Kadazan-Dusun leaders in Warisan – Darell Leiking and Peter Anthony – were vital in persuading the Kadazan-Dusun to support the party.

Even though UPKO claims to be a multiracial party, it is heavily Kadazan-Dusun-based. Its decision to rebrand in June 2020 did not diminish UPKO's outlook as a Kadazan-Dusun-based party. UPKO's dismal performance speaks volumes of the party's lack of popularity in the Kadazan-Dusun areas. By associating itself with Warisan, whom PBS and STAR Sabah accused of being an 'illegal-friendly' party, UPKO had exposed itself to virulent attacks from PBS and STAR Sabah supporters. Furthermore, most Kadazan-Dusun are unhappy with UPKO for causing the collapse of the BN-led government in GE14. For some, UPKO's decision was akin to the collapse of the PBS-led government in 1994 due to defections.

The Kadazan-Dusun were looking for a local-based party that could defeat Warisan which had failed to resolve the issue of illegal immigrants in Sabah.[27] Having failed to come up with a comprehensive plan to manage the

[25] An anonymous third year Kadazan-Dusun university student, personal communication, 24 September 2020.

[26] An anonymous Kadazan-Dusun independent candidate, personal communication, 20 September 2020.

[27] An anonymous Kadazan-Dusun party volunteer, personal communication, 11

growing number of undocumented migrants and to dismiss the perception that Warisan was 'pro-illegals', Warisan had been made the 'whipping boy'. Chin wrote:

> Warisan['s] problem with the heartland [Kadazan-Dusun] community starts from the widely held belief that Warisan is a party sympathetic to illegal immigrants (PTI). PTI are undocumented migrants from the Southern Philippines, said to have been naturalised as Malaysians for decades in order to help the federal government skew the electoral roll in favour of Muslims. Shafie himself was accused of being pro-PTI because his extended family allegedly came from the Southern Philippines. This image was not helped by rumours he had promoted mostly Bajau and Suluk people in the civil service, from his political base, Semporna, which he did little to dispel. The [Kadazan-Dusun] polity is very sensitive to these sorts of rumours. Many [Kadazan-Dusun] are angry that PTI have 'taken over their land' yet the Warisan allowed these rumours to fester unchallenged.[28]

The GRS consistently brought up the PTI (*pendatang tanpa izin* or illegal immigrant) issue throughout the campaign to create fear and linked it to Warisan. During our casual conversation with people in Sook and Nabawan, we found that they were very cynical about Warisan's purported plan to address the PTI issue. They believed that if the Pas Sementara Sabah (PSS or Sabah Temporary Pass) proceeded as planned, it would exponentially increase the number of illegal immigrants in Sabah. They also believed that the PSS would pave the way for the undocumented migrants to apply for citizenship.

While Warisan's campaign themes of 'unity' and 'nation-building' were acceptable to most people in the urban areas, the Kadazan-Dusun were unperturbed and viewed the slogan with suspicion.[29] First, the Kadazan-Dusun have never had any issue with the concept of unity, as the state's religious and racial tolerance is well-known throughout the country. Yet some Kadazan-Dusun viewed the attempt to promote the idea of unity as an attempt to unite the Kadazan-Dusun with the PTI.[30] The sweeping

---

October 2020.

28 James Chin. 'Commentary: Sabah's surprise results'.

29 An anonymous Kadazandusun party volunteer, personal communication, 11 October 2020.

30 Ibid.

message of unity did not resonate well among most Kadazan-Dusun voters in the interior. Even though some did not reject it outright, they questioned Warisan's lack of urgency in tackling their dire economic needs; they instead accused Warisan of promoting something that has no urgency in their community.

The Result

PRN2020 was somewhat unique as at least 16 parties contested against each other, including 56 independents. There were also multi-cornered fights in all 73 seats. Traditionally, multi-cornered fights give the advantage to BN, as they split the votes. In GE14, multi-cornered contests benefitted not just BN but Warisan, PH and STAR Sabah.[31]

The results show that PRN2020 was a contest between GRS and Warisan. The other small parties were spoilers and most of their candidates lost their deposits. Warisan obtained 32 seats, GRS 38 and independents three. PCS, LDP and other local-based political parties failed to secure any seats.

Most of the seats in the Kadazan-Dusun areas were won by PBS and STAR Sabah (Table 2). Overall, following the trend of GE14, GRS managed to maintain its strong presence in the Kadazan-Dusun areas. Warisan and its allies only managed to win five seats with UPKO winning just one.

In terms of popular votes, GRS obtained about half compared with Warisan and its allies, which took 31.6 per cent (Table 3). In fact, GRS managed to increase its popular vote by 4.7 per cent. There is no marked change, however, in terms of the popular votes obtained by Warisan. PBS and STAR Sabah maintained their popularity among the Kadazan-Dusun voters, obtaining 20.3 and 18.1 per cent of the popular votes respectively.

[31] Tony Paridi Bagang and Arnold Puyok. 'Sabah: the End of BN and a New Order?'. in *The Defeat of Barisan Nasional*, Francis E. Hutchinson and Hwok Aun Lee (eds.) (Singapore: ISEAS, 2019), 402-422.

Table 2: Number of Seats Won According to Party/ Alliance in the Kadazan-Dusun Constituencies

Party	Seat Won
Warisan	3
PKR	1
UPKO	1
Gabungan Rakyat Sabah (GRS)	
UMNO/BN	1
Bersatu/PN	3
STAR Sabah/PN	5
PBS	6
Independent	3

Source: Authors' calculations from the Election Commission of Malaysia. Accessed at https://dashboard.spr.gov.my/#!/home.

Table 3: Party/Alliance and Popular Votes in the Kadazan-Dusun Constituencies

Party	Popular Votes (%)
Warisan	14.6 (32.6)
PKR	7.0
UPKO	11.0
Total	32.6
Gabungan Rakyat Sabah (GRS)	
BN	12.0
PN	20.3
PBS	18.1
Total	50.4 (45.7)
Others	17.0

Note: Numbers in parentheses show the popular votes obtained in 2018

Observations in Selected Kadazan-Dusun Seats

To understand the results, we draw from our fieldwork. The focus of our observations was on seats considered as 'highly competitive'. In this chapter, we detail three seats – Kiulu, Tambunan and Moyog. We also did fieldwork in Matunggong, Keningau, Tenom and Nabawan. There were 24 Kadazan-Dusun seats altogether. We defined a Kadazan-Dusun seat as one predominantly occupied (by more than 51 per cent) by the Kadazan-Dusun as an ethnic entity.[32]

Table 4: Winning Party in Kadazan-Dusun Seats

Constituency	Party Won
Bangkoka	BN
Pitas	Independent
Matunggong	PBS
Bandau	(Bersatu) PN
Tandek	PBS
Kadamaian	UPKO
Tamparuli	PBS
Kiulu	PBS
Inanam	PKR
Moyog	Warisan
Limbahau	Warisan
Kundasang	PBS
Karanaan	(Bersatu) PN
Paginatan	(Star) PN
Tambunan	(Star) PN
Bingkor	(Star) PN
Liawan	(Bersatu) PN
Malalap	Warisan
Kemabong	Independent
Tulid	(Star) PN

[32] The KDCA constitution, Article 6 (1) defines the Kadazan-Dusun as the definitive indigenous peoples of Sabah comprising 40 dialectical ethnic groups.

Constituency	Party Won
Sook	(Star) PN
Nabawan	(Bersatu) PN
Telupid	PBS
Kuamut	Independent

Source: Authors' compilation from the Election Commission of Malaysia. Accessed at https://dashboard.spr.gov.my/#!/home.

One of the highly competitive seats was Kiulu, contested by Madius Tangau and the incumbent Janiston Bingkuai, PBS's information chief. The other candidates contesting here were from LDP and PCS as well as an independent. Madius contested in Kiulu for the first time. Being a party president and a member of the state cabinet under Warisan, Madius was initially tipped to win, albeit with a slim majority. The former STAR Sabah leader who contested under the party in GE14, Terrence Sinti, gave his support to Madius and campaigned aggressively for UPKO.[33] Madius's campaign theme was on development, promising to develop Kiulu as a popular tourism spot.

Janiston focused his campaign on the '*misompuru*' or unity pact between PBS, UPKO and PBRS, covenanted prior to GE14. Janiston accused Madius of breaching the '*misompuru*' after supporting Warisan and its allies. The people here seemed to reject Madius mainly due to his abandoning of BN to support Warisan. For many, this was history repeating itself. In 1994, the PBS-led government collapsed after its key leaders ditched the party. One of the leaders was Bernard Dompok who formed the Sabah Democratic Party (UPKO's precursor), which later became part of BN. UPKO's decision to rebrand received mixed reactions from the Kadazan-Dusun. Those already in UPKO were supportive of UPKO becoming a multiracial party. For others, however, the decision had diminished UPKO's reputation as a Kadazan-Dusun-based party fighting for the interests of the community.

Apart from the attack on Madius, PBS also accused Warisan of being pro-PTI.[34] The PTI issue is very close to Sabahans and in particular the

[33] Terence Sinti contested under STAR Sabah in GE14. Despite losing, he still managed to secure 2,457 votes. Terence quit STAR Sabah in 2019 to join UPKO.

[34] 'Battle for Kadazandusun votes grows intense,' *The Star*, 21 September 2020, https://

Kadazan-Dusun. As mentioned above, in the Kimanis by-election, the voters rejected Warisan because of the PTI and PSS issues. Despite Warisan's efforts to explain the rationale behind the PSS, the Kadazan-Dusun voters in Kimanis seemed to have already made up their minds.[35]

The impact of Pairin's presence when campaigning for Janiston could also be felt. In Pairin's speech, he reminded the people about PBS's struggle to fight against a 'cruel' state government that had stifled religious freedom and failed to resolve the issue of undocumented migrants.[36] Pairin, therefore, stressed that it was important to vote for PBS to save Sabah from the influx of 'illegal immigrants' and other security concerns which Warisan had failed to address. It could not be denied that PBS's campaign messages resonated well with most voters in Kiulu. Meanwhile, Madius campaigned hard to justify UPKO's association with Warisan, but the general sentiments here show that the people were not receptive to him. Madius, whom many tipped as the favourite to win, failed to capture Kiulu from PBS. Janiston retained the seat by a majority of 1,221 votes.

Another competitive seat was Moyog, one of the state seats under the Penampang parliamentary seat. Jenifer Lasimbang of Warisan won the seat in GE14 with a majority of 4,442 votes, defeating UPKO's Donald Mojuntin. This time, Jenifer gave way to Darell to contest. Darell faced six challengers from STAR Sabah, PCS, LDP, PBS, PPRS and an independent. Most of the candidates campaigned heavily on issues related to flooding, poor village roads, youth employment and women's empowerment. A casual conversation with several people in Penampang revealed that most were not satisfied with Darell's performance as a Member of Parliament, particularly in upgrading the village roads. Their other complaints were that despite having a federal minister and an assistant minister in the state Cabinet, Moyog was still lagging far behind in terms of infrastructural development

---

www.thestar.com.my/news/nation/2020/09/21/battle-for-kadazandusun-votes-grows-intense.

35 Durie Ranie Fong and Jason Santos, 'There were telltale signs Warisan would lose in Kimanis, say analysts,' *Free Malaysia Today*, 19 January 2020, https://www.freemalaysiatoday.com/category/nation/2020/01/19/writing-is-on-the-wall-for-warisan-after-defeat-in-kimanis-say-analysts/.

36 Ricardo Unto, 'PBS won't withdraw from seats: Pairin', *Daily Express*, 22 September 2020, https://www.dailyexpress.com.my/news/158684/pbs-won-t-withdraw-from-seats-pairin/.

compared with other towns around Kota Kinabalu.[37] Furthermore, road conditions are bad in many villages such as Kg (Kampung) Buayan, Kg Terian and Kg Pongobonon. These villages can only be accessed via highly modified four-wheel-drive vehicles.

The multi-cornered contest in Moyog did not affect Darell that much as he won the seat with a majority of 5,935 votes. His main rivals from STAR Sabah (Joe Suleiman) and PBS (John Chryso) were only able to obtain 2,502 and 1,175 votes respectively. Despite dissatisfaction with his performance, the voters were not easily swayed by the issues brought up by Darell's rivals. Criticisms against Darell's performance during his tenure as federal minister did not affect him at all. Many wanted him to represent the voice of Moyog in the state legislative assembly. They believed that Darell could still contribute significantly to developing Moyog. Based on our observations, the support for STAR Sabah was stronger in upper Moyog, if the visibility of the party's flags and posters was anything to go by. Darell's support was mostly felt in the lower Moyog, indicating that his supporters were mainly urban dwellers living within the vicinity of Penampang proper. UPKO played an instrumental role in Warisan's victory as UPKO had a large following in Moyog.

Another competitive seat was Tambunan – considered a landmark of Kadazan-Dusun ethnonationalism. It is also the birthplace of PBS and the *Huguan Siou*, Joseph Pairin Kitingan. His brother, Jeffrey, retained the Tambunan seat with a majority of 6,792 votes. Jeffrey has been regarded as a Sabahan nationalist known for his 'Sabah for Sabahans' struggle since the mid-1980s. Jeffrey's focus on raising regional sentiments was effective in mobilising support, particularly among the less sophisticated and pliant voters. The 'Kitingan factor' has indeed played a salient role in contributing to STAR Sabah's victory in Tambunan.

The extent of Jeffrey's popularity could be seen in the results: STAR Sabah's close challenger from UPKO, Laurentius Nayan Umbu, did not manage to unseat Jeffrey, garnering only 1,899 votes. The other four candidates lost their deposits. Another candidate, Silverinus Bruno, who was slated to contest under the PBS had pulled out from the race to avoid a clash with Jeffrey.[38] PN Secretary-General Hamzah Zainuddin brokered the

---

[37] Anonymous (senior party leader), personal communication, 24 September 2020.

[38] Tarrance Tan, 'PBS withdraws from two seats,' *The Star*, 22 September 2020, https://

consensus between STAR Sabah and PBS at the eleventh hour. In return, Jeffrey agreed to withdraw his support for the independent candidates in Api-Api and Bengkoka. Our observations on 24 September showed party workers taking down PBS's posters and banners, replacing them with larger posters and banners of Jeffrey and Prime Minister Muhyiddin Yassin. STAR Sabah not only retained Tambunan but also did well outside of its traditional stronghold in Keningau, winning in Sook and Tulid under the Pensiangan parliamentary constituency.

Conclusion

This chapter shows that voting in the Kadazan-Dusun areas is still influenced by personality politics, patronage and ethnonationalism. Personality politics and patronage play a complementary role. In Kadazan-Dusun politics, personality politics is shaped by the leaders' past legacy, contributions and the traditional titles they hold. The influence of the Kitingan brothers among many Kadazan-Dusun in the interior is still strong. Warisan and UPKO lack these types of personalities useful to arouse sentiments and mobilise political support.

Patronage politics is strengthened as GRS was regarded as a kind of saviour during this pandemic period. As most Kadazan-Dusun live in rural areas and are in dire need of economic assistance, most were appreciative of the various forms of monetary aid distributed by GRS and wanted such aid to be continued. Those who continued to support GRS were also hopeful that by continuing to support the PN-led federal government, they would one day see their villages' infrastructures developed and upgraded.

Ethnonationalism in Kadazan-Dusun politics is expressed mainly through these issues: the Kadazan-Dusun lack of political representation, loss of cultural significance and the threats posed by 'outsiders'. UPKO and its leaders were victims of collateral damage after they chose to support Warisan – accused by some Kadazan-Dusun ethnonationalists as 'pro-illegal immigrants' and an outsider party. While such an accusations are not necessarily true, Warisan's inability to address the problem of undocumented migrants head-on raised doubts about its ability in managing Sabah's security. By promoting the 'us' versus 'them' mentality against Warisan, the

---

www.thestar.com.my/news/nation/2020/09/22/pbs-withdraws-from-two-seats.

ethnonationalists were successful in preventing most of the Kadazan-Dusun from supporting the party, thus winning the state elections for themselves.

Chapter 14

Islam and Muslim Politics in Sabah's 2020 State Election

Mohd Rahimin Mustafa

Introduction

On 7 October 2020, Dr Aliakbar Gulasan, the Sabah secretary of the Malaysian Islamic Party (PAS), was appointed to the Gabungan Rakyat Sabah (GRS)-led state assembly.[1] There was public outcry over the appointment, given that PAS had not contested in PRN2020. This response highlighted the underlying opposition of some Sabahans towards the party's appeal to religion.

Few understand, however, the mobilising role Islam has long played in Sabah politics. In fact, Muslim religious leaders and organisations have been an integral part of Muslim Bumiputera politics in Sabah's politics since before Sabah joined Malaysia. As Muslim Bumiputera politics has shifted, with divisions, new parties and alliances emerging, political Islam's influence has expanded, with candidates and parties appealing to religion in their engagement with Muslim Bumiputera voters. Mobilisation around political Islam was also decisive in shaping PRN2020. Both Warisan and Muslim Bumiputera parties in GRS fielded candidates with religious credentials, assuring that many with strong roots in the Islamic community were elected to office.

This chapter describes the roots of political Islam in contemporary Sabah and traces its developments. It shows that while Islam has gained a

[1] The Sabah Constitution allows the victor of the election to appoint six additional assemblypersons.

more prominent voice in politics and its influence has expanded, Islamic voices are pluralistic, representing a variety of different perspectives in Sabah's political life. Yet this pluralism also divides the Muslim Bumiputera, weakening the coherence of attempts to represent the Muslim community at large. This was clear in PRN2020. This analysis draws from my experience as a research associate at Sabah Strategic Studies Institute (Institut Kajian Strategik Negeri Sabah, IKSAS), a PAS research centre in Sabah, over the last three decades.

Early Muslim Politics in Sabah

Scholars have argued that Islam has played an important role in the fight against colonial rule in Malaysia. Nationalism and the struggle against Western imperialism became intertwined with Islam and historians have argued that the same dynamic was at play in Sabah, as Muslims came to challenge British rule. From Datu Tating in 1775, who fought the British presence, to leaders such as Sharif Usman (1845) in Marudu, Pengiran Usop (1846) in Kimanis, Haji Saman (1846) in Membakut River, Datu Baginda Putih (1879) in Sandakan, Pengiran Samah (1884) in Gomantong, Pengiran Syahbandar Hashim (1889) in Sungai Padas, Paduka Mat Salleh (1894), Timus and friends (1900), Mat Satur (1900) and Sharif Ali (1915) in Pandasan, Kota Belud.[2] According to Jamdin Buyong, it was the spirit of Islam which contributed to these Muslims rising up against the British, in part because they did not want to accept non-Muslim foreign powers.[3]

Despite British control, Islamic scholars (*ulama*) continued to visit Borneo to carry out Islamic preaching without fear of the British colonial presence. For example, Tuanku Sharif Kedah, an *ulama*, was born in Jiyad, Mecca, and was educated by religious scholars from the archipelago. He then travelled to Malaya, Sarawak, Brunei and finally arrived in Labuan in 1896. In the village of Batu Arang Kedah, Tuanku Sharif set up a mosque and made it a centre for the dissemination of Islamic knowledge. Another *ulama*, Haji Yaakob Haji Ali from Pasir Mas Kelantan, travelled and

---

2 William H. Treacher, *British Borneo Sketches of Brunei, Sarawak, Labuan, and North Borneo* (Kuala Lumpur: Silverfish Books, 2020), 16.

3 See Jamdin Buyong, 'Islam Membentuk Tamadun Penduduk Sabah: Sejarah dan Kejayaan,' in A.F. Omar et al. (ed) *Islam di Sarawak dan Sabah* (Bangi: Fakulti Pengajian Islam UKM & Kuching: Jabatan Agama Islam Sarawak, 2003), 189.

preached in Kedah and Melaka before arriving in Brunei in the 1880s. In 1917, Haji Yaakob migrated to North Borneo and settled down next to the Putatan Mosque, becoming a well-known religious teacher in the area. After five years in Putatan, Haji Yaakob was appointed the religious teacher and *imam* (who leads Muslim in prayer) at the Jesselton Mosque, located in the capital of Sabah. With the height of knowledge possessed by Haji Yaakob, his influence expanded to the west coast of Sabah, making him a famous scholar in Sabah at that time.[4] After his death, the *da'wah* (conversion) effort was continued by his son Imam Suhaili Haji Yaakob. He was later involved in the founding of Khairat Jumaat Muslimin (the Muslim Welfare Group, KJM) in 1947 after the demise of the Parti Kebangsaan Melayu Jesselton (Malay Nationalist Party Jesselton, PKMJ) and Barisan Pemuda (The Youth Front, BARIP).[5]

The development of a formal Islamic education system in Sabah only happened around the 1950s. The British North Borneo Chartered Company (BNBCC) first opened an Islamic religious school for the children of local Muslim Bumiputera leaders in Sandakan at the end of 1881,[6] but shut it down shortly afterwards due to a lack of response and funds. The leaders' children were, however, given informal education at the mosque or the village headman's house. None of them left to pursue education regionally or abroad as a result of this programme. Religious education continued, however, in local communities. In Malaya, the religious educated classes,

---

4 See A.S. Abdul Latif, 'Ketokohan Ulama Bapa-Anak di Sabah: Imam Haji Yaakub dan Imam Haji Suhaili,' in A.F. Omar at al. (ed), *Islam di Sarawak dan Sabah*, 240.

5 The struggle of PKMJ and BARIP was an integral part of the struggle to liberate North Borneo (the former name of Sabah) from British occupation. Their leaders were influenced by Indonesia, so the BARIP flag uses the red *saka* (*sang saka merah*). BNBCC, PKMJ and BARIP competed for influence with leadership problems finally burying PKMJ and BARIP. It is believed that Muslim Bumiputera leaders changed their strategy by forming a religious association to unite all Muslims after this competition. They believed that only unity would make them stronger in fighting for their rights from the British.

6 See 'North Borneo Education Department - Triennial Survey 1958-1960'. The first Governor of North Borneo, W.H. Treacher, worked for the colonial government and withdrew money, provided land and donated money from his salary to set up the school. He selected a religious teacher named Sheikh Abdul Dulunan to teach and build a mosque. Refer to Mohd Nor Long, *Perkembangan Pelajaran di Sabah* (Kuala Lumpur: Dewan Bahasa dan Pustaka, Kementerian Pelajaran Malaysia,1978) 7.

known as *kaum muda* (young group),[7] played a role in bringing awareness to the Muslim community through reformist Islam or the Islamic *Islah* movement.[8] They consisted of individuals who sought knowledge from the Middle East and India and were exposed to the global *Islah* movement.

These groups wanted fellow Muslims, particularly the Malays, to progress and develop to help change their perceived attitudes of negligence and complacency. To do this, it was argued that Malays themselves needed to provide adequate education to their children to compete with the other races that were perceived to be more financially privileged in Malaya. This group blamed traditional *ulamas* who mixed matters of *bid'ah* (innovation in religious matters) and *khurafat* (superstition), narrowing the teachings of Islam to the confines of mosques and suraus. Their belief was that Islam as a religion had the potential to bring progress to the Malays, to be on par with other nations, and wider religious education was an integral part of this progress.

In an effort to disseminate the ideas and thoughts of the *kaum muda*, newspapers, magazines and books became the main medium in the growing awareness among Muslims in Malaya, Singapore, Sumatra and Borneo. For example, the magazines *al-Ikhwan* (1926) and *Saudara* (1928) pioneered by Syed Sheikh Ahmad al-Hadi, discussed the question of the political, economic and social awakening of the community and called for Muslims to rise up against British colonial rule. Through newspapers, a social organisation called Persaudaraan Sahabat Pena Malaya (PASPAM, Malayan Pen-pal Brotherhood) was formed in 1934 which aimed to improve the literacy rate in Malaya.[9]

PASPAM branched out to North Borneo in 1937, known in different localities as Persatuan Sahabat Pena Tawau (PASPAT), Persaudaraan Sahabat Pena Labuan (PASPAL) and Persaudaraan Sahabat Pena Sabah (PASPAS) in Kota Kinabalu. The formation of these branches in Sabah, Sarawak and Brunei allowed Sabah's Muslim community to become active in politics

---

7 See Kamarul Afendey Hamimi & Ishak Saat, *Kaum Muda di Tanah Melayu 1906-1957* (Tanjong Malim: Penerbit Universiti Pendidikan Sultan Idris, 2020), 5.

8 See Azmah Abd. Manaf, *Malaysia: Gerakan Kesedaran & Nasionalisme* (Kuala Lumpur: Universiti Sains Malaysia and Utusan Publications & Distributors, 2016) 12.

9 See Eko Prayitno Joko et al., *Gerakan Berpolitik Bumiputera Islam di Sabah (1938-1963)* (Kota Bharu: Kedai Hitam Putih, 2018), 40-41.

and established the political character of the organisations, in line with the emergence of political parties in Malaya such as the United Malays National Organisation (UMNO) and the Parti Kebangsaan Melayu Malaya (Malay Nationalist Party, PKMM).

Meanwhile, another political organisation that emerged at the end of 1946 in Borneo was BARIP, founded by Bruneian teachers. BARIP grew rapidly with several newly opened branches in Labuan, Jesselton and Papar.[10] This forged greater unity between the diverse Muslim Bumiputera in Sabah and strengthened support to liberate Sabah from British colonial rule. However, these groups did not last long due to internal problems and the intervention of the British, who tried to undermine their work.

Since the beginning of the administration of the BNBCC in 1881, the local Muslim community leaders, known as the *Orang Kaya Kaya*, were members of the Native Chief Advisory Council, and urged British officials to introduce an Islamic legal system to manage matters related to Muslims, separate from Native Laws. This included issues such as marriage, divorce, inheritance, *waqf* property, *sharia* (also spelled '*syariah*') courts and so on. The Putatan Islamic Association (PIP)[11] leader Awang Sahari Abdul Latif felt that Muslims in Malaya needed their Islamic religious affairs governed under the Islamic Religious Council of State. In Sabah, religious affairs were administered by the *imams* appointed by British officers. The powers of the *imams* were only limited to issues of marriages and deaths, while matters such as the division of inheritance had to be referred to the Native Court with *imams* acting as witnesses or prosecutors.[12] The administrative role of religious leaders in Sabah was noticeably less pronounced than that in Malaya.

Muslim Bumiputera in Sabah, however, wanted a greater voice, expressed in the emergence of Islamic associations in Sabah after the Second World War. Realising the importance of a strong Muslim body, Muslim leaders[13] from different districts in Sabah united by merging smaller existing

---

[10] See Zaini Haji Ahmad, *Pertumbuhan Nasionalisme di Brunei (1939-1962)* (Kuala Lumpur: ZR Publications, 1989), 26.

[11] Founded by Awang Sahari Abdul Latif together with several community leaders in Putatan in 1959, aimed at guiding Muslims to follow the teachings of Islam through religious school activities and Islamic *da'wah*.

[12] See Emin Madi, *Sinar Perjuangan USIA* (Kota Kinabalu: USIA, 2009), 10.

[13] Awang Sahari from PIP, OKK Zainal Kerahu (Persatuan Islam Tawau, PIT) and Mohd

Islamic associations into a large coalition at the state level. In 1969, after examining the 20 points of the 1963 Malaysia Agreement (MA63) closely and noticing the absence of Islam as the official religion of the state,[14] a congress was held at the Kota Kinabalu Community Hall to unanimously approve the establishment of the United Sabah Islamic Association (USIA) with the aim of fighting for the recognition of the Muslim community in Sabah.

Muslim Bumiputera Politics After Independence

History has shown that unity between Muslim Bumiputera in Sabah was difficult to achieve. The struggles of political parties in Sabah, were more generally tied to the different representations of religion, race, language, descent and culture, with the belief that diversity was bad for political unity.[15] In the context of Sabah politics, the three relevant cleavages are between the Muslim Bumiputera, Non-Muslim Bumiputera and the Chinese.[16] Muslim politics in Sabah cannot be separated from the influence of national politics, especially from Peninsular Malaysia. Yet there were, however, different local influences that shaped its evolution. Sabah's political history was divided between two major political influences, the Sultanate of Brunei and Sulu,[17] making it difficult for any type of unity between Sabah Muslims to exist, except religious unity. The Brunei influence, for example, was concentrated along the west coast, with Sulu shaping the developments on the east coast – reinforcing different local identities and competition.

This lack of unity did not prevent Muslim Bumiputera from being active

---

Kassim Haji Hashim (Persatuan Islam Sabah, PIS). Ibid., 17.

14 Jamdin Buyong (1995) in *Islam di Sabah Peranan Putatan Dalam Perkembangannya*, writes that the leaders of PIP and PIS were desperate to find a new path towards Islamic unity because they realised that in the 20-point agreement, Sabah did not have an official religion as enshrined in the Federal Constitution. With this response, the PIP leader, in his general meeting on 10 March 1968, decided to merge all Islamic associations in Sabah.

15 Kartini Aboo Talib Khalid, 'Masyarakat Sivil di Malaysia Isu dan Strategi', paper presented at UKM-UNESCO Asia Pasific Conference on History, Politics, Strategic Studies and Climate Change, Universiti Kebangsaan Malaysia, November 2010, 229.

16 See Ismail Yusoff, *Politik dan Agama di Sabah* (Bangi: Penerbit UKM, 2004) 26.

17 See D.S Ranjit Singh, *The Making of Sabah 1865-1941 The Dynamics of Indigenous Society* (Kota Kinabalu: Bahagian Kabinet dan Dasar JKM, 2011 (3rd)) 6.

in politics. From the discussion over the formation of Malaysia, Sabah's religious groups played a prominent role in Muslim Bumiputera political parties. BARIP, led by the nationalist Cikgu Harun Aminurrashid, played an important role in the establishment of PKMM branches in Borneo. Cikgu Harun's biggest contribution was the establishment of Parti Rakyat Brunei (Brunei People's Party, PRB) in 1956,[18] a political ally to Parti Rakyat Malaya (Malayan People's Party, PRM), which was led by Ahmad Boestaman. The failure of these parties to gain traction weakened Muslim Bumiputera influence during the subsequent negotiations for independence.

When the proposed establishment of the Melayu Raya or Malaysia on 27 May 1961 was brought forward by then Malayan Prime Minister Tunku Abdul Rahman, the only party that appeared to represent the majority of Muslims in Sabah was the United Sabah National Organisation (USNO). The presence of USNO was highly anticipated by the Muslim community as their political platform was to defend and improve the lives of those living in poverty, and to represent the Muslim Bumiputera community.[19] USNO tapped into Islamic community organisations such as PIP, Persatuan Islam Sabah (PIS)[20] and Persatuan Islam Tawau (PIT),[21] then called USIA. Putatan, Tawau and Kota Kinabalu established long traditions connected to religious organisations. Sabah independence-era political parties such as USNO, United National Kadazan Organization (UNKO), United Pasok Momogun Organization (UPMO), Borneo Utara National Party (BUNAP), the Democratic Party (DP) and United Party (UP) were race-based political parties. As they were inseparable from primordial sentiments, religion was part of their mobilisation. For USNO the appeal was to Muslims through political Islam, while UNKO appealed to Christians through church networks, thus tying religion to the ethnic foundation of politics in the state.

[18] H.Z. Haji Ahmad, *Pertumbuhan Nasionalisme di Brunei* (1939-1962), 50.

[19] See H. Aziz, *USNO dan BERJAYA Politik Sabah* (Kuala Lumpur: Dewan Bahasa dan Pustaka, 2015) 41.

[20] Founded by Yusoff Shamsudin in 1959, then led by Kassim Haji Hashim based in Jesselton (Kota Kinabalu). It fought for the interests of Islam, provided Islamic education as well as established and managed mosques and suraus, *waqf* property and established relationships with other Islamic associations.

[21] Founded in 1956 and was chaired by Abdul Karim Abdul Rahman and assisted by Kassim Kamidin. Just like PIP and PIS, PIT also fought for the interests of Tawau Muslims through Islamic education and *da'wah*.

USNO followed a similar organisational and ideological foundation to that of UMNO, believing in ethnonationalist politics. Persatuan Islam Se Tanah Melayu (later Parti Islam SeMalaysia or Pan-Malaysian Islamic Party, PAS) also tried to spread its wings to Sabah in 1964 by establishing the Persatuan Islam Seluruh Sabah (All Sabah Islamic Association or PAS Sabah).[22] However, the desire was thwarted when PAS President Dr Burhanuddin al-Helmi was arrested under the Internal Security Act (ISA) in January 1965. Islam was a central pillar of USNO, which portrayed itself as an Islamic association,[23] and the same goes for other political groups like USIA that have functioned as non-governmental organisations (NGOs) in Sabah. *Ulamas* and religious intellectuals from such organisations used their influence to carry out *da'wah* missions throughout the state, to influence the Sabah Alliance government to achieve greater Islamic ideals. A number of famous Sabah politicians and statesmen have been associated with these circles, such as Datu Mustapha Datu Harun[24] and Mohd Said Keruak,[25] former Chief Ministers, and others who have also held ministerial positions; Mohd Yassin Hashim, Habib Abdul Rahman Habib Mahmud, Salleh Sulong and Harris Mohd Salleh.[26] These personalities were involved in Islamic work in Sabah and were considered political elites with ties to USNO during that period.

---

22 See 'PAS ada Chawangannya di-Sabah—Bakar Hamzah,' *Berita Harian*, 17 November 1964 and 'An Islamic Opposition Party in Formed in Sabah,' *The Straits Times*, 30 December 1964.

23 Robert Stephen Milne & K.J. Ratnam, *Malaysia – New States in a New Nation, Political Development of Sarawak and Sabah in Malaysia* (London & New York: Routledge, 2016), 129.

24 Datu Mustapha was the founder of the USNO party, USIA and was the first governor of the state of Sabah. He later became the third chief minister from 1967 to 1975. After the fall of USNO he continued to lead USNO and USIA until USNO was dissolved in 1990 to make way for UMNO to enter Sabah. He is known as the 'Father of Sabah's Development'.

25 Mohd Said Keruak was a senior leader representing USNO who joined the cabinet of Chief Minister Donald Stephens (Fuad) in 1963. He remained in the cabinet of Chief Ministers Peter Lo and Datu Mustapha and later became the fourth Chief Minister of Sabah in 1975-1976. In 1987 he was appointed governor of the state of Sabah until 1994.

26 Harris Mohd Salleh was the vice president of USNO and the sixth chief minister, while Mohd Yassin Hashim was the vice president of USNO. Habib Abdul Rahman, Secretary General of USNO and Salleh Sulong was the chief of USNO Youth. All were the first vice presidents of USIA.

The organisations increased in influence under the USNO government. The big victory in the state elections of October 1971 gave a strong mandate to Datu Mustapha to continue to lead the Sabah Alliance to govern the state government for a second term. This opportunity was capitalised on by USIA to strengthen the position of Islam in Sabah. Among the contributions during the period was the establishment of the Sabah Islamic Religious Council or Majlis Ugama Islam Negeri Sabah[27] (MUIS) and enshrining Islam as the official religion of the state of Sabah in 1973.[28] With the establishment of MUIS, *da'wah*, through the government machinery, became more prominent in the management and administration of Islamic religious affairs and Islamic law, the development and administration of mosques, surau and religious schools, as well as Islamic education at all levels for the Muslim community.[29]

Among the issues of concern for the Sabah Alliance government was the need to build enough religious schools to provide formal Islamic education for future generations. Around the 1950s, before the establishment of USIA, there were only eleven religious schools funded by the Muslim community throughout Sabah. By the 1970s, several religious secondary schools emerged such as Sekolah Menengah Islamiah Tawau (1970), Sekolah Menengah Agama Negeri (SMAN) Toh Puan Hajah Rahmah (1975) and Sekolah Menengah Kebangsaan Agama (SMKA) Limau-Limauan (Now SMKA Tun Datu Mustapha), Kinarut (1977). These religious schools played a major role in producing *ulama*, politicians, intellectuals, government officials, religious teachers and preachers for Sabah. Prior to the existence of these schools, the government, through the Sabah Foundation, would send religious school students to higher education institutions in Peninsular Malaysia. Others would continue onto foreign universities, most notably, Al-Azhar University in Egypt, and universities in other countries including Saudi Arabia, Jordan and Indonesia.

---

27 MUIS is a statutory body, established in 1971 with the aim of managing the governance of Islamic affairs as a whole and acting as a maker and implementer of Islamic policy in Sabah.

28 The State Assembly (DUN) sitting on 23 September 1973 approved amendments in the State Constitution Article 5(A), which recorded Islam as the state religion without restricting religious freedom, see Emin Madi, *Sinar Perjuangan USIA*, 93.

29 Najion Jamil, *Pembentukan Malaysia dan Impaknya Terhadap Perkembangan Islam di Sabah* (Kota Kinabalu: Jabatan Hal Ehwal Agama Islam Negeri Sabah, 2010) 18.

The role of foreign-trained scholars would increase in Sabah. In the year 2000, alumni of Al-Azhar in Sabah formed the Persatuan Alumni al-Azhar Sabah (Sabah al-Azhar Alumni Association).[30] It was officiated by Sabah Chief Syariah Judge Aidi Mokhtar who was himself an Al-Azhar alumnus. Many of these alumni would go on to become elected representatives in the Sabah state assembly, such as Ustaz Mohd Suhaili Said, representing BN (UMNO), who won in Tunku during the 2004 General Election (GE) and Ustaz Mohd Arifin Mohd Arif, who won the Membakut seat under the same BN (UMNO) flag in the next election. Subsequent elections saw many more Al-Azhar graduates being involved.

The emergence of Angkatan Belia Islam Malaysia (Muslim Youth Movement of Malaysia, ABIM) in Sabah in the early 1980s brought another approach to *da'wah* activities in Sabah, and introduced youths from secondary school students, tertiary institutions and teaching colleges to join religious programmes. ABIM activists from the peninsula brought over *tarbiah* and *da'wah* programmes to schools, which later encouraged many students to become ABIM activists themselves.[31] One of the important contributions of ABIM activities in Sabah was their involvement in developing PAS in Sabah, especially among ABIM activists from Sandakan, Tawau and Kota Belud. Their efforts eventually helped Sabah PAS get officially launched on 19 May 1986.[32]

Anwar Ibrahim's move from ABIM to UMNO in 1982 also affected Sabah, when a group joined PAS Sabah while remaining loyal to Anwar and ABIM. ABIM then took action by becoming a partner in nation-building efforts, known to many as the 'ABIMisation' of UMNO,[33] and saw a number of ABIM activists absorbed into government strategic agencies, such as the Biro Tata Negara (National Civics Bureau, BTN). One example is Sapawi

---

30 The author was present at the invitation of one of the alumni members, Ustaz Abidin Omar, who was then the principal or *mudir* at Sekolah Menengah Islamiah Papar.

31 Based on the author's own interactions with these organisations, most of them are civil servants such as lecturers, teachers and government officials, who were first involved with ABIM in the peninsular as leaders and activists.

32 Hamzah Abdullah, *Sejarah penubuhan PAS Sabah*, personal communication, 7 July 1999.

33 See Shaharuddin Badaruddin. *Masyarakat Madani dan Politik, ABIM & Proses Demokrasi* (Shah Alam: IDE Rsearch Center Sdn Bhd, 2016), 53-68.

Ahmad, who was appointed as the first director of BTN in Sabah.[34] Sapawi later contested in Sipitang seat representing BN (UMNO) in the 1994 state elections, making him the first ABIM Sabah cadre to become a member of the State Assembly in Sabah.

Starting from the mid-1970s there was increased diversity in the representation of the Muslim Bumiputera in Sabah, which would expand in later years. A pattern emerged where Islamic political elites would position themselves with a party they could cling on to as their vehicle to their next destination. After the 1976 USNO defeat, for example, there was a shift in the support of Muslim voters in favour of Sabah People's United Front (Parti Bersatu Rakyat Jelata Sabah, BERJAYA). USNO only won three state seats in the 1981 election.[35] When an internal crisis plagued BERJAYA in 1984, involving Chief Minister Harris Mohd Salleh and his minister Joseph Pairin Kitingan, BERJAYA lost power to Pairin's United Sabah Party (Parti Bersatu Sabah, PBS) in the state election of 1985. The 1985 results saw the majority of Muslim voters backing USNO, with a minority voting for BERJAYA.[36] PBS's victory sparked an awareness among the Muslim Bumiputera political elites for the need to strengthen their position after losing a series of snap state elections in 1986.[37] The events of 1985 and 1986 prompted PAS to take steps to expand its wings to Borneo. It participated in the 1986 elections, fielding three candidates in Kota Belud, Kimanis and Jambongan. The political elites' support of USNO and BERJAYA began to shift towards PAS and was seen as a signal to UMNO to follow in the footsteps of PAS, and to also open a branch in Sabah.[38] After 1985, there was a realignment, with efforts to unite all the divided Muslim Bumiputera political groups to unite for the future of Islam in Sabah. This curtailed the expansion of PAS in Sabah. In 1990, the UMNO Supreme Council officially expanded its wings

---

34 See *Sejarah ABIM Sabah*, https://abimsabah.org.my/sejarah-abim-sabah.

35 The results were BERJAYA (44), USNO (3), SCCP (1), see Anwar Sullivan & Cecilia Leong, *Commemorative History of Sabah* (Kota Kinabalu: Sabah State Government, 1981), 168e.

36 The result were PBS seats (25), PASOK (1), USNO (16), BERJAYA (6), see Yahaya Ismail, *Politik Islam di Sabah* (Kuala Lumpur: Dinamika Kreatif Sdn Bhd, 1986), 49.

37 The results were PBS (34), USNO (12), BERJAYA (1) and SCCP (1). Ibid. 50.

38 See Musli Oli, *Dilemma Melayu Sabah* (Kota Kinabalu: Pengedar Buku Mas, 1997), 60.

to Sabah.[39] Through 2018, UMNO became the main vehicle representing Muslim Bumiputera in the state, connecting with the religious organisations and strengthening the religious bureaucracy.

In 2018, Warisan/PH took over the state government. GE14 showcased the diversity of views in the Muslim Bumiputera community and their political divisions. UMNO's defeat signalled the familiar pattern of Muslim elites finding new political vehicles, a trend that continued into the 2020 state elections.

Muslim Bumiputera in PRN2020

PRN2020 was the first major election that tested the strength of the Muafakat Nasional (MN), a political alliance between PAS and UMNO, and the Malay Muslim super-majority Perikatan Nasional (PN) government of Muhyiddin Yassin. The politics of Muslim unity gained ground after GE14, beginning in the August 2018 Selangor by-election of Sungai Kandis,[40] followed by a mass rally to protest the proposed ratification of the International Convention on the Elimination of All Forms of Racial Discrimination (ICERD) on 8 December 2018, which culminated in the *Charter Muafakat Nasional* in the *Himpunan Penyatuan Ummah* (Muslim Unity Assembly) on 15 September 2019 in Kuala Lumpur. This sentiment for Muslim unity also underscored support for the 'Sheraton Move' in February 2020.

As the Sabah snap poll was called, it was not clear that unity of the *ummah* pioneered by PAS and UMNO, and capitalised on by Muhyiddin, would be able to rally the support of Sabah Muslim voters. Tensions were growing between the political parties in PN, especially between UMNO and Bersatu.

PRN2020 offered 73 state seats with the addition of 13 new seats, namely 45 Muslim Bumiputera majority seats, 17 non-Muslim Bumiputera majority seats, five Chinese majority seats and six mixed seats which were contested

---

[39] Chamil Wariya, *UMNO Sabah, Mencabar dan Dicabar* (Kuala Lumpur: Penerbit Fajar Bakti Sdn Bhd, 1992), 13.

[40] See Mohd Iskandar Ibrahim, 'PRK Sungai Kandis titik permulaan persefahaman UMNO-PAS', *Berita Harian*, 31 July 2018, https://www.bharian.com.my/berita/politik/2018/07/455894/prk-sungai-kandis-titik-permulaan-persefahaman-umno-pas8.

by political parties and independent candidates. Since the state election of 1967 and up to 2013, the parties that controlled the majority of Muslim Bumiputera voters were USNO and UMNO. Although there are other parties that won over Muslim Bumiputera votes as the strength of USNO declined, with votes going to BERJAYA and PBS, such support was only temporary. After the 2008 General Election, Muslim Bumiputera support for UMNO began to erode and by the next election, its support shifted to other parties such as PKR and PAS. The prominence of former UMNO Vice President Mohd Shafie Apdal helped Warisan in successfully breaking UMNO's 24-year dominance over Sabah Muslim Bumiputera politics. GE14 dealt a fatal blow to UMNO's hegemony, with more than half of their seats lost to Warisan. From 30 Muslim Bumiputera seats controlled by UMNO in 2004, Warisan managed to grab 18 Muslim Bumiputera seats, making Warisan the major political party for the community in Sabah.

After the fall of the BN government in 2018, Sabah UMNO began to split, with leaders and elected representatives defecting, among them a group led by Sabah UMNO Liaison Committee Chairman Hajiji Noor along with nine state assembly persons (ADUNs), five Members of Parliament, 21 UMNO Division Heads and two Sabah UMNO senators who later joined Bersatu on 25 March 2019.[41] Bung Moktar Radin and Musa Aman were left as UMNO's sole representatives in the Dewan Rakyat (House of Representatives) and the state legislative assembly. For UMNO Sabah to rise again, they needed to be given full autonomy to enable Sabah leaders to determine the direction of the party, determine political partners and select election candidates without the intervention of UMNO in Kuala Lumpur.[42] Without the autonomy, local leaders argued, Sabah UMNO would be ridiculed as a Peninsular-based party by their opponents.

The birth of Bersatu Sabah in April 2019 meant that Muslim Bumiputera politics was now divided between at least three large groups, namely

---

41 See Ruzaini Zulkepli & Fifi Harteeny Marzuki, '13 wakil rakyat UMNO Sabah, termasuk pengerusi negeri keluar parti,' *Astro Awani*, 12 December 2018, https://www.astroawani.com/berita-politik/13-wakil-rakyat-umno-sabah-termasuk-pengerusi-negeri-keluar-parti-193406.

42 Bernama, 'Perhimpunan Agung UMNO 2019 lulus kuasa autonomi UMNO Sabah,' *Sinar Harian*, 7 December 2019, https://www.sinarharian.com.my/article/60940%20/%20KHAS%20/%20UMNO%20/%20Perhimpunan-Agung-UMNO-2019-lulus-kuasa-autonomi-UMNO-Sabah.

UMNO, Warisan and Bersatu in addition to PKR, PAS, USNO and Parti Cinta Sabah (PCS). As an UMNO splinter party, UMNO's relationship with Bersatu was lukewarm on the eve of polls, as many from UMNO joined Bersatu, campaigned for the support of Sabahans to join Bersatu, registering more than 100,000 new members within a year and thereby cutting into UMNO's political base.[43] The tensions between other political parties appealing to Muslim Bumiputera were also evident, with PKR and Warisan head-to-head as to who should lead the national opposition and the relationship with Tun Mahathir. Parties were grappling with these divisions as the election approached.

For PRN2020, a grand coalition known as the Gabungan Rakyat Sabah (GRS) was formed, including two different coalitions: namely PN which comprised Bersatu, STAR, SAPP and PAS, and BN, which comprised UMNO, PBRS and MCA. PBS also joined GRS. The formation of GRS consolidated the BN-allied groups with PAS, PBS and STAR to face their main rivals Warisan Plus. The battle was not just about who would govern, but who would win over the majority of Muslim Bumiputera voters. For Warisan, the contest would test their support among Muslim Sabahans.

Warisan had worked to buttress its support among Muslim Bumiputera while in office. It did so through its appointees on religious matters. The participation of Al-Azhar graduates strengthened Islam in local government administration, specifically for relevant Islamic agencies such as the Jabatan Hal Ehwal Agama Islam Negeri Sabah (JHEAINS),[44] Jabatan Kehakiman Syariah Negeri Sabah,[45] MUIS, Pejabat Mufti Negeri Sabah[46] and

---

[43] Ruzaini Zulkepli, 'Kemasukan ahli baharu tanda Bersatu semakin diterima di Sabah - Hajiji.' *Astro Awani*, 5 July 2020, https://www.astroawani.com/berita-politik/kemasukan-ahli-baharu-tanda-bersatu-semakin-diterima-di-sabah-hajiji-249916.

[44] A Sabah state government departmental agency, established in 1996 to implement the policies of MUIS. The rationale for the establishment of JHEAINS is in line with its role as the implementing and enforcement agency for MUIS and in line with the enactment of the administration of Islamic law in Sabah.

[45] The Sabah State Syariah Judiciary Department has the role of administering the affairs of *sharia* court cases involving Muslims to obtain justice and defences that are in accordance with the provisions of the law.

[46] The Sabah Mufti's Office is an institution whose role is to issue *fatwa*, be the main reference point on religious issues including current issues and a place for research, expansion and dissemination of Islamic knowledge.

Perbadanan Baitulmal (Baitulmal).[47] Under the Warisan/PH government, for the first time, religious graduates were appointed as full ministers, with the appointment of former Sabah Chief Syariah Judge Aidi Mokhtar as Sabah Minister of Law and Native Affairs. As a graduate of Al-Azhar University with experience in the judiciary, Aidi changed policies, among them the establishment of the Lembaga Pengurusan Wakaf Negeri Sabah[48] in addition to the restructuring of MUIS and Baitulmal. Aidi also plans to set up a mosque, *surau* and cemetery management board to better the management of religious institutions.

Another important contribution was made by responding to the call by Sabah *ulama* and intellectuals for *fiqh Sabahi*, an idea that was first introduced in 2017. *Fiqh Sabahi* is a concept whereby all matters related to Islamic law, *da'wah*, and religious education are adapted to the environment of the community of various races, ethnicities, cultures and religions in Sabah.[49] It involves rationalising the diverse views and interpretations of religious scholars and assesses the appropriateness of these different interpretations for Sabah. The Warisan/PH government continued this ongoing dialogue.

This outreach to the Muslim Bumiputera community extended into the election. The polls saw the broad participation of Muslim Bumiputera parties and candidates, including Islamic NGO activists, graduates of religious schools and universities, or those with family backgrounds among *ulama* and preachers in Sabah. The line-up included four big guns with resources and national standing: UMNO, Bersatu, Warisan and PKR, with smaller local parties. PAS Sabah did not participate in the election this time after failing to get support from UMNO and Bersatu to enter the contest.[50] In contrast with PAS Sabah, Parti Amanah Negara (Amanah) was allocated the Tanjung Keramat seat as part of Warisan Plus.

---

47 Baitulmal functions are to collect and administer money or movable or immovable property, *waqf* property and vows, as well as develop it for the economic, social and welfare development of Muslims in the state of Sabah, in accordance with Islamic Law.

48 The Sabah State Waqf Management Board was established in 2018, with the role of developing property and endowment products, which will be managed by MUIS. It is able to reduce dependence on government assistance to build houses of worship, educational institutions and that benefit the community in the state.

49 Aziz bin Haji Jaafar, '*Perutusan*', Buletin PMNS, Bil 1/2018, https://mufti.sabah.gov.my/images/laman-utama/penerbitan/fail-pdf/Buletin_PMNS_Bil1.pdf.

50 Between 1986 and 2018, PAS consistently participated in Sabah elections.

We see the pattern noted above, with religious leaders and organisations tying themselves to different political parties, fielding candidates with strong religious roots in the community. The number of Islamic leaders that participated was high, with a total of four USIA leaders, three ABIM activists and four graduates of Al-Azhar University. A total of 19 candidates had strong religious roots contesting in 18 different seats, 25 per cent of the overall seats and 45 per cent of Muslim Bumiputera majority seats. Table 1 offers details of their participation.

Table 1: Islamic NGOs, Religious Teaching Institutions and Ulama Families Candidates

State Seat	Candidate	Religious Background
N.09 Tempasuk	Mustapha @ Mohd Yunus bin Sakmud (PKR)	Former Deputy Chief of ABIM Sabah (2007-2010)
N.11 Kadamaian	Raiting @ Mohd Farhan (Bebas)	Alumni Universiti al-Azhar, Egypt Former Head of Information PAS Kota Belud Division
N.22 Tanjung Aru	Mohd Reduan Hj Aklee (BN-UMNO)	Alumni SMKA Limau-Limauan
N.23 Petagas	Awang Ahmad Shah Awang Sahari (Warisan)	Great-grandson of well-known Sabah *ulama*, Imam Haji Yaakob Haji Ali The son of a famous USIA preacher, Awang Sahari Abdul Latif
	Arsit Sedi (PN-Bersatu)	Deputy President of USIA
	Ahmad Farid Sainuri (PCS)	Deputy Chief of ABIM Sabah Son of former first Chief of ABIM Sabah, Sainuri Yahmin
N.24 Tanjung Keramat	Rosday @ Rosdy Wasli (Warisan-Amanah)	Member of Parti Amanah Negara Sabah Chapter
N.29 Pantai Manis	Azmih bin Junaidi (USNO)	Former committee member of Yayasan Amal Malaysia Sabah
N.30 Bongawan	Ag Lahap bin Ag Bakar @ Ag Syairin (BN-UMNO)	Alumni Universiti al-Azhar, Egypt Former Religious Administration Officer of JHEAINS

State Seat	Candidate	Religious Background
N.31 Membakut	Mohd Arifin Mohd Arif (PN-Bersatu)	Alumni, Universiti al-Azhar, Egypt Alumni Sekolah Menengah Agama Toh Puan Hajah Rahmah Former Deputy Director of JHEAINS
N.32 Klias	Abdul Rahman bin Md Yakub (PKR)	Former Deputy Chief ABIM Sabah
N.42 Melalap	Jamawi Jaafar (BN)	Chief Youth of USIA Alumni SMKA Limau-Limauan (Now SMKA Tun Datu Mustapha)
N.46 Nabawan	Abdul Ghani Yassin (PN-Bersatu)	Supreme Council Member of USIA Chief Division of USIA Pensiangan
N.49 Labuk	Sh Suhaimi bin Sh Miasin (USNO)	Former Universiti al-Azhar student, Egypt
N.53 Sekong	Alias bin Sani (Warisan)	Former Deputy Chairman of Parti Amanah Negara Sabah chapter Former Internal Security Act (ISA) detainee 2003-2007 who linked with Jemaah Islamiah (JI). He was the principal of As-Salam school, Sandakan, an educational institution that was built in 1989.
N.60 Tungku	Assaffal Alian (Warisan)	Alumni SMKA Limau-Limauan
N.62 Silam	Abdul Hakim Gulam Hassan (PN-Bersatu)	Former Chief Youth of USIA Former Deputy President of USIA Son of a well-known religious teacher in Sabah's east coast, Haji Muda (Haji Ghulam Hassan Ali Akbar)

State Seat	Candidate	Religious Background
N.68 Apas	Amrullah Kamal (Warisan)	Chairman of Tawau Islamiah School Alumni Association
	Nizam Abu Bakar Titingan (PN-Bersatu)	Tawau Islamiah School Alumni Association Son of PIT chairman, Abu Bakar Titingan

Source: Suruhanjaya Pilihan Raya (SPR), ABIM (online), USIA (online), *New Sabah Times*, *Harakah Daily*, alumni al-Azhar, alumni SMKA Tun Datu Mustapha Limauan and Alumni SMAN Toh Puan Hajah Rahmah.

PRN2020 candidates with Islamic religious backgrounds drew on a variety of sources: from prominent religious teaching families to ties with religious education (as teachers in religious schools as well as from their own religious training), representatives of Islamic NGOs and those from government religious departments. This breadth of engagement highlights the deep roots of the ties between Islam and politics in Sabah. Interestingly, candidates with religious backgrounds from different political backgrounds largely did not contest against each other, except in Petagas.

The unity in terms of how candidates with religious backgrounds contested did not extend to the results. The Muslim Bumiputera vote is divided, arguably more than before. Warisan continues, however, to hold the largest support in Muslim Bumiputera seats. The PRN2020 results saw GRS competing closely with Warisan in Muslim Bumiputera majority constituencies, with Warisan winning 20 seats, while UMNO won 14 seats and Bersatu nine seats. UMNO failed to make significant gains, winning only 14 seats out of the 30 Muslim Bumiputera seats it contested, one less than the number they obtained in GE14. PBS and independent candidates Ruslan Muharam and Ruddy Awah managed to win the traditional USNO and UMNO seats in Lumadan and Pitas, showing the decline of support among Muslim Bumiputera for UMNO. The party was not able to recover from its 2018 political defeat. The success of Warisan in winning 20 Muslim Bumiputera seats out of 45 seats suggests that the Borneo Agenda is growing and gaining a place in the hearts of Muslim voters. PKR failed to make gains using candidates with religious credentials, despite having featured two experienced ABIM Sabah figures. Smaller local parties who also fielded many Muslim Bumiputera candidates such as PCS and USNO failed completely to win any seats, as shown in Table 2.

Table 2: Results of Muslim Bumiputera Seats, 2008-2020

Party	GE2008		GE2013		GE2018		PRN2020	
	CONTEST	WIN	CONTEST	WIN	CONTEST	WIN	CONTEST	WIN
WARISAN	0	0	0	0	34	18	39	20
UMNO	30	30	29	28	29	15	30	14
Bersatu							17	9
PBS	1	1	1	1	1	1	4	1
BEBAS					5	0	30	1
UPKO	2	2	2	2	2	2	3	0
LDP	2	2	2	2	2	0	24	0
PKR	32	0	26	1	2	0	2	0
Amanah					1	0	1	0
PCS					5	0	45	0
USNO					2	0	45	0
PAS	2	0	9	0	17	0	0	0
Total		35		34		36		45

Source: Election Commission

There is greater pluralism in the representation of Muslim Bumiputera voters. Table 3 below shows that Muslim Bumiputera voters divided their support between Warisan, UMNO, Bersatu, PBS and even independent candidates. The creation of more Muslim Bumiputera seats in the UMNO-originated delineation exercise that was championed by Warisan in 2018, however, has increased the number of Muslim Bumiputera seats.[51] This has allowed parties aligned together in GRS and PN – UMNO and Bersatu – to collectively win the most Muslim Bumiputera seats: a total of 23, with PBS and the GRS-aligned independents moving the total to 25 seats, as shown in Table 3. The addition of new seats has changed the balance of Muslim Bumiputera representation. The results also show that Warisan and UMNO support did not change significantly. Rather the biggest winner among Muslim Bumiputera parties was the newcomer Bersatu.

[51] The increase in Muslim Bumiputera seats involves nine out of 13 seats, namely N.2 Bengkoka, N.6 Bandau, N.8 Pintasan, N.13 Pantai Dalit, N.17 Darau, N.24 Tanjung Keramat, N.51 Sungai Manila, N. 58 Lamag and N.61 Segama.

Table 3: Results by Ethnic/Religious Group, 2018 & 2020

ETHNIC GROUP	GE	UMNO	Bersatu	Warisan	PBS	STAR	PBRS	UPKO	PKR	DAP	IND	TOTAL
Muslim Bumiputera	2018	15	0	18	1	0	0	2	0	0	0	36
	2020	14	9	20	1	0	0	0	0	0	1	45
Non-Muslim Bumiputera	2018	1	0	2	5	2	1	3	0	0	0	14
	2020	0	1	2	6	5	0	1	0	0	2	17
Chinese	2018	0	0	0	0	0	0	0	0	5	0	4
	2020	0	0	0	0	0	0	0	0	5	0	5
Mixed	2018	1	0	1	0	0	0	0	2	1	0	6
	2020	0	1	1	0	1	0	0	2	1	0	6
TOTAL	**2018**	**17**	**0**	**21**	**6**	**2**	**1**	**5**	**2**	**6**	**0**	**60**
	2020	**14**	**11**	**23**	**7**	**6**	**0**	**1**	**2**	**6**	**3**	**73**

Source: Election Commission

Despite greater competition between Muslim Bumiputera parties, there remains pressure for Muslim Bumiputera unity. Although the Muafakat Nasional (MN) was not formally formed in Sabah, its spirit existed, albeit informally. It started in Sabah with the January 2020 Kimanis by-election, and then impacted PRN2020 where several UMNO, Bersatu and PAS divisions established cooperative relations through welfare programmes and party gatherings, such as divisional general meetings throughout Sabah. In Kalabakan, for example, UMNO and PAS came forward to help 100 flood victims in the village of Pasir Putih, Tawau. Similarly, UNMO has also invited PAS division leaders to attend the UMNO Division Delegates Meeting, including PAS Semporna, Silam, Tawau, Kota Belud, Kudat, Putatan, Sepanggar, Kinabatangan, Keningau, Kalabakan and so on. PAS's decision not to participate in PRN2020 further points to MN's commitment to reducing vote splitting among Muslim voters.[52] There were concerns that any splitting of votes would reduce the chances of UMNO and Bersatu achieving national victory in the next election, especially as tensions between UMNO and Bersatu continue to simmer. Among the initial successes achieved by the partners was the absence of three-cornered fights between UMNO and Bersatu in all the contested seats in PRN2020. The responsiveness of PAS in mobilising its entire machinery to help UMNO and Bersatu candidates campaign has created a win-win atmosphere, especially in giving confidence to PAS supporters and undecided voters. Based on interviews with party members, PAS was seen to contribute to the victory of Pintasan, Liawan, Karambunai Lamag and Tanjung Keramat.[53] One of the factors that contributed to the victory of UMNO and Bersatu was the close cooperation between the three parties, with their respective machinery moving as a team. In Putatan, for example, UMNO, Bersatu and PAS leaders (Jeffrey Nor Mohammad, Arsit Sedi and Muhammad Akmal Othman) were present at the friendly ceremony and launch of Bersatu state election machinery at N.24 Tanjung Keramat. This cooperation underscores the central role that concerns about Muslim unity play in Sabah and

---

[52] See Abdul Rahemang Taiming, 'PRN Sabah: PAS harap tiada pertembungan tiga penjuru,' *Harian Metro Online*, 8 September 2020, https://www.hmetro.com.my/mutakhir/2020/09/618298/prn-sabah-pas-harap-tiada-pertembungan-tiga-penjuru.

[53] This extends the number of seats listed in Bridget Welsh, 'The PAS Factor in Sabah Polls', *Malaysiakini*, 2 October 2020, https://www.malaysiakini.com/columns/545038.

Malaysia's national politics. The lack of unity, however, also played a role. Disgruntlement with not being able to field a PAS candidate in Kukusan contributed to Bersatu's loss in this seat.

Concluding Reflections

Sabah's political history has seen the people of Sabah willingly change governments, from one party to another. This happened again in PRN2020. The level of individual loyalty to a party is not high. For example, UMNO Sabah had 556,616 members in 2019,[54] but the number of members did not guarantee UMNO's victory in the 2018 and 2020 elections. A political party is like a vehicle, which, if damaged, can no longer reach its destination and will need to be replaced. Many continue to see UMNO as a vehicle damaged by Musa Aman and, to a lesser extent in Sabah, by Najib Razak. Members have shifted their support to Warisan and more recently Bersatu, despite still maintaining UMNO membership. Muslim Bumiputera voters are willing to divide the vote and move their vote towards other political vehicles. This has been the case in the past in Sabah politics, from USNO and BERJAYA, and it continues. In the current context of greater political competition and party fragmentation, this means that in order to hold power with political stability, Sabah's Muslim Bumiputera parties will need to find partners with whom to form a government. With the erosion of UMNO's political support, the era of a single dominant Muslim Bumiputera party is essentially over. Calls for unity can only yield results if there is a spirit of compromise between Muslim Bumiputera parties and with parties of the other communities.

Islam continues to play an important role in Sabah, as we see from the prominence of candidates with Islamic credentials and the close relations between political parties and Islamic organisations. The calls for Islamic representation in Sabah remain intertwined with ethnonationalist representations. There are, however, more diverse sources of Islamic political representation. PAS's inclusion in the state assembly is part of this diversity.

Looking forward, the relationship with Islamic leaders is changing. GE14 and the ouster of UMNO represented a change in the feudal structure

[54] See Mohamad Fadil, 'Umno Sabah yakin lebih 500 ribu ahlinya tetap setia, kata Bung Moktar'. *Free Malaysia Today*, 7 April 2019, https://www.freemalaysiatoday.com/category/bahasa/2019/04/07/umno-sabah-yakin-lebih-500-ribu-ahlinya-tetap-setia-kata-bung-moktar/.

of politics. As in peninsula Malaysia, the traditional feudal political culture of the Malay-Muslims is clashing with new values and pressures from globalisation.[55] The Muslim Bumiputera leadership in Sabah is also changing. The generation of USNO so dominant in the 1970s and 1980s leadership has faded. We are now seeing competition between Sabah UMNO leaders such as Hajiji Noor, Masidi Manjun, Bung Moktar Radin, Mohd Shafie Apdal, Dr Yusof Yaacob, Salleh Keruak and Azizah Mohd Dun. They too will face pressures as UMNO loses support and competition between them intensifies. Many of these leaders have been in the state political arena for too long. The influx of younger millennial voters will form a larger group of young voters, and of course these voters will be an important factor in future voting patterns.

With new voters comes new values, such as calls for more mature politics, corruption-free politics, good governance and unity. PRN2020 witnessed many of these new goals alongside older messages. Young people are more issue-oriented, and their idea of survival is less about how they survive *vis-à-vis* other communities but whether there is efficiency in the delivery system and greater justice in governance. The persistent support for states' rights for Sabah – seen in the strong Warisan vote – speaks to these calls for fairness. Muslim Bumiputera Sabahans continue to strive for common prosperity, just like the Malay proverb '*duduk sama rendah, berdiri sama tinggi*' (to have people of the same social status). This suggests that the calls for justice and fairness at the roots of Islamic politics in Sabah from the colonial era live on.

55 A.N. Sulaiman, 'Budaya Politik Dalam Masyarakat Majmuk Di Malaysia', in *Etika dan budaya berpolitik dari perspektif Islam*, edited by Abdul Monir Yaacob and Suzalie Mohamad (Kuala Lumpur: Institut Kefahaman Islam Malaysia (IKIM), 2002), 54.

Conclusion

Sabah's Covid-19 Election Aftermath: Beyond New (and Old) Political Alignments

Bridget Welsh, Benjamin YH Loh and Vilashini Somiah

As the polls closed and the results were counted in Sabah's 2020 election, the aftermath began. Traditionally, after elections in Sabah, attention turns to the immediate developments, as governments are formed and reformed (through party defections) and the rewards of victory are distributed. Meanwhile, the federal gaze usually returns to their priorities on the Peninsula. This election did not follow this pattern – the effects of the Sabah 2020 polls continued to be felt across Malaysia for months to come. The election aftermath in many ways overshadowed the election itself.

Our conclusion starts with a discussion of the immediate consequences of Sabah's 2020 election (PRN2020). To do this we look at the devastating effect that the election had as a Covid-19 super-spreader event, as well as its political implications locally and nationally. Covid-19 cases spiked, and within five months 290,837 people had been infected and 1,002 had died from the virus.[1] While cases declined from the peak of the third wave of

---

1 Figures are taken from World Health Organisation reports: 'Malaysia: Coronavirus Disease 2019 (COVID-19) Situation Report - Weekly report for the week ending 13 September 2020,' World Health Organisation, 13 September 2020, https://www.who.int/malaysia/internal-publications-detail/covid-19-in-malaysia-situation-report-17; 'Malaysia: Coronavirus Disease 2019 (COVID-19) Situation Report – Weekly report for the week ending 28 February 2021,' World Health Organisation, 1 March 2021, https://www.who.int/malaysia/internal-publications-detail/covid-19-in-malaysia-situation-report-34

5,738 on 30 January 2021, the third wave continued well into 2021. Sabah's cases were among the highest in Malaysia during that period.[2]

At the same time, Sabah's state election resulted in new political alignments and strained older alliances. The election showcased the ongoing political competition and fragmentation at the state and federal levels whilst also contributing to it. Political polarisation and instability are ever-present, with the federal-state relationship under more intensive scrutiny. Promises of a better resolution for long-standing grievances and Sabah's development needs remain outstanding in spite of the realignment of the state government to federal power. For some, in the wake of the initial lacklustre response from Gabungan Rakyat Sabah (GRS) to the health and economic effects of Covid-19, there are concerns that the pressing issues facing the state are receiving inadequate attention.

The power configuration of elites, especially in their relationship with the federal government, is the preoccupying narrative associated with the Sabah state election. Scholars have raised two issues – the relationship with federal power and political instability.[3] These 'game of thrones' discussions are indeed a prominent feature of analyses of Sabah politics – but they should not overshadow attention to changes and governance challenges within Sabah itself. This collection drew attention to conditions in Sabah – the demands of a younger population, the seriousness of the politicisation of irregular migrants and undocumented persons, high unemployment and persistent poverty, political divisions among Sabahans, coupled with more social activism and political engagement, just to name a few. The chapters showed how local conditions shaped the election and are influencing Sabah politics more generally. While not dismissing the importance of federal-state relations, PRN2020 was ultimately won (and lost) by conditions within the state itself. We close by bringing together these different perspectives on the election and lay out our alternative framework for understanding politics in Sabah, emphasising the politics of survival.

---

2 For details on Covid-19 cases in Sabah, see: https://covid19.sabah.digital/covid19/

3 See Anantha Raman Govindasamy, 'The Sabah State Election: A Narrow Win and Precarious Mandate for the New Government', *ISEAS Perspective* 2020/131, 17 November 2020, https://www.iseas.edu.sg/wp-content/uploads/2020/11/ISEAS_Perspective_2020_131.pdf and Arnold Puyok, 'The Fall of Warisan in Sabah's Election: Telltale Signs, Causes and Salient Issues', *ISEAS Perspective* 2021/8, 29 January 2021, https://www.iseas.edu.sg/wp-content/uploads/2021/01/ISEAS_Perspective_2021_8.pdf

A Covid-19 Shadow

When the election was called, Sabah's Covid-19 numbers were low, reaching only 394 since the start of the year with only 25 cases in July 2020. The country had come out of national lockdown and had managed to get the first and second waves of the virus under control. Sabah was seen then as among the states that had performed the best in controlling the virus.[4]

This would change. Five days before nomination day on 7 September, case numbers began to rise. On the day before nomination day 167 cases were reported in Sabah, arising from a detention centre in Lahad Datu. The case total for the country was the highest it had been since June, when Malaysia's first major lockdown ended.[5] Throughout the PRN2020 campaign case numbers remained modest but steadily increased, with the majority of the cases found along Sabah's east coast.

Chart 1: Sabah Covid-19 Reported Cases

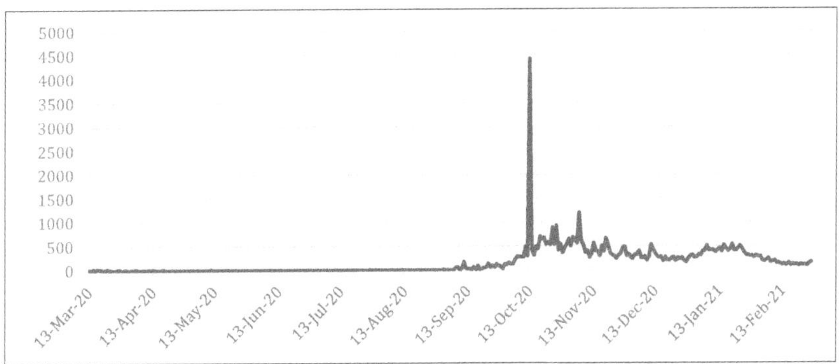

Source: Ministry of Health[6]

Through lenses of suspicion, many in Sabah viewed the cases as a 'federal conspiracy' accentuated by the fact that many initial cases were being found in federally managed detention centres such as those in Tawau

4 See Bridget Welsh, 'The Unsung Role of States in Battling Covid-19,' *Malaysiakini*, 3 July 2020, https://www.malaysiakini.com/columns/532836

5 '187 new Covid cases, 167 in Sabah,' *Free Malaysia Today*, 11 September 2020, https://www.freemalaysiatoday.com/category/nation/2020/09/11/182-new-covid-19-cases-167-in-sabah/

6 This chart is collated from daily announcements.

and Lahad Datu[7] – places where irregular migrants and undocumented persons, or as some Sabahans saw it, 'illegals', were being held.[8] The Muhyiddin government' response of imposing a quarantine announcement two days before polling for anyone who was returning from Sabah was cynically interpreted as a measure to dissuade Sabahans in Peninsular Malaysia from returning to vote. That the majority of these outside voters were assumed to favor Warisan Plus only compounded the cynicism. Calls went out to encourage voting as polling day approached and concerns about safety heightened.

Rising Covid-19 numbers quickly overshadowed the election outcome. Malaysia's post-Sabah third wave was devastating, with the nation's overall cases reaching over 300,000 by March, initiating a second national lockdown in January 2021. The situation in Sabah was dire – its healthcare system was pushed to breaking point such that the government had to move away from its policy of hospitalising all cases. At its height, Sabah's case numbers reached 4,433 in one day on 13 October, two and a half weeks after the elections. The situation in Sabah went from bad to worse as soon as the polls closed. Combined with heavy downpours that caused a series of massive floods, just days after the election, it felt that the people of Sabah could not catch a break as they were subjected to health emergencies and natural disasters. The impact of this was severe as over 350 Sabahans reportedly lost their lives to the coronavirus through February,[9] thousands were displaced by floods, and the livelihoods of millions hurt by the second national lockdown.

The blame for the Covid-19 crisis in Sabah has centred on politicians, who were targeted for not following the standard operating procedures (SOPs) in campaigning.[10] Others placed fault on the federal government's

---

[7] This originally was part of the Benteng Lahad Datu Cluster. See: 'Covid-19: outbreak spreads from lockup to prison,' *Malaysiakini*, 3 September 2020, https://www.malaysiakini.com/news/541207

[8] Bridget Welsh, 'The Covid Factor in the Sabah polls,' *Malaysiakini*, 24 September 2020, https://www.malaysiakini.com/columns/543948

[9] See: https://covid19.sabah.digital/covid19/

[10] 'Suhakam: Politicians, Campaigners least compliant with Covid-19 SOPs during Sabah polls,' *Malay Mail*, 21 January 2021, https://www.malaymail.com/news/malaysia/2021/01/21/suhakam-politicians-campaigners-least-compliant-with-covid-19-sops-during-s/1942682

failure to adopt strict quarantine protocols on returnees from Sabah – who were released after the results of a first test administered at the airport cleared.[11] It is irrefutable that the Sabah election was a super-spreader event. But the expedient and sweeping blame of politicians is inaccurate as it fails to acknowledge the role of supporters in the campaign and to recognise the local factors that contributed to the spread of the virus within Sabah itself. These include the handling of cases in detention centres, the exclusion of irregular migrants (seen to be as high as 1 out of 3 persons in Sabah) from affordable healthcare and the inadequate provision of healthcare facilities, as well as the laggard response of the federal and state governments to the healthcare crisis after the election.

The response to Covid-19 in Sabah was inadequate. Initial focus was on laying and deflecting blame rather than attending to the problems created by the third wave of the virus. This was not helped when the newly minted chief minister, Hajiji Noor, was hospitalised for Covid-19 himself, leaving GRS without clear leadership.[12] Warisan Plus's response was also missing as the opposition seemed to be licking its wounds after defeat. Calls to send more supplies and medical support were not heeded and the rising number of Covid-19 deaths in Sabah did not elicit adequate concern among federal authorities. With a strict lockdown affecting livelihoods, little federal government aid was forthcoming as Sabahans themselves had to largely bear the burden of the Covid-19 election aftermath. Malaysians outside of Sabah generously offered assistance for medical equipment and, importantly, Sabahans themselves came together to fill gaps in governance.[13] Five months later the health situation stabilised, although the economic hardships remain. For many Malaysians and Sabahans alike, the election will

---

11 Imran Ariff and Nicholas Chung, 'Government missteps to blame for Covid-19 surge, says experts,' *Free Malaysia Today*, 7 October 2020, https://www.freemalaysiatoday.com/category/nation/2020/10/07/government-missteps-to-blame-for-covid-19-surge-say-experts/

12 Muguntan Vanar, 'Sabah CM Hajiji tests positive for Covid-19,' *The Star*, 9 October 2020, https://www.thestar.com.my/news/nation/2020/10/09/sabah-cm-hajiji-tests-positive-for-covid-19

13 For a good overview of these initiatives see Tanya Jayatalika: 'How You Can Empower Sabah communities affected by Covid-19,' *Malaysia Tatler*, 22 October 2020, https://my.asiatatler.com/society/how-you-can-help-empower-communities-in-sabah-affected-by-covid-19-third-wave

be remembered for the painful Covid-19 aftermath, rather than the election campaign and outcome.

Political Spillovers

For political elites, however, the election marked changes in the country's fluid political waters with the ripple effects extending from Tambunan and Kota Kinabalu to Putrajaya and Kota Bharu. The Sabah polls was a contest in which the fortunes of both federal and state power were openly intertwined. This has been the case since 2008, but in this state election, with ongoing political instability and no federal elections to hide it from view, every victory in every seat was going to count – and it did.

Sabah's polls witnessed a shift in the battle between the long-governing Barisan Nasional (BN) and Pakatan (both Rakyat [2008–2015] and Harapan [2017–present]). After nearly two decades of political momentum, Pakatan lost ground. This long-standing contest stretched from 1999 in various coalitions, with Pakatan gaining political traction since 2008, culminating in the post-GE14 change of government. PRN2020 was a defeat for Malaysia's traditional Pakatan opposition, as Harapan's Sabah allies failed to hold onto power. This result came after Harapan itself lost power at the federal level in the February 'Sheraton Move'. The Warisan Plus coalition – comprised of Warisan, the Democratic Action Party (DAP), People's Justice Party (PKR) and United Progressive Kinabalu Organisation (UPKO) – lost by six seats. Sabah's results clearly show that Harapan and its allies face serious challenges in winning power, especially after its short tenure in office.

This collection has provided insights into some of the reasons why Warisan Plus lost support – its management of the economy, its outreach to ethnic communities, and its communication and overpromises. Philip Golingai's chapter shares the perspectives of those in the contest itself, while other chapters by Chan Tsu Chong, James Alin and Marcilla Malasius, Tony Paridi and Arnold Puyok, and Mohd Rahimin Mustafa offer analyses of issues on the ground. The lack of support from Mahathir's government, especially the pushing for the entry of Bersatu into Sabah, cannot be dismissed as well. It is not clear whether Sabah's 2020 polls reflect just a step backwards for the Pakatan coalition – as was the case with the 2016 Sarawak polls – or a more fundamental change in political fortunes for Harapan and its allies. Bridget Welsh's analysis of voting results shows that much of the support remained with Warisan Plus/Harapan in a polarised electorate, but not enough to win power. GRS was able to cobble together a broader coalition of parties and to bring out the vote it needed in its traditional base.

What made the difference for Pakatan after the 2016 Sarawak election was the lessons the opposition learned. The opposition came together to build alliances and put aside personality differences in forming an alliance with Warisan. It also adopted new leadership for the coalition. Looking at Sabah's campaign dynamics within the history of the opposition, PRN2020 showcased the internal problems of Harapan and its allies. For example, seat negotiations among partners delayed Warisan Plus's ability to cooperate on the ground. The candidate list had to be announced without PKR's candidates.[14] During the campaign, parties operated predominantly in silos, defending their own seats rather than working together. And, the leadership issues that haunted the Harapan coalition – namely tensions between Mahathir Mohamad, Anwar Ibrahim and their camps – were evident. Leaders and some parties did not trust each other. In fact, relations worsened when another one of Anwar's 'I got the numbers' performances a few days before polling day overshadowed Shafie Apdal's campaign to secure victory. Leadership competition rather than cooperation undercut Warisan Plus's campaign, and with its defeat, there are lasting resentments. The relationship between Warisan Plus and PKR nationally remains strained with Warisan moving to decouple from an Anwar-led Harapan. Minimally, Sabah's polls enhanced the fragmentation among allies tied to Harapan. Unlike after the defeat in Sarawak 2016, the opposition has yet to learn its lessons.

The same can be said for Barisan Nasional and UMNO, which has had over two years to reflect on why they lost power. Many Sabahans felt this battle against BN/UMNO was over with GE14, which was primarily an anti-UMNO vote. In Sabah these resentments had been galvanised around former Chief Minister Musa Aman's tenure, but they had deep historical roots. Particularly salient were perceptions of demographic, religious and political displacement of the KDM communities, concerns with corruption and a failure to provide Sabah with its perceived share of resource revenues. In the January Kimanis by-election, UMNO started making a political

---

14 Tarrence Tan and Kristy Inus, 'Warisan Plus anounces candidates, leaves out PKR as discussion still ongoing,' *The Star*, 10 September 2020, https://www.thestar.com.my/news/nation/2020/09/10/warisan-plus-announces-candidates-leaves-out-pkr-as-discussions-still-ongoing

comeback in Sabah, paralleling their gains in by-elections in Peninsular Malaysia in 2019. Ironically, it used an ethnicised appeal around the displacement of the KDM community to do so, tapping into resentments over irregular migrants.[15] When the PRN2020 results were counted, they had won 14 seats, showing that they were still a major political force in Sabah, that the efforts to displace the party had failed. Musa, while still an important leader, was not directly in the new leadership mix. His opting not to contest strengthened UMNO electorally. Importantly, however, UMNO lost three seats compared with GE14 and although it secured the most seats among the GRS component parties, it was not asked to lead the next Sabah government. UMNO was back, but in a subsidiary role.

UMNO has shown since September 2020 that it is uncomfortable in this position – with the Sabah election serving as a catalyst for wider divisions within the Perikatan Nasional (PN). In March 2021 UMNO announced it would not go into GE15 as part of the PN coalition – showcasing arguably one the most important national consequences of Sabah's polls: persistent divides among Malay political parties.[16] In another ironic twist, despite initial behind-the-scenes shouting, the relationship between UMNO and Bersatu in Sabah remains strong, in part due to long-standing cordial personal ties among leaders in the two parties (who were after all in the same party before the defections to Bersatu) and in part due to a recognition that they are dependent on each other to stay in power.[17] This could change, however, with a new federal government and more open differences between Bersatu and UMNO at the federal level potentially making relations at the state level untenable.

By comparison, the Barisan Nasional coalition was not back at all in Sabah. While UMNO used the cover of BN in its 2020 campaign, not promoting UMNO directly, none of the component parties in BN won (with

---

[15] Bridget Welsh, 'Kimanis: An UMNO Revival?' *Malaysiakini*, 21 January 2020, https://www.malaysiakini.com/columns/507936

[16] Adib Povera, Nuradzimmah, & Dawn Chan 'UMNO assembly approves motion to cut ties with Bersatu,' *New Straits Times*, 28 March 2021, https://www.nst.com.my/news/politics/2021/03/677744/umno-assembly-approves-motion-cut-ties-bersatu

[17] 'Bersatu-UMNO Cooperation in Sabah unaffected by federal power development, says Hajiji, Bung Moktar,' *The Edge Markets*, 6 March 2021, https://www.theedgemarkets.com/article/bersatuumno-cooperation-sabah-unaffected-federal-political-development-say-hajiji-bung

the MCA and PBRS the only other parties in BN contesting). The Sabah parties that had been part of BN left. PBS was on its own in the election but decided to join Muhyiddin's umbrella GRS coalition. UPKO, formerly of BN, had left in 2018. Along with a weaker UMNO, the BN coalition that they led was even weaker, effectively non-existent in Sabah. The growing weakening of BN has extended from 2008, but has arguably only increased with non-Malay political parties gaining fewer seats and government positions.

It was the new party, Bersatu, formed in Peninsular Malaysia in 2016 and only entering Sabah in 2019 with the backing of then-Prime Minister Mahathir Mohamad, which secured victory. With Muhyiddin's support during PRN2020 and the winning of 11 seats, Bersatu established a foothold in Sabah, effectively making it a national party. Most of those elected were former UMNO stalwarts with roots to the previous Sabah Muslim Bumiputera-based party, United Sabah National Organisation (USNO).[18] Nevertheless, Bersatu secured the top leadership position – Hajiji Noor – replicating the current national pattern. The strengthening of Bersatu assures greater competition among Malay political parties, further reinforced by the decision by GRS to give an appointed seat to the Malaysian Islamist Party (PAS) after the election in return for the party not contesting in the actual polls. Malay parties in Sabah are fragmented, competing with each other, and will depend on elite cooperation to hold power and maintain political stability. The top position in Sabah appears now to be tied to who controls federal power.

GRS's victory would not have been possible, however, without the support of the two KDM-based parties PBS and STAR. While the campaign showed long-standing and unresolved differences between these traditional competitors, both secured electoral gains. Our analysis shows that Jeffrey Kitingan's STAR was especially decisive for shifts in voting and the final electoral outcome. In comparison with Malay political parties, the KDM-based parties have been able to put aside differences to assure that GRS stays in power. KDM parties have a history of being separate yet united under the BN umbrella, and have now found shelter in PN, for the meantime. Kitingan however is making a risky move by allying himself with federal power, after winning support politically by pushing for greater state's rights. With

[18] James Chin, 'The Sabah State election of 1994: end of Kadazan unity', *Asian Survey* 34, no. 10 (1994): 904-915.

Kitingan effectively the new *Huguan Siou*, leader of the KDM communities, a leadership baton has been passed on in the KDM communities, yet expectations remain high.

Elite politics in Sabah is, in many ways, as important as ever. In an UMNO-ruled Sabah there was a hierarchical political arrangement, yet one in which a politics of accommodation took place. Increasingly a willingness to accommodate eroded away and one-party dominance and the centralisation of power took root within Sabah, a process that parallels developments in Peninsular Malaysia. In contrast, PRN2020 has empowered elites *vis-à-vis* each other, requiring more accommodation within GRS and the empowerment of all the parties in the two major alliances: GRS and Warisan Plus. This has yet to happen with the new GRS Sabah government, and inadequately occurred under the previous Warisan/PH one. UPKO, for example, did not get enough support from Warisan to build its base outside of BN. Warisan/PH similarly did not get enough support from Mahathir's Harapan government. With instability a persistent reality in Peninsular Malaysian politics and ironically the even stronger ties to federal power on the part of a GRS-led Sabah government, state leadership is less risk-adverse, taking the lead from Putrajaya rather than from the concerns of voters within Sabah itself. Political instability reinforces low common denominator politics, and the persistent use of patronage practices that has undercut support for BN-aligned parties in the past. For Warisan Plus, the challenge will be whether it can keep its elites together in a period of political attrition. Elites, however, will be looking to each other, and cognisant that a new election and possible new alliances could also be on the horizon. Meanwhile, weaker parties engaged in greater competition with each other – at a time when financial constraints and the competition over patronage limits deliverables – will contribute to the persistence of ethnic politics. The outlook for political leadership across the political divides working for Sabahans as a whole is not promising. It is hard to do this in a context of political fluidity and where the elites are interested in their own political survival.

Politics of Survival from the Ground

Elite political survival is not an uncommon feature of Sabah politics. The frogging (defections) for political (and financial) security, the creation of new political parties (for opportunities for advancement and patronage) and the use of state resources to fund political careers is well honed. These stories are also well-known. What is less understood is how concerns for survival play a political role among ordinary Sabahans; how their realities and the perceptions of those realities shape how they engage in politics and the choices they make at the polls.

We suggest that in order to better understand Sabah's politics it is important to put the circumstances voters face centre stage and to acknowledge the agency of Sabahans in making choices about their perceived interests. For too long Sabahans are seen as being acted upon, rather than acting for themselves. Sabahans face their own survival politics, arising from conditions in Sabah itself – its role as a periphery, the local narratives accompanying the realities of insecurity and the different inter-group dynamics within the state. Scholars have long stressed the importance of local conditions in Sabah, a theme that emerges from many of the authors in this collection.[19] In particular, they have emphasised the ethnic identities of the main communities, following in a tradition of understanding Malaysian politics through an ethnic lens.[20] The focus is on communities *vis-à-vis* 'others', rather than the dynamic exchange between, among and within ethnic groups. There is little attention to other political identities, be it gender, generational or class divisions, or how smaller ethnic groups fit into Sabah's broader societal milieu.[21] This book, through greater attention to Sabah's complexities, aims to move the discussion forward more holistically. In understanding how ordinary voters in Sabah engage politics and seek their own survival, it is useful to begin to unpack these 'other' Sabah local conditions.

---

19 For recent examples, see: Mohamad Nawab Mohamad Osman, 'A Transitioning Sabah in a Changing Malaysia', *Kajian Malaysia* 35, no. 1 (2017): 23-40; Farish A. Noor, 'The 13th Malaysian general elections from a Sabah perspective', *The Round Table* 102, no. 6 (2013); James Chin, 'Sabah and Sarawak in the 14th General Election 2018 (GE14): local factors and state nationalism', *Journal of Current Southeast Asian Affairs* 37, no. 3 (2018): 173-192.

20 Arnold Puyok and Tony Paridi Bagang, 'Ethnicity, Culture and Indigenous Leadership in Modern Politics: The Case of the KadazanDusun in Sabah, East Malaysia', *Kajian Malaysia: Journal of Malaysian Studies* 29 (2011): 177-97.

21 Increasingly, there is more attention to the rural status of voters. See: Arnold Puyok 'The Fall of Warisan in Sabah's Election: Telltale Signs, Causes and Salient Issues', *ISEAS Perspective*, 2021/8, 29 January 2021, https://www.iseas.edu.sg/wp-content/uploads/2021/01/ISEAS_Perspective_2021_8.pdf

As part of Borneo, Sabah (along with Sarawak) has long been Malaysia's 'remote other'. The peripheral nature of Sabah's politics goes well beyond geography.[22] Political institutions, from political parties to the bureaucracy, are comparatively weaker. While Sarawak invested in professionalising its civil service, this did not happen to the same extent in Sabah. Some of those from Peninsular Malaysia assigned to work in Sabah are not necessarily the strongest in the service, evident for example in the high absenteeism among teachers.[23] Many of those from Sabah who work in the civil service are also often not adequately recognised for their service and skills. Weaker political institutions have implications. Public service delivery is lacking. This was most evident during the third wave of Covid-19, which highlighted how limited access to healthcare is, especially across Sabah.[24] Borders remain porous – a factor that perpetuates long unresolved issues of migration. And, there are large administrative gaps tied to inadequate staffing and resources. Sabahans – especially many of those in the rural areas – do not have the same quality of governance that other Malaysians do.[25]

Unequal access to governance coincides with different notions of belonging and experiences of marginalisation. Largely left out of national history books and without the same level of services and development, Sabahans have been made to feel that they are on the periphery.[26] There are perceptions of being outsiders in the group, outsiders in Malaysia, and for some, outsiders within Sabah itself. While still proud to be Malaysian,

---

22 Sabahans are taking to social media to discuss politics. See: Benjamin YH Loh and Kevin Zhang, 'Sabah Elections 2020: Sentiments Trending on Social Media', *ISEAS Perspective* 2020/106, 23 September 2020, https://www.iseas.edu.sg/wp-content/uploads/2020/09/ISEAS_Perspective_2020_106.pdf

23 Muguntan Vanar, 'Teacher sued for not teaching', *The Star*, 31 October 2018, https://www.thestar.com.my/news/nation/2018/10/31/teacher-sued-for-not-teaching-exstudent-says-educator-denied-her-rights-to-learn-the-subject/

24 Tharanya Arumugam and Veena Babulal, 'Sabah at crossroads in Covid fight', *New Straits Times*, 30 October 2020, https://www.nst.com.my/news/nation/2020/10/636573/sabah-crossroads-covid-fight

25 James Chin, 'Is Malaysia heading for 'BorneoExit'? Why some in East Malaysia are advocating for secession', *The Conversation*, 25 September 2020, https://theconversation.com/is-malaysia-heading-for-borneoexit-why-some-in-east-malaysia-are-advocating-for-secession-146208

26 James Chin, quoted in Clarence Chua, 'The myth of the Malaysian dream', *New Naratif*, 9 September 2017, https://newnaratif.com/journalism/the-myth-of-the-malaysian-dream/

many Sabahans do not have the same connection to Malaysia as those in Peninsular Malaysia.[27] For indigenous Sabahans, their traditional connection has been with their land. With greater displacement from the land, these ties have also eroded.[28] This strain on families has been compounded by children having to leave Sabah to make a living. For migrant communities, many of whom have been in Sabah for decades and have multiple generations of children and grandchildren in Sabah, there is stigma and the challenge of documentation and acceptance.

It is thus not a surprise that there is greater insecurity. Some of this insecurity is starkly evident in the living socio-economic conditions – the lack of water, poor quality of housing and grossly inadequate roads. With one in five households in poverty, too many Sabahans struggle to survive – to feed their families and themselves.[29] Children in the rural areas often do not have the same access to education, with stunted growth and malnutrition far too prevalent.[30] Political engagement for many poor Sabahans is an extension of meeting everyday needs. For those looking for social mobility, Sabah's economy is not growing at a rate that accommodates the need for jobs, resulting in large out-migration. The economic growth that is taking place is uneven and not creating jobs at the wage levels to cover expenses.[31] This is not to deny economic growth in recent decades,

---

27 Lee Hock Aun, 'Borneo Survey: Autonomy, Identity, Islam and Language/Education in Sabah', *ISEAS Perspective* 2018/31, 13 April 2018, https://www.iseas.edu.sg/images/pdf/ISEAS_Perspective_2018_21@50.pdf

28 Amity A. Doolittle, *Property and politics in Sabah, Malaysia: Native struggles over land rights* (Washington: University of Washington Press, 2011).

29 Department of Statistics Malaysia, *Household Income and Basic Amenities Survey Report by State and Administrative District Sabah, 2019*, https://www.dosm.gov.my/v1/uploads/files/1_Articles_By_Themes/Prices/HIES/HIS-Report/HIS_Sabah.pdf Avila Geraldine, 'Sabah Ranks as Malaysia's Poorest State, Again', *New Straits Times*, 20 September 2020, https://www.nst.com.my/news/nation/2020/09/625711/sabah-ranks-malaysias-poorest-state-again and Martin Ravallion, *Ethnic Inequality and Poverty in Malaysia Since 1969*, No. w25640. National Bureau of Economic Research, 2019.

30 Wan Manan Wan Muda, Jomo Kwame Sundaram and Tan Zhai Gen, *Addressing Malnutrition in Malaysia*, Khazanah Research Institute, September 2019, http://www.krinstitute.org/assets/contentMS/img/template/editor/Discussion%20Paper_Addressing%20Malnutrition%20in%20Malaysia.pdf

31 Idris, Rafiq, and Kasim Mansur, 'Sabah Economic Model: An Overview', *International Journal of Academic Research in Accounting Finance and Management Sciences* 10, no. 3 (2020): 475-484.

but to acknowledge that the distribution of this growth, largely from oil and gas, palm oil and tourism, has not corresponded with the needs of a largely young population seeking a better future.

PRN2020 was Malaysia's first pandemic election, and this heightened the socio-economic insecurities. When elections were called in September 2020, the debilitating economic effects of the lockdown from March through June were still present. This accentuated the impact of Muhyiddin's Bantuan Prihatin Nasional relief initiative, as there was a need for voters to adopt strategies and find resources to manage the pandemic's impact. Arguably, the socio-economic insecurities that are usually present were even more prominent in PRN2020.

Many political commentators have long highlighted that Sabahans appear to vote against their self-interest, electing officials and parties that perpetuate patterns of weak governance.[32] The tumultuous nature of Sabah politics is often attributed to voters being easily bought and lacking in agency or rationality in political support, often voting along paternalistic lines. Our assessment of the situation argues that there is agency amongst grassroots voters, but there are also different rationalisations. Voters in Sabah's peripheries, especially those away from the urban centres of Kota Kinabalu and Sandakan, see political engagement as a means for their survival. The small payouts from political representatives do more to improve their daily lives, as opposed to voting for a party that will fight for better oil royalties, reject the building of a dam on the other side of Sabah, or restore the 1963 Malaysia Agreement (MA63). The fight for more autonomy and reduced subservience to the federal government are seen as distant battles amongst elites.[33] For many on the ground, the issues that dominate the reporting on campaigns are not seen as substantively shaping their ways of life.[34] Voters in Sabah's peripheries connect to issues that provide

---

32 See James Chin, 'Commentary: Sabah's surprise results – and how Warisan lost big in state elections', *Channel News Asia*, 28 September 2020, https://www.channelnewsasia.com/news/commentary/sabah-election-results-how-warisan-lost-big-grs-won-huge-13156026 and Joe Samad, 'Reflections on the Sabah election outcome', *Free Malaysia Today*, 30 September 2020, https://www.freemalaysiatoday.com/category/opinion/2020/09/30/reflections-on-the-sabah-election-outcome/

33 See Faisal S. Hazis, 'Domination, Contestation, and Accommodation: 54 Years of Sabah and Sarawak in Malaysia', *Southeast Asian Studies* 7 no. 3 (2018): 341-361.

34 Arnold Puyok 'The Fall of Warisan in Sabah's Election: Telltale Signs, Causes and

meaning and offer security, the familiar personality or party, the candidate from close and trusted personal social networks and those that best promise opportunities to reduce insecurity.

What further complicates Sabah's politics is that there are differences in which party and personalities best offer security. Some opt for those of the past, while others look to new opportunities through the new political entrants on offer. Voters relate to different definitions of security beyond the socio-economic conditions and ties noted above. These are intertwined with local narratives.

Among the many narratives, three stand out, as they are highly emotive. The first is well-known: divisions over the changing demography of Sabah tied to the 'Project IC' of the 1980s.[35] The KDM communities and Chinese Sabahans hold long-standing resentments against how the social fabric of the state was changed, seen to suit the interests of federal power and to transform Sabah into a replica of the pattern dominant in Peninsular Malaysia.[36] While the reality on the ground is more complex, with the communities and areas affected by migration facing their own hardships, the problems of unregulated migration and undocumented persons weigh down Sabah's development. One in three people in Sabah are estimated to be non-citizens, with most being part of the undocumented community.[37] Vilashini Somiah and Aslam Abd Jalil's chapter describes many of the challenges. Statelessness and stigma coexist with perceptions of invasion and trauma. The insecurities connected to migration and the large numbers of undocumented persons have become a convenient political tool to leverage in political campaigns, one that was wielded effectively as part of the arsenal in PRN2020. For voters engaged in Sabah's politics of survival, they are forced to choose sides – a choice which authors such as Trixie Tangit in her chapter on younger Sabahans suggest they wrestle with.

Salient Issues' *ISEAS Perspective* 2021/8, 29 January 2021, https://www.iseas.edu.sg/wp-content/uploads/2021/01/ISEAS_Perspective_2021_8.pdf

35 RCI Commissioners. *Report of the Commission of Enquiry on Immigrants in Sabah*, (Kota Kinabalu, Malaysia, 2014), http://legacy.sapp.org.my/rci/RCI-Eng.pdf

36 James Chin, 'Exporting the BN/UMNO model,' in Meredith Weiss (ed.), *Routledge Handbook of Contemporary Malaysia* (London: Routledge, 2015), 83-92.

37 Department of Statistics Malaysia 2020 census projections based on the 2010 census estimate 29% of the population is non-citizens.

A second local narrative involves the place of religion, or rather the place of political Islam and Christianity in Sabah.[38] Views on the dominant role of Islam compete with views of the accommodation of all faiths, with similar parallels to the imposition of a Peninsular Malaysia model for Sabah where Islam is given a special position. This was not the case when Sabah helped form Malaysia in 1963 and it was only in 1973 that Islam became the state religion. A majority of Sabahans oppose this decision.[39] The disagreements about how to accommodate different religions were part of the 2020 campaign narratives – the message of 'unity' and equality from Warisan Plus was juxtaposed against the unspoken alternatives of hierarchy and exclusion – with those alternatives perceived as manifesting in the appointment of a PAS assemblyman by GRS after the election. Survival is not just about economic conditions, but ways of life and practising faith – for some voters their choices are tied to protecting their faith.

Finally, there are the competing narratives about the relationship with the federal government. Safety either comes from being on the same side as federal power or from possessing greater autonomy. Despite its natural resources, Sabah lacks the same level of reserves and revenue bases as Sarawak. The federal government provides necessary resources. While most voters recognise that they will not see much of these resources, given systemic corruption, many see the need to be 'on the same side' as federal power. Others disagree, arguing for a fairer distribution and more decentralisation of power. At the core of these different Sabahan perspectives are views of how Sabah can and should survive (and thrive). What has not fundamentally changed, however, is how the federal government sees Sabah. Rich in resources and opportunities, Sabah is perceived through a feudal lens, something that should follow and serve its lord from afar.

These different aspects of survival – marginalisation on the periphery, insecurities and local narratives – often conflict with each other. Many KDM voters in PRN2020, for example, voted for the familiar and trusted personalities in their support for PBS and STAR in the conditions of the

38 Arnold Puyok, 'Rise of Christian political consciousness and mobilisation', in Weiss, *Routledge Handbook of Contemporary Malaysia*, 60-72.

39 Lee Hock Aun, 'Borneo Survey: Autonomy, Identity, Islam and Language/Education in Sabah', *ISEAS Perspective* 2018/31, 13 April 2018, https://www.iseas.edu.sg/images/pdf/ISEAS_Perspective_2018_21@50.pdf

pandemic, and punished Warisan Plus – especially UPKO – for failing to deliver acceptable changes to the emotive issue of undocumented persons. By prioritising these dimensions of survival, they are now wrestling with concerns about PAS and perceptions of an Islamist agenda gaining a political foothold in Sabah as well as the greater federal footprint of the GRS government. Central to all of these contradictory choices is the role of Sabahans' own agency within their own rationalisations.

Tying Chapter Threads

Throughout this book, we have strived to present the different voices of Sabah from as many perspectives as possible. While many of us do not necessarily agree or subscribe to the same views, we believe in the need to see different perspectives and to widen the discussion of Sabah politics. In editing this book, we have found ourselves reflecting on the arguments and challenging assertions made by our authors. Many have raised issues and concerns that have necessitated the need to reassess what we know about Sabah and to reorient our understanding of Sabah. These chapters shed light on the struggles, challenges and inspirational efforts of Sabah's various communities (outside of the usual Kota Kinabalu bubble) as they experienced a state election during a global pandemic. In facing these uncertainties, we found common themes that are shared amongst these pieces.

The ever-changing nature of Sabah politics has resulted in a long-fragmented and increasingly polarised political landscape which has produced weak governments that constantly fear being displaced. Thus, elected representatives and political parties focus on making use of state resources and policies that reinforce their own and their party's positions rather than effectively focussing on the welfare of the people of Sabah. Several chapters have underscored this situation and how this context has paralysed the state apparatus from performing its duties. Even prior to the Warisan/PH administration, restoration of MA63 has always been a priority for any Sabah government to improve the welfare of the state, but as Johan Arriffin Samad points out, recent Sabah administrations have been ineffective at wrestling autonomy from Putrajaya. Given the opportunity after GE14 (with Warisan being an ally of PH yet remaining distinct and separate), Warisan was not able to produce changes that would have fundamentally eroded some of Peninsular Malaysia's hegemony over Sabah.

Ironically, it was the fellow Borneo government of Sarawak that helped thwart a constitutional amendment introduced by a Sabahan – then Law Minister Liew Vui Keong, who passed away after the election. Warisan's time in government, as James Alin and Marcilla Malasius conclude in reference to unemployment policy, was focussed on setting up new programmes and fulfilling promises. Like previous administrations, Warisan/PH would try to reinvent the wheel in addressing unemployment and setting unreachable targets.

Despite its shortcomings, Warisan/PH was just one in a long line of administrations that has wrestled with making major reforms and bringing about development for Sabah. We see that the people of Sabah have therefore taken it upon themselves to do what their governments have been derelict in for so long. As argued by Beverly Joeman, Nelson Dino and Asraf Sharafi Mohammad Azhar, civil society organisations (CSO) have been championing the rights of Sabahans for decades. By fighting for controversial issues such as protecting indigenous rights and migrant populations, CSOs have been challenged by various administrations, even those who had earlier supported them. Their expanding role in Sabah speaks to the greater agency of Sabahans on the ground.

Different communities within Sabah have different approaches in engaging with the state. As discussed by Undi Sabah in the chapter by Mahirah Marzuki, Fiqah Roslan and Auzellea Kristin Mozihim, youths in Sabah have been widely ignored and not given platforms to engage with politics. Sabah youths have long felt disenfranchised as the state does not execute policies or provide opportunities that support youths. Youths are keen to upend and change the system from the ground up. Chinese Sabahans, according to Oh Ei Sun and Amanda Yeo, have instead focussed on reducing their reliance on the state, which is in stark contrast to Chinese communities in other parts of Malaysia. In growing more independent this community is not as concerned or affected by weak governments. Their independence extends to their economic activities, which go on irrespective of the party in office.

The chapters have also shed light on various issues and convenient political targets during elections. It is important to understand why these stereotypes, misconceptions and issues have plagued public discourse in Sabah for such a long time and how scholarship can elevate the discourse and move it forward. Benjamin YH Loh and Yi Jian Ho discuss this in their analysis of Sabah's social media space. The presence of irregular migrants – labeled PTI/PATI or 'illegals' – has become a perpetual problem that needs fixing. As long as this issue persists without compromise and sustainable solutions, it will divide Sabahans and undercut its potential movement forward – impacting all residing in Sabah. Malaysia's third wave of Covid-19 cases, tied to PRN2020, showed clearly the costs of inadequate attention to migration and access to healthcare for all residents as it deepened the health crisis in the state.[40]

The writers of this book have shared their insights as to how Sabah's contemporary politics means different things to different demographics, which will be an ongoing dynamic for the coming years, as newer demographics emerge and take precedence. Sabah is a state with diverse intersecting political narratives which continue to develop, and it requires different interpretations, both old and new, especially regarding spatial, ethnic, economic, religious, gender, class and generational divisions. The authors in the collection have highlighted that with change in Sabah, the politics and the meaning of politics in Sabah is changing as well. So far, the results of the Sabah 2020 election have been primarily interpreted as a return to the past, a rejection of change.[41] Seeing Sabah from the ground, as this collection does, shows that in fact there are conflicting and competing developments – those embracing change, a product of changes and rejecting and resisting changes. These complexities and contradictory trends will require further analysis as they evolve. Our collection has kick-started the discussion, and hopefully this will expand further, moving forward.

---

[40] Andrew M. Carruthers, 'Movement Control and Migration in Sabah in the Time of COVID-19', *ISEAS Perspective* 2020/135, 17 November 2020, https://www.iseas.edu.sg/wp-content/uploads/2020/11/ISEAS_Perspective_2020_135.pdf

[41] Wong Chin Huat, 'Sabah State Election 2020: Did the Electorate Vote for Change?' *Platform: A Journal of Management and Humanities* 3, no. 2 (2020): 2-15.

Bibliography

Ahmad Nizamuddin Sulaiman. 'Budaya Politik Dalam Masyarakat Majmuk Di Malaysia'. In *Etika dan budaya berpolitik dari perspektif Islam*, edited by Abdul Monir Yaacob and Suzalie Mohamad. Kuala Lumpur: Institut Kefahaman Islam Malaysia (IKIM), 2002.

Allerton, Catherine. 'Contested Statelessness in Sabah, Malaysia: Irregularity and the Politics of Recognition.' *Journal of Immigrant & Refugee Studies* 15, no. 3 (2017): 250-68.

Aslam Abd Jalil. 'Malaysian Malaysia': the rise of xenophobia'. Strengthening Human Rights and Peace Research Education in ASEAN, 4 May 2020. https://shapesea.com/op-ed/malaysian-malaysia-the-rise-of-xenophobia/.

Awang Sahari Abdul Latif. 'Ketokohan Ulama Bapa-Anak di Sabah: Imam Haji Yaakub dan Imam Haji Suhaili.' In *Islam di Sarawak dan Sabah*, edited by A.F. Omar et al. Bangi: Fakulti Pengajian Islam UKM & Kuching: Jabatan Agama Islam Sarawak, 2003.

Azmah Abdul Manaf. *Malaysia: Gerakan Kesedaran & Nasionalisme*. Kuala Lumpur: Universiti Sains Malaysia and Utusan Publications & Distributors, 2016.

Azizah Kassim. 'Filipino Refugees in Sabah: State Responses, Public Stereotypes and the Dilemma over Their Future'. *Southeast Asian Studies* 47, no. 1. (2009): 52-88.

Azizah Kassim and Ragayah Haji Mat Zin. 'Policy on Irregular Migrants in Malaysia: An Analysis of Its Implementation and Effectiveness.' PIDS Discussion Paper Series, no. 2011-34 (2011).

Banaji, Shakuntala and Ram Bhat. *Whatsapp Vigilantes: An Exploration of Citizen Reception and Circulation of Whatsapp Misinformation Linked to Mob Violence in India*. The London School of Economics and Political Science (London: 2019). http://eprints.lse.ac.uk/104316/1/Banaji_whatsapp_vigilantes_exploration_of_citizen_reception_published.pdf.

Bagang, Tony Paridi and Puyok, Arnold. 'Sabah: the End of BN and a New Order?' In *The Defeat of Barisan Nasional: Missed Signs or Late Surge?*, edited by Francis E. Hutchinson and Lee Hwok Aun, 402-422. Singapore: ISEAS, 2019.

Barlocco, Fausto. 'An Inconvenient Birth. The Formation of a Modern Kadazan Culture and Its Marginalisation within the Making of the Malaysian Nation (1951-2007).' *Indonesia and the Malay World* 41 (119): 116-141.

———. 'The formation of the Kadazan: ethnic identities in precolonial, colonial and early postcolonial Sabah.' In *Identity and the State in Malaysia*, edited by Fausto Barlocco, 46-61. London: Routledge, 2013.

Bersih 2.0. Laporan Pemerhatian Pilihan Raya Umum Negeri Kali Ke-16. October 2020, http://www.bersih.org/wp-content/uploads/2020/10/Laporan-Pemerhatian-Pilihan-Raya-Umum-Negeri-Sabah-Kali-Ke-16.pdf.

Buyong, Jamdin. 'Islam Membentuk Tamadun Penduduk Sabah: Sejarah dan Kejayaan.' In *Islam di Sarawak dan Sabah*, edited by A.F. Omar et al. Bangi: Fakulti Pengajian Islam UKM & Kuching: Jabatan Agama Islam Sarawak, 2003.

Carruthers, Andrew M. 'Movement Control and Migration in Sabah in the Time of COVID-19.' *ISEAS Perspective*, 2020/135, 17 November 2020. https://www.iseas.edu.sg/wp-content/uploads/2020/11/ISEAS_Perspective_2020_135.pdf.

Chala, Teresa Maria. 'The 'green Gold' of Sabah: Timber Politics and Resource Sustainability.' The University of Melbourne, 2000.

Chamil Wariya. *UMNO Sabah, Mencabar dan Dicabar.* Kuala Lumpur: Penerbit Fajar Bakti, 1992.

Chin, James. 'The Sabah State election of 1994: end of Kadazan unity.' *Asian Survey* 34, no. 10 (1994): 904-915.

———. 'The Sarawak Chinese Voters and Their Support for the Democratic Action Party (DAP).' *Southeast Asian Studies* 34, no. 2 (1996): 399-400.

———. 'Going east: UMNO's entry into Sabah politics.' *Asian Journal of Political Science* 7, no. 1 (1999): 20-40.

———. 'Malaysian Chinese Politics in the 21st Century: Fear, Service and Marginalisation.' *Asian Journal of Political Science* 9, no. 2 (2001): 87-88.

———. 'Federal-East Malaysia Relations: Primus-Inter-Pares?' In *50 Years of Malaysia: Federalism Revisited*, edited by Ander J. Harding and James Chin, 152-85. Singapore: Marshall Cavendish Editions, 2014.

———. 'Exporting the BN/UMNO Model: Politics in Sabah and Sarawak.' In *Routledge Handbook of Contemporary Malaysia*, edited by Meredith Weiss, 83-92. London: Routledge, 2014.

———. 'From Ketuanan Melayu to Ketuanan Islam: UMNO and the Malaysian Chinese.' In *The End of UMNO*, edited by Bridget Welsh, 226-273. Petaling Jaya: SIRD, 2016.

———. '"Malay Muslim First": The Politics of Bumiputeraism in East Malaysia.' In *Illusions of Democracy: Malaysian Politics and People*, edited by Sophie Lemiere, 201-220. Petaling Jaya: SIRD, 2017.

———. 'Sabah and Sarawak in the 14th General Election 2018 (GE14): local factors and state nationalism.' *Journal of Current Southeast Asian Affairs* 37, no. 3 (2018): 173-192.

———. 'The 1963 Malaysia Agreement (MA63): Sabah And Sarawak and the Politics of Historical Grievances.' In *Minorities Matter: Malaysian Politics and People*, edited by Sophie Lemiere. Singapore: ISEAS–Yusof Ishak Institute, 2019.

———. 'GE14 In East Malaysia: MA63 and Marching to a Different Drum.' In *Southeast Asian Affairs* 2019, edited by Daljit Singh and Malcolm Cook, 211-222. Singapore: ISEAS-Yusof Ishak Institute, 2020.

———. 'Politics of federal intervention in Malaysia, with reference to Sarawak, Sabah and Kelantan.' *Journal of Commonwealth & Comparative Politics* 35, no. 2 (1997): 96-120.

———. 'Commentary: Sabah's surprise results – and how Warisan lost big in state elections.' *Channel News Asia*, 28 September 2020. https://www.channelnewsasia.com/news/commentary/sabah-election-results-how-warisan-lost-big-grs-won-huge-13156026.

———. 'Is Malaysia Heading for 'BorneoExit'? Why Some in East Malaysia Are Advocating for Secession.' *The Conversation*, 29 September 2020. https://theconversation.com/is-malaysia-heading-for-borneoexit-why-some-in-east-malaysia-are-advocating-for-secession-146208.

———. 'The Sabah State election of 1994: end of Kadazan unity.' *Asian Survey* 34, no. 10 (1994): 904-915.

Chin, James and Puyok, Arnold. 'Going Against the Tide: Sabah and the 2008 Malaysian General Election.' *Asian Politics & Policy* 2, no. 2 (2010): 219-35.

Chua, Clarence. 'The myth of the Malaysian dream'. *New Naratif*, 9 September 2017. https://newnaratif.com/journalism/the-myth-of-the-malaysian-dream/.

Department of Statistics, Malaysia. 'Yearbook Statistics Malaysia 2016.' 2017.

———. 'Official Portal: File External Trade Sabah 2017-2018' https://www.dosm.gov.my/v1/index.php?r=column/cone&menu_id=dTZ0K2o4YXgrSDRtaEJyVmZ1R2h5dz09.

———. 'Household Income and Basic Amenities Survey Report by State and Administrative District Sabah.' 2019.

———. 'Current Population Estimates, Malaysia 2020.' July 2020.

———. 'Household Income and Basic Amenities Survey Report 2019.' July 2020.

———. 'Laporan Sosioekonomi Negeri Sabah 2019.' 2020.

Doolittle, Amity A. *Property and politics in Sabah, Malaysia: Native struggles over land rights*. Washington: University of Washington Press, 2011.

Frimer, Jeremy A. and Skitka, Linda J. 'The Montagu Principle: Incivility Decreases Politicians' Public Approval, Even with Their Political Base'. *Journal of Personality and Social Psychology* 115, no. 5 (2018): 845–66.

Gale, Bruce. 'Politics at the Periphery: A Study of the 1981 and 1982 Election Campaigns in Sabah.' *Contemporary Southeast Asia*, 6, no. 1 (1984): 26-49.

Gearhart, Sherice and Weiwu Zhang. 'Gay Bullying and Online Opinion Expression: Testing Spiral of Silence in the Social Media Environment'. *Social Science Computer Review*, (23 September 2013): 18-36.

Glick, Henry Robert. 'The Chinese Community in Sabah and the 1963 Election.' *Asian Survey* 5, no. 3 (1965): 144-151.

Govindasamy, Anantha Raman. 'The Sabah State Election: A Narrow Win and Precarious Mandate for the New Government.' *ISEAS Perspective*, 2020/131, 17 November 2020. https://www.iseas.edu.sg/wp-content/uploads/2020/11/ISEAS_Perspective_2020_131.pdf.

Govindasamy, Anantha Raman and Lai, Yew Meng. 'GE14: The Urban Voting Pattern in P172 Kota Kinabalu and P186 Sandakan, Sabah'. *Jebat: Malaysian Journal of History, Politics & Strategic Studies* 45, no. 2 (2018): 298-318.

Government of Malaysia. *Report of the Commission of Enquiry on Immigrants in Sabah*. Kota Kinabalu, Malaysia, 2014. http://legacy.sapp.org.my/rci/RCI-Eng.pdf.

Granville-Edge, P. J. *The Sabahan: the Life & Death of Tun Fuad Stephens*. Kota Kinabalu, Sabah: The Family of Tun Fuad Stephens, 1999.

Haji Zaini Haji Ahmad, *Pertumbuhan Nasionalisme di Brunei (1939-1962)*. Kuala Lumpur: ZR Publications, 1989.

Hamdan Aziz. *USNO dan BERJAYA Politik Sabah*. Kuala Lumpur: Dewan Bahasa dan Pustaka, 2015.

Hazis, Faisal S. 'Patronage, Power and Prowess: Barisan Nasional's Equilibrium Dominance in East Malaysia'. *Kajian Malaysia* 33, no. 2 (2015): 1-24.

———. 'Domination, contestation and accommodation: 54 years of Sabah and Sarawak in Malaysia.' *Southeast Asian Studies* 7, no. 3 (2018): 341-36.

———. *Domination and Contestation: Muslim Bumiputera Politics in Sarawak*. Singapore: Institute of Southeast Asian Studies, 2012.

Hilsdon, Anne-Marie. 'Migration and Human Rights: The Case of Filipino Muslim Women in Sabah, Malaysia.' *Women's Studies International Forum* 29, no. 4 (2006): 405-16.

Hirschmann, Robert. 'Population distribution in Sabah Malaysia 2019-2020, by ethnicity'. *Statista*, 25 September 2020. https://www.statista.com/statistics/1041537/malaysia-population-distribution-ethnicity-sabah/.

Hoffstaedter, Gerhard. 'Place-Making: Chin Refugees, Citizenship and the State in Malaysia.' *Citizenship Studies* 18, no. 8 (2014): 871-84.

Hopkins, Julian. 'Cybertroopers and Tea Parties: Government Use of the Internet in Malaysia.' *Asian Journal of Communication* 24, no. 1 (2014): 5-24.

Inglehart, Ronald and Norris, Pippa. 'The developmental theory of the gender gap: Women's and men's voting behavior in global perspective.' *International Political Science Review* 21, no. 4 (2000): 441-463.

Iruthayaraj, P. Pappusamy, D. 'Migrant Workers Contribution towards the Malaysian Economic Transformation'. Asian Conference on Globalization and Labor Administration: Cross-Border Labor Mobility, Social Security and Regional Integration (2014). https://islssl.org/wp-content/uploads/2014/12/Pappusamy_2014_Asian_Conf.pdf.

Ishak, Mohamed Mustafa Bin. 'From Plural Society to Bangsa Malaysia: Ethnicity and Nationalism in the Politics of Nation-Building in Malaysia.' PhD diss., University of Leeds, 1999.

Isma Noornisa Ismail, Shanmuganathan, Thilagavathi and Shaari. Azianura Hani. 'Defying Out-Group Impoliteness: An Analysis of Users' Defensive Strategies in Disputing Online Criticisms.' *GEMA Online Journal of Language Studies* 20, no. 1 (2020).

Ismail Yusoff. *Politik dan Agama di Sabah*. Bangi: Penerbit UKM, 2004.

Jamdin Buyong. 'Islam Membentuk Tamadun Penduduk Sabah: Sejarah dan Kejayaan.' In *Islam di Sarawak dan Sabah*, edited by A.F. Omar et al. Bangi: Fakulti Pengajian Islam UKM & Kuching: Jabatan Agama Islam Sarawak, 2003.

Joe Samad. 'Reflections on the Sabah election outcome'. *Free Malaysia Today*, 30 September 2020. https://www.freemalaysiatoday.com/category/opinion/2020/09/30/reflections-on-the-sabah-election-outcome/

Johns, Amelia and Niki Cheong, Niki. 'Feeling the Chill: Bersih 2.0, State Censorship, and "Networked Affect" on Malaysian Social Media 2012–2018'. *Social Media + Society* 5, no. 2 (1 April 2019): 1-12.

Joko, Eko Prayitno, Othman, Zaini and Damit, Saat Awg. *Gerakan Berpolitik Bumiputera Islam di Sabah (1938-1963)*. Kota Bharu: Kedai Hitam Putih, 2018.

Kamarul Afendey Hamimi and Ishak Saat. *Kaum Muda di Tanah Melayu 1906-1957*. Tanjong Malim: Penerbit Universiti Pendidikan Sultan Idris, 2020.

Khalid, Muhammed Abdul and Yang, Li. 'Income Inequality and Ethnic Cleavages in Malaysia: Evidence from Distributional National Accounts (1984- 2014).' *World Inequality Database, Working Paper*, no. 2019/09 (2019).

King, Gary, Tanner, Martin A. and Rosen, Ori. *Ecological inference: New methodological strategies*. Cambridge University Press, 2004.

Kitingan, Jeffrey G. and Maximus J. Ongkili, eds *Sabah, 25 Years Later, 1963-1988*. Kota Kinabalu, Sabah: Institute for Development Studies (IDS), 1989.

Lasimbang, Helen Benedict, Wen Ting Tong and Wah Yun Low. 'Migrant Workers in Sabah, East Malaysia: The Importance of Legislation and Policy to Uphold Equity on Sexual and Reproductive Health and Rights.' *Best Practice Research Clinical Obstetrics & Gynaecology* 32 (2016): 113-23.

Lee, Hock Aun. 'Borneo Survey: Autonomy, Identity, Islam and Language/Education in Sabah.' *ISEAS Perspective*, 2018/31, 13 April 2018.

Leong, Pauline. *Malaysian Politics in the New Media Age: Implications on the Political Communication Process*. Singapore: Springer, 2019.

Lim, Regina. *Federal-state Relations in Sabah, Malaysia: The Berjaya Administration, 1976-85*. Singapore: Institute of Southeast Asian Studies, 2008.

Lind, Richard A. *My Sabah: Reminiscences of a Former State Secretary*. Kota Kinabalu, Sabah: Natural History Publications, 2003.

Linvill, Darren L and Warren, Patrick L. 'Troll Factories: Manufacturing Specialized Disinformation on Twitter.' *Political Communication* 37, no. 4 (2020): 447-67.

Loh, Kok-Wah Francis. 'A "New Sabah" and the Spell of Development: Resolving Federal-State Relations in Malaysia.' *South East Asia Research* 4, no. 1 (1996): 63-83.

———. 'Understanding politics in Sabah and Sarawak: an overview,' *Kajian Malaysia* XV, no. 1/2 (1997).

———. 'Developmentalism and the limits of democratic discourse.' In *Democracy in Malaysia: Discourses and Practices*, edited by Francis Loh Kok Wah and Khoo Boo Teik, 19-50. London: Curzon, 2002.

———. 'Strongmen and federal politics in Sabah.' In *Elections and Democracy in Malaysia*, edited by Mavis Puthucheary and Norani Othman, 71-117. Bangi: Penerbit Universiti Kebangsaan Malaysia, 2005.

———. 'Restructuring federal–state relations in Malaysia: from centralised to co-operative federalism?' *The Round Table* 99, no. 407 (2010): 131-140.

Loh, Benjamin YH and Zhang, Kevin. 'Sabah 2020 Elections: Sentiments Trending on Social Media.' *ISEAS Perspective*, no, 106 (2020).

Luping, Herman. 'The Making of a Kadazan Huguan Siou (Great Leader).' *Sarawak Museum Journal*, 21 no. 54 (1984): 83-87.

———. 'Sabah's Dilemma: The Political History of Sabah (1960-1994).' Kuala Lumpur: Magnus Books, 1994.

Madi, Emin. *Sinar Perjuangan USIA*. Kota Kinabalu: USIA, 2009.

'Malaysia: Agreement to Form Malaysia and Draft Constitution.' *International Legal Materials* 2, no. 5 (1963): 816-70.

Malaysia: Report of the Inter-Governmental Committee. Kota Kinabalu, Sabah: Government Printing Department, 1962.

Manaf, AA. *Malaysia: Gerakan Kesedaran & Nasionalisme*. Kuala Lumpur: Universiti Sains Malaysia and Utusan Publications & Distributors, 2016.

Milne, Robert S. and Ratnam, K. J. 'Patterns and Peculiarities of Voting in Sabah, 1967.' *Asian Survey* 9, no. 5 (1969): 373-381.

———. *Malaysia: New States in a New Nation, Political Development of Sarawak and Sabah in Malaysia*. London & New York: Routledge, 2016.

Milne, Robert S. 'Patrons, clients and ethnicity: The case of Sarawak and Sabah in Malaysia.' *Asian Survey* 13, no. 10 (1973): 891-907.

Mohd. Nor Long. *Perkembangan Pelajaran di Sabah*. Kuala Lumpur: Dewan Bahasa dan Pustaka, Kementerian Pelajaran Malaysia, 1978.

Mohamed Mustafa Bin Ishak. 'From Plural Society to *Bangsa Malaysia*: Ethnicity and Nationalism in the Politics of Nation-Building in Malaysia'. PhD diss., University of Leeds, 1999.

Mohamed Nawab Mohamad Osma,. 'A Transitioning Sabah in a Changing Malaysia.' *Kajian Malaysia* 35, no. 1 (2017): 23-40.

Mohamad Shaukhi Mohd Radzi, Ahmad, Syahruddin Awang and Sakke, Nordin. 'The Malaysian Islamic Party (PAS) in 14th General Elections (GE-14) in Sabah: A Study on Voting Patterns, Campaign Approaches and Society's Perceptions.' *Jurnal Kinabalu* (2018): 437-437.

Mohammad Agus Yusoff. 'The politics of centre-state conflict: The Sabah experience under the ruling Sabah Alliance (1963-1976)' *Jebat: Malaysian Journal of History, Politics & Strategic Studies* 26 (2020).

Muhamad M. N. Nadzri, 'The 14th General Election, the Fall of Barisan Nasional and Political Development in Malaysia, 1957-2018.' *Journal of Current Southeast Asian Affairs* 37, no. 3 (2019): 139-71.

Muhammed Abdul Khalid and Li Yang. 'Income Inequality and Ethnic Cleavages n Malaysia: Evidence from Distributional National Accounts (1984- 2014)'. *World Inequality Database*, Working Paper no. 2019/09 (April 2019). https://wid.world/document/9231/.

Musli Oli. *Dilemma Melayu Sabah*. Kota Kinabalu: Pengedar Buku Mas, 1997.

Muzaffar, Chandra. *Protector? An Analysis of Leader-Led Political Relationships in Malay Society*. Penang: Aliran Press, 1979.

Najion Jamil. *Pembentukan Malaysia dan Impaknya Terhadap Perkembangan Islam di Sabah*. Kota Kinabalu: Jabatan Hal Ehwal Agama Islam Negeri Sabah, 2010.

Neoh, Joshua. 'Apostasy and Freedom of Religion in Malaysia.' In *Freedom of Religion or Belief*, edited by Paul Babie, et al., 363-385. Edward Elgar Press, 2020.

Noelle-Neumann, Elisabeth. 'The Spiral of Silence a Theory of Public Opinion.' *Journal of Communication* 24, no. 2 (1974): 43-51.

Noor, Farish A. 'The 13th Malaysian General Elections from a Sabah Perspective.' *The Round Table* 102, no. 6 (2013): 541-48.

Ong, Andrew. 'Sabah Voters Are Kind to Defectors.' *Malaysiakini*, 27 September 2020. https://www.malaysiakini.com/news/544239.

———. 'Eight Takeaways from Sabah Polls.' *Malaysiakini*, 29 September 2020, https://www.malaysiakini.com/news/544494.

Pappusamy, P. Iruthayaraj D. 'Migrant Workers Contribution Towards the Malaysian Economic Transformation.' Asian Conference on Globalization and Labor Administration: Cross-Border Labor Mobility, Social Security and Regional Integration Manila, Philippines, 2014.

Puyok, Arnold. 'Voting Pattern and Issues in the 2006 Sarawak State Assembly Election in the Ba' Kelalan Constituency.' *Asian Journal of Political Science* 14, no. 2 (2006): 212-228.

———. 'Political Development in Sabah, 1985-2010: Challenges in Malaysian Federalism and Ethnic Politics.' *Irasec's Discussion Papers* #9 (2011). http://www.irasec.com/documents/fichiers/44.pdf.

———. 'Kota Marudu and Keningau, Sabah: Personality, Patronage and Parochial Politics.' In *Electoral Dynamics in Malaysia*, edited by Meredith Weiss, 181-196. Petaling Jaya/Singapore: SIRD/ISEAS, 2014.

———. 'Rise of Christian political consciousness and mobilisation.' In *The Routledge Handbook of Contemporary Malaysia*, edited by Meredith Weiss, 60-72. London: Routledge, 2015.

———. 'The Appeal and Future of the "Borneo Agenda" in Sabah.' In *Coalitions in Collision: Malaysia's 13th General Elections*, edited by Johan Savaranamuttu et al., 173-92. Singapore: ISEAS, 2016.

———., 'Political Turmoil in Sabah: Attack of the Kataks,' *ISEAS Commentary*, 2020/113, 5 August 2020. https://www.iseas.edu.sg/media/commentaries/politicalturmoil- in-sabah-attack-of-the-kataks/.

———. 'The Fall of Warisan in Sabah's Election: Telltale Signs, Causes and Salient Issues' *ISEAS Perspective*, 2021/8, 29 January 2021 https://www.iseas.edu.sg/wp-content/uploads/2021/01/ISEAS_Perspective_2021_8.pdf.

Puyok, Arnold and Bagang, Tony Paridi. 'Ethnicity, Culture and Indigenous Leadership in Modern Politics: The Case of the Kadazandusun in Sabah, East Malaysia.' *Kajian Malaysia* 29, Supp. 1 (2011): 177-97.

Puyok, Arnold and Sukhani, Piya Raj. 'Sabah: Breakthrough in the Fixed Deposit State.' *The Round Table (The Commonwealth Journal of International Affairs)*, no. 2 (2020).

———. 'Ethnic Factor in the 2008 Malaysian General Election: The Case of The Kadazan Dusun (KD)' *Sabah Jebat: Malaysian Journal of History, Politics & Strategic Studies* 35 (2020).

———. 'Political Turmoil in Sabah: Attack of the Kataks.' *ISEAS Commentary* 2020/113, 5 August 2020. https://www.iseas.edu.sg/media/commentaries/political-turmoil-in-sabah-attack-of-the-kataks/.

———. 'What issues matter to local voters and Why?: Electoral politics in Ranau, Sabah.' *Journal of Borneo-Kalimantan* 4, no. 1 (2018): 20-27.

Pye, Lucian. *Politics, Personality and Nation-Building: Burma's Search for Identity.* New Haven: Yale University Press, 1962.

Rafiq Idris and Kasim Mansur. 'Sabah Economic Model: An Overview.' *International Journal of Academic Research in Accounting Finance and Management Sciences* 10, no. 3 (2020): 475-484.

Ravallion, Martin. *Ethnic Inequality and Poverty in Malaysia Since 1969*. No. w25640. National Bureau of Economic Research, 2019.

Rodziana Mohamed Razali. 'Addressing Statelessness in Malaysia: New Hope and Remaining Challenges.' Working Paper Series No. 2017/9, (2017). https://files.institutesi.org/WP2017_09.pdf.

Romzi, Ationg Azlan, Gansau, Jualang and Totu Andreas. 'Ethnohistorical Analysis on the Resurgence of Multiracial Political Ideology through "Sabah for Sabahan" Slogan in Sabah, Malaysia.' In ASEAN/Asian Academic Society International Conference, 186-94. 2018.

Sabihah Osman. 'Sabah state elections: implications for Malaysian unity.' *Asian Survey* 32, no. 4 (1992): 380-391.

Sadiq, Kamal. 'When States Prefer Non-Citizens over Citizens: Conflict over Illegal Immigration into Malaysia.' *International Studies Quarterly* 49, no. 1 (2005): 101-22.

Samsudin A. Rahim. 'Social Media and Political Marketing: A Case Study of Malaysia During the 2018 General Election'. *Advances in Social Science, Education and Humanities Research* 241 (2018).

Sandhu, Kernial Singh. 'Introduction: Emergency Settlement in Malaya'. In *Chinese New Villages in Malaya: A Community Study*, edited by Shirle Gordon, xxix-lxv. Singapore: Malayan Sociological Research Institute [MSRI], 1973.

Saravanamuttu, Johan, 'Beyond the End of 'New Politics' in Malaysia…Is There Hope?' *Aliran*, 4 September 2020. https://aliran.com/newsletters/beyond-the-end-of-new-politics-in-malaysia-is-there-hope/

Scott, James. 'Patron-Client Politics and Political Change in Southeast Asia.' The *American Political Science Review* 66, no. 1 (1972): 91-113.

———. *Weapons of the Weak: Everyday Forms of Peasant Resistance*. New Haven: Yale University Press, 1985.

Selway, Joel Sawat. 'Cross-Cuttingness, Cleavage Structures and Civil War Onset.' *British Journal of Political Science*. 41, no. 1 (2011): 111-38.

Shaharuddin Badaruddin. *Masyarakat Madani dan Politik, ABIM & Proses Demokrasi*. Shah Alam: IDE Rsearch Center Sdn Bhd, 2016,

Shaharuddin Maaruf. *Concept of a Hero in Malay Society*. Petaling Jaya: SIRD, 2014.

Singh, D.S Ranjit. *The Making of Sabah 1865-1941 The Dynamics of Indigenous Society*. Kota Kinabalu: Bahagian Kabinet dan Dasar JKM, 2011.

Sinpeng, Aim, Gueorguiev, Dimitar and Arugay, Aries A. 'Strong Fans, Weak Campaigns: Social Media And Duterte in the 2016 Philippine Election.' *Journal of East Asian Studies* (2020) 1-22.

Somiah, Vilashini. 'Romantic Whispers: When Relationships Mobilise Political Agency in the Sabah Elections.' In *Minorities Matter: Malaysian Politics and*

People Volume III, edited by Sophie Lemiere, 36-51. ISEAS–Yusof Ishak Institute, 2019.

———. 'We Can't Talk About the Terrorists: An Ethnography of Silence in The East Coast of Sabah.' *The Panjialam Monographs*. Kuala Lumpur: Iman Research. 20 December 2017.

———. 'What Is the MA63? And Why It Is Important to Sabah and Sarawak.' *New Naratif*, 8 October 2020. https://newnaratif.com/comic/what-is-ma63/.

Smith, Anthony D. *Nationalism: Theory, Ideology, History*. Cambridge: Polity Press, 2001.

Statistics Yearbook Sabah 2017, Kuala Lumpur: Department of Statistics Malaysia, 2018.

Storm, Servaas. 'Structural Change.' *Development and Change* 46, no. 4 (2015): 666-99.

Sullivan, Anwar & Leong, Cecilia. *Commemorative History of Sabah*. Kota Kinabalu: Sabah State Government, 1981.

Tangit, Trixie. *Ethnic labels and identity among Kadazans in Penampang, Sabah (Malaysian Borneo)*. PhD thesis. Australian National University (ANU). 2017.

———. 'Broader Identities in the Sabahan Ethnic Landscape: "Indigenous" and "Sabahan".' *Borneo Research Bulletin* 49 (2018).

Teoh, Crystal. 'We have a Zero Reject Policy, so what's next?' *Centre for Public Policy Studies*, 1 April 2019. https://cpps.org.my/publications/we-have-a-zero-reject-policy-so-whats-next/.

Thornett, Robert C. 'Chinese Malaysian university students discover a world of opportunities venturing abroad, transcending affirmative action quotas at home.' *The Solutions Journal* 10, no. 4 (2019).

Treacher, William H. *British Borneo Sketches of Brunei, Sarawak, Labuan and North Borneo*. Kuala Lumpur: Silverfish Books, 2020.

United Nations High Commissioner for Refugees. 'Ending statelessness in Malaysia.' UNHCR, 2020. https://www.unhcr.org/endingstatelessness-in-malaysia.html.

United Nations Human Rights. 'Statement by Philip Alston, United Nations Special Rapporteur on extreme poverty and human rights, on his visit to Malaysia, 13-23 August 2019'. Ohchr.org, 23 August 2019. https://www.ohchr.org/en/NewsEvents/Pages/DisplayNews.aspx?NewsID=24912&LangID=E.

United Nations Human Rights. 'Figures at a Glance in Malaysia'. UNHCR, 2020. https://www.unhcr.org/en-my/figures-at-a-glance-in-malaysia.html.

Wan Manan Wan Muda, Sundaram, Jomo Kwame and Tan, Zhai Gen. *Addressing Malnutrition in Malaysia*. Khazanah Research Institute. September 2019. http://www.krinstitute.org/assets/contentMS/img/template/editor/Discussion%20Paper_Addressing%20Malnutrition%20in%20Malaysia.pdf.

Weingrod, Alex. 'Patrons, Patronage and Political Parties.' *Comparative Studies in Society and History* 10, no. 4 (1968): 377-400.

Weiss, Meredith L. *The Roots of Resilience: Party Machines and Grassroots Politics in Southeast Asia*. Cornell University Press, 2020.

Welsh, Bridget. 'Malaysia's Political Polarization: Race, Religion and Reform.' In *Political Polarization in South and Southeast Asia: Old Divisions, New Dangers*, edited by Thomas Carothers and Andrew O'Donohue, 41-52. Carnegie Endowment for International Peace, 2020.

———. 'Is Sabah Ready for Political Change?' *Malaysiakini*, 26 April 2018. https://www.malaysiakini.com/columns/421636.

———. 'Kimanis: An UMNO Revival?' *Malaysiakini*, 20 January 2020, https://www.malaysiakini.com/columns/507936.

———. 'The Unsung Role of States in Battling Covid-19.' *Malaysiakini*, 3 July 2020. https://www.malaysiakini.com/columns/532836.

———. 'Sabah's new seats- a reassessment.' *Malaysiakini*, 9 September 2020. https://www.malaysiakini.com/columns/541922.

———. 'All in the Family: Candidates and Contests in Sabah Polls.' *Malaysiakini*, 14 September 2020. https://www.malaysiakini.com/columns/542581.

———. 'Old and New Politics Blend in Sabah.' *Malaysiakini*, 18 September 2020. https://www.malaysiakini.com/columns/543140.

———. 'Warisan Swing: How It Helped "win" Sabah in GE14.' *Malaysiakini*, 24 September 2020. https://www.malaysiakini.com/columns/543711.

———. 'The Covid Factor in the Sabah polls.' *Malaysiakini*, 24 September 2020. https://www.malaysiakini.com/columns/543948.

———. 'Why Warisan Plus Lost – a Preliminary Analysis.' 28 September 2020. https://www.malaysiakini.com/columns/544346.

———. 'The PAS Factor in Sabah Polls.' *Malaysiakini*, 2 October 2020, https://www.malaysiakini.com/columns/545038.

Welsh, Bridget and Cheng, Calvin. 'Emerging Humanitarian Covid-19 Crisis in Sabah.' *Malaysiakini*, 25 October 2020, https://www.malaysiakini.com/columns/548026.

Weiss, Meredith. *The Roots of Resilience: Party Machines and Grassroots Politics in Singapore and Malaysia*. Singapore: NUS Press, 2020.

Wong, Chin Huat. 'Sabah State Election 2020: Did the Electorate Vote for Change?' *Platform: A Journal of Management and Humanities* 3, no. 2 (2020): 2-15.

Wong, Tze Ken Danny. 'Weaker Kingmakers? Chinese Politics in Sabah under Mahathir.' In *Reflections: The Mahathir Years*, edited by Bridget Welsh, 199-209. Washington DC: Johns Hopkins SAIS, 2004.

Yeoh, Tricia. *Reviving the Spirit of Federalism: Decentralisation Policy Options for a New Malaysia*. IDEAS, April 2019. https://www.ideas.org.my/wp-content/uploads/2019/04/PI59-Reviving-the-Spirit-of-Federalism.pdf.

———, *Federal-State Relations under the Pakatan Harapan Government*. Singapore: ISEAS-Yusof Ishak Institute, 2020.

Zaini Haji Ahmad. *Pertumbuhan Nasionalisme di Brunei (1939-1962)*. Kuala Lumpur: ZR Publications, 1989.

Zhang, Kaiping and Rene F Kizilcec. 'Anonymity in Social Media: Effects of Content Controversiality and Social Endorsement on Sharing Behavior.' Eighth International AAAI Conference on Weblogs and Social Media, AAAI Publications, 2014.

List of Contributors

Aslam Abd Jalil is a PhD candidate at the University of Queensland. His research interests are refugee studies and labour migration. Aslam has also completed a Master's degree in Public Policy from the University of Malaya and a Bachelor's degree in Business from the Australian National University.

James Alin has been a member of the Faculty of Business, Economics and Accountancy, Universiti Malaysia Sabah, since 2003. His journal publications are related to issues of seaweed economics, labour issues and the conservation of wildlife and natural areas. James also writes for local newspapers and Internet news portals. He holds two external appointments: as a Senior Research Fellow and Adjunct Professor in the Center for Strategic Policy and Governance, Palawan State University, the Philippines and as an Adjunct Professor and Senior Research Fellow in the Centre for Local Government, University of New England Business School, Australia.

Asraf Sharafi Mohammad Azhar (Asraf Sharafi) is from Kedah and is currently residing in Tuaran, Sabah. He is the Bersih 2.0 Programme Coordinator and has been active in social movements in Sabah since 2011. He writes poetry as well as analyses on politics and electoral reform.

Auzellea Kristin Mozihim currently works in the government sector as a teacher and has been teaching for five years. She is now enrolled in a Master's in Administrative Science researching the policy process of the Kadazan-Dusun language in schools. Apart from being the researcher for Undi Sabah, she is also the co-founder for Edufication, a platform where teachers can engage in education discourse. Her passion in education, politics, and policies looks at how youths as young as 15 should be empowered in obtaining political literacy and inculcating mature political judgment. Working in the education sector has opened her eyes to acknowledging the potential that youths have, if only they are given the proper knowledge and tools to evaluate government policies and political affairs.

Tony Paridi Bagang has a Master's degree in Public Administration from Universiti Sains Malaysia and is currently attached to the Faculty of Administrative Science and Policy Studies, Universiti Teknologi MARA Sabah. He has contributed to several edited volumes including *Electoral Dynamics in Malaysia: Findings from the Grassroots* (2014), *Constitutional Asymmetry in Multinational Federalism. Federalism and Internal Conflicts* (2019) and *The Defeat of Barisan Nasional: Missed Signs or Late Surge?* (2019). He is now completing his PhD at Universiti Malaysia Sarawak, Kuching.

Chan Tsu Chong is a socio-political activist currently based in Melaka, Malaysia. He recently gained his Master's in Asian Politics from the School of Oriental and African Studies, University of London. Formerly, he was the Outreach Officer in Bersih 2.0 and has been involved in various electoral reform campaigns. He continues to contribute towards political reforms in Malaysia at the policy and grassroots level.

Nelson Dino is a poet and social activist. Raised in Sandakan, he uses his love for the literary arts, particularly poetry, short stories and novels, to promote social change. He has written extensively about Suluk visual arts and culture. His Master's thesis, which is an iconological study of various motifs found on the *ukkil*, the Suluk art of carving, is now being turned into a book and will be published soon. He is passionate about learning the arts and culture of many other races in Malaysia. He believes in cultural knowledge building as a way towards achieving awareness, appreciation, and harmony among different peoples. He is a recipient of the Sabah Literary Prize, 2018. His two novels are published by the Institute of Language and Literature, Malaysia (DBP): *Janikar Oh Janikar* (2020) and *Sapi Mandangan dan Apuk Daguan* (2018). His three books of poetry were published in Jakarta, Indonesia in 2017 and 2018 respectively.

Fiqah Roslan currently works as a reporter at a local news daily. Her experience in journalism catalysed her interest in advocacy, particularly involving youths. Prior to entering the workforce, she first gained exposure to advocacy through Green Leaf Theatre House, a Sabah-based non-governmental organisation. In her involvement with Green Leaf, she works with youths to create awareness and foster a better understanding of societal issues, using theatre as a medium. Together with a group of journalist colleagues, she is also a writer and contributor for Borneo Speaks, a platform founded by Sabahan journalists as a form of alternative media telling Sabahan and Bornean stories. Most recently, she serves as a Research and Content Engineer for Undi Sabah.

Philip Golingai is a news editor at The Star Media Group. He writes two columns, 'One Man's Meat' on Wednesdays for *The Star Online* and 'It's Just Politics' for *The Star* on Sunday. He was the Asia News Network editor and *The Star's* Thailand correspondent in Bangkok from 2006 to 2010. He has won four Malaysia Press Institute Awards.

Yi Jian Ho is a Research Associate at the Jeffrey Cheah Institute on Southeast Asia. His areas of focus are on governance, international relations and comparative politics. He holds a Master's degree in International Relations from the Australian National University under the Hedley Bull Scholarship and a Bachelor's in Political Science from the National University of Singapore as an ASEAN Scholar. He has experience in advocacy and think tank work, with selective publications on Malaysian socio-economics, migration, electoral politics, energy and South China Sea security.

Benjamin YH Loh is a media scholar who employs digital ethnography to study emergent cultures and the digital public sphere. Having received his PhD in Communications and New Media from the National University of Singapore, he focuses much of his work on the confluence of technology and society, with a particular focus on minority and marginalised communities. He is currently a senior lecturer at the School of Media and Communication, Taylor's University.

Beverly Joeman is a Kadazan from Penampang who believes in defending fundamental civil liberties. She is a mom to three gorgeous children, the Program Coordinator for the CSO Platform for Reform under Pusat Komas, the current BERSIH 2.0 (Sabah) Vice Chair, a Supreme Council Member of Kadazan Society Sabah (KSS), and an Executive Committee Member of Gabungan Bertindak Malaysia, in that order. She also dabbles in writing satirical prose and poems that reside in her notebook.

Mahirah Marzuki just passed her Bar in Sabah and currently works as a civil litigation lawyer. She is the Program Coordinator of Undi Sabah as well as a researcher. Her interest in activism was sparked when she joined the Sabah Human Rights Centre, understanding and assisting on issues of marginalised communities. She is also passionate about parliamentary reforms, being involved in the Senate 18 Campaign aiming to lower the age of eligibility for the Senate. Her involvement in the Policy and Research Team in the Malaysian Youth Delegation, which focuses on climate change, helps her understand that a lot of issues plaguing society are, more often than not, intersectional. She constantly strives to listen, understand and empower the people around her to be more involved in shaping the direction of her beloved home state.

Marcilla Elmy Malasius graduated with a Master's degree in Economics in 2018 from the Faculty of Business, Economics and Accountancy, Universiti Malaysia Sabah. She is now in her second year as a PhD candidate in Human Resource Economics, working on the Beveridge Curves for Malaysia, Sabah and Sarawak. Her more recent publication was on solid waste management in Kota Kinabalu, Sabah.

Arnold Puyok is currently the Deputy Dean (Research and Commercialisation) and Senior Lecturer in Politics and Government Studies at the Faculty of Social Sciences and Humanities, Universiti Malaysia Sarawak. Dr Puyok's research articles on contemporary Malaysian politics, especially Sabah and Sarawak have been published in *Asian Journal of Political Science*, *Journal of Contemporary Southeast Asia*, *Kajian Malaysia*, *Asian Politics and Policy*, and *Journal of Borneo-Kalimantan*. Dr Puyok's first book is *Electoral Dynamics in Sarawak: Contesting Developmentalism and Rights* (SIRD/ISEAS, 2017) which he co-edited with Meredith L. Weiss. In 2014, together with like-minded Sabahans from various professional backgrounds, Dr Puyok established the Society Empowerment and Economic Development of Sabah (SEEDS) an NGO dedicated to creating a moderate and progressive society in Sabah (https://www.facebook.com/seedssabah1/).

Oh Ei Sun is senior fellow at the Singapore Institute of International Affairs, and Principal Adviser to the Pacific Research Center of Malaysia. He was visiting professor at Hang Seng University of Hong Kong and senior fellow at the S. Rajaratnam School of International Studies, Nanyang Technological University, Singapore. Previously Ei Sun was political secretary to the Prime Minister of Malaysia. A justice of the peace, Ei Sun is a council member of the Commonwealth Magistrates' and Judges' Association. He is also an avid commentator and columnist on politics, economics and current affairs for various international media. Ei Sun was Administrative Officer at the International Telecommunication Union, and scientific and legal consultant to the United Nations Office for the Coordination of Humanitarian Affairs in Geneva, Switzerland. Ei Sun studied at the University of California, USA, where he earned his JD, MBA, MSc, BSc (aeronautical and mechanical engineering) and BA (German).

Mohd Rahimin Mustafa is a business entrepreneur. He is currently a student at the School of Distance Learning, University Sains Malaysia, pursuing a Bachelor of Social Science Research (Honours). He has been active in Sabah politics and his current research interests are electoral politics and the politics of Islam in Sabah. He is a Research Associate of Institut Kajian Strategik Negeri Sabah (IKSAS or Sabah Strategis Studies Institute) affiliate the PAS, Parti Islam Malaysia or Malaysian Islamic Party.

Vilashini Somiah is a Sabahan anthropologist who received her PhD from the National University of Singapore. Currently a Senior Lecturer at the Gender Studies Programme at the University of Malaya, her work focuses primarily on underrepresented narratives of women, youth, migrants and marginalised Borneans living in the interiors. With over a decade of research experience behind her, Dr Somiah has also produced interdisciplinary research in the fields of history, politics and socio-economics. Outside of academia, she writes ethnographic articles on the local socio-political landscape.

Trixie Tangit is a Senior Lecturer in the Faculty of Social Sciences and Humanities, Universiti Malaysia Sabah, Malaysia. She received her PhD in Anthropology from the Australian National University, her Master's in Linguistics from the University of Hawaii and her Bachelor's in Child Development, emphasising in community services, from Michigan State University. Prior to her foray into academia, she worked extensively with NGOs both in Malaysia and Australia in the areas of language rights and indigenous advocacy (Kadazan-Dusun Language Foundation; Reconciliation Australia), and the empowerment of women and female children (Good Shepherd Services Malaysia). Realising that the ballot box does not solve problems; rather, people do, Trixie's keen engagement with youths is aimed at bringing their voices to the fore, encouraging youths to spark a new consciousness in the Sabahan and Malaysian political landscapes.

Bridget Welsh is an Honorary Research Associate with University of Nottingham Asia Research Institute Malaysia (UoNARI-M), a Senior Research Associate of the Hu Feng Center for East Asia Democratic Studies of National Taiwan University and a Senior Associate Fellow of the Habibie Center. She specialises in Southeast Asian politics, with a focus on Malaysia, Myanmar, Singapore and Indonesia. After receiving her PhD in political science from Columbia University, she taught at John Cabot University, Ipek University, Singapore Management University, SAIS (JHU) and Hofstra University. She is a Senior Advisor for Freedom House, a member of the NED's International Research Council and a core member of the Asian Barometer Survey.

Amanda Yeo Yan Yin is a Research Analyst at EMIR Research, Malaysia. Prior to researching socio-economic issues in Malaysia, she served as Private Secretary to both the Minister of Youth and Sports of Sabah and Minister of Health and People's Well-Being of Sabah. Amanda's thought-leadership articles and research pieces have been published by the likes of *Bernama*, the *Malay Mail*, *The Star*, *Focus Malaysia* and *Singapore International Foundation*. With her passion for integrating Malaysia and ASEAN into China-United States interactions, she was selected as the Malaysia Founding Chapter Leader at the Young SEAkers and as one of the 100 Southeast Asian delegates for the YSEALI Good Governance and Civil Society Regional Workshop. Amanda earned her Master's in International Relations at the S. Rajaratnam School of International Studies, Nanyang Technological University, Singapore and a Bachelor's in Economics and Finance from the University of London.

www.ingramcontent.com/pod-product-compliance
Lightning Source LLC
Chambersburg PA
CBHW060135280326
41932CB00012B/1529
* 9 7 8 9 8 1 4 9 5 1 6 8 5 *